Development on the Ground

The central concepts of development on the ground focus on how economic activities come into being and grow as concrete, localized structures of production, work, and interaction. This book deals with the practical and policy problems of promoting economic development from the ground up in low- and middle-income countries, concentrating specifically on the logic and dynamics of cities and regions as the basic building blocks of the development process. Garofoli and Scott have gathered together a series of outstanding essays by academics and policy experts from around the world, showing how the theory of local economic development has major significance for countries in the world periphery.

These essays offer a general conceptual discussion of the role of clusters, networks, and regions in the growth and development of low- and middle-income countries, focusing specifically on such diverse issues as the role of technology and labor markets in local economic development, regional dynamics in mixed economies, the logic of value chains, the effects of globalization on cities and regions in the world periphery, and the possibilities and limitations of cluster-based strategies of economic development. The essays in this volume deal with various countries in Africa, Asia, and Latin America, arguing that development is not only a function of macroeconomic processes, but also proceeds from the ground up via the emergence of localized clusters of production and their associated socio-economic infrastructures.

This book will be invaluable to policy-makers as a guide to understanding and dealing with a wide diversity of development issues, as well as to academics seeking fresh conceptual and analytical approaches to these issues.

Allen J. Scott is Distinguished Professor at the Department of Public Policy and the Department of Geography at the University of California – Los Angeles. **Gioacchino Garofoli** is Professor of Economics at the University of Insubria in Italy.

Routledge advances in management and business studies

Development on the Ground

Clusters, networks and regions in emerging economies

Edited by Allen J. Scott and Gioacchino Garofoli

Routledge
Taylor & Francis Group

LONDON AND NEW YORK

First published 2007
by Routledge
2 Park Square, Milton Park, Abingdon, Oxon OX14 4RN

Simultaneously published in the USA and Canada
by Routledge
711 Third Avenue, New York, NY 10017

Routledge is an imprint of the Taylor & Francis Group, an informa business

First issued in paperback 2011

Transferred to Digital Printing 2009

© 2007 Selection and editorial matter, Allen J. Scott and Gioacchino
Garofoli; individual chapters, the contributors

Typeset in Times by Wearset Ltd, Boldon, Tyne and Wear

British Library Cataloguing in Publication Data
A catalogue record for this book is available from the British Library

Library of Congress Cataloging in Publication Data
A catalog record for this book has been requested

ISBN13: 978-0-415-77118-4 (hbk)
ISBN13: 978-0-415-51276-3 (pbk)
ISBN13: 978-0-203-96166-7 (ebk)

Contents

Contributors

Justin Barnes. Research Associate, School of Economics, University of Cape Town, South Africa.

Nacer El Kadiri. Professor, Institut National de Statistique et d'Economie Appliquée, Rabat, Morocco.

João Furtado. Assistant Professor, Department of Production Engineering, Polytechnic School, State University of São Paulo, Brazil.

Renato Garcia. Assistant Professor, Department of Production Engineering, Polytechnic School, State University of São Paulo, Brazil.

Gioacchino Garofoli. Professor, Department of Economics, Insubria University, Italy.

Thi Bich Van Ho. Lecturer, Faculty of Management Science, National Economics University, Hanoi, Vietnam.

Jean Lapèze. Professeur Associé, Université Pierre Mendès-France, Grenoble, France.

Isaac Minian. José María Luis Mora Extraordinary Chair in International Economics, Facultad de Economía, Universidad Nacional Autónoma de México, México City, Mexico.

Dorothy McCormick. Associate Professor and Director, Institute for Development Studies, University of Nairobi, Kenya.

Mike Morris. Research Professor, School of Economics, University of Cape Town, South Africa.

Balaji Parthasarathy. Assistant Professor, International Institute of Information Technology, Bangalore, India.

Rajah Rasiah. Professor of Technology and Innovation, Faculty of Economics and Administration, University of Malaya, Kuala Lumpur, Malaysia.

Hubert Schmitz. Professor, Institute of Development Studies, University of Sussex, Brighton, United Kingdom.

Allen J. Scott. Distinguished Professor, Department of Policy Studies and Department of Geography, University of California, Los Angeles, United States.

Abdelkader Sid Ahmed. Professor, Institut pour le Développement Economique et Social, University of Paris I, Panthéon Sorbonne, Paris, France.

Wilson Suzigan. Professor, Department of Science and Technology Policy, Institute of Geosciences, State University of Campinas, Brazil.

Antonio Vázquez-Barquero. Professor, Department of Economics, Universidad Autonoma de Madrid, Spain.

Jici Wang. Professor, Department of Urban and Regional Planning, Beijing University, Beijing, China.

Shahid Yusuf. Economic Adviser, Development Economics Research Group, World Bank, Washington, DC, United States.

Preface

Some of the most intractable theoretical and policy questions today reside in the sharp contrasts that exist between different parts of the globe in stages of development and standards of living. These contrasts occur at diverse levels of spatial scale, from the continental, through the national, to the local or regional. The underlying logic of inequality is manifest in distinctive ways at each of these levels, so that in each case something unique is revealed to us about the nature of the problem at large. The local or regional scale, however, is of special interest and importance, notably because it offers us a direct perspective on what might be called *development on the ground*, i.e. the creation and maintenance of physical production systems in geographic space combined with the application of policies and strategies that secure expanding pools of competitive advantages at selected locations.

These aspects of the development problem are of high significance whether we are dealing with backward regions in more economically advanced parts of the world, or with regions in less economically advanced countries. The regional dimension calls all the more urgently for scrutiny because it has for the most part been marginalized in much mainstream thinking and policy-making about economic development. Yet regions are both actual and latent repositories of remarkable economic energies. In particular, many regions are sites at which multifaceted positive externalities and increasing returns effects are generated, and they frequently serve as broad platforms from which individual firms can effectively contest national and global markets. Growing regions also function as conduits through which important developmental energies diffuse outward across a wider territorial expanse and, hence, as privileged sites through which accelerated national economic growth can sometimes be accomplished.

This book is an attempt to address and resolve some of the vital problems raised by these preliminary remarks. Above all, the chapters that follow are focused on dilemmas of regional development in low- and middle-income countries in various parts of Africa, Asia, and Latin America. In recent years, a body of conceptual and empirical testimony to the dynamic role of regions in these countries has started to accumulate, and the present volume is an attempt to carry forward and consolidate this trend.

An important feature of the arguments put forth here is that they deal not only with intra-regional dynamics of economic growth, but also with the increasing integration of regional economic systems in less developed countries into the global economy. At the same time, the discussion focuses resolutely on the proposition that markets alone cannot be relied upon to engender an expanding employment base and rising incomes in less developed countries, and that selected policy interventions are essential for promoting these goals. The shape and form of appropriate policies for achieving successful development on the ground are, therefore, closely scrutinized in what follows.

The book is based on the proceedings of a workshop held over the period from August 30 to September 5, 2005. The workshop was funded by the Rockefeller Foundation, and was housed at the Foundation's Study and Conference Center at the Villa Serbelloni, Bellagio, Italy. We wish to thank the Foundation for its generosity in supporting the workshop and for enabling us to bring together an exceptional team of scholars and policy practitioners from all over the world to discuss diverse issues of economic development from a regional perspective. We also express our gratitude to the Center for Globalization and Policy Research at the University of California–Los Angeles and the Research Center on the Internationalization of Local Economies (CRIEL) at the Università degli Studi dell'Insubria for supplementary funds toward the publication of the present volume. We extend a special word of thanks, as well, to Scott Goldfine for his masterful editing of the final draft of the book, a doubly daunting task in view of the complexity of the material in hand and the fact that a very high proportion of the authors of these chapters are not native English speakers.

The final results of this collective effort, we believe, are of far-reaching consequence not only for continued theoretical and empirical work, but also for practical policy formulation in regard to development in poorer parts of the world. It is our hope that the book will stimulate further research into the burning questions raised when the problem of development is viewed through the lens of regional growth and differentiation, and that it will encourage, in particular, further rethinking of these questions in relation to the threats and opportunities that appear continually on the horizon as globalization runs its course.

Allen J. Scott and Gioacchino Garofoli

Part I

Region-centric concepts of development

1 The regional question in economic development

Allen J. Scott and Gioacchino Garofoli

Introduction

The role of regions as engines of economic development and growth has been widely recognized in recent years, and abundant documentation now exists on many of the most successful examples of this phenomenon in different parts of North America and Western Europe. The present discussion is focused on the more problematic case of regional development in low- and middle-income countries. We aim to demonstrate the relevance of a region-based approach to practical policymaking in these countries and its potential for improving their developmental prospects. At the same time, the discussion provides an opportunity for pinpointing a number of areas where the theory of development in general might be extended and strengthened.

In order to initiate the argument, a series of simple remarks may be articulated about the logic of economic development in general, and especially about the critical stage characterized by Rostow (1960) as take-off, when a given social formation starts to emerge from stagnation into the early phases of economic growth. Thus, many less developed economies are caught in vicious circles as represented by chronic labor surplus situations (Lewis, 1954), low-level equilibrium traps (Leibenstein, 1954), critical shortages of entrepreneurial talent and skilled labor, overdependence on primary products, and so on. In such cases, take-off is unusually hard to achieve, though growth can sometimes be initiated by certain kinds of push effects that open up promising developmental pathways (Murphy *et al.*, 1989; Rosenstein-Rodan, 1943).

Whatever the initiating factors of take-off may be, processes of cumulative causation will often set in as industrialization advances. As this occurs, intensifying flows of externalities and associated increasing-returns effects help to propel development forward. The same types of flow are apt to result in the concentration of economic growth in just a few regions, especially in take-off situations. Geographic concentration is consolidated by the locational strategies of producers who cluster together in order to translate latent benefits of these sorts into the realizable form of agglomeration economies. Of course, market coordination is essential for efficient resource allocation in cases like these, though externalities and increasing-returns effects significantly limit the overall efficiency-seeking powers of simple atomized competition. For these reasons alone, joint or collective action is required in order for rapid growth to be achieved.

In a globalizing world, national economic autarchy becomes less significant than it once was, especially where vigorous export-orientation policies are in place, and in these circumstances, small or less developed countries can afford to pursue strategies of specialized national/regional development to a degree that greatly exceeds what was once thought possible or advisable.

These remarks can be summarized in the proposition that economic development is critically dependent on the formation of dense industrial regions and cities, and that appropriate policies can greatly enhance the beneficial outcomes of this relationship. Of late years, numerous econometric studies have been published providing confirmation that economic growth and industrial agglomeration are indeed persistently and positively intertwined with one another. Even in low- and middle-income countries much evidence of this type has been forthcoming of late, as exemplified by the work of Becker *et al.* (1992), Henderson (1988), Henderson and Juncoro (1996), Lee and Zang (1998), Mills and Becker (1986), Mitra (2000), and Shukla (1988), among many others.

A brief perspective of development theory

Regions are not just passive receptacles of industrialization. Any region where industrial investment is proceeding also has some chance of emerging as a dynamic nexus of positive externalities and agglomeration economies. In turn, these outcomes will greatly enhance overall productivity and growth (though disabling negative externalities may also come into being if policy-makers fail to act). In low-income countries, the regional expressions of this process are particularly insistent because the restricted availability of capital for large-scale infrastructural investments means that development is all the more likely to be confined to a limited number of locations.

The contemporary literature ascribes the positive externalities and increasing-returns effects typically found in regionalized industrial systems to three main sets of socioeconomic relations.

First, networks of specialized but complementary producers are commonly found at the core of any burgeoning economic complex. These networks abound with external economies of scale and scope. For example, the presence of many different providers of goods and services in the local area means that producers can rapidly satisfy many crucial but unpredictable input needs. Equally, a high level of proximity between producers and their suppliers and subcontractors makes it possible for the former to adjust their input schedules frequently in response to market vagaries. Second, dense local labor markets invariably come into being in the vicinity of employment centers, and they too generate multiple increasing-returns effects. Thus, the presence of many workers in a given place enhances job-matching activities, reduces search costs, and facilitates the emergence of joint training efforts. Third, processes of creativity, innovation, and learning are often quite intense in regions marked by production networks and local labor markets of these sorts. These processes are most likely to occur in transactions-intensive complexes, especially where interaction is based on frequent face-to-face relationships combined with active exchange of information. Above and beyond these external economies, the mutual proximity of many different interrelated firms and workers helps to reduce overall transport and communications costs, and ensures the rapid flow of circulating capital. Regionalized industrial systems, in other words, have a marked propensity to function as fountainheads of dense multifaceted agglomeration economies and efficiency effects.

The published research on how these main sources of agglomeration economies operate in practice is immense. Detailed accounts can be found, for example, in Cooke and Morgan (1998), Garofoli (1983, 1992), Porter (2001), Scott (1988, 1998), and Storper (1997). Agglomeration economies become even more potent when set in a dynamic framework where networks, local labor market structures, and innovation processes evolve and interact with one another in a logic of circular and cumulative causation. By the same token, agglomeration economies are purely social creations. More to the point: development at any given location is not always or necessarily contingent on the existence of some prior, naturally given *comparative* advantage. On the contrary, development can also occur – and increasingly does occur – on the basis of endogenously built up *competitive* advantages in specific regional contexts.

In an older version of development theory and practice based on growth-pole and growth-center analysis as laid out by Perroux (1961) and Boudeville (1966), the more advanced regions in less developed countries were seen above all as focal points for capital-intensive industrialization based on large lead plants. The propulsive effects flowing from these plants, in combination with import substitution policies in response to perceived unequal returns from trade between North and South *à la* Prebisch (1959) and Singer (1950) were then expected to be the vehicle for eventual national economic independence. In today's world, where export orientation is generally taken to be a preferred pathway to economic growth, developing regions sometimes advance even on the basis of small-scale labor-intensive industries, of sorts that were previously thought to be the very antithesis of modernization, like clothing, shoes, jewelry, or furniture (cf. Cadène and Holmström, 1998; Cawthorne, 1995; Schmitz, 1995; Scott 1994). Development strategies today are less and less concerned with the establishment of an autarchic and balanced national economy, than they are with the search for a niche within the global division of labor. By the same token, one of the principal problems that developing areas face is to find and maintain market outlets in the global economy that are not already dominated by producers with early-mover advantages. A successful strategy of export orientation offers the further advantage that by widening final markets it also brings in its train an intensification of increasing-returns effects in producing regions.

Appropriate collective action can greatly magnify the agglomeration economies of developing regions. One obvious opportunity for such action is presented by the many market failures to which all industrial clusters are subject, but that are especially severe in developing countries. Another is related to the dysfunctional effects of social breakdown in areas of dense polarized growth. Yet another – above all in take-off situations where markets are often weakly developed at best – is based on the need to ensure some degree of complementary investment in the regional economy in order to foster accelerated growth. Moreover, once any regional economy enters into a spiral of cumulative causation, further forward evolution occurs in a path-dependent process where all elements of the system become mutually constitutive of one another in round after round of growth and development.

For example, a supply of entrepreneurs is essential for economic advances to continue; invariably, individuals can be found in the local area with distinctive personal features that equip them at the outset for the task of entrepreneurship. Contrary to purely behaviorist theories, however, entrepreneurs are also in part *made* within the evolving economic system as fresh structural spaces open up and as advantageous new prospects appear on the horizon. Irrespective of their personal attributes, individuals who are already caught up in the regional economy are notably well positioned to perceive and to seize these opportunities. But path dependency means that lock-in of the regional economy to suboptimal outcomes is an open possibility, and that some sort of collective steering mechanism may also be required in order to avoid the worst pitfalls of this condition. An immediate corollary of the above remarks, as we argue more closely below, is that the pro-market, anti-interventionist stance of the Washington Consensus and its avatars offers a severely deficient view of all that is at stake in the quest for development (Stiglitz, 2002).

In the same way, region-based economic growth and development are deeply dependent on complex socio-cultural processes of human mobilization and transformation. Regional production systems and their associated communities of workers are the locus of idiosyncratic social routines and conventions, and these phenomena are vital to processes of acculturation and habituation. To be sure, they are also sometimes rife with dysfunctional features. In low- and middle-income countries, moreover, the coming together of many jobless and underemployed individuals in dense urban settlements often results in costly social pathologies, particularly where hyper-urbanization occurs (cf. Wheaton and Shishido, 1981). Yet once this point has been conceded, and in contrast to the anti-urbanist views of development theorists such as Lipton (1977), the arguments already laid out suggest that the high road to development and growth is still more likely to pass through the admittedly troublesome way station of large-scale urbanization than it is through a dynamic of spatially dispersed and decentralized investment.

Macroeconomic structure and regional development

The national economy as a framework for regional stability and growth

Much of the time, we think of the economy of any country as a purely macro-economic phenomenon (e.g. national GDP, unemployment, inflation, export performance, and so on), but we often fail to grasp its full meaning because we tend to abstract away from its underlying geography. While the macroeconomic level is obviously of major importance in its own right, we should not overlook the fact that it is also in part constituted as an association of individual regional economies, each with its own system of synergies and collective order. This remark underlines the increasingly urgent need to explore the relationship between national economic development processes and the regional bases of both growth and decline. The point is of major importance in any attempt to understand the difficulties encountered in practical experiences of economic development and in implementing more effective strategies of regional planning.

In macroeconomic approaches, two different kinds of development paths or strategies can often be observed. The first involves an emphasis on accumulation in the manner of Nurske (1958) and Destanne de Bernis (1966, 1967). Here, the role of the economic surplus is paramount (and, indirectly, income distribution as well) and the trade-off between consumption and investment becomes a major object of policy concern. Empirically, developing countries with high rates of GDP growth tend to be marked by high ratios of investment to income, often exceeding the 20 percent mark. The second tends to be favored by adherents of the Washington Consensus. It preaches a doctrine of economic austerity and flexibility, i.e. the imperatives of low wages and competitive labor markets, the removal of political barriers to profitability, the dismantling of social protection policies, market discipline, and so on. However, this second kind of model has led to much social unrest, increasing inequalities, and economic instability in many of the countries where it has been applied, and as we have seen, it erroneously dismisses *on principle* the usefulness of collective action as a condition of development.

Nowadays, it seems increasingly clear that economic development cannot be managed at the macroeconomic level alone. Whereas there is broad acceptance that macroeconomic stability is a prerequisite for development to occur, there is also widening agreement that the fundamentals of the macroeconomic order (inflation, budget deficits, public debt, trade balances, and so on) are not in and of themselves sufficient to fulfill the objectives of economic development. Critical elements of the development process such as learning, innovation, upgrading of productive structures, labor training, and so on, are significantly related to the aptitudes of local and regional decision-making systems and to the behavior of individual firms. These kinds of outcomes depend heavily on strategic capability implementation at the local level and not just on macroeconomic actions like the devaluation of the national currency or the reduction of import tariffs.

The structural adjustment programs proposed by international agencies like the World Bank and the International Monetary Fund in the 1980s typically over-looked or under-emphasized this important issue. Thus, macroeconomic stability and coherent macroeconomic fundamentals are necessary but not sufficient conditions of development, and even recent European experiences confirm the same point. In fact, an overly aggressive macroeconomic policy will often have dele-terious effects on many regions, undermining the very search for growth and development. Premature or poorly executed market-opening measures are examples of this kind of failure. Centrally mandated development policies are, in any case, usually ill equipped to respond to the detailed idiosyncrasies of indi-vidual regions and industrial communities.

The mesolevel: resources and institutions

The economic health of regional economic systems depends, in particular, upon the progressive accumulation of knowledge and practical competencies. These phenomena emerge in significant degree out of creative interactions among local actors and the continuous production of external economies in the regional milieu. This process of accumulation, together with its encouragement of innovation and new entrepreneurship is the consequence of a dynamic economic and social environment, itself dependent on the capability of finding new opportunities and of exploiting specific social and cultural assets. Any capability of this sort is typically a socially constructed territorial resource; it is the outcome of a regional development process forming a space of human interplay and learning. For these reasons, the density of social and economic relationships is of paramount importance, as is the complementary role of institutions foster-ing positive interactions between the different spheres of regional life (industry, research, education, and so on) and supporting transfers of knowledge and experiences, thereby helping to upgrade the productive capability of local firms.

In successful experiences of economic development, then, governments at every level have invariably been of crucial importance, not only as agencies of coordination, investment, and system steering, but also as guarantors of the legal and social infrastructure that provides the basis for effective operation of market exchange relationships. In fact, without a network of collective order – whether it is government agencies as such, or (as is increasingly the case in contempor-ary capitalism) diverse institutions and organizations of civil society – economic life of any degree of complexity must necessarily collapse. This proposition follows not only from the market failures that are endemic in contemporary society, but also and more importantly from the inability of the atomized system of social and property relations that characterizes civil society in capitalism to reproduce itself unproblematically through time. The conflicts, collisions, diverging interests, and general immobilization that would necessarily follow from any dissolution of institutional and political order would almost certainly result in rapid economic decay.

More specifically and concretely, governmental and nongovernmental agencies are needed at the local level to mobilize investment capabilities and human competencies, and to provide various kinds of bottom-up support. They are needed to facilitate information flows, to underpin learning processes, to encourage local entrepreneurial cultures and network interaction, and, in general, to manage the complex systems of synergies and externalities (both positive and negative) that typically emerge as regional economic systems start to develop and grow.

The discussion above takes on added force in light of contemporary trends toward globalization and international economic integration. These trends help reinforce agglomeration in favored areas (by extending the market range of producers) and they highlight the tendency of the national economy to assume the form of a mosaic of regional structures of production and entrepreneurship. By contrast, they also lead to an intensification of the developmental predicaments faced by many less favored areas, as the latter struggle both to build their own productive capacities, and to find appropriate niches in wider markets. In either case, the relevance of the *mesoeconomic* level (i.e. the space of the local productive system, below the level of the national economy but above the level of the individual firm) is critical to any concrete program of development. This mesoeconomic level is a site of critical mass residing in the dense polarized systems of firms and workers that represent the basic condition for the emergence of multifaceted agglomeration economies (through the linkages between firms, the structure of local labor markets, and the different organizations that hold strategic knowledge).

The importance of critical mass for the achievement of economic development was proposed more than a half-century ago in the "big push" approach of Rosenstein-Rodan (1943). A geographical perspective on development leads to the notion that "regional push" effects are also a significant issue (Scott, 2002). The prime function of such effects is not so much to secure static efficiency levels, but more importantly to set virtuous circles of cumulative causation in motion. In some of its original formulations, the idea of critical mass (big push theory, balanced growth, growth poles) was linked to capabilities for spending and coordination on the part of central government, but gave little or no attention to participation on the part of small and medium enterprises. An extreme case in this regard is represented by Algeria in the era of import substitution.

For a brief period in the 1970s, the notion of critical mass in development practice was downplayed by major international agencies in favor of so-called polarization-reversal policies. However, these policies failed dramatically precisely because networks of firms and their associated labor markets work most productively and innovatively where they achieve some minimal level of regional concentration. Thus, again, and in view of the successful experiences of bottom-up development in many different parts of the world (both in more and less developed countries), we must take into account the extraordinary opportunities for growth offered by intervention in local economic systems with their distinctive endogenous dynamics. Nevertheless, we must reaffirm the need for a coherent general framework of national and regional economic policies, involving different levels of government. This remark points to the importance of capabilities linking macroeconomic objectives with mesoeconomic processes. Shortfalls of these capabilities account for many failures of development programs hitherto.

The region as a reservoir of competitive advantages

Economic development is always simultaneously a process of territorial adjustment, and it takes on geographic expression in many different shapes and forms. One of the most important expressions of this link between territory and development consists of dense regional agglomerations of capital and labor. Three major conditions help to reinforce this specific type of link, namely; (i) the existence of regional resources that cannot be easily transferred elsewhere (Colletis and Pecqueur, 1995); (ii) the emergence of a system logic binding firms and workers together into a functioning economic order; and (iii) the formation of project capacity, that is, an ability to deal with internal crises and to react to external challenges, which requires, in turn, the establishment of coherent mechanisms of local economic governance. We can describe this kind of territorial development in terms of the theory of local productive systems (Garofoli, 1983). The literature on local productive systems stems initially from the analysis of a small number of successful industrial districts in economically advanced countries in the 1970s and 1980s, but it has continued to evolve in various directions, including an important step forward into issues of endogenous development (Garofoli, 1991, 1992; Courlet, 2001; Vazquez Barquero, 2002).

By building on our arguments above, we can generalize the concept of local productive systems to any organizational model of economic activity rooted in geographic space and marked by the presence of specific resources, tacit knowledge (Becattini and Rullani, 1993), external economies, and mechanisms of social regulation. In this kind of system, the character of the local milieu depends crucially on a number of interrelated variables, namely:

1   *Production organization*, i.e. the operational structure of the local economic system, as reflected in rules and modes of management that allow for *divisions of labor* among firms. As we have already seen, this in turn fosters the formation of productive linkages, social relationships, and cooperation rules. Where trust and loyalty prevail, costs of inter-firm transacting are significantly reduced.

2   *Professional skills and competencies* are reproduced in the local area, both formally and informally. Social interaction and learning foster the acquisition of skills, and progressive learning stimulates new interests and abilities.

3   *Localized diffusion of knowledge and information* (about productive and managerial techniques, market outlets, local resources, competencies, and so on). Local modalities of competition and cooperation shape the diffusion of knowledge, on an involuntary basis in the first instance, on a voluntary basis in the second. Knowledge about local business conditions becomes a common heritage, a true public good.

4 *Structures of social regulation* help to solve common problems in the local productive system and to negotiate points of political tension. These structures assume many different guises: governmental agencies, civil associations, private–public partnerships, and so on.

These points lead on to the related issue of endogenous development, i.e. the notion that the local productive system possesses a degree of autonomy in regard to its internal structure and evolutionary course. This degree of autonomy derives from the decision-making capacities of individual and institutional actors in the local area, and from their ability to control and internalize flows of knowledge. Endogenous development is, in fact, based on the formation of "social capability" at the level of the community of firms and institutions operating in the local sphere, through the progressive construction of critical regional assets (Garofoli, 1991, 1992) of the sorts identified above. To be sure, endogenous regional development does not imply regional closure or imperviousness to external influences. On the contrary, it goes hand in hand with the insertion of the local productive system in a wider economic environment with multiple impacts via the emergence of new technologies, market shifts, national legislation, and so on. Endogenous development, in other words, refers simply to those elements of the productive system that, by reason of their collective order and mutual synergies, are imbued with certain powers of local social choice and self-determination.

This argument becomes clearer when we turn our attention to the role of innovation in local economic development. Innovation is – at least in part – territorial in nature by reason of the interaction mechanisms and learning process that drive it forward, and that they themselves have a distinctive spatial expression. This general point can be found in a variety of theoretical contributions from the growth pole concept of Perroux (1955, 1961) (with its emphasis on lead firms as sources of new product innovation) to more recent ideas about regional innovation systems as proposed by analysts like Asheim (1999), Bureth-Llerena (1993), or Gaffard (1992). In the latter perspective, technological innovation derives from territorially specific processes through the interaction of individuals and institutions in the course of everyday work and life. Territorial economic innovation and development are also and of necessity path dependent (cf. Freeman, 1982; Nelson and Winter, 1982).

Two further distinctive lines of analysis have developed around the issue of the relations between innovation and territorial development. These can be identified in terms of (i) the technological district (Antonelli, 1986), and (ii) the *milieu innovateur* as formulated by Aydalot (1986), Camagni (1991), and Maillat and Perrin (1992). In the technological-district approach, the process of technological change is driven primarily by the existence of dense interactions between firms located in close proximity to one another. In the *milieu innovateur* approach, innovation is seen as resulting from an environment made up of the local productive system together with its various social and political appendages. The notions of technological district and *milieu innovateur* are, of course, very close to one another. They share in common an evolutionary and nonlinear conception of technology and development; and they explicitly recognize the effects of spatial proximity in processes of technological innovation, and the importance of externalities (Courlet and Soulage, 1995).

These remarks now bring us full circle back to the question of spatial clustering, bearing in mind the words of Lundvall and Johnson (1994) that "in a world of learning economies the specialization of firms and countries becomes increasingly important for economic performance." In short, the clustering and specialization of firms are critical foundations of competitiveness and innovation, and the region is a true (but not the only) nexus of economic development. We must not forget, however, that local productive systems are also sites of widespread, sometimes massive, market failure, so that collective action is called for as a means of dealing with resulting problems of inefficiency and misallocation. Much market failure in these systems consists of suboptimal information flows, inadequate supplies of skills and competencies, and under-provision of certain critical services in circumstances where requisite scale thresholds are not satisfied by local conditions. Examples of this latter condition can be found in deficiencies regarding knowledge about distant or emerging markets, failures in the transfer of technological know-how, or low levels of access to financial resources for small and medium enterprises.

Problems like these call for different forms of governmental action and institution-building in civil society. These instances of collective action are in turn subject to processes of *institutional and regional* learning, much like the so-called experimental regionalism as set forth by Sabel (1995). In the latter case, regions function like laboratories in which social experiments based on *learning-by-doing* and *learning-by-monitoring* are carried forward to various stages of completion by different corporate bodies.

The global dimension

Geographic agglomeration may be an indispensable adjunct to competitiveness for many industries, but without complementary mechanisms for the distribution of final outputs on wider markets, its full powers must remain stillborn. In numerous instances, especially in less developed countries, final markets do not extend in spatial terms much beyond some provincial or national frame of reference. However, the most successful and innovative agglomerations in less developed countries today are increasingly caught up in export-orientation programs through which their products are projected onto the global stage. Globalization is both a promise and a threat. It opens up the prospect of lucrative export opportunities over a vast diversity of market niches; but it also brings producers in developing countries into head-to-head competition with one another, especially given that so much of their advantage on world markets resides in their employment of cheap labor. The great expansion of Chinese exports over the 1990s, and the deleterious impact of this expansion on the exports of many other developing countries, exemplifies this observation with some force (cf. Scott, 2005). Agglomeration is thus all the more important to the stragglers because it tends to offer at least some degree of competitive edge, in terms of both productive efficiency and possibilities for product differentiation.

Global flows of products from industrial agglomerations in less developed countries can be usefully categorized in terms of three broad types, i.e. direct exports to final markets, intra-firm trade, and flows associated with outsourcing activities. Direct exports of low- and medium-priced products from less to more developed countries represent a small but growing share of world trade. Intra-firm trade occurs between the different units of large corporate organizations. In this case, products flow from dependent branch plants in low-wage countries to facilities located for the most part in North America, Western Europe, and Japan, where finishing, marketing, and distribution activities are carried out. These plants have a great affinity for locations in special economic zones, export processing zones, maquiladoras, and the like, as well as in specialized agglomerations where they can tap into an assortment of local productive assets. Outsourcing or production sharing involves the putting out of work by firms (such as branded manufacturers, wholesalers, retailers, and so on) in high-wage countries to independent contractors in low-wage countries. Outsourcing activities are increasing at a rapid rate as the costs of international transacting continue to decline, and as entrepreneurs in low-wage countries learn how to produce to global standards. Bair and Gereffi (2003) argue that large multinational firms are actually tending to relinquish branch plant operations in favor of outsourcing, which generally entails much lower fixed costs.

As long ago as the late 1970s, intimations of widespread international subcontracting and production sharing were already apparent in the shift of low-skill, low-wage work in industries like clothing and electronics assembly to the so-called world periphery, and in the concomitant intensification of advanced design and production activities in core countries. The seminal work on the issue at the time was the book by Fröbel *et al.* (1980), in which the term the "new international division of labor" was coined to designate the hypothesized changing production relations between rich and poor countries. As useful as this term was, and is, it tends to impose an unduly schematic rigidity on thinking about the economic geography of contemporary globalization. We prefer to invoke the notion of a worldwide mosaic of regional economies at various levels of development and economic dynamism and with various forms of economic interaction linking them together. This notion allows us to describe global geographic space as something very much more than just a division between two (or three) broad developmental zones, and to acknowledge the numerous counterexamples to the predictions of the theory of the new international division of labor that are to be found in the contemporary world. These include – among others – the persistent growth and development of clusters of low-wage sweatshop industries in high-wage countries, and steadily increasing numbers of dynamic technology-intensive poles in low-wage countries.

Lall (1991) has pointed out that the received theory of international trade assumes *tout court* that if any firm can match world prices, then there is no reason why it cannot immediately sell its output on external markets. In practice, international trade is far from being generated by self-realizing supply–demand mechanisms like a simple textbook model, especially when the source areas lie in less developed countries. Even in the case of direct trade, the existence of some sort of intermediate marketing and distribution capacity is a prerequisite for supply and demand to interconnect with one another.

Where outsourcing is involved, the need for mediating arrangements is even more pressing given that firms at both ends of the trading relationship must constantly engage in extensive scanning, monitoring, and coordination of their inter-relationships. For this reason, any analytics of trade in general, and international production sharing in particular, must take seriously not only the measurement of physical flow, but also the institutional frameworks that sustain this flow. In this regard, the notion of the *value chain* is of key importance, with its double resonance signifying both movements of product between an origin and a destination, and a set of social relationships by means of which these movements are managed in quantitative and qualitative terms through time (Gereffi, 1994). Moreover, just as increasing-returns effects can be detected within the institutional structures of agglomeration, so do they emerge in value chains as well, above all in regard to search and monitoring costs, and learning-by-exporting processes. Agglomeration and trade, in short, are mutually reinforcing phenomena, which may be why we find that for many products, only a few countries dominate world export patterns at any given moment in time (Lall, 1998).

Gereffi (1994, 1999) suggests that we need to distinguish between producer-driven and buyer-driven types of value chain. The former type is found in large-firm manufacturing sectors such as the automotive or aircraft industries, where suppliers generally have the resources to mount their own distribution and marketing networks. The latter is more commonly associated with small-firm sectors where manufacturers lack the resources to undertake distribution and marketing functions themselves. Buyer-driven trade is dominant wherever production-sharing arrangements prevail in the guise of putting out by big-brand manufacturers, wholesalers, and chain retailers to firms in low-wage countries. International putting out activities can range from simple assembly tasks to more complicated operations, all the way up to full-package subcontracting in which the buyer simply lays out the design specifications of the final output and the manufacturer then executes the entire physical process of production, including the acquisition of basic material inputs. The output is then marketed under the buyer's brand.

Gibbon (2001) and Sverrison (2004) argue that we also need to recognize a third type of chain involving trader-driven exchange. Case studies reveal that in both the more and less economically advanced countries of the world, brokers, export agents, and traders frequently play an important role in promoting links between producers and buyers. The "impannatori" in the industrial district of Prato, Italy, are a case in point (cf. Becattini, 1987), as are the celebrated traders of Hong Kong and Taiwan (Hsing, 1999). Intermediaries like these are all the more important because they provide a means whereby even small firms in the more advanced countries can work with offshore producers in the developing world, whether by direct acquisition of final outputs or by putting out selected work tasks.

These comments focus only on cost, and abstract away from other important factors such as trustworthiness and product quality. However, value chains – or rather, the governance dimensions of value chains – are precisely a means of ensuring that these other factors remain within some sort of tolerance range. This is especially important where production-sharing relationships are in play (cf. Schmitz, 2004). In contrast to spot markets, production sharing almost always entails heavy front-end search costs together with recurrent monitoring costs to ensure smooth ongoing relations (Grossman and Helpman, 2005). The literature reveals that many different types of value chains are underpinned by long-term collaborative relations that help to compensate for market failure problems. Rauch (2001, p. 1180) has written that "[social] networks facilitate trade by building or substituting for trust when contract enforcement is weak or nonexistent." Network institutions, in other words, contribute to the suppression of opportunistic behavior and ensure at least minimal standards of performance by all parties concerned. For major buyers, these standards concern the critical variables of product quality, price, and delivery time (Egan and Mody, 1992).

Collaborative interactions and long-term relationships have been shown, in addition, to be important conduits through which many different forms of process and product upgrading occur in industrial clusters in developing countries (cf. Bair and Gereffi, 2003; Bazan and Navas-Alemán, 2004; Gereffi, 1999; Humphrey and Schmitz, 2002; Schmitz and Knorringa, 2000). Upgrading in these cases occurs not only as a consequence of informal flows of information from more to less experienced firms, but also as a result of deliberate interventions on the part of the former as they seek – in their own interests – to induce their partners to improve their manufacturing capabilities.

Institutions and markets: regional development strategies

Dense regional production systems are major elements of the development process in general, and critical engines of productivity in particular. Markets are essential moments in this dynamic, but so too is the joint extra-market generation of virtuous circles, positive externalities, and competitive advantages. This extra-market dimension is of special significance in regions in low-wage countries where neither industrialization itself nor the social context of industrialization, has attained to any strong degree of self-reproduction. Because of these features, there is always and necessarily a collective set of interests at stake (as well as purely individual interests) in local economic development and growth. This means, in turn, that a tissue of institutional arrangements and an apparatus of policymaking are crucial for success. The urgency of effective collective action in less developed countries is all the more intense because the emergence of negative externalities is likely to be especially damaging to local economic prospects.

These remarks, obviously, represent a direct challenge to neoclassical development theorists like Krueger (2000) or Lal (1983) who see extra-market intervention in economic affairs as being doomed of necessity to irrationality; but our observations here need to be taken seriously insofar as pervasive externalities and other market failures can indeed be shown to prevail in regional economic systems. Included in these failures are deficits in the politico-institutional arrangements on which the existence of markets depends in the first place.

More specifically, coordinating and steering mechanisms need to be constructed in order to deal with such issues as the efficient provision of infrastructure, the enhancement of information flows (in both production networks and local labor markets), agglomeration-specific training and research programs, social welfare, and so on. There is also an important part to be played by local institutions in helping to instill interrelated firms with useful norms of trust and collaboration, and, in situations where firms are too small or too unqualified to take the initiative themselves, to provide what Brusco (1992) calls "real services," including the gathering of data on export markets. Additionally, institutional guidance of the path-dependent process of cumulative causation can sometimes help to avert lock-in of the local economy to various kinds of low-level equilibrium traps. Market relations, capitalist forms of property, and macroeconomic stability provide a framework that potentiates success in take-off situations, though it bears repeating that these phenomena themselves are dependent variables within the overall developmental process.

In particular, at the regional level, a finely balanced and mutually sustaining mix of emerging market relations and institutional order is indispensable. And not just any institutional order will do, of course. Depending on their precise design, institutions can significantly promote or significantly hinder development, and hence issues of institutional quality (transparency, accountability, flexibility, competence, etc.) call for very careful attention above and beyond the particular strategic goals these institutions are meant to achieve (Rodrik, 1999). Among other things, institutions need to be sensitive to local social idiosyncrasies, and they need to be continually readjusted as the economic system (both local and national) evolves through time.

Actual development experiences provide a number of lessons about the general objectives that regional policymakers might usefully pursue in low-income countries. Above all, policymakers need to focus intently on ensuring that the following dimensions of a healthy regional economy are in place, and that forms of public support are geared to overall collective efficiency. The best general mode of approach, therefore, will usually be from the bottom up rather than from the top down.

1   The shoring up of critical localized masses or agglomerations of firms and workers is essential to the achievement of accelerated growth and development. Agglomeration encourages the division of labor and the formation of value-added networks. These processes also promote entrepreneurial spin-off and new firm startups.

2 Concomitantly, the encouragement of intensified backward and forward inter-linkages is a major factor in development (Hirschman, 1958, 1977). In this way, dynamic specialization and complementarity effects are generated as well as extended channels of interaction through which information is transmitted between firms.

3 Labor training programs are of primary significance in any agglomeration, especially in view of the chronic market failures that characterize the supply of appropriate skills and sensitivities.

4 The production and internalization of knowledge externalities is crucial. This process can in significant ways be managed by local agencies via incentives to greater information exchange and adjunct network services. Industrial innovation and upgrading can be enhanced by regional institutions offering agglomeration-specific intelligence and advice

5 In developing countries, it is especially important to promote the access of industrial clusters to international markets. This proposition indicates that strategic goals need to be focused not only on individual agglomerations, but also on the value chains that enable individual producers to contest far-flung markets and to broaden their overall industrial and commercial experiences (Gereffi *et al.*, 2005).

The broad aim of these objectives is to allow selected regional production systems to achieve a high degree of endogenous development as identified at an earlier stage in this chapter. Endogenous development, in turn, implies the realization of a certain degree of autonomy of the regional growth process, as represented by a series of outcomes involving improvements in engineering and design, increased capacities for product differentiation, intensified marketing expertise, and so on. More generally, this process amounts to progressive improvements in the quality of human resources and management, and the creation of dynamic competitive assets through circular and cumulative causation. All of this re-emphasizes the central role played by dynamics of social transformation and, in particular, the critical function of intermediate institutions able to identify common needs and to organize collective action in the face of actual and latent crises.

We have argued that much important new light can be thrown on development theory and practice by taking the regional question seriously. This proposition holds for economies at every level of per capita income, but it is especially pertinent to the case of economies poised at the stage of take-off where resources are scarce and competitiveness is limited. We have also argued that a policy-friendly approach offers useful lines of attack on economic backwardness, though finding exactly the right mix of arrangements to fit any concrete situation obviously presents enormous challenges. All-purpose boilerplate approaches are certainly unlikely to be successful in any long-run perspective. By the same token, the approach to development broadly sketched out here calls for a process of creative self-discovery. In this manner, with the passage of time, hitherto unsuspected local talents and potentialities are apt to be discovered and

mobilized, in line with the idea that economic development means "the utilization of unused, hidden resources" (Hirschman, 1958). Last, but not least, we
must take into account the overarching need for coordination of the national and
regional dimensions of development policy. One vital manifestation of this need
can be found in the circumstance that the formation of dense industrial agglomerations in any country often brings in its train persistent interregional income
inequalities, above all in countries at an intermediate stage of development
(Williamson, 1965). Scott and Storper (2003) have argued that exacerbated
regional inequalities may lead to political tensions that in turn can threaten
further economic advances. In circumstances like these, both social justice and
the ultimate workability of the region-centric development model make it
imperative for compensating macroeconomic policies of redistribution to be put
into place. Redistribution, however, is not simply a burden on the wealthier
regions of the national space-economy, for it also helps broaden the overall
extent of the market and, eventually, to encourage the formation of new proto-
agglomerations.

A world of regions?

We have laid out two main propositions at some length. First, we have tried to
demonstrate that the model of local productive systems as worked out for the
more advanced economies of North America and Western Europe has – with
suitable modifications – considerable relevance to the analysis of less advanced
economies in Africa, Asia, and Latin America. Second, we have proposed that
policymakers in low-income countries need urgently to take this circumstance
into account, and that considerable enhancement of economic-development
strategies can be expected by more vigorous pursuit of the region-centric
approach. At the same time, we have insisted on the continuing need to pay
attention to macroeconomic issues, and to ensure that appropriate coordination
of the macroeconomic and mesoeconomic levels of policymaking is secured.

The overall discussion ultimately points in the direction of a global economy
that is also in part an ensemble of local economies, or, in its most dramatic form,
a worldwide network of city-regions (Scott et al., 2001). The old postwar international order with its developmental geography rooted in a core–periphery
system seems more and more to be giving way to a new geography in the shape
of a global mosaic of regional economies. Likewise, the dynamics of economic
take-off and development in many countries increasingly revolve around
regional concentrations of production and work, and the orientation of markets
to export opportunities. If this analysis is correct, it suggests that selected urban
areas on the current margins of world capitalism are likely eventually to accede
as vigorous nodes to the expanding worldwide network of city-regions. Places
like Seoul, Taipei, Hong Kong, Singapore, Mexico City, São Paulo, and others
have already moved far along this developmental pathway. Many others now
appear to be in the early phases of their own assimilation into the global division
of labor. These city-regions represent privileged growth places within individual

national territories, and they are the principal nodal points through which wider developmental impulses diffuse to less urbanized areas.

That said, not all parts of the less developed world are susceptible to this process of transformation; some seem to remain immune from any kind of meaningful economic take-off; others industrialize up to a certain point and then stagnate or reverse direction. Hence, interspersed through our hypothesized worldwide mosaic of regional productive systems, we are likely to continue to find stubborn pockets of resistance to development, the left-behinds of the global economy. Perhaps the most pressing development-policy problems of all are posed by this perplexing situation.

References

Antonelli, C. (1986) *L'Attività Innovativa in un Distretto Tecnologico*, Fondazione Agnelli, Torino.

Asheim, B. (1999) The territorial challenge to innovation policy: agglomeration effects and regional innovation systems, in B. Asheim and K. Smith (eds.) *Regional Innovation Systems, Regional Networks and Regional Policy*, Edward Elgar, Cheltenham.

Aydalot, P. (ed.) (1986) *Milieux Innovateurs en Europe*, GREMI, Paris.

Bair, J. and Gereffi, G. (2003) Upgrading, uneven development, and jobs in the North American apparel industry, *Global Networks*, 3, pp. 143–169.

Bazan, L. and Navas-Alemán, L. (2004) The underground revolution in the Sinos Valley: a comparison of upgrading in global and national values chains, in H. Schmitz (ed.) *Local Enterprises in the Global Economy: Issues of Governance and Upgrading*, Edward Elgar, Cheltenham.

Becattini, G. (ed.) (1987) *Mercato e Forze Locali: il Distretto Industriale*, Il Mulino, Bologna.

Becattini, G. and Rullani, E. (1993) Sistema locale e mercato globale, *Economia e Politica Industriale*, 80, pp. 25–48.

Becker, C.M., Williamson, J.G. and Mills, E.S. (1992) *Indian Urbanization and Economic Growth since 1960*, Johns Hopkins University Press, Baltimore.

Boudeville, J.R. (1966) *Problems of Regional Economic Planning*, Edinburgh University Press, Edinburgh.

Brusco, S. (1992) Small firms and the provision of real services, in F. Pyke and W. Sengenberger (eds.) *Industrial Districts and Local Economic Regeneration*, Internal Labour Organization, Geneva.

Bureth, A. and Llerena, P. (1993) Système local d'innovation: approche théorique et premiers résultats empiriques, *Industrie et Territoire: Les Systèmes Productifs Localisés*, IREPD, Université Pierre Mendès France, Grenoble.

Cadène, P. and Holmström, M. (eds.) (1998) *Decentralized Production in India: Industrial Districts, Flexible Specialization, and Employment*, Sage Publications, New Delhi.

Camagni, R. (ed.) (1991) *Innovation Networks: Spatial Perspectives*, Belhaven Press, London.

Cawthorne, P. (1995) Of networks and markets: the rise and rise of a south Indian town: the example of Tiruppur's cotton knitwear industry, *World Development*, 23, pp. 43–57.

Colletis, G. and Pecqueur, B. (1995) Dinamica territorial y factores de la competencia espacial, in G. Garofoli and A. Vazquez Barquero (eds.), *Desarollo Economico Local en Europa*, Economistas Libros, Madrid.

Cooke, P. and Morgan, K. (1998) *The Associational Economy: Firms, Regions, and Innovation*, Oxford University Press, Oxford.

Courlet, C. (2001) *Territoires et Régions*, L'Harmattan, Paris.

Courlet, C. and Soulage, B. (1995) Dinamicas industriales y territorio, in G. Garofoli and A. Vazquez Barquero (eds.) *Desarollo Economico Local en Europa*, Economistas Libros, Madrid.

Destanne de Bernis, G. (1966) Industries industrialisantes et contenue d'une politique d'intégration régionale, *Economie Appliquée*, No. 1.

Destanne de Bernis, G. (1967) Les industries industrialisantes et l'intégration économique régionale, *Economie Appliquée*, Nos. 3–4.

Egan, M.L. and Mody, A. (1992) Buyer-seller links in export development, *World Development*, 20, pp. 321–334.

Freeman, C. (1982) *The Economics of Industrial Innovation*, Pinter, London.

Fröbel, F., Heinrichs, J. and Kreye, O. (1980) *The New International Division of Labor*, Cambridge University Press, Cambridge.

Gaffard, J.C. (1992) *Territory as a Specific Resource: the Process of Construction of Local Systems of Innovation*, Latapses, Nice.

Garofoli, G. (1983) *Industrializzazione Diffusa in Lombardia*, Franco Angeli, Milano.

Garofoli, G. (1991) *Modelli Locali di Sviluppo*, Franco Angeli, Milano.

Garofoli, G. (ed.) (1992) *Endogenous Development and Southern Europe*, Aldershot, Avebury.

Gereffi, G. (1994) The organization of buyer-driven global commodity chains: how US retailers shape overseas production networks, in G. Gereffi and M. Korzeniewicz (eds.) *Commodity Chains and Global Capitalism*, Greenwood Press: Westport.

Gereffi, G. (1999) International trade and industrial upgrading in the apparel commodity chain, *Journal of International Economics*, 48, pp. 37–70.

Gereffi, G., Humphrey, J. and Sturgeon, T. (2005) The governance of global value chains, *Review of International Political Economy*, 12, pp. 78–104.

Gibbon, P. (2001) Upgrading primary production: a global commodity chain approach, *World Development*, 29, 345–363.

Grossman, G.M. and Helpman, E. (2005) Outsourcing in a global economy, *Review of Economic Studies*, 72, pp. 135–159.

Henderson, J.V. (1988) *Urban Development: Theory, Fact, and Illusion*, Oxford University Press, New York.

Henderson, J.V. and Juncoro, A. (1996) Industrial centralization in Indonesia, *World Bank Economic Review*, 10, pp. 513–540.

Hirschman, A.O. (1958) *The Strategy of Economic Development*, Yale University Press, New Haven.

Hirschman, A.O. (1977) A Generalized Linkage Approach to Development with Special Reference to Staples, *Economic Development and Cultural Change*, 25, supplement.

Hsing, Y.T. (1999) Trading companies in Taiwan's fashion shoe networks, *Journal of International Economics*, 48, pp. 101–120.

Humphrey, J. and Schmitz, H. (2002) How does insertion in global value chains affect upgrading in industrial clusters? *World Development*, 36, pp. 1017–1027.

Krueger, A.O. (2000) Government failures in development, in J. Frieden, M. Pastor and M. Tomz (eds.) *Modern Political Economy and Latin America*, Westview, Boulder, Colo.

Lal, D. (1983) *The Poverty of Development Economics*, Institute of Economic Affairs, London.

Lall, S. (1998) Exports of manufactures by developing countries: emerging patterns of trade and location, *Oxford Review of Economic Policy*, 14, pp. 54–73.

Lall, S. (1991) Marketing barriers facing developing country manufactured exporters: a conceptual note, *Journal of Development Economics*, 27, pp. 137–150.

Lee, Y.J. and Zang, H. (1998) Urbanization and regional productivity in Korean manufacturing, *Urban Studies*, 35, pp. 2085–2099.

Leibenstein, H. (1954) *A Theory of Economic-Demographic Development*, Princeton University Press, Princeton.

Lewis, W.A. (1954) Economic development with unlimited supplies of labour, *Manchester School*, May, pp. 139–191.

Lipton, M. (1977) *Why Poor People Stay Poor: a Study of Urban Bias in World Development*, Temple Smith, London.

Lundvall, B.A. and Johnson, B. (1994) The learning economy, *Journal of Industrial Studies*, 1, pp. 23–41.

Maillat, D. and Perrin, J.C. (1992) *Entreprises Innovatrices et Développement Territorial*, GREMI, Neuchâtel.

Mills, E.S. and Becker, C.M. (1986) *Studies in Indian Urban Development*, Oxford University Press, New York.

Mitra, A. (2000) Total factor productivity growth and urbanization economies: a case of Indian industries, *Review of Urban and Regional Development Studies*, 12, pp. 97–108.

Murphy, K.M., Schleifer, A. and Vishny, R.W. (1989) Industrialization and the big push, *Journal of Political Economy*, 97, pp. 1003–1026.

Nelson, R. and Winter, S. (1982) *An Evolutionary Theory of Economic Change*, Harvard University Press, Cambridge.

Nurske, R. (1958) *Problems of Capital Formation in Underdeveloped Countries*, Basil Blackwell, Oxford.

Perroux, F. (1955) Note sur la notion de pôle de croissance, *Economie Appliquée*, 7, pp. 307–320.

Perroux, F. (1961) *L'Economie du XXᵉ Siècle*, Presses Universitaires de France, Paris.

Porter, M.E. (2001) Regions and the new economics of competition, in A.J. Scott (ed.) *Global City-Regions: Trends, Theory, Policy*, Oxford University Press, Oxford.

Prebisch, R. (1959) Commercial policy in the underdeveloped countries, *American Economic Review, Papers and Proceeding*, 44, pp. 251–273.

Rauch, J.E. (2001) Business and social networks in international trade, *Journal of Economic Literature*, 39, pp. 1177–1203.

Rodrik, D. (1999) *The New Global Economy and Developing Countries: Making Openness Work*, Overseas Development Council, Washington, DC.

Rosenstein-Rodan, P. (1943) Problems of industrialization of Eastern and South-Eastern Europe, *Economic Journal*, 53, pp. 202–211.

Rostow, W.W. (1960) *The Stages of Economic Growth: A Non-Communist Manifesto*. Cambridge University Press, Cambridge.

Sabel, C.F. (1995) Experimental regionalism and the dilemmas of regional economic policy in Europe, paper presented to the OECD International Seminar on local small firms and job creation, Paris, June 1–2.

Schmitz, H. (1995) Collective efficiency: growth path for small-scale industry, *Journal of Development Studies*, 31, pp. 529–566.

Schmitz, H. (ed.) (2004) *Local Enterprises in the Global Economy: Issues of Governance and Upgrading*, Edward Elgar, Cheltenham.

Schmitz, H. and Knorringa, P. (2000) Learning from global buyers, *Journal of Development Studies*, 37, pp. 177–204.

Scott, A.J. (1988) *New Industrial Spaces: Flexible Production Organization and Regional Development in North America and Western Europe*, Pion, London.

Scott, A.J. (1994) Variations on the theme of agglomeration and growth: the gem and jewelry industry in Los Angeles and Bangkok, *Geoforum*, 25, pp. 249–263.

Scott, A.J. (1998) *Regions and the World Economy: the Coming Shape of Global Production, Competition, and Political Order*, Oxford University Press, Oxford.

Scott, A.J. (2002) Regional push: the geography of development and growth in low- and middle-income countries, *Third World Quarterly*, 23, pp. 137–161.

Scott, A.J. (2005) The shoe industry of Marikina City, Philippines: a developing country cluster in crisis, *Kasarinlan: Philippine Journal of Third World Studies*, 20, pp. 76–99.

Scott, A.J., Agnew, J., Soja, E.W. and Storper, M. (2001) Global city-regions, in A.J. Scott (ed.) *Global City-Regions: Trends, Theory, Policy*, Oxford University Press, Oxford.

Scott, A.J. and Storper, M. (2003) Regions, globalization, development, *Regional Studies*, 37, pp. 579–593.

Shukla, V. (1988) *Urban Development and Regional Policy in India: an Econometric Analysis*, Himalaya Publishing House, Bombay.

Singer, H.W. (1950) The distribution of gains between investing and borrowing countries, *American Economic Review, Papers and Proceedings*, 40, pp. 473–485.

Stiglitz, J.E. (2002) *Globalization and its Discontents*, Norton, New York.

Storper, M. (1997) *The Regional World: Territorial Development in a Global Economy, Perspectives on Economic Change*, Guilford Press, New York.

Sverrison, Á. (2004) Local and global commodity chains, in C. Pietrobelli and Á. Sverrison (eds.) *Linking Local and Global Economies: The Ties that Bind*, Routledge, London.

Vazquez Barquero, A. (2002) *Endogenous Development*, Routledge, London.

Wheaton, W.C. and Shishido, H. (1981) Urban concentration, agglomeration economies, and the level of economic development, *Economic Development and Cultural Change*, 30, pp. 17–30.

Williamson, J.G. (1965) Regional inequality and the process of national development: a description of the patterns, *Economic Development and Cultural Change*, 13, pp. 3–45.

2 Endogenous development
Analytical and policy issues

Antonio Vázquez-Barquero

Introduction

We find ourselves at the beginning of the twenty-first century and economic development continues to be a central question in countries that must fulfill basic needs, improve economic and social well-being, and reduce poverty.

Since the mid-1970s, important transformations have affected the process of economic growth and, thus, the development policies. On the one hand, the forms of firm organization have changed (more flexible and integrated within the territory today) as well as the firm location patterns, which are transforming the spatial development models. Furthermore, urban growth is encouraging the appearance and development of city networks and their insertion in the globalization process. Last of all, many countries have begun political and administrative decentralization processes, which allow the cities and urban regions to assume, to a greater or lesser degree, new competences in the definition, implementation, and management of economic policy.

The fall of the Soviet Union and countries associated with it has accelerated the integration of the international economic system. At the same time, it has clearly shown that the capitalist system, while stimulating the growth and structural change processes, also maintains enormous inequalities in income distribution, with high poverty and unemployment rates. The regions, cities, and countries answer this challenge with local development initiatives that have spontaneously emerged, mainly in Latin American and Asian regions and cities, and to which much attention is being paid by international organizations.

This chapter is about endogenous development, and it aims to describe it as both an approach capable of analyzing the economic dynamic and structural change, and as a valid instrument for action. It argues that local development policy, which appeared as a spontaneous response to increased competition and globalization, tries to stimulate the forces and mechanisms that shape capital accumulation and economic development.

The chapter is organized as follows: After arguing that the concept of development changes as society changes, an analytical definition of endogenous development is presented. Following this, some local initiatives in developing countries are described, and a conceptualization of territorial development policy is proposed. The chapter ends with some final comments on endogenous development.

Economic development: an evolutionary approach

The concept of economic development evolves and changes as countries, regions, and cities face and solve new problems, and as innovation and knowledge are spread through the economic and social organizations. This occurred with the theories of Adam Smith and the classics since the latter third of the eighteenth century, during the industrial revolution, when the formation and expansion of the national markets took place. The same occurred with Schumpeter in the early twentieth century, at the time of the electrical revolution, when inventions and innovations transformed the manufacturing economy, giving way to a profound restructuring of the productive activity, and economic integration took shape with the increase in international trade, the intensification of capital flows, and the expansion of multinational corporations (MNCs).

During the last quarter of the twentieth century, the question reappears during a new phase of the market integration process and the irruption of the new information and communication technologies that lead to the information revolution. At the center of the theoretic consideration is, as in the past, the question of increased productivity and the mechanisms that favor the growth and structural change processes of the economies.

After World War II, a singular approach to economic development led by Abramovitz (1952), Arrow (1962), Kuznets (1966), Lewis (1954) and Solow (1956), among others, appears. This concept of development refers essentially to growth and structural change processes that seek to satisfy the needs and demands of the population and improve their standard of living, and it specifically proposes increased employment and the reduction of poverty.

In order to achieve economic development, increased productivity in all productive sectors is necessary: in agriculture, industry, and services activities it is required. The improvement in the productive-factors returns is what permits diversified production and satisfies new demands for manufactured products and services. Increased productivity depends on how labor and the other productive factors combine, on how the equipment goods, machinery, and production methods are used, and on how knowledge is introduced and energy applied within the productive process.

In sum, increased long-term production (per capita) is possible thanks to the accumulation of capital and to the application of innovation and knowledge in the productive process. Technological change allows for the introduction of new combinations of productive factors, and these increase the productivity of labor, which in turn, increases income.

A new scenario for development begins with the new phase of economic integration during the late 1980s; when the growth models inspired by the fundamentalism of capital are no longer useful. This is so, not only because the breakdown of the Soviet Union and the fall of the Berlin wall proved the superiority of the market economy over a planned economy, but also because the policies carried out in many developing countries and implemented by international aid programs from the developed countries and international organizations failed, as Easterly (2001) points out.

Since the 1980s, Schumpeter's ideas (1934, 1939), as well as those of others who contributed in the post-war years to what Krugman called "The Great Development Theory," return. Among the different approaches that have emerged during the past 20 years is the reintroduction of Solow's growth model on behalf of the new generation of growth theorists like Romer (1986) and Lucas (1988). At the same time, as pointed out by Garofoli (1991, 1992), since the early 1980s, a new approach appears that can be called *endogenous development*. It considers development as a territorial process (not a functional process) that is methodologically based on case studies (not on cross-section analysis) and that considers development policies are more efficient when carried out by local actors (not by the central administrations).

Giorgio Fuá (1994), intellectually linked to Abramovitz, maintains that the development capacity of an economy depends on the immediate sources of growth, such as the size of the working population, the number of hours worked, and the availability of equipment goods and social capital. The factors Fuá defined as structural – such as entrepreneurial and organizational capability, trained labor and skills, environmental resources, and the functioning of institutions – are what are really decisive for sustainable development.

Philippe Aydalot (1985), a follower of Perroux and Schumpeter, adds that the development processes have three main characteristics. First, he refers to the fact that the development actors must be flexible productive organizations, as occurs with the small and midsize firms, capable of overcoming the rigidity of large Fordist organizations. In this way, the economies would obtain better results, particularly in times of rapid change in both the milieu and the market. Second, and more strategic, he defends diversity in techniques, in products, in tastes, in culture, and in policies, which facilitates opening up various development paths for the different territories according to their own potential. Third and last, and more instrumental, he states that development processes are the result of having introduced innovations and knowledge through the investments made by the economic actors. This is a process that is territorial in nature given that it is a result of the forces that shape the milieu in which the firms are inserted; in other words, thanks to the interaction of the actors that shape what Aydalot calls *innovative milieu*.

This approach shows that development does not necessarily have to be focused in large cities, but rather is diffused in urban centers of different size, as explained by Giacomo Becattini (1979), a specialist on Marshall. The entrepreneur (both individual and collective) plays an outstanding role in industrial development and becomes the motor force of growth and structural change due to his creative capacity and innovative nature (Fuà, 1983). Fuà and Becattini add, however, that the firms are not isolated entities exchanging products and services in abstract markets, but are located in specific territories and are part of the productive systems, and are strongly integrated within the local society. In other words, society organizes itself for the purpose of producing goods and services more efficiently, which gives way to industrial districts and clusters of small and midsize firms, which then brings out network economies within the territory.

John Friedman and Walter Stöhr open up this approach and look at development policy from a territorial perspective. They give great importance to the local actors' initiatives through their investment decisions and participation in the definition and implementation of policies (Friedman and Weaver, 1979). They also point out that the economic progress of a territory is only possible when the firms and actors within the territory interact, organize themselves, and invest with the view of developing the local economy and society. Following this line of thought, they put forward "bottom-up" development strategies that allow mobilized and channeled resources and development potential within the territory (Stöhr and Taylor, 1981).

The endogenous development approach is, therefore, characterized by specific features (Vázquez-Barquero, 2005). First of all, endogenous development refers to the capital accumulation process of specific localities and territories. It deals with development processes based on local savings and investment, although private and public resources can be driven from other places and localities; it pays attention to the territory's capacity for the diffusion of innovation throughout the local productive system and the role played by that system. It argues that the efficient use of the territory's development potential is conditioned by the functioning of institutions. Endogenous development, therefore, is a territorial approach to economic growth and structural change, based on the hypothesis that the territory can be understood as the territorial community's network of interests and, therefore, can be perceived as an actor for local development (Massey, 1984).

Endogenous development: an analytical framework

As argued elsewhere (Vázquez-Barquero, 2002, 2005), the endogenous development approach is a useful interpretation for understanding long-term economic growth and the behavior of productivity. It argues that economic development comes about as a result of the economic forces not explicitly included in the production function (flexible organization of production, diffusion of innovation, the territory's urban development and the change and adaptation of the institutions) that generate capital accumulation and increasing returns.

How do the forces that facilitate growth of productivity and economic development work? Which are the mechanisms through which the tendency toward the steady state is neutralized? How can the determinant forces of capital and knowledge accumulation be activated? How do the hidden economies that exist within productive and urban systems emerge? What about the reduction of transaction and production costs caused by the institutional model?

One of the central forces of the capital accumulation process is the organization of the productive system, as seen in advanced countries and in late developed economies during the past 20 years (Becattini, 1979; Piore and Sable, 1984; Saxenian, 1994; Scott, 1988). The question lies not in whether the productive system of a locality or territory is formed by large or small firms, but rather in the organization of the production system and its effects on the behavior of productivity and competitiveness.

Thus, local productive systems, clusters and industrial districts are forms of organization of production, based on the division of labor between firms, and on the local exchange system. They are organizational models that allow the generation of increasing returns when the interaction between firms permit the emergence of scale economies, usually concealed in the productive system, and ultimately one of the development potentials of the local economies (Becattini, 1997).

The backbone of a local productive system (particularly in the case of industrial clusters) is the existence of a network of industrial firms. An industrial network (Hakansson and Johanson, 1993) is made up of actors (the firms in the local productive system), resources (human, natural, infrastructural), economic activities (productive, commercial, technical, financial, social, legal), and their interrelations (interdependence and exchanges). The relations within the network lead to the exchange of products and services among the actors, and also of technological knowledge and behavioral codes (Becattini, 1997).

Furthermore, the adoption of more flexible forms of organization in large firms and groups of firms makes them more efficient and competitive; and new territorial strategies, involving networks of subsidiary plants, make them more autonomous and more integrated within the territory. The greater flexibility of large firm organization allows them to make more efficient use of the territorial attributes and so obtain competitive advantage within the markets (Bellandi, 2001; Vázquez-Barquero, 1999). Finally, some multinational corporations have embedded themselves as leading partners in knowledge-intensive clusters of developed regions and cities (Castells, 1996; Dunning, 2001).

The formation and expansion of networks and flexible firm systems, the interaction of the firms with local actors, and strategic alliances allow the productive systems to generate economies of scale (external and internal, depending on the case) in production and research and development (when the alliances affect innovation), and reduce firms' transaction and production costs.

The introduction and diffusion of innovation and knowledge is, in turn, another mechanism for increased productivity and economic development, since it stimulates economic growth and the structural change of the productive system (Schumpeter, 1934; Freeman and Soete, 1997).

Economic development and the dynamics of production depend on the introduction and diffusion of innovation and knowledge, which impel transformation and renovation of the local productive system. Aydalot (1986) maintains that local firms are the instruments through which innovations and knowledge are introduced into development processes. Their creativity is conditioned by the territory's experience and tradition. In other words, knowledge, accumulated in firms and organizations, is one of the mainstays of development and the local milieu may serve as an incubator of innovation (Maillat, 1995).

From this perspective, innovation is a collective learning process among the actors within the milieu in which the firms make investment and location decisions (Cooke and Morgan, 1998). Thus, we are dealing with learning processes, rooted in the society and the territory, in which coded knowledge, or production "recipes," and tacit knowledge embodied into human resources are diffused within the network as a result of relations among the actors. Consequently, processes of technological change and innovation are interactive, and regional systems of innovation play a strategic role in both the learning process and the diffusion of innovation (Asheim *et al.*, 2003; Lundvall, 1992).

The adoption of innovation allows firms to widen their range of products and create larger groups and construct smaller plants, which are more efficient economically, and reinforce internal scale economies. Furthermore, innovations allow firms to define and carry out strategies focused toward exploring and opening up new products and factors markets. The adaptation of technologies favors differentiation of production and creates scope economies. In short, the introduction and diffusion of innovations and knowledge leads to improvement in the stock of technological knowledge of the productive system, which creates external economies, for the benefit of all sorts of firms in the system.

In sum, the diffusion of innovation and knowledge throughout the productive fabric allows each firm within the cluster to reap internal and external economies of scale and scope. Thus, the productivity and competitiveness of the local firms and economies are increased (Roseger, 1996).

In today's scenario, characterized by globalization of production and exchange and greater services activities, cities continue to be the favorite space for economic development, for it is there where the investment decisions are made and where industrial and service firms are mainly located (Lasuen, 1973; Scott, 1998).

Historical evidence shows that sustained per capita income growth is accompanied by higher levels of urbanization, specifically in its initial phases. After the industrial revolution in England, increasing productivity and expansion of urban production were driven by the introduction of innovation. Changes in firm activities and city systems can be understood as the temporal and spatial effect of adopting innovation. It was Perroux (1955) who, by means of the growth pole theory, argued that economic development and urbanization are the consequence of innovation. Economic development and urbanization are, therefore, two sides of the same coin.

Cities are a place for endogenous development. They generate externalities that lead to increasing returns, they have a diversified productive system that drives the economic dynamic, they provide space for networking in which relations among actors leads to the diffusion of knowledge, and they stimulate the innovation and learning processes of firms (Quigley, 1998; Glaeser, 1998). Cities are places for the creation and development of new industrial and service spaces due to their capacity to generate externalities and allow hidden economies to emerge (Scott, 1988; Hall, 1993).

Development acquires significance within the territory and, in organized societies, it is articulated through the urban system. A well-structured urban system, made up of city networks, encourages the exchange of goods and services, stimulates the performance of firms, and promotes a satisfactory evolution of the labor market, while the presence of adequate economic (transportation, communications, energy) and social (health and education) infrastructures facilitates the appearance and development of external economies, and, therefore, sustainable development. As suggested by Camagni (1992; 1994), at the present time this can be thought of in terms of polycentric urban models, of a sort of urban armature, which tends to function more and more as a network.

Last of all, development processes are not isolated and have deep institutional and cultural roots (Lewis, 1955; North, 1990 and 1994). The development of an economy is always led by the local actors who organize themselves in order to carry out their projects. Thus, cities and regions stimulate the development of specific forms of organizations and institutions that respond to the needs of the economic and social actors, and which will either facilitate economic activity or obstruct it.

The emergence and consolidation of local productive systems arose in areas in which the social and cultural systems are strongly rooted within the territory (Fuà, 1988; Putman, 1993). On the other hand, increased competition in the markets requires efficient responses and strategic cooperation of actors and local organizations, and as pointed out by Cooke (2002), the development of clusters in "knowledge-based" economies requires social capital (norms of reciprocity and trust) and collective learning. Thus, the emergence of multiple institutions from the plurality of actors has led to effective strategic responses to the new needs posed by economic, social, and political dynamics. In the most innovative cities and regions, institutional relations have become more complex and the number of actors and institutions has multiplied. This has led some authors (Amin and Thrift, 1993) to refer to this process as *institutional thickness*.

Economic development, therefore, takes strength in those territories with evolved, complex, and flexible institutional systems. Its strategic relevance lies in that institutional change and development allows for the reduction of transaction and production costs, strengthens trust among the economic and social actors, expands networks and cooperation between actors, and reinforces learning and interaction mechanisms. That is to say, the institutions condition the behavior of productivity, and therefore, the economic development process.

Finally, diffusion of innovations and knowledge, flexible organization of production, and urban and institutional development generate increased efficiency in the performance of the productive system. Each one of these mechanisms becomes an efficiency factor in the process of capital accumulation, to the extent that they stimulate economies of scale and scope, and reduce transaction costs, all of which bring about increased productivity and returns (Vázquez-Barquero, 2002).

Local response to global challenge

The high unemployment and poverty rates reached in the 1980s made for profound change in development policies (Stöhr, 1990; Vázquez-Barquero, 1993). The new development policies represent a spontaneous response on behalf of the local communities for the purpose of neutralizing the negative effects of globalization, and of the productive adjustment on employment and the population's standard of living.

Given the need to restructure their productive systems in order to face increased competition and changes in the market conditions, many of the economies of developing countries are carrying out local development policies (Albuquerque, 2001; Aghón *et al.*, 2001; Altenburg and Meyer-Stamer, 1999). Faced with the limitations of the macroeconomic policies for solving the problems associated with poverty, job creation, and improved social welfare, the local and regional actors tried to correct the adjustment processes. Through their actions, they tried to increase the productivity of the farms and the industrial and services firms, and improve competitiveness in the national and international markets of firms located within their territories.

Fostering firms' development and cluster

Local initiatives are very diverse in nature (Vázquez-Barquero, 2005). Yet, the basic characteristic of the new development policy is that an important part of the local initiatives are designed to spur on the forces and mechanisms that are decisive factors in the capital accumulation process. One of the objectives of local initiatives is the startup and development of firms and the formation of firm networks. In Rafaela, Argentina, an industrial district under productive restructuring (Ferraro and Costamagna, 2000), the Centre for Entrepreneurial Development was created in 1996, financed by the Inter-American Development Bank (IDB) as well as by local firms and the municipality. The Centre gives technical and financial assistance to local and regional firms, which will allow them to improve their production, have a greater presence in the markets, and increase the internationalization of small firms.

On the other hand, in the Sierra de los Cuchumatanes, in Guatemala, on the border with Chiapas (Cifuentes, 2000) during the 1990s, cooperatives and associations were recovered and began to acquire full legal capacity (Formal Organization of Agricultural Producers). These organizations also resuscitated the experience and knowledge of self-management that existed within the local population, but was lost during the civil war. Moreover, more informally structured organizations, or interest groups, were encouraged, which brought together people with common productive and commercial interests.

As indicated by Scott (2005), the improvement of the cooperative base of the shoe production cluster in Marikina (Philippines) is one of the objectives of the group of shoe manufacturers. The Marikina Footwear and Leather Goods Manufacturers Cooperative, for example, provides financial services to members of the cooperative; among which are "the right to take out loans, to purchase raw materials at a reduced price, and to discount letters of credit." The cooperative has a footwear brand (B&G) that the members may use when manufacturing their shoes. The cooperative provides distribution and marketing services to its members.

The government of Penang, in Malaysia, created the Penang Development Center (PDC), whose main objective is to promote socioeconomic development, including the attraction of export-oriented MNCs. The PDC played an important role in the creation of the electronic cluster in Penang with an important presence of MNCs (Clarion and National Semiconductors, Intel, Motorola, Hewlett-Packard, AMD, Hitachi) located during the 1970s, and consumer electronics firms (such as Sony, Toshiba, Pensangko, Komag, Seagate, and others) located during the 1980s and 1990s.

PDC helped stimulate the formation of firm networks, and differentiate and diversify the productive fabric, particularly after the late 1980s. A productive fabric has been created in which the domestic SMEs have established ties among themselves and with the MNCs. Yet, the lack of coordination on behalf of the government of Penang with the federal government of Malaysia restricted the development of local initiatives in order to upgrade human resources and diffuse innovation within the local productive fabric (Rasiah, 2007).

Finally, during the past decade in Latin America, Asia, and Africa, various forms of micro-credit and financial support to micro-firms and small businesses have appeared (Lacalle, 2002; Armendáriz and Murdoch, 2001). The Grameen Bank, created in 1974, is a story of success. In 1999, it had more than 2.3 million clients (95 percent women) and a volume of loans in excess of $2.715 billion. It is estimated to have helped 12 million people in Bangladesh. In turn, International Action, founded in 1961, has a network of 19 credit offices in Latin America, with more than 380,000 clients (57 percent women) and more than $335 million in loans.

There are many experiences in fulfilling local firms' needs and demands for services in Latin America (Muñoz, 2000; Londoño, 2000). In 1992, the Municipal House of the Small Businessman (Casa Municipal del Pequeño Empresario) in the town of Rancagua, Chile, was established to promote qualification in business management and render technical and financial assistance to micro-firms and small businesses. The Program for the Support of Small and Medium-size Firms (Programa de Apoyo a la Pequeña y Mediana Empresa) in Antioquía, Colombia, aims to provide small textile and clothing industry entrepreneurs with knowledge of textile materials and design as well as technical consulting and export assistance through a strategic alliance with the Export and Fashion Institute.

In Porto Alegre, the prefecture, in collaboration with private economic and social actors, founded the community credit institution PORTOSOL, a nonprofit company with two main principles: the combination of real guarantees and solidarity bonds, and the provision of services to small businessmen.

Diffusion of innovation and knowledge

Another major axis of the new development policy is the diffusion of innovation and knowledge throughout the local productive fabric, as can be seen in the initiatives that work in territories with very different productive dynamics and levels of development. Thus, in Rafaela, the Rafaela Regional Centre (Centro Regional de Rafaela), a part of the National Institute of Technology, was created in 1997, which provides services such as analysis and laboratory tests, research and development of products, technical assistance to local firms, and training to qualified workers.

A particularly interesting case is that of the Technological Centre do Couro, Calçado e Afins (CTCCA) of Novo Hamburgo, Rio Grande do Sul in Brazil. This is a private, nonprofit institution established in 1972, which was founded for the purpose of helping the shoewear firms at the beginning of their export activity by providing services that would allow them to maintain the quality standards required by international markets. After 30 years it has become an institution capable of stimulating research activity and product and process development in the shoe industry of Brazil.

In Asia, both in developed as well as emerging countries, the technological policy is at the core of the development programs. In Japan, the policies in support of technology during the 1980s were focused toward promoting structural change in underdeveloped regions, through the support of high technology activities in peripheral locations. In China, the Scientific and Technological Park Zhong Guan Cun in Beijing, has become, since 1999, an example of how to combine training with scientific research, both with the creation and diffusion of innovations. In its central area are located 2,400 firms and public centers, a result of the investments of multinational corporations like IBM, Microsoft, HP, Oracle, Siemens, Motorola, NTT, Fujitsu, Panasonic, Samsung, and Mitsubishi, among others.

Last of all, the Malaysia Technological Park, located within the "Multimedia Super Corridor" in the outskirts of Kuala Lumpur, Malaysia, was created in 1996 as an instrument for converting Malaysia into an economy focused on the production of high technology and knowledge-intensive goods and services. This complex provides firms with services and infrastructures that stimulate the creation and diffusion of technological innovation and knowledge. It gives technical and financial services to entrepreneurial initiatives that wish to transform an innovative idea into a business; it helps in the implementation of research projects through its biotechnology division (in the fields of molecular biology, biochemistry, pharmacology, and food sciences); it provides training services in the fields of engineering, biotechnology, and information technology; and it provides fully equipped floor space and services to firms that wish to locate in an environment focused toward a knowledge economy.

Building up infrastructures for local development

Initiatives targeting the building up of infrastructures and social overhead capital are traditional instruments for urban and regional development. Investment in economic overhead capital is at present a long-term policy response to the challenges of globalization and competition between cities. In Asia, during the past 15 years, important investments in infrastructures (such as international airports, ports, roads, underground, high-speed railways) have taken place in leading cities like Bangkok, Kuala Lumpur, Seoul, Beijing, and Shanghai. The purpose is to make these global city-regions more attractive to inward investment and global capital, and as a result intercity networks are taking shape (Scott *et al.*, 2001; Douglas, 2001).

Furthermore, in Latin America, practically all the local development experiences involve improving accessibility, meeting the needs of social overhead capital, and making cities more attractive places in which to live and produce. The Villa el Salvador initiative (located in Southern Lima, Peru) bases its strategy on the creation of an industrial park in order to provide industrial land, equipment, and the services required by micro-firms and small and medium-sized firms (Benavides and Manrique, 2000). The Local Economic Development Program of the mayor's office in Medellin, Colombia, includes urban and metropolitan infrastructure projects.

The concern for sustainable development has led cities to create imaginative projects like that of Curitiba, Brazil (Cambell, 2001; World Bank, 1999) where, during the late 1990s, a project was launched that tries to integrate urban infrastructure actions (construction of a road that facilitates communication among 14 neighborhoods in the periphery of the city) with business initiatives based on equipment goods (community huts) in which micro-firms and small enterprises can be installed with the support of the services available through professional and entrepreneurial training. The urban transport system was transformed into a surface metro system and it is considered the main element of the urban development model. The innovations introduced in the urban transport of Curitiba have been imitated in other cities of Latin America, such as the surface metro, Transmilenio, in Bogotá, Colombia.

An example of measures that act on the economic, social, and physical system of a city as a whole is the remodeling of Puerto Madero, in Buenos Aires, located between Rio de la Plata and the historic city center, which allowed the incorporation of the old port into the city. The initiative put a stop to the degradation of a space that had ceased its urban function and recycled it by enhancing leisure activities (cafes, restaurants, bars), the location of educational and entrepreneurial services activities, and quality housing. This spurred an economic motor force for the city, at a time when the economy of the city was very weak. The transformation of the old seaport into an urban area, housing key activities for its economic development, is accompanied by the recuperation of its architectural heritage.

To neutralize the negative effects of social exclusion, cities have launched urban development initiatives such as neighborhood restructuring in Caracas, Venezuela (Baldó and Villanueva, 1996; Villanueva, 1998). A good example is the Catuche project of 1993, an initiative that relied on the Jesuit Fathers of the Pastora to provide this marginal neighborhood with the basic services and social capital needed to improve the environment and living conditions of the population. Some of the most important actions of this initiative are the environmental clean-up of the Catuche River, improved neighbor relations, the building or reconstruction of public services and new housing, and the promotion of micro-firms to carry out the construction jobs. The project was managed by the Consortium of the Quebrada de Catuche, made up of members from the Catuche community, representatives from the group of promoters, and professional participants. It was funded by the Caracas municipal government, the national government, and nongovernmental organizations.

New governance for local development

At the center of new development policy are actions aimed at improving the organization of development in the city or region in order to give an efficient answer to the problems and challenges ahead.

The development of a locality or territory is organized by the decisions of the public and private agents. Frequently, as occurred in Bogotá, in Rosario, and in Quezaltenango, in the early stages of the local development policy, local leaders stimulate the implementation of local initiatives, but they should count on explicit or tacit support from other local actors as well.

In Latin America, as in Asia, endogenous development policy is also based on initiatives where social and economic projects are coordinated through new forms of governance, such as partnerships among public and private actors, international agencies, or nongovernmental organizations. In Villa El Salvador, the Autonomous Authority of the Cono Sur Industrial Park (Autoridad Autónoma del Parque Industrial del Cono Sur) was founded and brings together public and private agents working to develop the Industrial Park. In Jalisco, Mexico, local entrepreneurs, including executives of MNCs as well as the public actors, participate in the creation of local networks of suppliers.

The development of city institutions has also become one of the characteristic features of the Development Policy of Rafaela (Costamagna, 1999). Strategic planning helps cities and regions define goals and initiatives, like in Rosario, Argentina.

The definition, design, and promotion of local development initiatives and strategies is also strongly supported by international organizations like the Organization for Economic Co-operation and Development (OECD), the European Union, the United Nations Program for Development (UNDP), the International Labour Organization (ILO), and the World Bank, since the early 1990s. Various UN agencies, often through joint programs with other agencies and entities, propose the creation and promotion of Local Economic Development Agencies (LEDA) in developing countries and in transition economies for the purpose of promoting the economic activity and improving the standard of living in cities and regions with economic and social problems (Canzanelli, 2003).

Today, there are 42 LEDA agencies in Central America, the Balkans, and Africa, which work with a great deal of autonomy. These are nonprofit organizations, with mixed public and private capital, whose objective is to create and develop the environment necessary for firm startups and to provide support services for the economic development of the territory, as well as for social inclusion. Thus, the LEDA support the development of networks of local actors, thereby allowing a degree of local autonomy in development decisions and stimulating innovation processes.

The Local Human Development Program now underway in Cuba since late 1998, promoted by the UNDP and the ILO, is an example of the new forms of international cooperation that has advanced the introduction and diffusion of relevant innovations, particularly in the field of cooperation practices (Panico *et al.*, 2002). It has helped bring about important changes in cooperation through the articulation of resources from various international agencies, from governments, and other public and private organizations, as well as enhancing decentralized cooperation. Furthermore, it has led to innovations and transformations in the local development processes with the forming of municipal and provincial workgroups for the design and carrying out of local initiatives, and the startup of the Rotation Fund for Initiatives of Local Economic Development, a tool for financing small and medium-sized local firms.

In this general framework, Old Havana has become an example of good practice with respect to development policy through multilateral finance, thanks to the stimulus of the City Historian's Office, which works as a development agency. Among the more important initiatives are: the rehabilitation of the historic heritage, the improvement of urban infrastructures, support to tourist activities, the recovery of craftsmanship (such as the sisterhood of embroidery and weavers), and the improvement of social services (for the elderly and handicapped children).

Endogenous development policy

As seen above, endogenous development policy meets a relevant function in the economic development processes, for it acts as a catalyst of the development mechanisms through local initiatives. It facilitates entrepreneurial development and the creation of firm networks, it encourages the diffusion of innovation and knowledge, improves urban diversity, and stimulates the development of the institutional fabric. In other words, the new development policy tools favor the improvement of the functioning of each one of the determining forces of capital accumulation and economic development.

One of the main objectives of the new development policy is to foster the continuous improvement of entrepreneurial resources. All of the local initiatives propose, as their main objective, to promote the startup of new firms and the upgrading of the entrepreneurial and organizational capacity of their economic agents. As mentioned above, firm incubators, business innovation centers, and initiatives that encourage the entrepreneurial capacity of social target groups like young people and women are some of the tools that are implemented in developing countries. Furthermore, in recent years, the firm attraction policy has reappeared. The "endogenization" of modern large firm activity within the territory has been helped through new forms of regulation, such as territorial agreements, that facilitate relations between external firms and the territory.

Additionally, the initiatives for the creation and diffusion of innovations also play a central role in the new development policy. For decades, one of the pillars of restructuring and modernization of local economies has been to facilitate the adoption and adaptation of technology through instruments such as innovation centers, scientific parks, technological parks, and technology institutes. Among their objectives was to stimulate the transfer and diffusion of innovations within the productive fabric, favor the startup and development of high-tech firms, and, ultimately, fulfill the firms' needs and demands for technological services, at a time in which increased competition requires improved technology.

The urban development of the territory is one of the main features of the new development policy. On one hand, the initiatives focuses toward making cities more attractive for living and for producing include providing equipped land to firms, reinforcing the urban transport and communications system, improving the social capital of cities, and recuperating the historic and cultural heritage and making them more sustainable. On the other hand, the creation of services such as fairs or business centers, urban marketing through image campaigns, and the construction of emblematic buildings makes the city more attractive, encourages inward investment, promotes the demand for urban services, and, in sum, activates the urbanization processes. In any case, the adaptation of norms and regulations to the needs and demands of firms and citizens, as well as improved public services, foster city networks and favor the urban development of the territories.

From another point of view, the new development policy is based on a new form of regulation and relations between the economic, social, and political actors. It is a new form of governance that designs and carries out policies based on the negotiation of specific agreements between the public and private actors, nongovernmental organizations, and international agencies. The implementation of the actions is made through specific intermediary agencies promoted and managed by the local actors. Lastly, partnership and networks among firms and organizations are the most common forms of cooperation: partnership leads the transactions based on formal agreements among local actors; networking is less extended at this time.

The new development policy is, also, an instrument that tries to integrate the various types of actions in such a way that it is more closely adjusted to the needs of the productive systems and to the demands of the firms and citizens. Its objective is to act in a combined manner on all of the mechanisms and forces of development, trying to create and improve the synergy, in such a way that the conditions for the sustained growth of productivity are created, and the sustainable development of each locality or territory is stimulated.

In short, what give an innovative character to the endogenous development policies are, among others, the following characteristics:

- It is an economic development policy (industrial, technological, training, environmental) designed and carried out by the municipal governments and regions (within the general macroeconomic framework), financed by different areas of the state, nongovernmental organizations, and international agencies, and that occurs for the first time since modern economic policy existed.
- It is a policy that has surged spontaneously and that has a direct effect on the development forces, as explained above, which allows us to say that it has economic rationality. Although the central administrations of many countries don't always consider this kind of policy relevant, international organizations (such as UNDP, ILO, IDB, EU) use it more and more often for putting into effect the aid to development (decentralized aid). This permits them to overcome the limitations of the "financial deficit" approach, characteristic of the previous period where fundamentalism of capital was the development model that inspired international aid policy.
- It is a development policy that seeks the creation of local wealth and employment, and not a redistributive policy, as was the case in the 1950s, 1960s, and 1970s (both social and welfare policies; as with macroeconomic policies, central administration does it better). It is, essentially, a policy directed toward fostering the startup and development of firms in an ever more integrated and competitive world. Thus, it is not a welfare policy, even though social aspects are kept in mind, such as increased employment and improved income and well-being for the population of specific territories.
- It is a policy in which organized civil society designs and controls the development policy (through instruments like strategic planning and management) and in which the local actors participate in the management of the development tools; such as, for example, occurs in the CTTCA of Novo Hamburgo, with the participation of the entrepreneurs in the technical boards (fashion, machinery, human resources training, or environment).

However, what lessons can be learned from the results obtained with these types of policies? Which are the factors, if any, that condition the final results? Why do some instruments work and others don't? Why have some of the territories had better results than others?

It is difficult to answer these types of questions with a limited knowledge of the evolution of the endogenous development policies and their instruments, the result of occasional studies or specific technical visits. Nevertheless, there is an issue that affects the success of the policies and the results of the instruments used in a remarkable way. That is that the actions and initiatives should obey a specific strategy and development policy in each city or region that defines the main objectives and actions to be accomplished, because economic development is a result of the interaction of the economic forces. When this is not the case, it is only by chance that the results can meet expectations.

The success of the policy depends, therefore, on the adaptation of the actions to the economic and social conditions of each locality or territory. Endogenous development policies take on different shapes in the old industrialized regions, such as the Grand ABC in São Paulo, Brazil, that is now experiencing strong industrial restructuring processes; in endogenous industrialization areas, such as Rafaela in Argentina, the State of Santa Catarina in Brazil, or Marikina in the Philippines, where production service activities are more and more developed; or in rural areas with development potential, such as the region of the Sierra de los Cuchumatanes in Guatemala, where they are in the first stages of the industrial development process.

Nevertheless, the success of the development instruments depends on the existence of a market for the services that the business centers, the technological institutes or the development agencies can offer, and that which has not already been covered by private firms or by organizations similar in nature to what the policy pretends to create. Good practice recommends that, from its creation, every development tool should precisely define its target group, the needs to be covered, the objectives that the services should reach, and the necessary technical facilities that should be supplied to the clients.

These types of considerations will, for example, lead to accepting the fact that scientific and technological parks are instruments for the diffusion of innovations in a specific entrepreneurial fabric. Thus, when an entrepreneurial fabric is being created, as occurs in the cases of the Technological Park in Malaysia or the Scientific Park in Beijing, and the target group to which this action is directed is not sufficiently precise, the results, in terms of creation and development of innovative firms, may be found lacking with respect to the project. The selection criteria for initiatives in the firm incubator of the Scientific Park of Beijing are rather ambiguous. They mix aspects such as technical and economic viability of the projects and its innovative nature, with aspects related to the academic interest of the projects, which is an issue outside the functioning of the instrument that may have a negative effect on the efficiency of the instrument, and, thus, for the results that could be expected from the firm incubator.

The management of local initiatives and development tools is an issue that seriously affects the results of the development policy. Policy success rests on the strength of the commitment with the project and the motivation of the promoters. In order to reach the objectives, the expressed or tacit support of the organizations and firms that are part of the top management of the city or region is necessary. Furthermore, the people responsible for the management of the agencies and service centers must necessarily have experience in the management of intermediary organisms, as well as a strong ethical commitment to the values that regulate the market system. Because of this, the bad results of the development actions and the faulty working of the instruments are often associated with management deficiencies. In this sense, it is very important that, as occurs in the Novo Hamburgo Technological Center, the firms that use the services, the clients of the agency, have a presence in the management councils of the center.

With respect to the financial aspects of the project and the financial means of the services to be made available to the firms, they should be clearly established before the development initiatives and tools are set in motion. Thus, the best practices recommend that the business centers, the technological institutes, or the training centers be created based on a firm's plan for the center that is clear, coherent, consistent, and realistic, and establish the financial needs, the financial objectives, their own resources devoted to the financing of the center, and the actions for attracting outside resources. A high degree of internal cohesion between the financing of the development strategy and the foreseeable results of the services supplied should exist from the start; although it would be necessary to adjust the development strategy to the changes in the environment and to policy performance as a result of carrying out the projects. Local development agencies are usually nonprofit organizations that pretend to cover the financial needs by charging for services rendered, which is often an unobtainable objective, but this does not mean that the managers of the policy tool should not be focused in that direction.

Last of all, the state's central administration has an important role to play in the application of the endogenous development policy, both on the technical as well as on the financial level. Although endogenous development policy cannot be understood as a state policy, given that it has appeared spontaneously as an answer on behalf of the municipalities and regions to the productive adjustment problems and to social exclusion, good practice again recommends that the central administrations should take it on as its own, since it is in line with its objectives of growth, increased productivity, and productive adjustment. This could be put forward as an action, as done by international organizations, financing the endogenous development actions and tools, and specifying the requirements for local initiatives in order to be eligible for state financing.

Final comments

This chapter argues that the sustainable development of countries, regions, and cities does not depend exclusively on the level of savings and investment of each economy, but mainly on the functioning of the forces that condition capital accumulation and economic development. Because of this, the chapter argues that these forces are: entrepreneurial development and the formation of firm networks, diffusion of innovation and knowledge, urban development of the territory, and the change and adaptation of institutions. The combined action of all the forces and their interactions produce a synergic effect that stimulates sustained growth of productivity and economic and social progress.

Therefore, endogenous development policy that has appeared spontaneously meets a relevant function in the economic development processes, since it acts as a catalyst of the development mechanisms through the local initiatives. It facilitates entrepreneurial development and the creation of firm networks, it encourages diffusion of innovations and knowledge, it improves urban diversity, and it stimulates the development of the institutional fabric. In other words, the new development policy attempts, precisely, to improve the functioning of each one of the forces that determine capital accumulation and economic development.

Thus, the endogenous development approach distinguishes between economic growth (changes in economic variables that take place in the short term, for example, the increase in GDP) and economic development (the qualitative transformation of the economy and society). It points out that the economic development of cities, regions, and countries takes place as a result of the changes in the institutions, in technology, in culture, in social relations, and in the organization of production. The very same development processes, in turn, affect all of these dimensions.

References

Abramovitz, M. (1952) Economics of Growth, in B.F. Haley (ed.) *A Survey of Contemporary Economics*, Richard D. Irwin, Homewood, Ill.

Aghón, G., Alburquerque, F., and Cortés, P. (2001) *Desarrollo Económico Local y Descentralización en América Latina: Un Análisis Comparativo*, CEPAL/GTZ, Santiago de Chile.

Alburquerque, F. (2001) *Evaluación y reflexiones sobre las iniciativas de desarrollo económico local en América Latina*, Mimeograph, Consejo de Investigaciones Científicas, Madrid.

Altenburg, T. and Meyer-Stamer, J. (1999) How to Promote Clusters: Policy Experiences from Latin America, *World Development*, 27, pp. 1693–1713.

Amin, A. and Thrift, N. (1993) Globalization, Institutional Thickness and Local Prospect, *Revue d'Economie Regional et Urbain*, 3, pp. 405–427.

Armendáriz de Aghion, B. and Murdoch, J. (2001) *The Economics of Microfinance*, MIT Press, Cambridge.

Arrow, K.J. (1962) The Economic Implications of Learning by Doing, *Review of Economic Studies*, 29, pp. 155–173.

Asheim, T.B., Isaksen, A., Nauwelaers, C. and Tödtling, F. (eds.) (2003) *Regional Innovation Policy for Small–Medium Enterprises*, Edward Elgar, Cheltenham.

Aydalot, P. (1985) *Economie régionale et urbaine*, Economica, Paris.

Aydalot, P. (1986) *Milieux innovateurs en Europe*. Economica, Paris.

Baldó, J. and Villanueva, F. (1996) Plan de reestructuración de los barrios de la estructura urbana, in H. Garnica (ed.) *Los Barrios no tienen quien les escriba*, Diario El Universal, Dec. 9, pp. 1–4.

Becattini, G. (1979) Dal settore industriale al distretto industriale: alcune considerazione sull'unita di indagine dell'economia industriale, *Rivista di Economia e Politica Industriale*, 1, pp. 7–21.

Becattini, G. (1997) Totalità e cambiamento: il paradigma dei distretti industriali, *Sviluppo Locale* 4, 6, pp. 5–24.

Bellandi, M. (2001) Local Development and Embedded Large Firms, *Entrepreneurship & Regional Development*, 13, pp. 189–210.

Benavides, M. and Manrique, G. (2000) La experiencia de desarrollo económico local del distrito de Villa el Salvador, in G. Aghon, F. Alburquerque and P. Cortés (eds.) *Desarrollo Económico Local y Descentralización en América Latina: Un Análisis Comparativo*, CEPAL/GTZ, Santiago de Chile.

Camagni, R. (1992) Organisation économique et réseaux des villes, in P.H. Derycke (ed.) *Espace et dynamiques territoriales*, Economica, Paris.

Camagni, R. (1994) *Processi di utilizzazione e difesa di suoli nelle fasce periurbane*, Fundazione Cariplo, Milan.

Cambell, T. (2001) Innovation and Risk-taking: Urban Governance in Latin America, in A.J. Scott (ed.) *Global City-Regions. Trends, Theory, Policy*, Oxford University Press, Oxford.

Canzanelli, G. (2003) *The Role of International Organizations for the Promotion of Endogenous Development*, Mimeograph, University of Naples, Geneva and Napoli.

Castells, M. (1996) *The Information Age: Economy, Society and Culture. Volume I: The Rise of the Network Society*, Blackwell Publishers, Cambridge.

Cifuentes, I. (2000) *Proyecto Cuchumatanes. Transferencia de servicios técnicos a las organizaciones de productores*, Ministerio de Agricultura, Ganadería y Alimentación, Huehuetenango, Guatemala.

Cooke, P. (2002) *Knowledge Economies: Clusters, Learning, and Cooperative Advantage*, Routledge, London.

Cooke, P. and Morgan, K. (1998) *The Associational Economy. Firms, Regions, and Innovation*, Oxford University Press, Oxford.

Costamagna, P. (1999) *Iniciativa de desarrollo económico local. La articulación y las interaciones entre instituciones. El caso de Rafaela*, Mimeograph, CEPAL/GTZ Project, Santiago de Chile.

Douglas, M. (2001) Intercity Competition and the Question of Economic Resilience: Globalization and Crisis in Asia, in A.J. Scott (ed.) *Global City-Regions. Trends, Theory, Policy*, Oxford University Press, Oxford.

Dunning, J.H. (2001) Regions, Globalization, and the Knowledge Economy, in J.H. Dunning (ed.) *Global Capitalism at Bay?* Routledge, London.

Easterly, W. (2001) *The Elusive Quest for Growth: Economists' Adventure and Misadventures in the Tropics*, MIT Press, Cambridge, MA.

Ferraro, C. and Costamagna, P. (2000) *Entorno institucional y desarrollo productivo local. La importancia del ambiente y las instituciones para el desarrollo empresarial. El caso de Rafaela*, CEPAL, LC/BUE/R.246, Buenos Aires.

Freeman, C. and Soete, L. (1997) *The Economics of Industrial Innovation*, MIT Press, Cambridge, MA.

Friedmann, J. and Weaver, C. (1979) *Territory and Function*, Edward Arnold, London.

Fuà, G. (1983) L'industrializzazione nel nord est e nel centro, in G. Fuà and C. Zachia (eds.) *Industrializzazione senza fratture*, Il Mulino, Bologna.

Fuà, G. (1988) Small-scale Industry in Rural Areas: the Italian Experience, in K.J. Arrow (ed.) *The Balance Between Industry and Agriculture in Economic Development*, Macmillan, London.

Fuà, G. (1994) *Economic growth: a Discussion on Figures*, Istao, Ancona.

Garofoli, G. (1991) *Modelli locali di sviluppo*, Angeli, Milano.

Garofoli, G. (1992) *Endogenous Development and Southern Europe*, Avebury, Aldershot.

Glaeser, E. (1998) Are Cities Dying? *Journal of Economic Perspectives*, 12, 2, pp. 139–160.

Hakansson, H. and Johanson, J. (1993) The Network as a Governance Structure. Interfirm

Cooperation Beyond Markets and Hierarchies, in G. Grabher (ed.) *The Embedded Firm. On the Socioeconomics of Industrial Network.* Routledge, London.

Hall, P. (1993) Forces Reshaping Urban Europe, *Urban Studies*, 30, 6, pp. 883–898.

Kuznets, S. (1966) *Modern Economic Growth*, Yale University Press, New Haven.

Lacalle, M.C. (2002) *Microcréditos. De pobres a microempresarios*, Ariel, Barcelona.

Lasuen, J.R. (1973) Urbanization and Development. The Temporal Interaction Between Geographical and Sectoral Clusters, *Urban Studies*, 10, pp. 163–188.

Lewis, A. (1954) Economic Development with Unlimited Supplies of Labour, *The Manchester School of Economic and Social Studies*, 22, pp. 139–191.

Lewis, A. (1955) *The Theory of Economic Growth*, George Allen & Unwin, London.

Londoño, C. (2000) Iniciativas de cooperación para el desarrollo económico local en Antioquia, in G. Aghon, F. Alburquerque, and P. Cortés (eds.) *Desarrollo Económico Local y Descentralización en América Latina: Un Análisis Comparativo*, CEPAL/GTZ, Santiago de Chile.

Lucas, R.E. (1988) On the Mechanics of Economic Development, *Journal of Monetary Economics*, 22, 1, pp. 129–144.

Lundvall, B.A. (ed.) (1992) *National Systems of Innovation: Towards a Theory of Innovation and Interactive Learning*, Pinter, London.

Maillat, D. (1995) Territorial Dynamic, Innovative Milieus and Regional Policy, *Entrepreneurship & Regional Development*, 7, pp. 157–165.

Massey, D. (1984) *Spatial Divisions of Labour. Social Structures and Geography of Production*, Macmillan, London.

Muñoz, C. (2000) Programa "Rancagua emprende": una experiencia de desarrollo económico local en Chile, in G. Aghon, F. Alburquerque and P. Cortés (eds.) *Desarrollo Económico Local y Descentralización en América Latina: Un Análisis Comparativo*, CEPAL/GTZ, Santiago de Chile.

North, C.D. (1990) *Institutions, Institutional Change and Economic Performance*, Cambridge University Press, New York.

North, C.D. (1994) Economic Performance Through Time, *The American Economic Review*, 83, 3, pp. 359–368.

Panico, C., Fleitas, R., and Vázquez-Barquero, A. (2002) *Local Human Development Programme in Cuba. External Evaluation Report*, UNDP, Havana.

Perroux, F. (1955) Note sur la notion de pôle de croissance, *Économie Appliquée*, 7, pp. 307–320.

Piore, M. and Sabel, C.F. (1984) *The Second Industrial Divide*, Basic Books, New York.

Putman, R. (1993) *Making Democracy Work*, Princeton University Press, New Jersey.

Quigley, J.M. (1998) Urban Diversity and Economic Growth, *Journal of Economic Perspectives*, 12, 2, pp. 127–138.

Rasiah, R. (2007) Clusters and Regional Industrial Synergies: The Electronics Industry in Penang and Jalisco, in A.J. Scott and G. Garofoli (eds.) *Development on the Ground: Clusters, Networks, and Regions in Emerging Economies*.

Romer, M.P. (1986) Increasing Returns and Long Run Growth, *Journal of Political Economy*, 94, pp. 1002–1037.

Roseger, G. (1996) *The Economics of Production and Innovation*, Butterworth-Heinemann, Oxford.

Saxenian, A. (1994) *Regional Advance, Culture and Competition in Silicon Valley and Route 128*, Harvard University Press, Cambridge.

Schumpeter, J.A. (1934) *The Theory of Economic Development*, Harvard University Press, Cambridge [1st edition in German, 1911].

Schumpeter, J.A. (1939) *Business Cycles*, McGraw-Hill, New York.

Scott, A.J. (1988) *New Industrial Spaces*, Pion Ltd, London.

Scott, A.J. (1998) *Regions and the World Economy*, Oxford University Press, Oxford.

Scott, A.J. (2005) The Shoe Industry of Marikina City, Philippines: A Developing-Country Cluster in Crisis, *Kasarinlan: Philippine Journal of Third World Studies*, 20, 2, pp. 76–79.

Scott, A.J., Agnew, J., Soja, W.E. and Storper, M. (2001) Global City-Regions, in A.J. Scott (ed.) *Global City-Regions. Trends, Theory, Policy*, Oxford University Press, Oxford.

Solow, R. (1956) A Contribution to the Theory of Economic Growth, *Quarterly Journal of Economics*, 78, pp. 65–94.

Stöhr, W.B. (ed.) (1990) *Global Challenge and Local Response*, Mansell, London.

Stöhr, W.B. and Taylor, D.R.F. (eds.) (1981) *Development from Above or Below?* J. Wiley and Sons, Chichester.

Vázquez-Barquero, A. (1993) *Política Económica Local*, Pirámide, Madrid.

Vázquez-Barquero, A. (1999) Inward Investment and Endogenous Development. The Convergence of the Strategies of Large Firms and Territories? *Entrepreneurship and Regional Development*, 11, pp. 79–93.

Vázquez-Barquero, A. (2002) *Endogenous Development*, Routledge, London.

Vázquez-Barquero, A. (2005) *Las Nuevas Fuerzas del Desarrollo*, Barcelona, A. Bosch.

Villanueva, M. (1998) Proyecto Quebrada de Catuche. Programa de habilitación física de barrios (PROHABITAT), unpublished paper, Seminar on Programas Sociales, Pobreza y Participación Ciudadana en Caracas, Banco Interamericano de Desarrollo, Cartagena.

World Bank (1999) *World Bank Report*, Washington, DC.

Part II

Regional development in the Middle East and Africa

3 The Arab world

The role of regional production systems in catch-up and convergence

Abdelkader Sid Ahmed

Introduction

The aim behind the Barcelona, Spain, agreements signed in November 1995 was to bring the countries on the southern and eastern borders of the Mediterranean into line with northern Europe, and thus create a zone of shared prosperity in the Mediterranean basin. Eleven years later it seems clear that this objective is likely to become a dead letter. The promised financial investments and complementary technological aid still stagnate at around 1 percent of total EU world investment, revealing the low attraction of the Arab region. With a few exceptions, Arab growth has been at a virtual stop since the middle of the 1980s. The result is that, in spite of numerous resources, including important financial ones, the hopes for catch-up and revenue convergence between the two sides of the Mediterranean expressed in the Barcelona project are now postponed.

This somber view is shared by the EU. Within the general framework of the June 2004 EU expansion, the EU proposed a new project of "strategic partnership" to its partners on the other side of the Mediterranean. The central proposal of this project, formulated at the Conference of Euro-Med Foreign Affairs Ministers held in Dublin, Ireland, in May 2004, concerned a new "neighborhood" policy aimed at creating environments favorable to investment. In proposing this new neighborhood approach, the EU confirmed that it was ready to *share everything except its institutions*. Europe offered the advantages of security, stability, and prosperity, but based the offer on the condition that the Arab countries accept a certain number of "common values," ranging from the respect of human rights to lasting development. The Arab countries were asked to submit the project proposals they considered essential if their economies were to be put on a two-digit durable growth course. This was the necessary condition postulated for catch-up and convergence at Barcelona. The proposals were to be based on global macroeconomic growth policies aimed at stability and convergence, coupled with the promotion of regional production systems developed in the light of what has been learned in these areas during the previous decade.

Growth and development in the Arab world: assessment and perspectives

The boom of the 1950s, 1960s and 1970s

Arab countries experienced important economic and social progress in the 1950s, 1960s, and 1970s. Between 1960 and 1985, the Middle East and North Africa enjoyed a per capita annual growth rate of 3.7 percent. This was, however, below the 4.3 percent growth rate of Far East Asia.

During these three decades, most Arab economies followed an interventionist and redistribution type development model (Richards and Waterbury, 1996), a model that encourages the role of the state in the fixing of economic and social priorities via a mechanism of centralized economic planning, agrarian reforms, and the nationalization of foreign and private assets. On a social and political level, the state played an essential role in the development of education, housing, health, and food subsidies. Controlled hierarchic unions and professional associations were encouraged. Within this model, the state was seen as the instrument of social transformation, political mobilization, and general economic redistribution.

The massive public investment in infrastructure, health, and education, together with the creation of state companies in the protected industrial sector, acted as a strong stimulus for industrialization in the 1960s, bringing the annual GDP growth per worker to 6 percent. The considerable oil revenues maintained this boom throughout the 1970s in spite of the extremely high levels of capital accumulation and an increase in the negative total factor productivity (Sid Ahmed, 2000). There was a massive increase in public sector employment, while opportunities for migration abroad, including migration between Arab countries, opened up significantly.

The collapse of oil prices and the economic crisis of the 1980s and 1990s: the natural resources curse

When the price of hydrocarbons decreased, it became increasingly difficult for institutions to respect their social contracts. The collapse of oil revenues, together with the drastic reduction in demand for migrant labor, led to a dramatic fall in the number of workers leaving for other countries and a more competitive international environment. At the same time, the domestic regulatory environments discouraged private investment and blocked the development of export-oriented industrial sectors and the integration of regional markets in global markets. With the increasing macroeconomic imbalance, particularly indebtedness, rates of investment declined in the 1980s by as much as 75 percent on a per worker basis. Between the 1970s and 1980s, all countries experienced a considerable decrease in the accumulation rate, and the vast majority registered a decline in the growth of total factor productivity. There was, thus, a collapse in the output growth per worker, an annual decrease of 3.5 percent in comparison with the 1970s.

The cycle of boom, bust, and weak recovery is linked to the so-called *natural resources curse* thesis. Long-term GDP growth is weaker in countries with abundant natural resources. The positive external shocks resulting from the export of natural resources increase the demand for non-tradable products and attract qualifications, investments, and entrepreneurial capacities in the tradable goods sector; all of this moreover, in an "overheated" environment where the expenditure boom leads to a loss of competitiveness resulting from the reassessment of the real exchange rate. The tradable sector shrinks, leading to de-industrialization and de-agriculturization (modern sector), and a reduction in the global growth rate.

Today, it is widely accepted that the main problem with *resource booms* is that economies with resources conduct negative economic policies for a longer period than economies with fewer resources. In a study carried out on six big, newly industrialized countries (Korea, Taiwan, China, India, Brazil and Mexico), Auty demonstrated that countries with few resources and potentially weak markets are those that have been most successful in their industrialization. For example, Korea and Taiwan have been more successful than India and China (which have strong potential markets) and more successful than Brazil (which has abundant resources). This is in spite of the fact that the last two groups, especially those countries with abundant resources, have been exposed to a wider range of industrialization projects.

Auty drew the following conclusion: the more natural resources a country has,

* the longer it will tolerate lax macroeconomic policies;
* the more time it will take to reach mature industrialization;
* the longer it will tolerate and allow rent-seeking groups to take root in the country; and
* the more exposed it will be to a slowing-down process, and to erratic type growth.

(Auty, 1994, pp. 24; 2001)

In their analysis of the links between big push, natural resource booms, and growth Sachs and Warner (1999) and Sachs (2001) took to task the hypothesis that the "big push" was ineffective in situations with private macroeconomic policies (Mahon, 1992). In their comparison of the recent evolution of the Far East Asian group and that of Central and Latin American countries, Weiss and Jalilian emphasized the inadequate role played by the manufacturing sector as a growth engine in the two Americas. As the manufacturing industry declined as a percentage of total activity (including during periods of economic expansion), a structural shift appeared in several countries during the 1990s (Weiss and Jalilian, 2004). What is new in some Latin American economies is that the manufacturing sector apparently started to slow down while revenue per person was still relatively low.

Arab growth during the past four decades can be evaluated by analyzing traditional growth fundamentals, and also by looking at associated factors such as geography, ecology, resources, demographic transitions, and conflicts (Elbadawi, 2005).

Determining factors for growth in the Arab world

High growth is associated with a number of factors: a stable macroeconomic environment, appropriate human capital or manpower, institutions that guarantee property rights, an efficient, lean government, etc. The catch-up hypothesis postulates among other things that poor countries should grow more rapidly than rich countries because of the decreasing productivity of capital resulting from the capital intensity of higher revenue (Loayza and Soto, 2002; Elbadawi, 2005).

Concerning the effects of convergence in the areas of human and social capital, revenue per person in the Arab world has significantly increased, mainly because of the high performance registered during the first three decades. Excluding the high revenues of the oil economies, revenue in the rest of the Arab world – especially in the DAEs (diversified Arab economies) and the primary export Arab economies (PEAEs) – has remained at a much lower level than the average revenue of East Asia.

The ratio of government consumption in the GDP is quite clearly disproportionate. The amount increased from 17 percent in the period 1960–1984, to 26 percent in the period 1985–2000. Even for the DAE and the PEAE, where the public sector was substantially reduced, this participation remained much higher than in East Asia. This is particularly alarming since it mainly concerns general public expenditure with few social returns. Theoretically, heavy participation is associated with bloated administration and high taxes, which, in turn, act as a break on expansion in the private sector (Loayza and Soto, 2002). This participation might have been acceptable during the boom when the traditional redistribution interventionist model type system was in operation in the region, but it was no longer possible when the cycle was inverted. In the Arab region, it was difficult to question such participation because of the expectations and preferences concerning the social contract; governments that reduced their social programs were confronted with serious social and political conflicts and opposition movements (Harik and Sullivan, 1992). Finally, macroeconomic stabilization and crisis-related variables, inflation, parallel market premium on foreign exchange, regular bank crises, and balance of payments all affect cyclical output variability as well as long-term growth.

Other growth factors

Another important factor is *demographic transition*. When a country enters a period of demographic transition and the potentially active population increases in proportion to the rest of the population, a demographic window of opportunity opens; a "demographic gift" becomes available (Williamson and Yousef, 2002). In the absence of strong growth, this opportunity may well remain virtual, and lead to social crisis and increasingly high unemployment. The impact of demographic transition on growth is reflected in the extent to which the rate of growth of the active population exceeds the growth rate of the global population. Egypt and the Maghreb countries have entered this phase of transition, but in the Arab region, although the economically active population increased at the rapid rate of 2.74 percent during the years 1960–2000, global population also increased substantially, thus reducing the economic gift in relation to that of East Asia.

Significance and limits of economic reforms

The Arab countries began to reform with the utmost reticence; indeed, if they reformed at all it was because most of them were forced to do so following the mid-1980s crisis. The existence of the social contract resulting from the redistributive interventionist model and the impact of a soft budget constraints situation: oil revenues, nationals working abroad, diverse financial aids, and exogenous variables in the local economies guaranteed a minimum revenue for governments, and diminished the intensity and urgency of the demand for reform (Barkey, 1992; Luciani, 1994; Vanderwalle, 2003). These flows softened the effects of economic stagnation and although governments adopted a limited number of reforms, they put off the difficult decision to adjust their structure and adapt the social contract to the situation prevailing at the beginning of the millennium (Yousef, 2004). It was moreover difficult to organize the link between economic reform and political reform, an instrumental connection accepted by many countries. The social contract was an obstacle to the reduction of the role played by the state in the economy and in the public sector, and it also acted as a brake on all possibility of economic reorganization and political reform (Kienle, 2001; Yousef, 2004).

Faced with this opposition and the violence of extremist groups, governments reacted by resorting to their old strategy of political control. Concern with national security became the overriding factor, and as had been shown in the past, such concerns put a stop to economic reforms (as for example in Egypt, Tunisia, and Algeria). In the 1980s and 1990s, the priority had been political liberalization, a precondition for the economic reform of the countries. In the middle of the 1990s, this priority was reversed.

Globalization, trade and employment

The Arab world did not take advantage of the expansion in world trade, especially the major flows of direct foreign investments (FDI), with the result that the region became one of the least integrated in the global economy (Hakimian and Nugent, 2004). This was true even within the Arab region itself. In 1999, Aarts concluded that, in terms of regionalization, the Middle East could be considered as the exceptional case, one which was always out of step with the march of history, eternally immunized against the tendencies affecting the rest of the world (Aarts, 1999, p. 991). In spite of the high number of hydrocarbons exported by the region, the ratio of foreign trade in the GDP diminished from 100 percent of the GDP in the middle of the 1970s (one of the highest at the time) to 60 percent in the mid-1980s, after which it stagnated and only began to improve very recently. Apart from oil, exchanges declined from 53 percent of the GDP at the beginning of the 1980s to 43 percent in 2000, and even interregional trade stagnated at 10 percent of total trade. This was in part due to the "trade regimes," among the most protective in the world, with an average weighted tariff of 17 percent for the region. During the period 1985–2000, the rates of exchange stayed consistently overvalued at a minimum average of 22 percent during the period (Nabli and Veganzones, 2004).

These barriers to exchange, a poor business climate, and the restrictions concerning participation in foreign capital in a number of key sectors, such as banking and finance, discouraged the FDIs (an average of 1 percent of EU world investment). The mediocre performance of Arab labor markets reflects the inability of the previous development model to benefit from demographic changes and an expanded, better-educated workforce. The future appears extremely gloomy. In 2000, the region's workforce totalled 104 million workers, and it is estimated that it will reach 185 million by 2020 (Williamson and Yousef, 2002). The creation of 80 million jobs as well as the absorption of the unemployed implies that the new employment level should be doubled during the first two decades of the third millennium, or that a number of jobs equivalent to the number created between 1950 and 2000 should be created during the next 15 years.

Catch-up and convergence: the role of regional productive systems in the Arab economies

This analysis of the Arab economies underlines the limits of the development experienced during the past 40 years, but it also reveals the considerable potential for growth that exists today. Two particularly negative elements for the success of catch-up policies have been identified: the weak integration of the Arab region in the global economy and the high level of unemployment.

The limited integration is reflected in the region's virtual inexistence in cross-border production-sharing networks, which, as has been demonstrated, have become an important growth engine in global commerce (Hummels *et al.*, 2001), and in the virtual absence of FDIs, which provide *savoir faire* and technological know-how. These limits are aggravated by the fact that several factors lie at the base of the low impact of trade in the region. Apart from hydrocarbons, exports are concentrated on resource-based, low value-added products. The expansion of such products has only a very low impact on employment (Pietri, 1997). In those countries with abundant hydrocarbons, exports of manufactured products are concentrated on highly capitalized, downstream energy industries and have little impact on employment (refined products, gas, fertilizers, and plastic). Since the region does not participate in international production networks, exports do not benefit from vertical trade expansion, nor do they benefit from FDIs constituted by the complement of the increased participation in global production networks. The weak response of domestic and foreign investment to trade liberalization has acted as a brake on job creation. The situation is further strained by the absence of any kind of innovation or educational system geared to the acquisition of qualifications.

The aim is to examine both the experiences and achievements of the newly industrialized countries (NICs), and the setting up of regional productive systems in the developed countries, and to see what could be done in the Arab region to reduce the problems cited previously and facilitate the region's catch-up and convergence within the global economy. The emergence during the 1960s and 1970s of so-called "diffuse" local examples of industrialization in northeast Italy drew attention to the tremendous potential for development that, given the right conditions, can be achieved locally (Garofoli, 1996). One of the most important conditions is the know-how accumulated over the centuries in different domains.

The strategy proposed for Arab countries is the following: first, different ways and means of readapting the accumulated know-how at the regional level need to be identified; second, an analysis should be carried out of how such know-how can be improved through the use of those new techniques and innovations, including technological innovations, which could put new life into development at different levels, but particularly at the local and regional level.

The regional push

In 1990, Porter postulated that the geographic concentration of industries in a national economy plays an important role in the identification of sectors that have a competitive advantage within the international economy (Porter, 1990, p. 790). During the same decade a new idea emerged, that of a fundamental transition from Fordist mass production to more flexible production methods, *flexible specialization*). The mounting uncertainty of markets and technical change strain internal scale economies; this leads to horizontal and vertical disintegration, and an externalization of production. This results in greater flexibility, which enables companies to satisfy differentiated demand and to adapt better to market forces (Humphrey, 1995). In cases where there are many relations and where transaction costs are low, externalization is positively associated with agglomeration. The latter facilitates transactions between producers, since their proximity enables them to adapt needs to capacities at a reduced cost, and at the same time it increases the number of opportunities (Scott and Storper, 1992, p. 13). This move toward flexible specialization results in the emergence of new industrial districts and renewed interest in regional agglomeration (Sabel, 1989).

Scott defines a region as "an area of sub-national extent focussed on a central urban agglomeration or agglomerations to gather with an immediately surrounding hinterland" (Scott, 2002, p. 137). He observed that regions played this role not as "passive geographic receptacles of productive activity," but "as powerful instruments shaping how development and growth have actually occurred."

Scott partially explains this situation in terms of the "differential natural endowments" of the regions, but also in terms of "emergent effects," that is their ability in specific circumstances to "generate significant economic synergies."

During the past 20 years, numerous articles have confirmed the importance of the region as a "nexus of critical development processes," to use Scott's formula (2002, p. 138). At first, the literature only concerned regions in the north (Western Europe and America), but recently it has begun to deal with an increasing number of regions in developing countries.

At the same time, researchers began to consider the idea that regions in newly developing countries might similarly act as a development engine for their economies, and to analyze the type of public policies necessary for such an experiment. As Scott notes, certain well-defined regions are ready to exercise "powerful push effects" on national development and growth (regional push effect, 2002, p. 138).[1]

He was, of course, referring to certain regions. Some regions are trapped by previous development processes that today prevent all moves toward a big push. The state of Kerala in India, for example, demonstrates the paradoxical situation of a state of development where there are remarkable social achievements but relative industrial backwardness resulting from a "path dependent process of industrialization." Decisions made in the 1930s concerning investment priorities accorded to chemical industries and the choice of hydroelectricity, which were considered at the time as a good basis for industrialization, continue to weigh on Kerala's industrial growth. As Thomas notes, "With policy decision in the 1930s, industrial structure in Kerala came to be locked into a pattern that offered very little potential for inter-industry inter-linkages and industrial growth" (Thomas, 2005, p. 763).

The three industrial districts of Santa Catarina in Brazil provide another example of path-dependent process. The performance of these districts was good while the market remained closed. For various reasons, a maximum number of activities were internalized, leading to the emergence of an "extremely non-cooperative business culture," one that is not easy to modify when the situation changes, when the market opens, and there are increasing competitive pressures. Firms adjust from their established practices to the new conditions (Meyer-Stamer, 1998, p. 1495). Clustering both impedes and supports adjustments to the "dramatically changing framework conditions." At the beginning, in cases where path-dependent behavior is favored, it impedes adjustment: rather than taking the risk of trying a completely different policy, the firm follows its well-established behavioral pattern more intensively. This phenomenon is even reinforced by clustering. During the first stage firms observe what is happening. Clustering can subsequently facilitate adjustment as long as the key actors understand the limits of path-dependent behavior. It is a question of moving from the passive to the positive advantages of clustering.[2]

The passive advantages of clustering principally concern the offer of specialized suppliers, business service firms, and qualified employment, all of which are constants in regions where interaction between firms is very weak. The positive advantages include the strengthening of core competencies through out-sourcing and subcontracting to specialized suppliers, as well as a systematic effort to upgrade the learning-by-interacting benefits of close cooperation between firms, and a dense flow of information as well as the "creation of specific supporting institutions" (Meyer-Stamer, 1998, p. 1508). In the case of the Brazilian example already referred to, the pioneer firms of the textile district experienced first the period of passive advantages and then that of active advantages.

Local production systems: a lesson for developing countries, especially Arab countries

The phenomenon of clusters originated with A. Marshall. As early as 1912, he demonstrated that clustering could help companies (especially the very small ones) to remain competitive (Becattini, 2002). The agglomeration of firms engaged in similar or linked activities could, he maintained, generate a whole network of local external economies, thus reducing the production costs within the cluster. The advantages gained included a pool of specialized workers, easier access to suppliers, specialized services, and a better diffusion of knowledge.

When considering this list of advantages, the question arises as to how this kind of territorial organization can be reproduced in environments and situations, such as the developing countries where the necessary conditions do not exist, except in the case of *rentier* economies. A certain amount of research was carried out in the 1990s regarding districts in the developing countries and their creation. This coincided with the growing optimism caused by the perspectives of small industrialists exporting in the developing countries. These studies showed that clustering helped small companies overcome the constraints of growth and competition on distant markets. The crucial concept of collective efficiency was highlighted, a concept resulting from the combination of two effects: the comparative advantage derived from external economies, and collective action (which led certain authors to speak of collective efficiency) (Schmitz and Nadvi, 1999).

The performance level of the clusters, the duration of their dynamism, their capacity to regenerate, and particularly their ability to adapt to the pressures of competition all depend on the combination of the two active and passive components: collective action and the producer's rents. The concept of collective efficiency is useful when evaluating the performance of companies that cooperate, but it does not take into account external links. The nature of such links, with foreign buyers for example, can be crucial for the expansion of clusters. It would seem moreover that a strategy of adjustment to external challenges might well necessitate more than local firms simply acting collectively, for it brings up the whole question of the role to be played by local government. The first practical studies carried out in the developing countries showed that, in certain cases, agglomeration could promote technical learning and innovation trajectories (Humphrey, 1995).

Elements of the political economy of agglomeration: experiences in the developing countries

The issues concerning the growth, exports, and role of small and medium-sized companies in the developing countries is now being viewed from a different angle than the one applied to the local production systems (LPS). This new approach first began with studies of small firms in Italian industrial districts and with research into how the experience of such firms could be applied to developing countries. Research on new models of industrial organization was also carried out (Humphrey, 1995). The studies sought to determine whether such industries exist in developing countries. If so, how exactly do they emerge, how do they evolve, and what blocks their emergence? Initial research was carried out within the framework established by Piore and Sabel 1984, followed by research by Pedersen *et al.* (1994), Bessant and Kaplinsky (1995), and Schmitz and Musyck (1994). Research was subsequently conducted on the relevance of clustering to the NICs, with numerous methodological and theoretical studies and debates.[3] The following main points emerged from these different studies (Schmitz and Nadvi, 1999, p. 1504):

The phenomenon of clustering is becoming more and more frequent in the developing countries and occurs in a relatively large number of countries. The growth experience of these clusters varies considerably. At one end of the spectrum there are the craft industry clusters (for example the African districts), which are not very dynamic and demonstrate limited innovative capacity (Oyeleran-Oyeyinka, 1997; McCormick, 1999). At the other end are clusters that managed to reinforce and extend inter-firm work division, and which were able to increase their competitiveness and enter the world markets.[4] Even the successful clusters differed from the Italian model. These districts are very heterogeneous, and small and medium-sized industries were able to emerge and play a crucial role in the organization and administration of the clusters.[5] In this respect, the experience of developing countries differs from that of the Italian model of the 1970s and 1980s.

The experience of the developing countries shows that although the Italian model constitutes a useful starting point, it is vital to take into account the differences between countries and to understand how firms and sectors are transformed. This explains the emphasis put on the change trajectories used by firms that reorganize their production, and by firm clusters (Humphrey, 1995, p. 149). This dynamic approach helped reveal the processes leading to success or failure, and the debate concerning perspectives for small and medium-sized company growth and exports in the developing countries was revived. Some researchers believe that in the Italian situation the role of the small and medium-sized companies in the districts was overestimated, whereas big firms were underestimated. Their role was thus established for exporting clusters in Brazil and Pakistan (Schmitz, 1995; Nadvi, 1999b) and also in China (Thompson, 2000, 2002). The striking fact is the crucial role played by clustering in the launching of the industrialization process itself, through the mobilization of unused local resources (both human and financial). Clustering facilitates gradual special-ization and investment. Since they do not have to acquire all the equipment needed for the production process, producers can limit themselves to a few stages of the process. Thanks to workshops specialized in repairing and improv-ing existing equipment it is possible to reduce technological discontinuities; hence, the possibility of investment.

At the same time, the needs for circulating capital are reduced because of the proximity within the cluster of suppliers of raw materials and specialized equip-ment. This also means that stocks can be kept low. Human capital needs are also reduced. Investments made by certain producers in one area of qualifications are made profitable by investments carried out by other producers in other areas of qualification. Specialization does not entail isolation, for without interaction, products and services cannot be sold. The risk is also reduced because of work division (since emphasis is put on one particular aspect of manufacturing com-petence) and the local external economies. Collective action also helps reduce the jump each individual industrialist has to make (for example, the case of the surgical instrument cluster in Sialkot, Pakistan).

In short, clustering facilitates the mobilization of financial and human resources and divides investment up into small riskable steps. The creation of one company acts as a stepping-stone for the next one. Links are created that enable small companies to move up the hierarchy and develop. And so a process is created in which companies create for each other opportunities for the accu-mulation of capital and qualifications (Schmitz and Nadvi, 1999, p. 1506)

If clustering facilitates this strategy, it does not guarantee growth. This is particularly true in Africa. In his study of the Kamukunji cluster for metal trans-formation in Kenya, McCormick discussed the "groundwork" (first stage clus-ters) and emphasized the weakness of links for intermediary goods, technological spillover, bilateral liaisons, and a common labor market. He reached the same conclusion for the "Eastlands" clothes cluster (McCormick, 1999, pp. 1538–1539). As has been shown by young Indonesian clusters, collective efficiency only emerges under certain conditions. Clusters limited to the local market only experience an *involution* type of growth; agglomeration attracts tradesmen but does not necessarily forge effective trading links with more distant markets (Weijland, 1999*)*. But the revenue level of rural clusters depends on their connections with *distant markets* (Knorringa, 1993). On a more general level, the weakness of distribution networks in the developing countries acts as an important brake on growth, as shown in the case of South Africa and the east of Africa (Pedersen, 1997).

The development of districts in the developing countries and the challenge of globalization

What *factors* determine the growth path of clusters and lead to an understanding of their trajectories? Schmitz and Nadvi refer to "Turning points" (1999, p. 1507). Recent studies have emphasized the double challenge of liberalization and globalization faced by clusters today. A number of common features that go beyond the specific characteristics of individual cases emerge from these studies, such as the increasing pressures on local firms to adopt global standards (including quality, response deadlines, and flexibility standards). This is the case for clusters that have reached a level of maturity and that enjoy significant external economies. From a methodological point of view, it is useful to distinguish between three types of clusters, with specific complex policies (Altenburg and Meyer-Stamer, 1999, p. 1693).

To begin with, there are the service clusters of micro- and small companies featuring favorable macroeconomic conditions rather than entrepreneurial ability and dynamism. Their potential, in terms of competition, is limited; support for them is aimed at improving their chances of survival (job creation) through policies aimed at breaking the vicious circle connected with poor qualifications and low investment. The second category includes more advanced clusters (differentiated mass producers). These clusters, which were set up as a substitution for importation during the period of industrialization, are today confronted with the challenges caused by transition to open economies. Their challenge is the creation of environments that stimulate learning, innovation, and constant production development.

The third group concerns transnational company clusters (Felker, 2003), which are dominated by foreign firms not only at the setting-up stage, but also for the production of components. They are real shop-windows for what is "best" in manufacturing, something that can stimulate local firms by integrating them in the supply chains of transnational companies. These clusters are involved in complex activities such as the electronics and car industries, oriented to exporting. Robots and the very latest technologies are necessary for the final assembly process and the production of the majority of components. Technological mastery of such processes is difficult and the economies substantial. The entry barriers are generally too high for local firms, thus limiting the possibility of their integration in the district. For the most complex components, the big assembly companies that constitute the kernel of the district give preference to suppliers from their own country when setting up production facilities at the local level. This reflects the increased centralization of product design and standardization at the global level, but also often the lack of competitive industrialists in the majority of developing countries (Altenburg and Meyer-Stamer, 1999, p. 1703) for small and middle-sized companies. The low level of embeddedness in their local affairs' organizations constitutes one of the big differences between the developing countries and Europe and the United States. Another difference is that transnational company clusters can often only pursue standardized operations, which, although admittedly sometimes quite complex, *do not require innovative local settings*, i.e. settings that foster innovation. Research and development and design are conducted in the parent company, and only later transferred to the NICs. This was the case for the automobile component districts in the northeast of Mexico, from Puebla to the center, and of the electronic product districts in Guadalajara (Altenburg and Meyer-Stamer, 1999, pp. 1704–1705).

Two trajectories stand out with regard to manufacturing capacities in old and new shoe-exporting countries. Clustering in Italy, Brazil, and Taiwan initially facilitated a "measured" growth, while specialization, synergy, and cooperation facilitated the gradual accumulation of qualifications and capital (Chon, 1996). A significant proportion of the small companies developed into midsize companies, and even big companies. Local exports and embeddedness progressed in parallel. Growth stopped when the new producers entered the world market, where there was a different growth path. This concerned recent producer regions and big companies, which had recently begun shoe production and which had the size and capacity to export very soon after they were created. In fact, these new producer regions were simply an extension of the former districts. The latter continued to operate, but more slowly and in different ways.

The key characteristic of this second trajectory is the importance of the cheap labor factor, whereas in traditional clusters it is the entrepreneurial capacities and technical qualifications that are crucial. The clearest case is China, where exports progressed at a phenomenal rate (Sonobe *et al.*, 2002; Zhang and Xiabao, 2003; Steinfield, 2004; Lemoine and Unal-Kesenci, 2004). The Chinese success cannot be explained simply in terms of abundant cheap labor; the technological know-how of Taiwan, which China had close links with, proved decisive. Taiwan enabled China to benefit from the entrepreneurial and technological competence it had built up, and from its shoe-marketing networks throughout the world (Chon, 1996). The same process is today operating in Vietnam, via Taiwanese joint ventures. As with China, components are sent from Taiwan. The Taiwanese rapidly set up assembly factories in Vietnam fearing that European commercial restrictions might affect exports from China (Schmitz and Knorringa, 2000, p. 192).

The emergence of new competitors generated by old clusters was not limited to the Far East Asian zone. The same tandems appeared elsewhere. Italy/Romania (often with foreign investment) (Caroli and Fratocchi, 2000; Garavelo and Navaretti, 2001) and south and north Brazil both followed the tandem model of Taiwan/Vietnam and China. In this case, the choice of localization was determined by labor costs and reasonable *proximity* of components. The original Italian, Taiwanese and south Brazil clusters provided the capital production capacities and the connections with buyers and components. A certain division of labor appeared between the old and the new districts; the former were geared to relatively urgent high-quality orders, produced by small and medium-sized industries, or by largely decentralized firms.

A third trajectory has recently appeared where the buyers themselves install the production premises. These results need to be compared with Gereffi's conclusions in his study of the clothing industry and the "manufacturing triangle" (1999). The triangle was based on the idea that American or other buyers placed orders with industries in emerging countries that had previously benefitted from relocations in the clothing industry. The latter, in turn, shifted the orders to their offshore subsidiaries in countries where salaries were low, i.e. China, Indonesia, or Vietnam. Gereffi argues that this transfer toward the manufacturing triangle contributed to the insertion of many countries in production and exporting networks. The phenomenon noted in the shoe industry is similar, except for the inspection role reserved for the "old manufacturers." They make sure that the purchasing standards of price, quality, and delivery are respected in the "other locations" of the developing countries. In this case, the role of the old manufacturers is to transfer qualifications and the organization of production, particularly in the early stages (Schmitz and Knorringa, 2000, p. 194; Thompson, 2002; Felker, 2003).

In the creation of manufacturing plants, producers first develop at the local level (first trajectory) and then, in certain cases, move out and develop further afield. Because of the problem of insufficient production of components for the manufacture of shoes, India failed to become an export leader and integrate the second trajectory. This was in spite of the country's long history of manufacturing, its abundant source of cheap labor, and its access to high quality leather. There were several reasons for this: mediocre infrastructure that limited exchanges; problems with customs; weak component production facilities (well below those in Italy and Taiwan); a rigid labor market; and workers' lack of interest in external training (Schmitz and Knorringa, 2000).

From districts to translocal international networks: value chains and the "external push"

There is a clear convergence between the conclusions derived from the experience of clusters and those of global value chains. The cluster theory goes beyond A. Marshall's analysis of the effects of agglomeration, and states that, in certain cases, agglomeration can promote a trajectory of technical training and innovation (Humphrey, 1995). More recently, another theory postulates that whereas the physical agglomeration might be a necessary condition, it is not in itself sufficient. Apart from conditions linked to global macroeconomic policies, cluster growth can only happen if an "external push" exists, *alongside favorable conditions* for the creation of local and extra-local networks. Among the conditions for an extra-local network, the one concerned with exporting networks is vital. Cluster experience has shown that the process of upgrading implies in parallel a process of differentiation. In other words, exclusion becomes the hidden face of upgrading (Gibbon, 2001, p. 349) once the buyers instigate the upgrading process.

An analysis in terms of global value chains offers a new perspective for developing countries in their upgrading strategies. Two aspects deserve to be discussed here. First, is the possibility of generalizing perspective, which concerns global value chains where retail traders play a central role. The perspectives offered by other buyer-driven chains remain, for the moment, uncertain in those cases where agents other than traders (for example international trading firms) intervene.

In the category of first chains, underlying conditions exist that promote high level upgrading and differentiation between producers and suppliers from the south. During the 1960s and 1970s, an important acceleration factor within the clothing chain in the emerging Asian countries was the multifiber agreement and its encouragement of buyers and producers of all countries to promote external- ization of activities, leading to the "manufacturing triangle." This upgrading tra- jectory remains frozen in contemporary international poles for the clothing industry: Mexico, Turkey, Eastern Europe, and North Africa, poles which are involved in various free-exchange agreements and which are today threatened by China's entry into the World Trade Organization. This has led to increased externalization of assembly by leading brand buyers from the north (Levi- Strauss for example), an area where growth possibilities are limited (Gibbon, 2001, p. 349). NICs should, therefore, promote economic activities in those sub- sectors where global chains promoted by retailers from the north exist, by selec- tively helping local companies reinforce their links with leader firms on world markets, by supporting local institutions that can generate projects, and by encouraging inter-firm training schemes, etc.

The value chain refers to the whole range of activities needed for the concep- tion of a product or service, from the intermediary phases of production (imply- ing a combination of physical transformation and linked services) to the final phase of presenting it to the consumer, and the post-phase of how it is disposed of after use (Gereffi and Korzenewicz, 1994; Gereffi, 1995, 1999). Production is just one of the aspects of added value. At every stage of the chain there are a number of different activities.

The concept of value chain is being increasingly used, particularly in the area of inter-firm relations.[6] The basic idea is that the design and commercialization of products implies a whole range of activities carried out by different com- panies (Dolan and Humphrey, 2000, pp. 148–149). This concept has been defined in different ways in the literature; Porter speaks of *chain of values* and *systems of values* in his analysis of company strategies for the management of inter-firm relations; he states that the comparative advantage is a growing func- tion of the way a company manages the whole system (Porter 1990, p. 44). The most common concept is the inter-firm liaison chain, which can be applied to a variety of situations and emphasizes specific relationships and their character- istics.

Gereffi went further with the analysis, and introduced three new ideas. First, the chain often implies across-frontier coordination of the activities of independ- ent firms. Second, on a governance level, he notes that big retail trade firms and leading brands create highly coordinated inter-firm networks. Most goods and services trade today is internalized in the system of international production. This commerce is organized inside multinational firms – one might almost say internationalized firms – in an organizational framework that links them by means of a whole system of contractual arrangements and "sourcing." Most international trade is somewhere between markets and hierarchies.

Finally, Gereffi brought to light the increasing role played by international buyers: retailers and leading brands in the commerce of labor-intensive manu- factured goods, for example the clothing industry (1995). He distinguishes between two types of product chains: producer-driven chains typical of intensive capital and technological factor industries managed by firms that control the crucial production and technological facilities, and buyer-driven chains where the retailers and big brands are in control of governance functions. Their activities are mainly concentrated in design, retail commerce, and marketing, but also in the organization of the chains themselves. They do not produce themselves, but decide what should be produced. These firms play a crucial role in the business opportunities offered to the developing countries, as has been demonstrated for the Brazilian shoe industry (Schmitz, 1995, p. 14 onwards) and for the Indian knitwear industry (Cawthorne, 1995, p. 46).

Firms like Nike and Benetton are good examples of this new type of production organization. They transform models across the world, unifying tastes and speeding up the rotation of products, by introducing products that have an increasingly short life. These new networks emphasize the key role played by the developed countries: the United States, Japan, the EU, etc. in the setting up of decentralized production networks in a large number of exporting countries where the big retail trade brands, designers, and trading companies intervene in important business companies (Felker, 2003; Smith *et al.*, 2002; Bair and Gereffi, 2001). This underlines the influence that the big consumer and distribution structures of these countries exercise on regional production in the Far East, for example a whole range of labor-intensive consumer goods industries, such as shoes and toys. This major organizational phenomenon is masked by the excessive emphasis placed on assembly industries.

Characteristics of network approaches

First, there is a high complexity of regional institutions involved (Bernard, 1996, p. 654). By emphasizing the move from "regional" to "global" through the localization of production and distribution structures in a wider context, these approaches clearly explain the historical regional creation originating in dynamic changes in regional profiles (Bernard, 1996; Felker, 2003). This enables us to understand the way a given economy enters processes implying regional projections. It should also provide an analysis explained in terms of regional and global localization, rather than in terms of linear path development by country based solely on macroeconomic data. In this case, the paradigm country is transcended, while factors specific to the local region and transnational structures are taken into account.

The value chain concept takes into account the changes that have occurred in the exchange of products like fresh fruit, tinned goods, or furniture, car components, horticultural products, cut flowers, and many others (Gibbon, 2001; Kaplinsky, 2000a and b; Palpacuer *et al.*, 2005; Giuliani *et al.*, 2005).

Suggestions for "regional push" and "external push" strategies in the Arab World: conclusion

Today, the general consensus is that regional agglomeration economies in the developing countries constitute a decisive lever in growth and development (Scott, 2002, p. 142). The effectiveness of "regional push" can be seen in the emergence of the East Asian region as a new growth pole in the world economy. This historic regional concentration of rapidly emerging economies in newly industrialized countries illustrates the relationship between the pattern of industrialization and regional localization (Sid Ahmed, 2004, p. 19). The decisive economic advantages registered when the leading countries (the first tier of the developing countries) moved from industries based on natural resources and manpower to high-productivity capitalistic industries enabled the less developed countries of the region to integrate this new regional work division by targeting activities linked with supply.

The Arab countries, big exporters of natural resources (especially exporters of hydrocarbons, like Indonesia and Malaysia), were unable to make the same kind of transition to intermediary goods and capital goods industries. It is true that, in contrast to what they had done for Japan and the first tier countries, Europe was unable to act as a growth engine for countries on the south shore of the Mediterranean, as is clearly shown by the low level of European investment in the Arab region (excluding hydrocarbons). In contrast to Asia, countries that had to redeploy at the top of the trading hierarchy and export more elaborate goods (an area where they had comparative advantages) and the major flows of direct foreign investment acted as an important motor, favoring the recycling of the comparative advantage via technology transfer, know-how, and qualifications.

This regional work division combining industrial and localization hierarchy is known as the "flying geese" development paradigm (Bernard and Ravenhill, 1995). The big electronic complexes of the Far East and East Asia stand out as the most impressive creations in this respect (Borrus, 1993; Lim, 1995; Machado, 1999). During the past 20 years, the crucial role played by clusters in a number of NICs has come to light. The phenomenon applies to artisan type as well as advanced industries, like electronics, financial services and knowledge industries. These industries increasingly coexist in the big cities of the Third World, for example in Hong Kong. Such complexes constitute dynamic endogenous paths in the industrialization of these countries. Such was the case for the Brazilian car industry, where the implementation of export industrialization strategies went hand in hand with the regional concentration of production activities.[7] The Asian countries succeeded in combining their initial low salary levels and the regional push with the intensification of spatial agglomeration and their insertion in the global economy, i.e. the external push.[8] Scott noted that these effects can be assimilated with endogenously created competitive advantages, and that this enables whole production groups to move ahead to the next stage of market contestation (Scott, 2002, p. 146), as was the case, for example, with Taiwanese machine tool manufacturers (Amsden, 1985).

In association with local clustering, direct foreign investment (FDI) plays an important role in the consolidation and reinforcement of the creation of regional production systems in the NICs (Liu, 2002; Xu, 2000; Lipsey, 2004). Clustering reinforces the impact of FDI resulting from the agglomeration growing through the various spillovers of host economy productivity. Further, Li and Liu believe there is a growing endogenous relationship between FDI and economic growth (Li and Liu, 2005). In the first case, FDI increases economic growth by generating technological diffusion from the developed world toward the NICs. The endogenous relationship is observed in a sample of 84 countries for the second part of the period (1970–1999), i.e. from the middle of the 1980s. FDI not only promotes economic growth itself, but it does so indirectly via its "interaction terms." Interaction with human capital or manpower has an important positive effect on growth in the NICs, while interaction with the "technological gap" is negative (Li and Liu, 2005, p. 393). FDI is a composite bundle of capital stock, know-how, and technology. It can increase the existing stock of knowledge in the host country through manpower training, the acquisition and diffusion of qualifications, and the introduction of alternative management practices and organizational arrangements (Uchida and Cook, 2005 p. 702ff.).

In fact, endogenous growth always supposes that there is a minimum of human capital and technology-absorptive activity from the start. On this minimum basis, the endogenous interrelationship between FDI and economic growth, the promotion of human capital, technological capacities, and economic development will lead to even more FDI. This, in turn, reinforces economic growth and increases the country's productivity and competitiveness. It appears moreover that the high concentration of FDI – a dozen or so developing countries – is due to their manpower capacities. With more manpower, they would attract more FDI (Noorbakhsh, Paloni, and Youssef, 2001).

Although Arab countries constitute 2 percent of world GDP, they only receive an average of 1 percent of world FDI. This FDI concerns six countries in the following sectors: hydrocarbons, petro-chemicals, textiles, and other mining products. A study carried out by Ali Sadik and Ali Bolbol showed that the spillovers expected from these FDIs did not materialize, even if the contribution of these FDIs to investment and growth was positive. The authors emphasize that the Arab world should first and foremost improve its total factor productivity. The incentives based on positive externalities from FDI are not economically justifiable, apart from the fact that they constitute a drag on light fiscal budgets (Sadik and Bolbol, 2001, p. 2122). The only exceptions are when either the FDI is located for export purposes so that competition on international markets induces foreign affiliates to be more productive and innovative, or when the technological gap between the foreign affiliates and the average domestic firms is considerable, such as in medium- to high-technology goods in the Arab world. In both cases, the efficiency gains of technology spillovers can be significant. But as the authors noted, with or without FDI, the Arab world vitally needs "an overall improvement in the quality and the environment of investment so that new capital expenditures would have higher social productivity" (Sadik and Bolbol, 2001, p. 2122), i.e. the necessary conditions for an external push must first be established.

If it is to be effective, regional push must not rely solely on agglomeration or clustering combined with collective efficiency. As they advance toward maturity, the most advanced clusters are confronted with upgrading, especially in the areas of technological learning and innovation. Big firms see their role increase within the clusters. The competitiveness of these firms, which were previously small, depends less on local sources, that is, on "collective efficiency." It has been shown that once they attain a certain size, firms depend less on their immediate environment (Audretsch and Feldman, 1996).

The real permanent advantages of clustering appear in the creation of knowledge and learning, as Maskell *et al.* recently repeated (1998). The advantages of the low cost of transaction resulting from a culture of "confidence" and good reciprocal understanding are far from negligible, but these external effects and increasing social yields should be seen as the by-products of the success of districts rather than their cause, as Bresnashan and others have shown (1998). Using Bangalore, India, as an example, big joint investments in infrastructure projects were largely induced by an environment where the demand for innovation was already high. It is unlikely that these projects were the major engine for regional industrial competitiveness, as the EC approach suggests (Caniels and Romijn, 2003b, p. 288). The accumulation of technological capacity is crucial for industrial growth and for the competitiveness of firms, particularly in the context of increasing international economic liberalization and integration.

The geographic clustering of an industry has little impact on regional economic prosperity in those cases where there is no potential for exploiting technological learning opportunities. In Pakistan, and particularly at Daska, firms had to face great pressure in order to invest in "technological effort" to respond to competition. In brief, there has to be an incentive or demand for technical improvement. The existence of such incitement in of itself enables firms to engage in training, recruitment, and workshop-level research. This is when the potential learning advantages of clustering materialize. If individual firms do not make the effort to improve their capacities, there is no cross-fertilization of knowledge and information through new ideas. In regions where markets are sluggish, the creation of districts on the basis of clustering is difficult, and clustering is not a panacea (Caniels and Romijn, 2003a, p. 149)

However, the Arab world cannot ignore the crucial role (within the framework of appropriate global and regional strategies) that agglomeration economies can play through the two complementary push effects: regional push and external push, thanks to growing externalities and yields resulting from proximity and collective efficiency (inter-firm flows), the dynamism of local labor markets, learning structures, innovation, and the insertion of global value chains, all of which are sources of convergence. The effects of "structural competitiveness" need to be added to this systemic competitiveness. Di Costa used this concept to explain the rapid development of the Korean steel industry (Di Costa, 1994).

The concept is based on three conditions: government autonomy with respect to lobbies, a sound economic policy, and indigenous technological capability (Di Costa, 1994, p. 44). These aspects have a great influence on the bargaining capacity of the state, as well as on autonomous investment decisions, labor control, the acquisition and absorption of modern technology, and finally, international competitiveness, which determines catch-up and convergence. The interest of this concept for the Arab world, where competitiveness is lacking, is that it suggests the kind of socio-institutional and economic policy contexts that are often necessary to foster competitive industries (Sid Ahmed, 1998, 2004).

This debate brings us back to the nature of government, in particular the inescapable role of "the developmental state" (Amsden, 1997; Leftwich, 1995) in a world that is not the same as that of Adam Smith. His laissez-faire theories were prescribed for a country at the world technological frontier (Britain). In the present case, the post-war industrial policies of latecomer countries were initially conceived for firms and industries that needed to reduce the wide technological and qualifications gap that existed between them and the advanced countries. Important building bottlenecks like the availability of finance, foreign exchange, up-to-date technologies, access to firm-specific knowledge of established companies, brand-name recognition, and, on a more general level, oligopolistic global competition, require, among other things, a revision that takes into account the historic role played by the developmental state in the latest technologies.

This situation is more or less the one that exists in the Arab world today; the only difference being that the region has so far been unable to implement the industrial policies needed to absorb qualified workers and the ever-growing active working population resulting from population growth. These industrial policies are also essential if the regional production systems that develop agglomeration economies are to reach "maturity level" and integrate world networks. Unless this happens, there is a real risk that the local production systems will revert, as occurred in both the developing countries and even in developed countries like Italy. It is not a matter of chance that, despite its rich historical heritage, the Arab region is the one area in the world where the innumerable precapitalistic informal clusters have not been able to experience the revolution of the "Third Italy" through their dynamism. The medinas of Fez, Sfax, Cairo, Aleppo, Tunisia, Tripoli and Lebanon exist, as do potential agglomerations – but often without collective efficiency, and so they remain enclaves in a formal economy with no "push" possibilities.

In the majority of Arab economies, not only is there no spatial planning; there is not even any recognized regional planning.[9] Regional planning was used as a support for the global economic development model. The area was only a tool used in the service of a general policy where the dividing up of revenue, including that of hydrocarbons, was of prime importance. The anti-"regional push" bias maintained by the hydrocarbon revenue remains as important as ever. The resulting "Dutch disease" not only undermined the competitiveness of non-resource tradable sectors and impeded economic diversification and growth

(Gelb *et al.*, 1988; Sachs and Warner, 1999; Sid Ahmed, 1998, 2005); it also generated corrosive effects on governance and accountability, and undermined the institutional foundation of growth.

The paradox is that the developed economies alone have been effective in taking advantage of revenue, particularly hydrocarbon revenue, by reinforcing their industrial and technical development, and thus escaping from the painful "petrol or industry" dilemma referred to as early as 1977 by Ellman and Barker and Brailovsky in 1981. The seriousness of the Dutch disease for the developing countries is that the reduction in the importance of the tradable goods sector in the initial stages of industrial development excludes all industrial learning by doing and learning, and therefore, all improvement in the comparative advantage of the country and all reduction of comparative disadvantage in the production of manufactured goods. The hypothesis (confirmed) being that technical progress will be faster in non-tradable sectors than in tradable sectors (Van Winjnbergen, 1984). In this case, external integration and job creation are postponed. Only those economies that are already industrialized and diversified, and that have considerable technological capacities and solid institutions escape this trap, as has been shown in particular in the examples of Great Britain, Norway, and Canada.

Gas revenues enabled Holland to totally change its capital vintage in an increasingly capitalistic direction, thus considerably reinforcing the economy's productivity and competitiveness. As for Norway, the negative impact of revenue on the less favored regions (depopulation in the north and the disappearance of certain activities, in particular fishing and agriculture) was neutralized by subsidizing tradable sectors (as Corden suggested) and by also subsidizing the maintenance of the population in the territory. The different biases against economic diversification and growth, and therefore against push,[10] combine to limit the region's international integration[11] and convergence.

In a study carried out in 1995 covering 122 countries, Sachs and Warner noted international convergence during the period 1970–1989 in those countries that satisfied openness criteria.[12] They refute the three dominant explanations concerning the absence of convergence. The first maintains that productive technology is intrinsically linked with leader technology: the rich become richer each time following increasing returns to scale in one form or another. The second maintains that convergence is a fact of life, but only between countries with a sound human capital base for using modern technology. The third holds that currently poor countries have a long-term potential income level, though countries tend to grow faster the greater the gap between their current income and their own long-run potential.

Sachs and Warner (1995, pp. 40–41) argue that the absence of convergence is above all due to wrong trade policies. According to them, convergence is possible for all countries, even those with an initial low level of qualifications, as long as they are open and integrated in the world economy. The convergence club is one where economies are linked together by international trade. The OECD, the EU, the economies at the end of the nineteenth century, the US, and the Japanese prefectures all tend to convergence. The differences in long-term income levels do not stem from fundamental tastes and technologies, but rather from policies concerning economics (Sachs and Warner, 1995, pp. 44–46). In the same perspective, Ben David shows that the incomes of countries that trade with each other more intensely converge (Ben David and Loewy, 1998). This is confirmed by Waltz in the case of the extension of the "Common Market" (Waltz, 1998).

On their side, O'Rourke and Williamson, who studied the impact of globalization on revenue convergence in the nineteenth century and the beginning of the twentieth century, also found a positive relationship, but their interpretation of globalization is to be seen more in terms of "trade boom, a mass migration and huge capital flows" (O'Rourke and Williamson, 1999, p. 167). These conditions are by no means found together in the Euro-Med zone. The study by Rodrik and others reaffirms the crucial role of institutions; that is of governance in convergence (Rodrik *et al.*, 2002) – an area in which the Arab world does not particularly shine.

Notes

1 Garofoli, 1996; Viesti, 2000; Becattini, 1999, 2002; Camagni and Maillat, 2006.
2 Schmitz and Musyck, 1994; Altenburg and Meyer-Stamer, 1999.
3 Van Dijk and Rabellotti, 1997; Meyer-Stamer, 1998; Sandee and Rietveld, 2001; Thompson, 2002. Sid Ahmed, 2001, 2004.
4 Schmitz, 1995; Nadvi, 1999a, 1999b; Thompson, 2002.
5 Schmitz, 1995; Nadvi, 1999a.
6 Gereffi, 1995, 1999; Kaplinsky, 2000a, 2000b; Gibbon, 2001; Gibbon *et al.*, 2005; Dolan and Humphrey, 2000: Hugues, 2000; Bair and Dussel, 2006.
7 The same observation has been made for the Indian car industry and the integration of the Indian economy in the world economy. A study of 50 component suppliers for two big car assembly firms in the automotive industry revealed that the dynamic industrial transformation in the 1990s significantly changed the nature, content, and range of skills of home suppliers.
8 This assumes, of course, that there are no immiserating growth effects, as often occurs in global chains and which results in producers benefitting less from the advantages of globalization. Kaplinsky has recently reported this phenomenon in the South African furniture industry.
9 Except during the past few years, for example in Morocco and Algeria.
10 In these conditions it is difficult to envision how, at the regional level, the change could be effected from a system of regional planning in the sole context of revenue distribution (Chaudhry, 1997) to one of territorial development favoring local actors and coordination and more concretely "meso-systems."
11 "Openness" shows the following characteristics: the degree of deviation of internal prices from external prices, an index of national policies shaping openness (tariffs, quotas, exchange rate overvaluation or undervaluation, incidence of controls on capital inflow or outflow) openness ratio, presence of foreign direct investment in total investment, importance of intra-industry trade relative to inter-industry (Giles and Mosk, 2004, p. 363).
12 Sachs and Warner consider an economy "closed" if one of the following conditions is present: (1) the average tariff rate exceeds 10 percent; (2) non-tariff barriers cover more than 40 percent of import; (3) socialist economy; (4) state monopoly of major exports; (5) the black market premium exceeds 20 percent.

References

Aarts, P. (1999) The Middle East: A Region Without Regionalism or the End of Exceptionalism, *Third World Quarterly*, Vol. 20 (5), pp. 911–925.

Altenburg, T. and Meyer-Stamer, J. (1999) How to Promote Clusters: Policy Experiences From Latin America, *World Development*, Vol. 27 (9), pp. 1693–1715.

Amsden, A. (1985) The Division of Labour Is Limited by the Rate of Growth of the Market: The Taiwan Machine Tool Industry in the 1970s, *Cambridge Journal of Economics*, Vol. 9, pp. 271–284.

Amsden, A. (1997) Editorial; Bringing Production Back in Understanding Government's Economic Role in Late Industrialization, *World Development*, Vol. 25 (4), pp. 469–481.

Audretsch, D. and Feldman, M. (1996) Innovative Clusters and the Industry Lifecycle, *Review of Industrial Organisation*, Vol. 11, pp. 253–273.

Auty, R. (ed.) (1994) Industrial Policy Reform in Six Large Newly Industrializing Countries: The Resource Curse Thesis, *World Development*, Vol. 23 (1).

Auty, R. (2001) *Resource Abundance and Economic Development*, Oxford University Press, Oxford.

Bair, J. and Dussel, P. (2006) Global Commodity Chains and Endogenous Growth: Export Dynamism and Honduras. *World Development*, Vol. 34 (2), pp. 203–222.

Bair, J. and Gereffi, G. (2001) Local Clusters in Global Chains: The Causes and Consequences of Export Dynamism in Torreon's Blue Jeans Industry, *World Development*, Vol. 29 (11), pp. 1885–1903.

Barker, T. and Brailovsky, V. (1981) *Oil or Industry? Energy Industrialisation and Economic Policy in Canada, Mexico, Netherlands, Norway and the United Kingdom*, Academic Press.

Barkey, H. (ed.) (1992) *The Politics of Economic Reform in the Middle East*, St. Martin's Press, New York.

Becattini, G. (1999) *L'industrializzazione leggera della Toscana ricerca sul campo e confronto delle idee*, F. Angeli, Milan.

Becattini, G. (2002) From Marshall's to the Italian Industrial Districts: A Brief Critical Reconstruction in Curzio and Fortis (eds.), *Complexity and Industrial Clusters: Dynamics and Models in Theory and Practice*, Physica-Verlag, pp. 83–103.

Ben David, D. and Loewy, M.B. (1998) Free Trade, Growth and Convergence, *Journal of Economic Growth*, Vol. 3, pp. 143–170.

Bernard, M. (1996) Regions in the Global Political Economy: Beyond Global–Local Divide in the Formation of the East-Asian Region, *Third World Quarterly*, Vol. 17 (4), pp. 625–649.

Bernard, M. and Ravenhill, J. (1995) Beyond Product Cycles and Flying Geese: Regionalism, Hierarchy and the Industrialization of East Asia, *World Politics*, Vol. 47 (2), pp. 171–210.

Bessant, J. and Kaplinsky, R. (1995) Industrial Restructuring: Facilitating Organization Change at the Firm Level, *World Development*, Vol. 23 (1), pp. 129–141.

Borrus, M. (1993) The Regional Architecture of Global Electronics: Trajectories, Linkages and Access to Technology in P. Gourevitch and P. Guerrieri (eds.), *New Challenges to International Cooperation Adjustment of Firms, Policies and Organizations to Global Competition*, University of California Press, San Francisco, Calif., pp. 41–80.

Camagni, R. and Maillat, D. (2006) *Textes réunis: milieux innovateurs et politiques*, Economica Anthropos, Paris.

Caniels, M.C. and Romijn, H. (2003a) Agglomeration Advantage and Capability Building in Industrial Clusters: The Missing Link, *The Journal of Development Study*, Vol. 39 (3), pp. 129–154.

Caniels, M.C. and Romijn, H. (2003b) Dynamic Clusters in Developing Countries: Collective Efficiency and Beyond, *Oxford Development Studies*, Vol. 31 (3), pp. 275–293.

Caroli, M.G. and Fratocchi, L. (2000). *Nuove tendenze nelle strategie di internalizzazione delle imprese minori.* Franco-Angeli, Milan.

Cawthorne, P.M. (1995) Of Networks and Markets: the Rise and Rise of a South Indian Town, the Example of Tiruppua's Cotton Knitwear Industry, *World Development*, Vol. 23 (1), pp. 43–57.

Chaudhry, K. (1997) *The Price of Wealth: Economic and Institutions in the Middle East*, Cornell University Press, Ithaca, NY.

Chon, S. (1996) Small and Medium-sized Entreprises in the Republic of Korea, Implications for the Development of Technology Intensive Industries, *Small Business Economics*, 8, pp. 107–120.

Di Costa, A.P. (1994) Structural Competitiveness and Development in South Korea, *The Journal of Development Studies*. Vol. 31 (1), pp. 44–82.

Dijk, M.P. Van and Rabellotti, R. (1997) Clusters and Networks as Sources of Cooperation and Technology Diffusion for Small Enterprises in Developing Countries, in M.P. Van Dijk and R. Rabellotti (eds.), 1997. *Enterprises Clusters and Networks in Developing Countries*. EADI Book serie 20, Franck Cass, London, pp. 1–10.

Dolan, C. and Humphrey, J. (2000) Governance and Trade in Fresh Vegetables; The Impact in Fresh Vegetables; The Impact of the African Horticulture Industry, *Journal of Development Studies*, Vol. 37 (2), pp. 145–176.

Elbadawi, I. (2005) Reviving Growth in the Arab World, *Economic Development and Cultural Change*, Vol. 53 (2), pp. 293–327.

Ellman, M. (1977) Report from Holland: the Economics of North Sea Hydrocarbons, *Cambridge Journal of Economics*, Vol. 1 (3), pp. 281–291.

Felker Gray, B. (2003) Southeast Asian Industrialisation and the Changing Global Production System, *Third World Quarterly*, Vol. 24, pp. 255–282.

Garavello, O. and Barba Navaretti, B. (eds.) (2001) *Investimenti esteri dele impresse italiane nei paesi emergente.* Giaffre, Milan.

Garofoli, G. (1996) Industrialisation diffuse et systèmes productifs locaux: un modèle difficilement transférable aux pays en développement, in L. Abdelmalki and C. Courlet (eds.), *Les nouvelles logiques du développement: globalisation versus localisation*, L'Harmattan, Paris, pp. 367–383.

Gelb, A.H. *et al.* (1988) *Oil Windfalls: Blessing or Curse?* Oxford University Press, Oxford.

Gereffi, G. (1995) Global Production Systems and Third World Development, in B. Stallings (ed.), *Global, Regional Response: the New International Context of Development*, Cambridge University Press, Cambridge.

Gereffi, G. (1999) International Trade and Industrial Upgrading in the Apparel Commodity Chain, *Journal of International Economics*, Vol. 48 (1), pp. 37–70.

Gereffi, G. and Korzenewicz, M. (eds.) (1994) *Commodity Chains and Global Capitalism*, Praeger, Westport.

Gibbon, P. (2001) Upgrading, Primary Production: a Global Commodity Chain Approach, *World Development*, Vol. 29 (2), pp. 345–363.

Gibbon, P., Thomsen, L. and Palpacuer, F. (2005) New Challenge for Developing Countries Suppliers in Global Clothing Chains: a Comparative European Perspective, *World Development*, Vol. 33 (3), pp. 409–430.

Giles, David, E. and Mosk, C. (2004) Introduction to Special Issue: Trade Openness and Economic Convergence, *The Journal of International Trade and Economic Development*, Vol. 13 (4), pp. 359–371.

Giuliani, E., Pietrobelli, C. and Rabellotti, R. (2005) Upgrading in Global Value Chains: Lessons from Latin American Clusters, *World Development*, Vol. 33 (4), pp. 549–575.

Hakimian, H. and Nugent, J. (eds.) (2004) *Trade Policy and Economic Integration in the Middle East and North Africa, Economic Boundaries in Flux*, Routledge, London.

Harik, I. and Sullivan, D. (1992) *Privatization and Liberalization in the Middle East*, Indiana University Press, Bloomington.

Hugues, A. (2000) Retailers knowledge and Changing Commodity Networks: the Case of the Cut Flower Trade, *Geoforum*, Vol. 31, pp. 175–190.

Hummels, D., Ishii, J. and Yi, K.M. (2001) The Nature and Growth of Vertical Specialization in World Trade, *Journal of International Economic*, 54, pp. 75–96.

Humphrey, J. (1995) Industrial Reorganization in Developing Countries, from Models to Trajectories, *World Development*, Vol. 23 (1), pp. 149–162.

Kaplinsky, R. (2000a) Globalisation and Unequalisation: What can be Learned from Value Chain Analysis, *Journal of Development Studies*, Vol. 37 (2), pp. 117–148.

Kaplinsky, R. (2000b) Spreading the Gains from Globalization: What can be Learned from Value Chain Analysis, *Journal of Development Studies*, Vol. 37 (2), pp. 117–146.

Kienle, E., (2001) *A Grand Delusion: Democracy and Economic Reform in Egypt*, I.B. Tauris, London.

Knorringa, P. (1993) *Lack of Interaction between Traders and Producers in the Agra Footwear Cluster*, Amsterdam Vrije Universiteit.

Leftwich, A. (1995) Bringing Politics back in: Towards a Model of the Development State, *The Journal of Development Studies*, Vol. 31 (3), pp. 400–428.

Lemoine, F. and Unal-Kesenci, D. (2004) Assembly Trade and Technology Transfer: the Case of China, *World Development*, Vol. 32 (5), pp. 829–850.

Li, X. and Liu, X. (2005) Foreign Direct Investment and Economic Growth: an Increasingly Endogenous Relationship, *World Development*, Vol. 33 (3), pp. 393–409.

Lim, L.Y.C. (1995) Southeast Asia: Success through International Openness, in Stallings, B. (ed.), *Global Change, Regional Response: the New International Context of Development*, Cambridge University Press, Cambridge.

Lipsey, R.E. (2004) Home and Host Country Effects of FDI, in R.E. Baldwin and L.A. Winters (eds.). *Challenges to Globalization*, University of Chicago Press, Chicago.

Liu, Z. (2002) Foreign Direct Investment and Technology Spillover: Evidence from China, *Journal of Comparative Economics*, Vol. 30 (3), pp. 579–602.

Loayza, N. and Soto, R. (2002) The Sources of Economic Growth: an Overview, in N. Loayza and R. Soto (eds.), *Economic Growth; Sources, Trends and Cycles*, Central Bank of Chile, Santiago, pp. 1–39.

Luciani, G. (1994) The Oil Rent, the Fiscal Crisis of the State and Democratization, in G. Salamé (ed.), *Democracy without Democrats?: The Renewal of Politics in the Muslim World*, I.B. Tauris, London, pp. 130–156.

Machado, K. (1999) Complexity and Hierarchy in the East Asian Division of Labour: Japanese Technological Superiority and ASEAN Industrial Development, in K.S. Jomo and G. Felker (eds.), *Technology, Competitiveness and the State: Malaysia's Industrial Technology Policies*, Routledge, London, pp. 65–97.

Mahon, E.J. (1992) Was Latin America too Rich to Prosper? *Journal of Development Studies*, Vol. 28 (2), pp. 241–264.

Maskell, P. and Malmberg, A. (1998) *Competitiveness, Localised Learning and Regional Development*, Routledge, New York.

McCormick (1999) African Enterprise Clusters and Industrialization: Theory and Reality, *World Development*, Vol. 27 (9), pp. 1531–1551.

Meyer-Stamer, J. (1998) Path Dependence in Regional Development: Persistence and Change in Three Industrial Clusters in Santa Catarina, Brazil, *World Development*, Vol. 26 (8), pp. 1491–1511.

Nabli, M. and Veganzones, M.A. (2004) Exchange Rate Regime and Competitiveness of Manufactured Exports, *Trade Policy and Economic Integration in the Middle East and North Africa*, in H. Hakimian and J. Nugent, op. cit., Chapter 2.

Nadvi, K. (1999a) The Cutting Edge: Collective Efficiency and International Competitiveness in Pakistan, *Oxford Development Studies*, Vol. 27 (1), pp. 81–107.

Nadvi, K. (1999b) Collective Efficiency and Collective Failure: the Response of the Sialkot Surgical Instrument Cluster to Global Quality Pressures, *World Development*, Vol. 27 (9), pp. 1605–1626.

Noorbakhsh, F., Paloni, A. and Youssef, A. (2001) Human Capital and F.D.I. in Flows to Developing Countries: New Empirical Evidence, *World Development*, Vol. 29 (9), pp. 1596–1611.

O'Rouke, K.H. and Williamson, J. (1999) *Globalization and History*, The MIT Press, Cambridge, Mass.

Oyeleran, O. (1997) *Nnewi: an Emergent Industrial Cluster in Nigeria*, Technopol Publishers, Ibadan.

Palpacuer, F., Gibbon, P. and Thomsen, L. (2005) New Challenges to Developing Countries Suppliers in Global Clothing Chains: a Comparative European Perspective, *World Development*, Vol. 33 (3), pp. 409–430.

Pedersen, P.O. (1997) Clusters of Enterprises within Systems of Production and Distribution: Collective Efficiency and Transaction Cost, in M.P. Van Dijk and R. Rabellotti (eds.), *Enterprise Clusters and Networks in Developing Countries*, Frank Cass, London, pp. 11–19.

Pedersen, P.O., Sverrinson, O., and Van Dijk, m.p. (eds.) (1994) *Flexible Specialization. The Dynamics of Small-Scale Industries in the South*, Intermediate technology Publications, London.

Pietri, A. (1997) Trade Strategies for the Southern Mediterranean, *OCDE Development Centre Technical Paper*, No. 127, Paris.

Porter, N. (1990) *The Competitive Advantage of Nations*, Free Press, New York.

Richards, A. and Waterbury, J. (1996) *A Political Economy of the Middle East*, Westview Press, Boulder, Colo.

Rodrik, D., Subramamian, A., and Trebbi, F. (2002) *Institutions Rules: the Primacy of Institutions over Geography and Integration in Economic Development*, Harvard University, Cambridge, Mass.

Sabel, C. (1989) Flexibility Specialization and the Re-emergence of Regional Economies, in P. Hirst and J. Zeitlin (eds.), *Reversing Industrial Decline*, Oxford, Berg, pp. 17–70.

Sachs, J.D. (2001) Natural Resources and Economic Development: the Curse of Natural Resources, *European Economic Review*, Vol. 45, pp. 827–838.

Sachs, J.D. and Warner, A. (1995) Economic Reform and the Process of Global Integration, *Brookings Paper on Economic Activity*, Vol. 1, pp. 1–118.

Sachs, J.D. and Warner, A. (1999) The Big Push, Natural Resource Booms and Growth,

Journal of Development Economics, Vol. 59 (1), pp. 49–76.

Sadik, A.T. and Bolbol, A.A. (2001) Capital Flows, F.D.I. and Technology Spillovers: Evidence from Arab Countries, *World Development*, Vol. 29, (12), pp. 2111–2127.

Sandee, H. and Rietveld, P. (2001) Upgrading Traditional Technologies in Small-Scale Industry Clusters: Collaboration and Innovation Adoption in Indonesia, *The Journal of Development Studies*, Vol. 37 (4), pp. 150–173.

Schmitz, H. (1995) "Small" Shoemakers and Fordist Giants: Tale of a Supercluster, *World Development*, Vol. 23 (1), pp. 9–29.

Schmitz, H. and Knorringa, P. (2000) Learning from Global Buyers, *Journal of Development Studies*, Vol. 37 (2), pp. 177–205.

Schmitz, H. and Musyck, B. (1994) Industrial Districts in Europe: Policy Lessons for Developing Countries, *World Development*. Vol. 22 (6), pp. 889–911.

Schmitz, H. and Nadvi, K. (1999) Clustering and Industrialization, *World Development*, Vol. 27 (9), pp. 1503–1514.

Scott, A.J. (2002) Regional Push: Towards a Geography of Development and Growth in Low and Middle Income Countries, *Third World Quarterly*, Vol. 23 (1), pp. 137–161.

Scott, A.J. and Storper, M. (eds.) (1992) *Pathways to Industrialization and Regional Development*, Routledge, London.

Sid Ahmed, A. (ed.) (1998) *Le Maghreb, rencontre avec le troisième millénaire: l'impératif de Barcelone: Rapport introductif*, pp.1–36. C.N.R.S. éditions, Paris.

Sid Ahmed, A. (2000) Economic Convergence and Catching-up in the Mediterranean: Diagnostics, Prospects and Limitations of the Barcelone Process and Elements for a Strategy, in H.G. Brauch, A. Marquina and A. Biad (eds.), *Euro-Mediterranean Partnership for the 21st Century*, Macmillan, London, pp. 147–163.

Sid Ahmed, A. (2004) *Le développement asiatique: quels enseignements pour les économies arabes?, éléments de stratégie de développement: le cas de l'Algérie*, ISPROM-Publisud, Paris.

Sid Ahmed, A. (2004) Technologies de l'information et développement économique local: enjeux et stratégie pour les régions et pays en développement du bassin Méditerranéen, in A. Sassu and A. Sid Ahmed (eds.), *Technologies de l'information et développement économique local*. Isprom- Publisud, Paris, pp. 19–69.

Sid Ahmed, A. (2005) Transforming Mediterranean Rentier Economies: Globalisation and Convergence, in M. Dauderstad (ed.), *Towards a Prosperous Wider Europe: Macroeconomic Policies for a Growing Neighborhood*, F. Ebert Foundation, Bonn, pp. 25–44.

Smith, A., Rainnie, A., Dunford, M., Hardy, J., Hudson, R. and Sadler, D. (2002) Networks of Value, Commodities and Regions: Reworking Divisions of Labour, *Progress in Human Geography*, Vol. 26 (1), pp. 41–63.

Sonobe, T., Hu, D. and Otsuka, K. (2002) Process of Cluster Formation in China: a Case Study of a Garnment Town, *The Journal of Development Studies*, Vol. 39 (1), pp. 118–140.

Steinfeld, E. (2004) China's Shallow Integration Networked Production and the New Challenge for Late Industrialization, *World Development*, Vol. 32 (11), pp. 1971–1987.

Thomas, J.J. (2005) Kerala's Industrial Backwardnass: a Case of Path Dependence in Industrialization, *World Development*. Vol. 33 (5), pp. 763–785.

Thompson, E.R. (2000) Business Integration Across the Hong-Kong Chinese Border: Patters and Explanations in the Garment-Industry, in D. Anderson and J. Poon (eds.), *Asia in Transition*, Macmillan, London.

Thompson, E.R. (2002) Clustering of Foreign Direct Investment and Enhanced Technology Transfer: Evidence from Hong-Kong Garment Firms in China, *World Development*, Vol. 30 (5), pp. 87–91.

Uchida, Y. and Cook, P. (2005) The Transformation of Competitive Advantage in East Asia: an Analysis of Technological and Trade Specialization, *World Development*, Vol. 35 (5), pp. 701–729.

Vanderwalle, D. (2003) Social contracts, institutional development and economic growth and reform in middle east oil exporters. Unpublished report, Dartmouth College.

Viesti, G. (2000) Le strade dello sviluppo: como sono i distretti industriali del made in Italy nelle mezzogiorno, *Economia e Politica industriale*, Vol. 6.

Waltz, U. (1998) Does an Enlargement of a Common Market Stimulate Growth and Convergence? *Journal of International Economics*, Vol. 45, pp. 297–321.

Weijland, H. (1999) Microenterprise Cluster in Rural Indonesia: Industrial Seedbed and Policy Target, *World Development*, Vol. 27 (9), pp. 1515–1530.

Weiss, J. and Jalilian, H. (2004) Industrialization in an Age of Globalization: Source Comparisons between East and Southeast Asia and Latin America, *Oxford Development Studies*, Vol. 32 (2), pp. 283–308.

Williamson, J.G. and Yousef, T. (2002) Demographic Transition and Economic Performance in the Middle East and North Africa, in I. Sirageldin (ed.), *Human Capital: Population Economics in the Middle East*, Cairo American University Press, pp. 16–36.

Winjnbergen, V.S. (1984) Inflation Employment and the Dutch Disease in Oil Exporting Countries, *Quarterly Journal of Economics*, May, pp. 233–250.

Xu, B. (2000) Multinational Enterprises, Technology Diffusion and Host Country Productivity Growth, *Journal of Development Economics*, Vol. 62 (2), pp. 477–493.

Yousef, T. (2004) Development, Growth and Policy Reform in the Middle East and North Africa since 1950, *Journal of Economic Perspectives*, Vol. 18 (3), pp. 91–116.

Zhang, K.H. and Xiabo, Z. (2003) How Does Globalisation Affect Regional Inequality Within a Developing Country? Evidence from China, *The Journal of Development Studies*, Vol. 39 (4), pp. 47–67.

4 The dynamics of territorial development in Morocco

Nacer El Kadiri and Jean Lapèze

Introduction

The adoption of local approaches by governmental authorities is a relatively recent phenomenon in Morocco. As a matter of fact, it is only after applying the Structural Adjustment Program (SAP), and noting its negative impact on social outcomes, that measures were adopted, both at the institutional and economical levels, in order to extend the local initiatives initially designed to alleviate the burden of accumulated social deficits.

Territorial policy is more and more significant considering the adoption of the first National Scheme for Town and Country Planning (Schéma National d'Aménagement du Territoire). The creation of new institutions for development (e.g. regional agencies of development, the Social Development Agency, Hassan 2nd Fund) corresponds to a will from the central administration to establish a closer relationship with local authorities, even though the newly created institutions tend to infringe on the prerogatives of these local authorities.

The local (or territorial) scale thus appears to be a major point of focus and a catalyst for the development process, even though policies at the local and global levels still remain widely uncoordinated. In this context, the concept of local development is rooted in a political reference shown in the decentralization policy that started in the 1970s and was accelerated in the 1980s. The government set up procedures for the institutional organization of local development, which were gradually entrusted to local communities. However, this process meets some difficulties in terms of practical implementation, as a result of institutional deficiencies as well as an obvious lack of human and practical means and resources, especially in rural areas. Furthermore, the interest for local development comes from an economic and social concern linked, on one hand, to the increase of poverty, particularly in rural areas, and, on the other hand, to the rise of unemployment, especially among young people.

Recently, a debate took place around the National Initiative for Human Development (NIHD) announced in May 2005. Even though it would be premature to state that NIHD will bring tangible solutions to development needs, it does reinforce the idea that solutions are to be found in the dialectical relationship between local and global levels of decision; that policies put forward to correct geographical and socio-economical imbalances can only be effective if they are led together with local organization structures, thus showing a strong political will from local authorities to take part in the territorial and national development process.

The analysis of the local development dynamic in Morocco responds to two main steps:

1 Rural areas have become the experimenting field for the local development concept.
2 The second step started with the growing urban problematic showing increasing areas of poverty surrounding large cities.

Therefore, the trends observed in the past ten years give some indications of the changes that are now taking place. Those changes are:

1 The progressive assignment of some public services to the private sector through granting and delegation policies.
2 The creation of new governmental agencies for development with great autonomy in fields so far reserved for the state's central administrations.
3 The creation of regional centers for investment in the form of "one-stop offices" aiming at stimulating investments and making administrative procedures easier for national and foreign companies.
4 The creation of the Mohammed V Foundation.
5 The regulation of decentralization transferring to regional assemblies and local communities' important tasks in the economical, cultural and social fields, thus putting forward a new approach in terms of local governing, including a growing concern for the concept of partnership.
6 The development of micro-credit.

Local and territorial development in Morocco: an outstanding approach

Greffe (1989) defines "local development [as being] a process of diversification and enrichment of the economic and social activities on a territory that starts from the mobilization and the coordination of its resources and its energies." For the United Nations Development Program (UNDP), it is

> the carrying out of quantitative and/or qualitative actions aiming at sustainably improving the living conditions of populations of a given region, whether this be on the institutional, geographical or cultural levels. It is a participatory and dynamic process belonging to the socio-economic development approach of the community through the mobilization and the share of responsibilities of an organized community, supported by, coordinated and across sector actions.

This approach is based on the one hand, in the involvement of the community in identifying and satisfying basic and other needs for its own development; and, on the other hand, on the improvement and organization of partnerships for the intervention of different actors from various economical, social, and cultural origins, in the development of the entire community.

We will assert here, together with Claude Courlet, that local development is "the expression of a creative solidarity generated through new social relationships as well as the will of the inhabitants of a given territory to develop local resources toward economical, social, and cultural development." The two terms "development" and "local" relate to the necessary articulation between two fundamental components: in the first place, duration, in the second, the delimitation of a "relevant" space. Consequently, the policies of local economic development encompass not only the carrying out of infrastructures and the creation of activities related to the promotion of employment, but also the creation and, above all, the organization of networks and partnerships among the actors of the territory.

In Morocco, most of the time the development projects were planned at a central level and carried out at the local level, the latter being considered based on administrative delimitations. Gradually, a growing awareness comes to the fact that "local development can only be carried out in a territory that corresponds to a space of solidarity, where the inhabitants have a common history to which they individually and collectively adhere, and where they wish to build together a future" (Courlet, 2001).

An awareness for a local approach

Today in Morocco, the local (and/or territorial) scale appears to be an important factor for development. The proliferation of various and diverse initiatives points to the awareness for the need to act at a local level. Nonprofit groups initially carried out these initiatives and associations, which, faced with the dissatisfaction of communities, played a major role in setting up projects of all kinds. The other organized members of the population (elected officials, professional organizations, administrations, financial institutions, etc.) joined the movement in order to bring answers to common topics such as the fight against poverty, social support of the populations from shantytowns and slums, the fight against unemployment, environmental protection, etc.

Consequently, the answers provided were concerned with the promotion of job-creating activities, the integration of women in the development process; the development of rural tourism, the creation of seed beds for manufacturing companies, as well as with the valorization of local agricultural productions. However, a quick look at history would help to understand fully the roots of these initiatives and how they are progressing.

Local management: going back to the roots?

Morocco has experienced important evolutions in the management of the local authorities throughout its history.

The local government before 1912

For centuries, Morocco has experienced a tradition of self-government by the tribal communities. An endogenous capacity of management concerning all aspects of collective life can be observed on a local level (management of water and pastures, organization of trade associations, etc.). At local level, the society was structured around religious (brotherhoods), social (tribes, confederations of tribes), political (Jemaâ), and economical (corporations) interests, such as shown in Figure 4.1. Nowadays, the structure of this traditional society carries on exist-ing in a rural world, where we meet stacked powers; often, the elites keep their dominant positions through the electoral system maintained under the influence of traditional powers.

Local government during the French protectorate

The colonial policy was aimed at dominating the territory in its entirety by sub-duing the populations to the direct control of the government through the payment of taxes. Under the protectorate, the "Region" was conceived and managed as an administrative territory to keep the population under control, rather than a framework for the design and implementation of development planning policies. It strictly answered to military requirements in order to control space and force all communities to submit to its decisions. In this respect, Morocco had been divided into four military zones (Fès, Meknès, Mar-rakech, Agadir) and three civil regions (Oujda, Salé, Casablanca). Here, local authorities were either left aside or used to fulfill the protectorate's objectives against the sultan's authority. Their structure is shown in Figure 4.2.

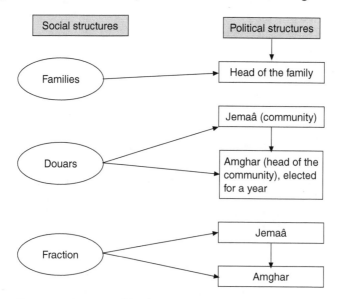

Figure 4.1 Structure of local government before 1912.

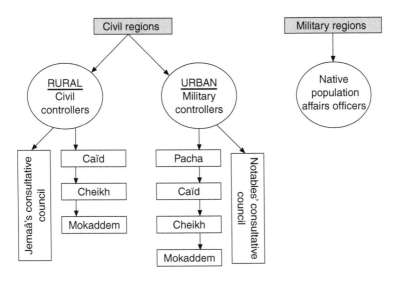

Figure 4.2 Structure of local government under the French protectorate.

The reconstruction

Reconstruction consisted in reviewing the whole administrative apparatus, in order to consider it from a development point of view, in a prospective way. Since 1959, Morocco has moved toward a modern practice of local autonomy through the creation of 800 basic territorial communities, the settling of an elective and pluralist system for the election of local councils, and the carrying of direct vote for all. Decentralization already acknowledged by the 1960s charter, however, maintains a heavy control upon the local authorities. Controls a priori and a posteriori limit the initiative of local elected officials and increase the authority of the state, to the detriment of carrying out local responsibilities. This situation lasted until the end of the 1970s.

For two decades, planning progressively affirmed the idea of the Region:

- The 1960–1964 plan linked overall development with the rise of local communities through regional planning considered as a means to contribute to the achievement of the objectives of the plan. However, the ambitions of the plan, with regard to regionalization, could not materialize and no action was ever carried out.
- With the 1968–1972 plan and the creation of seven economical regions, the Region was not exclusively considered through the prism of economical planning any more, but also under the angle of regional planning while taking into account space imbalances.
- In 1976, the law brought to communal councils the right "to design an

economical and social development plan for the municipality in accordance with the guidelines and objectives retained by the national plan."

However, decentralization as impelled by this act, failed to produce satisfactory results. First of all, its effects on the economical and social development, and the fight against the regional disparities, remained highly limited. Second, there was no efficient functional intermediary link between local and national levels. Furthermore, the level of devolution of the administration was low.

The present local government

The royal speech of 1984 announced a reconsideration of the statute of the Region, by creating regional structures "with legislative, financial and administrative competences," so landing a reference to the German Landers' model. But it was only in 1992 that the constitution provided Regions with the rank of local community, with that attribution confirmed by the constitution of 1996. In 1997, the law limited the institutional, structural, and legal framework by dividing the national territory into 16 Regions, equipped with legal entity and financial autonomy, as well as substantial prerogatives likely to make it an efficient tool for regional and local development (see Table 4.1).

In 1999, the formulation of a new concept of authority in the management of local businesses enlarged the sphere of activity of the authorities to social action and environmental protection; it also promoted partnerships with civil society. In 2002, a new municipal charter was promulgated. It reduced the supervision exerted by the Ministry of the Interior and widened the municipality's autonomy in regard to economical and social development, while founding an external inspecting body (Regional Courts of Accounts), (see Table 4.2).

On an economic level, questions related to investment and employment are of major concern within the political debate. The revival of economics to tackle social deficits explains the importance given to outline obstacles in the field of investment. The positioning of regional commissions for investment close to the governors' offices, just as the creation of new governmental agencies for development endowed with a greater autonomy in fields that so far were solely reserved to government's central administrations, meets those needs. So is the case of both the Development Agency for Northern provinces and the Develop-

Table 4.1 Attributions of the regional council

Title 2 of 1997's Dahir established three categories of attribution reserved for the regional council:

1 Competencies like carrying out the regional development plan, local taxation and the promotion of private investments
2 Attributions that can be transferred by the state with financial resources
3 Proposals for the actions in favor of the development of the Region, regional planning, and the creation of universities, hospitals, etc.

Table 4.2 Attributions of the municipal council (municipal charter of November 21, 2002)

Article 35: The municipal council . . . decides on measures to be taken to ensure the economical, social, and cultural development of the municipality.
Article 36: Economical and social development.

1 It considers and votes the plan for economic and social development of the municipality, in accordance with the national plan's aims and objectives.
2 It initiates any action suitable to support and promote the development of the local economy and employment.

   a It takes the required measures likely to contribute to boost its economic potential, particularly in agriculture, industry, handcraft, tourism, and services;
   b It takes necessary action to promote and encourage private investments, particularly the carrying out of infrastructures and equipment, settling of zones for economical activities, and improvement of companies' environment;
   c It decides on the participation of the municipality in the companies' investment tied to municipal, inter-municipal, prefectoral, provincial or regional interest;
   d It decides on the concluding of any agreement or convention for cooperation or partnership leading to the promotion of economical and social development, and sets up the conditions for the carrying out of the municipality's actions to be undertaken in collaboration or partnership with public administrations, local communities, public or private organizations, and social actors.

3 It sets, within the limit of its legal attributions, conditions for forests' conservation, exploitation, and development.

---

ment Agency for Southern provinces, and, more recently, the Development Agency for Eastern provinces. They all have broad prerogatives and are able directly or indirectly to carry out infrastructure projects in partnership with ministries and local communities. In the same way, the Social Development Agency was intended to support local initiatives for income production, most particularly in rural areas.

The current situation related to the organization of local government, such as shown in Figure 4.3, depicts four main preoccupations:

1 On the institutional level, Morocco puts forward a territorial policy based on a three-level structure: municipal, provincial and regional.
2 Politically, juridically, and even financially speaking, the whole of the structure lies upon the municipal authority as a fundamental foundation.
3 Concerning the provincial level, known as the intermediary level, it acts under state control, making it difficult to speak of a true decentralization, even though elected councils are juridically supposed to have some autonomy.
4 The regional framework is theoretically less dependent on the central government's control. The concept of Region/Space is closely related to that of economic and social development. Regional councils are naturally mainly concerned with their contribution to national planning; by the promotion of investments, the support for the creation of activities and

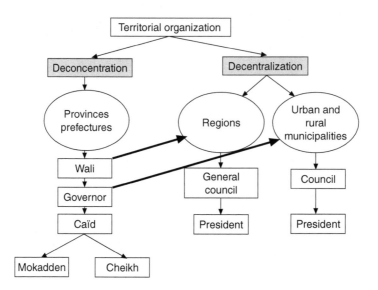

Figure 4.3 Structure of the present local government.

employment so supplying their own space with durable dynamics of development; and finally, by supporting the municipalities in order to help them face the requirements of providing equipment to their territory.

The last point leads us to consider who are the actors involved in this process and how it works.

The main actors of local development

The local communities

The promotion of the Region to the level of local community by the constitution of 1992 seems to be one of the most important reforms in recent years. At the level of basic local communities, several reforms have been undertaken that gave broad prerogatives to the councils. In addition to the Regions and municipalities, the provincial assembly has a competence defined by law most particularly related to regional development programs, creation and choice of managerial models for the prefectoral and provincial public services, and creation or contribution to development or planning companies.

National nongovernmental organizations (NGOs)

The participation of the civil society in the local development process is increasing as about 20,000 associations are now working in the development field. This expansion began at the end of the 1980s when the state began to withdraw from some social functions following the structural adjustment policy. The promotion of the associative sector was also backed by international organizations. Associations were first involved in informal education, health, and assistance of low-income populations (women, handicapped people, and abandoned children). They became more involved in the field of employment, promotion of small firms, and construction of basic rural infrastructures such as electrification, water supplies, and road building. Step by step, these associations became privileged partners of the authorities in the development field. Even though, to some extent, these associations substituted for the state, they proved to be a real power of proposal, promotion and initiative.

Nowadays, these NGOs are of very different kinds, but all of them are actively working in the fields of poverty relief and exclusion. Some of them were created with a great and durable support from international cooperation organizations, such as the Moroccan Association of Solidarity and Development (AMSED), which contributed to the implementation of micro-credit in 1993. These associations, which could be able to be an efficient relay for the state and financial institutions, very often suffer from a lack of financial means, organization and autonomy. Furthermore, they also need permanent and qualified staff.

The other actors

Operating through the international cooperation system, the main partners are: international NGOs (Enda-Maghreb, Handicap International, Catholic Relief Services, etc.), multilateral organizations (UNDP, UNICEF, UNFPA, ILO, etc.), and actors from decentralized cooperation (French, Italian, and Spanish Regions that signed cooperation agreements with Moroccan Regions).

Constraints on the promotion of local development

What is the real contribution of local development projects to resolve problems at the local and national scale? What is the effective way to act in order to increase dynamic growth and development? How can a shift from local to global approach of the territory be achieved?

If we want to address the issue of the effectiveness of local development actions in Morocco, we need to evaluate the ability of the territory's actors to work together in order to fulfill the individual and collective needs of the populations. However, at the local level we note, on the one hand, a great tendency toward bureaucratization of the municipal functions to the detriment of development tasks, while, on the other hand, leverages of development are insufficiently controlled and strategic considerations are often left aside regarding emergency matters. The latter goes together with a lack of means and competencies into local NGOs, as well as with a lack of cooperation among actors.

The task is not only to initiate local projects, but to accelerate local dynamics by creating a synergy among the actual potentialities of the territory (agricultural, industrial, tourist, and cultural resources) and its human resources (dynamism and qualification, entrepreneurship and cultural richness of the local populations), while being inserted within the orientations of the country's planning (infrastructures of communication, great economic guidelines, specific programs for mountain or rural areas), and its economic planning.

Localized productive systems (LPSs) in Morocco[1]

The overall situation

Morocco has gone through important changes during the past decade. Because of its fast-growing opening to the world and the worsening of social and regional imbalances, its development policy has to be seen differently. It has to be based on two remarkable phenomena: globalization and a new definition of the role of economic actors.

Local development and globalization

The signature of several free-trade agreements with the European Union, the USA, Turkey, and several Arab countries made Morocco part of the global market. This choice implies painful adaptations, particularly in industry, but also, in the long run, in the agricultural production process. However, the creation of increasingly differentiated regional structures, as well as specialized areas, implies that

> globalization must not be understood as a standardized process, and that territories and local areas still have their place in the national economy. Here appears a new difference between what is global and local. This new form of development combines complex multidimensional networks and appears to be very creative, while being both global and local at the same time. In this new approach of space, the economic linkages are no longer to be ruled by a logic of "proximity and encasing" [Russian dolls].
>
> (Courlet, 2005)

This also implies a change in the traditional approach. In the first place, it means moving from a simple geographical approach of space to an organizational approach of development. In the second place, it responds to a need to endow space with new strategic functions such as anticipation, observation, and prospective. Finally, these two points lead to an obligation to build a specific territorial offer displaying skills and excellence. We thus move from geography of costs to geography of skills.

The first part focuses on the growing interest for territory in Morocco, related to the principle of governance. The effectiveness of such method will, above all, depend on the power entrusted in regional councils and, more generally, in local territories. This implies an in-depth reorganization of the state and a redefinition of its representatives' prerogatives, within the framework of the democratization process. However, the Walis and governors keep exerting a strong determining role in the dynamics of territories despite the creation of the Regional Centers for Investment (RCI). Even though this shows the importance given by the state to a regional economic impulse, there is little or no place for democratic institutions. Given the fact that decentralization is a long-run process, the redefinition of governance as a centralized and state-run process leads to a new understanding of the state's role.

On one hand, local communities must benefit from various skills and know-how, and must be endowed with resources in order to create plurality of interests inside a given territory. On the other hand, the state will have to give up some key competencies to local territories. Thus, these competencies would be used in a different way and the state would enhance dialogue and consensus, initiating projects and playing the role of a referee.

Regional differentiation

The Moroccan economy is definitely fragile and strongly dependent on primary economic activities. The average GDP growth (around $40 billion) has lost momentum during the past 15 years, and is constantly less than 3 percent per year. As a matter of fact, per capita annual growth hardly exceeds 1.5 percent, in spite of the decreasing demographic growth. Industry and, more recently, tourism do not generate sufficient income for the taking off of the national economy even though both sectors appear to be modern and well developed. Poverty still affects an important proportion (around 25 percent) of the population in rural areas and represented nearly 45 percent of the whole population in 2004.

Industry concentrated on the Atlantic coast

Moroccan industry has shown its ability for job creation during the past 40 years, moving from 76,000 jobs in 1958 to 475,000 in 2002. Approximately 90 percent of labor is employed in small and medium firms. The industrial sector is based upon textile–clothing–leather activity that represents more than 46 percent (against 34 percent in 1980) of the industrial labor force, with 222,000 workers in 2002. The food industry represents around 19 percent of the industrial labor, whereas electric and electronic industries, mechanics, and metallurgy account for only 15 percent. The manufacturing industry was originally located in Casablanca, which represented in excess of 46 percent of the labor in 2002. However, we can see that this city is getting relatively less important than it used to be compared with other big cities such as Rabat-Salé and Tangier.

An LPS survey identified around 50 agglomerations of specialized industries that correspond with the noted description. These specialized industrial areas account for approximately 35 percent of the manufacturing labor force.

Combined, these similar or complementary activities create specific territories that are close to the concept of LPS:

- Fez for ceramics, tanning, and production of leather shoes, for cotton-spinning and other fibers and modern clothing industry;
- Safi for sea products' transformation;
- Marrakech for fruit and vegetables canning, cereals and semolina flours;
- Meknès for cereal and semolina flours, as well as the clothing industry;
- Casablanca for the hosiery and clothing industries;
- Casablanca again (Sidi Bernoussi) for the manufacturing of leather shoes;
- Rabat and Salé for the clothing industry.

LPS and economic development in Morocco

The usual definition of LPS is "an area characterized by the proximity of productive units in its broad meaning (industrial firms, handcrafting, tourism, services, training and research centers, interfaces, etc.) that are more or less intensively related" (Courlet, 2001). Indeed, LPS is comparable with many phenomena where territories and geographical proximity play an important role within the relationships among the actors of economical development. The intensity of the relationships among the manufacturing units depends, above all, on the organization of the production system. There are several types of relationships among production units: they can be formal, abstract, material, immaterial, commercial, and noncommercial. They can be related to material flows, services, labor force, technology, or knowledge.

In the present situation, LPS appears to be a well-adapted answer to globalization and to the problems industries have to face, particularly in terms of localization of their activities. This is the case with the clothing industry or tourism. Indeed, LPS relies on the assets of space proximity and local specificities. Thanks to privileged linkages among the services of firms, as well as their connection to a work pool, to research centers, or to the authorities, the economic development can expand to the territory.

LPS is, thus, a territory likely to bind economical and social development, but can also become part of new territorial projects defined by local actors. Moreover, it could constitute a framework for a new industrial policy at a micro-territorial scale. More than a sectoral network, it can be considered as a dynamic structure able to foresee the trends and to reinvent the economical development of a territory using its own resources for doing so.

From the local diagnoses carried out on ten territories, we found two different types of cases:

- A first case in which the production directly aims at a market's requirements and in which we find well-defined "product/market" dualities, such as clothing industries in Casablanca and Tangier, olive culture in Guercif, and market garden products and dairy products in Souss.

- A second case dealing with "service" or "product-service" dualities, such as mechanical subcontracting in Casablanca, tourism in Arfoud and new technologies of information in Casablanca

These different cases correspond more or less to the LPS situation. Clothing industries in Guercif and Tangier, to a lower extent, are organized in an *opened localized development context* linked to the strategies of big foreign companies willing to lower their head costs; they are simple specialized agglomerations not so close to real LPS. Olive cultivation in Guercif; the clothing industry, mechanical subcontracting, and technologies of information in Casablanca; tourism in Arfoud; and greenhouse and citrus cultivations in Souss-Massa are *systems emerging from spontaneous initiatives* showing a real potential of territorial mobilization of resources. However, they cannot be regarded as true LPSs, even if one cannot deny that their development transformed their settling areas into genuine employment pools, and led them to become areas of the highest levels of effectiveness.

In traditional agriculture (Souss-Massa region), where the "Douar"[2] still constitutes the framework of such systems, we find the existence of *peculiar LPS*. Given the tough natural environment and the lack of public development initiatives in their territories, their populations had to rely on themselves and draw on their ancestral culture of solidarity, mutual aid, and self-organization that initially makes collective interest prevail over that of the individual. These systems are mixing polycultivation and extensive breeding, and the organization in channels of production or trade is not significant. Because of a lack of basic resources, the agricultural income cannot cover the needs of the population. This is why it becomes vital for these systems to seek external sources of income.

In addition, the survey also divulged genuine LPS. Copper and leather-shoes industry in Fez, where one can see the cooperation among actors as well as the technical–economical complementarities among the activities, and where the territory (Medina[3]) plays a fundamental role. It is a place where spatial dynamics are linked with trade, know-how sharing, and proximity that generates solidarity. However, this system often goes through a situation of saturation and stagnation.

In Souss-Massa, the dairy industry can be considered a LPS. First of all, this is so for the great number of producers and their contribution to the supply side of the national milk market and derived products. It is also the case because it integrates all categories of stockbreeders in the area considered in this survey. In addition, the level and quality of the corporations and their strong attachment to the territory, as well as the integrated production–transformation–trade process, show what can be considered a LPS. The impact on employment, income, and living conditions of local populations is, thus, huge, and is now promoted as a model for social economy and local development.

Characteristics of the Moroccan LPS

An abundant but relatively costly labor force

Wages are higher than in many other developing countries. Competitors in the clothing industry, for example, such as Romania, Indonesia, China, and Syria, employ workers who earn half of Moroccan wages. In Turkey, Tunisia, and Jordan wages are approximately 40 percent lower. In fact, Moroccan wages are close to those given in the Czech Republic and Poland. This situation requires urgent strategic action so as to avoid competition being strictly based on costs. The authorities have to rely on other sources of competitiveness, such as speed in reaction, quality, and delivery delays. This reinforces the interest for cooperation among local firms and, for that matter, the creation of genuine LPSs.

In Morocco, the recruiting of labor is based on personal contacts, as a result of local and tribal relationships. In a small production unit, flexibility is also based on the abundance and availability of local human resources. The local job market complies with various types of employment (full-time and part-time jobs, as well as retirees) and with a very flexible system of work distribution. Private relationships are good for the negotiation between employers and employees as they prevent social conflicts.

Specialization facilitates the hiring of almost-illiterate workers who have technical skills and are able to move from one company to another according to their closeness within the territory. Thus, the companies, even the biggest ones, benefit from a favorable environment and do not need to invest in training programs for their workers. In addition, this abundant labor force leads companies to manufacture with intensive labor force policies rather than to innovate. This abundance of labor force is doubled in urban areas because of a strong flow of migrants. Furthermore, the importance of a strong informal sector worsens this tendency, thus weakening the local development process.

The relationship among firms

Observing European LPSs, we can easily notice that production is organized through horizontal cooperation among producers: the various tasks traditionally gathered within one firm are moved outside the company, based upon division of labor. The notion of "trade branch community"[4] here is very important. This notion implies firms use innovation technologies to send information to their subcontractors, which facilitates the learning process in small firms through the sharing of skills, specialization, and information. One of the advantages of such cooperation is the increase in competitiveness and profits.

Moroccan LPSs are slightly different, and it is more difficult to find a common description to all LPSs. In some cases, cooperation among firms (within industrial areas in Tangier, for instance) is getting increasingly strong. But relationships between small firms and big companies are not often based on a technical specialization of subcontractors, as is the case for the manufacturing industry. They are more likely to be based on a will to alleviate the constraints of the law, by using the very cheap local labor force, as is the case in Guercif with the clothing industry.

The role of intermediation institutions

Institutions of intermediation (chambers of trade, trade associations, technical and research centers, training centers, etc.) are necessary to LPSs. The governance within a LPS then becomes a process of coordination between the actions and the needs of economic actors within a territory, and accounts for a partnership among public institutions and private companies that involves local authorities.

The Moroccan LPS system is largely imitating LPSs in developed countries. Apart from certain professions (copper in Fez for example, or dairy production in Souss-Massa), the authorities suffer from a lack of skills and resources, and corporations do not have training programs (the Hotel Industries Association in Arfoud, the "Bourse Nationale pour la Soustraitance" for mechanics, etc.). Relationships with the authorities are not so important given the fact that small companies have a bad image of the state that is allegedly hampering their activity (fiscal laws, bureaucracy). In addition, local initiatives totally depend on the central authority. This is why one cannot really talk of a "local power" as is the case for European LPSs. Additionally, power centralization leaves little space for public institutions to act locally. Local initiatives still depend on the central government. This is why the meaning of local authority is not the same as in European LPSs, and is still to be developed in Morocco.

Hence, unlike LPSs in France or Italy, there is no real institutional environment for Moroccan LPSs. An LPS can be described as an abstract social environment, ruled by family values and neighborhood relationships, rather than a concrete background with norms to be complied with or organized institutions to tackle precise issues.

Typology of Moroccan LPSs

The survey made it possible to draw up, on the basis of that suggested by Gioacchino Garofoli (1983), a first typology of Moroccan LPSs. This typology indicates, under the common denomination of "LPS," increasing levels of complexity, from the simple coexistence in a given area of similar firms (areas of productive specialization) to "system areas" (close to the famous Italian industrial districts) in which there are strong institutional and industrial relationships among the firms, and within the regional environment.

Characteristics of Morrocan LPSs have been defined, on the one hand, through the relationships among companies, and on the other hand, through their ability to face competition thanks to the specific skills they own. Herein lies a difference between competitors' cooperation (trading in the same market) and cooperation linked to trade between two companies. Comparison between the observed Moroccan LPSs and those described by G. Garofoli are subjective, and must not be considered realistic. If we consider the "specialized production area" as the first level of LPS (level 0), and the system area as the most complex and integrated level (level 5), and if we consider that the LPS itself is the intermediate level, Table 4.3 indicates the results we get.

This first analysis shows what strategy could be undertaken for a LPS development program: one solution could be an increased coordination of local actions to create true system areas. However, the question is to find out up to what point this development policy is relevant. An important point is that the focus should not be put on a local development scheme as opposed to a national policy that would be based on a sectoral overview. Rather, it would be a local scheme that paves the way to a steady global development of the country. Remember that Morocco has a peculiar position in global trade, with intermediate wages, as well as a geographical and cultural proximity to Europe and, especially, Western European countries (France, United Kingdom, Spain).

Moreover, access to European markets is controlled by powerful companies that dominate the trade of goods as well as, very often, their spin-off processes (the car industry, for example). In the clothing industry, as in most industrial sectors, several organization systems coexist. It then becomes possible, but not certain, that one of them might take the lead over the others in the next few years. The structure of the clothing industry and its sub-sectors is linked to both the nature of the activity (with a fundamental difference between mesh, screens, and chain) and to the strategy of the European firms that place the orders. The move from traditional subcontracting to shared production, the focus set on quality, nature of price negotiation, length of lines, growing speed of pattern changes, and "time to market" requirements have a strong impact on the organization of production and the relationships among firms.

Many surveys show that several systems of organization in the relationships among firms coexist. There are at least four kinds of these systems. Some of the companies are only related to the ones that place the orders through traditional subcontracting: these latter ones send the plans for the cutting of fabrics, evaluate the time needed for production, and impose their prices for activities such as the sewing and packing of the finished products. Elsewhere, a hierarchical system is in place, with a subcontractor that negotiates with the contractors and then distributes work among subcontractors of lower rank. We also find systems of companies belonging to networks based on a strict division of labor, but that are, in fact, involved in the production process from the design of goods up to their final delivery. Here, their involvement is based on strong family relationships, with a leader who owns one or more companies of the network. This system strongly resembles the Motte system, which was developed in the north of France during the first half of the twentieth century.

Finally, we observe companies seeking to organize themselves in a network at different levels of channel production, doing so via cooperation among companies of comparable size and importance. This project of organization, defended by the Textile and Clothing Industry Association (AMITH), falls

Table 4.3 Positioning of the LPS according to the typology of G. Garofoli

	Firm complementarities	*Firm cooperation*	*Specific capabilities*	*Total*
Specialized production area	0	0	0	0
Guercif clothing industry	1	1	1	3
Tangier clothing industry	1	1	1	3
Casa subcontractors	2	2	3	7
Casa clothing industry	2	3	2	7
Souss Massa extensive agriculture	1	4	2	7
Arfoud. tourism	3	3	2	8
Souss-Massa intensive dairy industry	3	3	3	9
Casa information technologies	2	3	4	9
Guercif olive culture	3	3	3	9
LPS	2	4	4	10
Fez. handcraft	4	4	3	11
System area	5	5	5	15

under a prospect aiming at conciliating flexibility and reactivity to fashion, with the firms' competencies and a sufficient scale of production to be competitive.

Whatever the system is, they all go hand in hand with a certain territorial organization of production. Companies falling under the first system keep low relationships among themselves. They even refuse a certain closeness so as to keep safe from trade-union disputes and be able to preserve a low level of wages. On the other hand, companies that have to exchange much information, whose managers have to solve many problems of coordination, in particular at the time for renewal of goods (matter, color, shape of the manufactured goods), must be able to communicate easily among each other. A part of these communications can be done remotely, with the assistance of new technologies (the transmission by Internet of the plans of cutting given by foreign contractors, for example). But since the companies' executives need to act in concert to solve common problems, personal links as well as geographic proximity become necessary. Moreover, external customers, who want to find the companies they mean to deal with quickly, visit many companies.

One then easily understands the importance of the organization of true industrial parks, distributed with relevant supplies and able to organize contacts among the companies settled on the spot, as well as support relationships with the outside. The geographical proximity, thus, appears to be a determining factor for modernization and the leveling of industrial companies. It is the same for the sectors of services and agriculture, sectors where this geographical proximity is, moreover, linked to a natural patrimony (tourism, agriculture). Besides, many rural communities enjoy a plurality of local assets: a good physical environment, an ancient settlement, a long tradition of agrarian installation and social life, economic potentialities, and secular know-how.

These combinations help develop local dynamics. As shown in the case of the dairy production in Souss-Massa, some of these dynamics could be widened thanks to a well-adapted close support policy such as the LPS framework. As can be noted in the case of the tourist resorts in mountain or in some peripheral rural areas in France, the rural dimension of these territorial forms supports the introduction of a dialectical relationship between community isolation and an opening toward the outside world, so constituting one of the conditions for the existence of this type of system.

LPS and institutional approach

Nevertheless, it remains that LPSs in Morocco still rely on traditional organizations rather than political will, even though the present government is trying to modernize its own approach. As far as craft is concerned, activities rest on history, ancestral practices, traditional values, etc., inherited from the corporations. It is quite easy to build a LPS where the tradition implies a sharing of works, common practices and representations, etc. Rooted in history, most of the communities, such as in the Souss-Massa, have a tradition of solidarity, sharing local resources, and so on. In other words, the dynamics among actors remain independent from the institutional system, even though they need and wish support from the government or local authorities.

For the handicraft from Fez, the central administration working together with the corporations managed to move the activities from the Medina to an organized area with a center of resources. However, so far this is the only case in which the central state answers to the corporations' demands, thus showing the beginning of a wider movement starting with the National Initiative for Human Development.

Notes

1 This part is largely inspired by "the study on the basins of employment. Case of the LPS in Morocco," realized by C. Courlet, N. El kadiri, L. Jennan, A. Fejjal, L. Jaidi, L. Zagdouni, M. Hollard and M. Souissi, direction of the regional planning, Morocco, 2005.
2 Village.
3 The old city.
4 Communauté de branche de métier.

References

Courlet, C. (2001) *Territoires et Régions, les grands oubliés du développement économique*, L'Harmattan, Paris.
Garofoli, G. (1983) *Industrializzazione diffusa in Lombardia*, Milan, F. Angeli.
Greffe, X. (1989) *Guide du développement local et du développement social*, L'Harmattan, Paris.

5 Kenya's garment and metal industries

Global and local realities

Dorothy McCormick

Introduction

Businesses are formed and operate in particular environments that are both complex and continuously changing. Made up of institutions and their related organizations, together with stocks of physical assets, the business environment can be viewed as a system that facilitates, constrains, and ultimately shapes business activity.

Institutions can be named as global, regional, national, local, or sectoral. In one sense, institutions are always local because of the way they touch individual firms in particular places that are undertaking particular activities. Nevertheless, identifying their origins and scope, and examining the ways in which they converge in specific circumstances can be extremely useful in raising questions and revealing alternative courses of action.

This chapter attempts to address the "regional question" by focusing on a particular country in the eastern part of Sub-Saharan Africa. Sub-Saharan Africa is the least industrialized and least urbanized part of the world, and, therefore, represents a very important development challenge. The chapter uses two manufacturing activities in Kenya – garment production and metal fabrication – as lenses through which to view the institutional environment for business. It draws mainly on data gathered by a team of researchers who investigated a number of sectors (McCormick *et al.*, forthcoming). The chapter is written in seven parts. Following this introduction, the second part elaborates the chapter's analytical framework. The third part offers a brief overview of Kenya's present reality. The fourth part describes the study's methodology. The fifth and sixth examine the two sectors in some detail, while the final part summarizes the findings, offers conclusions, and raises further questions.

Business in a global-local world

This section establishes the theoretical context for the discussion of particular sectors, by considering the impact on production of first, globalization and global institutions, second, local realities, including both institutions and physical agglomerations of firms, and, finally, the nature of manufacturing and its place in chains of productive activities. Critical to the discussion is the understanding of institutions as the way things are done in a particular economic, political, or social activity. They are, as North (1990) has so aptly put it, the "rules of the game" that both facilitate and constrain human interaction.

Globalization

Globalization has been credited with creating a world in which – for good or for ill – individuals and groups are linked in a dense network of interactions. Greatly improved communications and transport systems have allowed these interactions to occur with a speed and frequency that would have seemed impossible only a few decades ago.

Nowhere is the process of economic globalization clearer than in what have come to be called "global value chains" (Gereffi, 1994; Gereffi *et al.*, 2001; Kaplinsky and Morris, 2001; McCormick and Schmitz, 2001; Gereffi and Memedovic, 2003). These chains of activities are required to bring a product from its conception to the final consumer and often have nodes in several countries. Design may take place in one country, raw material procurement in another, production in several others, and distribution may span several continents. The links in the chain may signify ownership, as in the case of multinational companies, but more often firms are joined by market or subcontracting relationships.

In the view of many, globalization reduces the importance of national boundaries and local cultures. The argument rests on what Voisey and O'Riordan (2001) call the rhetoric of political globalization. This is the belief that the nation-state's powers and abilities to control events are being eroded by the activities of actors other than governments that operate at an international level. These include organizations such as Greenpeace, the World Bank, and the International Monetary Fund, as well as multinational firms. Arguments for cultural globalization, on the other hand, are largely based on the impact of modern transportation and communication, which allows both people and ideas to flow easily around the world. The impact of television, the Internet, and mass tourism are most commonly cited as driving the world toward a single global culture (UNDP, 2004).

Local realities

Many observers argue for the continued importance of local realities. Without denying that globalization is real, these scholars highlight the role of local social, political, and economic institutions in shaping development generally and business in particular (Whitley, 1992; Cherni, 2001; Schmitz, 2004).

The conduct of business differs from one place to another. The differences are largely a function of varying economic, political, and social institutions that have evolved over time (Whitley, 1992; Evans, 1995; Fukuyama, 1995; McCormick and Kimuyu, forthcoming). The very limited analysis that has been carried out on African business systems suggests that they tend to be made up of fairly distinct fragments that are not well linked (Pedersen and McCormick, 1999). According to this analysis, the typical African production and distribution system consists of different segments, including a parastatal sector, formal large-scale private sector, and micro- and small-scale sector. The fragmentation is largely a function of the ways in which institutions governing business have evolved (or failed to evolve) over time. Institutions surrounding property rights, contract enforcement, the organization of work, the availability of information, and collective action affect industrial development. Weak and costly mechanisms for enforcing contracts, for example, encourage businesses to restrict their dealings to people whom they know personally or with whom they share ethnic or religious networks. When collective action is seen as a threat to the political regime, businesses may fail to build effective associations.

Social institutions of family, religion, and ethnic group provide the values and norms that underlie economic and political activity, and thereby shape business culture and practice. Individually and when taken together, these institutions help to explain the form and operations of business enterprises. They make some aspects of business work well, while presenting challenges for others. For example, in most African societies the family consists of a number of people of different generations, including parents, children, grandparents, uncles, aunts, and other more distant relatives. Children growing up in such an extended family learn from an early age that they are part of a "we" that is much larger than themselves (Mbiti, 1969; Kuada, 1994; Hofstede, 1997). One positive consequence of this is that it can create a sense of group loyalty in the workplace, and may be the basis for business partnerships among members of the same extended family. On the other hand, it has been observed that the extended family can make demands that drain resources and make it difficult for businesses to prosper.

A second local reality is the country's or region's level of economic and human development. Countries with low per capita income generally have little income with which to provide infrastructure and public services for industry. Furthermore, in poor countries, workers are often humanly poor, in the sense of having low incomes, low levels of literacy, and poor access to preventative and curative health care (UNDP, 2005).

Another manifestation of the importance of the local realities is the existence of clusters of firms with the potential to foster competitiveness and innovation (Schmitz, 1995; Schmitz and Nadvi, 1999; Scott and Storper, 2003). Defined as geographic and sectoral agglomerations of firms and anchored theoretically in arguments for the importance of local realities and local dynamics, enterprise clusters are by their very nature local phenomena (Marshall, 1890; Krugman, 1991; Schmitz, 2004). In theory, clusters reap the benefits of agglomeration economies. Appropriate joint action can complement these economies and magnify their benefits (Schmitz and Nadvi, 1999; Scott and Garofoli, this volume). Of particular importance in this context is emerging evidence that African clusters lack the positive externalities and joint action that figure prominently in clusters elsewhere.

Africa has few complex industrial clusters and many micro- and small enterprise clusters (McCormick, 1999). This appears to be due to a number of factors that combine to keep businesses small and poorly linked. Among these are underdeveloped trading networks, overabundance of labor, weak political and economic institutions, and lack of effective business associations (McCormick, 1999; McCormick *et al.*, 2003). The most universal benefit for locating in clusters is access to markets. In many cases, this means access to localized and low-income consumers and to traders who take products to similar markets elsewhere (McCormick, 1999). Despite the weaknesses of existing clusters, small producers favor them as places they believe will offer opportunities for joint action, technological upgrading, and the sharing of resources.

Manufacturing

Manufacturing – the transformation of raw materials into new products – is an activity with particular requirements for infrastructure, human resources, production and storage space, and capital equipment. In industrialized countries, government is responsible for providing both physical infrastructure and public services. Manufacturers expect that roads, bridges, and ports will be there and in good condition. They can count on reliable public services, including electricity, water, communications, and fire and police services. Such things cannot be taken for granted in poor countries where they are more often than not completely missing or functioning badly. This forces producers to provide or supplement the services through some sort of self-provisioning. It is common for manufacturers to sink their own boreholes, repair access roads, invest in generators to supplement erratic power supplies, and hire their own security services. Such arrangements, however, add to costs, making products more expensive and less competitive on international markets.

Manufacturers also need managers, supervisors, and production workers with appropriate combinations of formal education and technical skills. These are often more difficult to find in countries with low levels of human development, many of which also lack up-to-date training systems. Businesses complain that tertiary graduates in technical fields have little practical knowledge. This is usually attributed to budgetary constraints that have not allowed universities and polytechnics to update their technologies. The lack of appropriate training opportunities for production workers forces larger firms to mount their own in-house training programs. Micro- and small enterprises mostly rely on so-called "on-the-job training," which, in their case, is usually little more than supervised work.

Finally, manufacturers need physical capital in the form of factory buildings, warehouses, machinery, and other equipment. In many industries, setting up a factory represents a major commitment of both time and money. Studies of the impact of the regulatory regime on the time taken to start a business show striking differences among regions, with the East Asian newly industrialized countries (NICs) reporting fewer obstacles to business entry than either rich

Organization for Economic Cooperation and Development (OECD) countries or other developing or emerging economies (Kaufman, 2004). Many African countries report a significant burden of both central and local government regulation (Porter *et al.*, 2004). This obviously translates into both direct and indirect costs for business establishment and operation.

Manufacturing processes vary from Fordist assembly lines and integrated continuous processes, on the one hand, to "flexible specialization" and craft modes on the other (Piore and Sabel, 1984; Langlois and Robertson, 1995). Furthermore, firms may concentrate on the production of certain core items or they may be vertically integrated. During the import substitution era, African countries tended to develop a range of large vertically integrated manufacturers using the typical assembly-line division of labor. Such firms emerged at least in part because of the difficulty in importing raw materials and components because of the tariffs and quotas established to support import substitution. The smallest firms are mostly craft producers in which each worker makes an item from start to finish, though there are variations.

Sub-sector and even the specific products are important because they often determine the nature of the technology, labor force requirements, and the markets most easily accessed. On the other hand, the markets themselves are a significant factor in determining the organization of production. Global markets seek products of consistent quality, often produced in high volume, and at low unit costs. Consumers in developed countries are also increasingly concerned about the conditions under which goods are produced, both because of genuine interest in the workers' well being and out of concern for their own health and safety (McCormick and Schmitz, 2002).

In manufacturing, global and local realities often meet and sometimes conflict. The manufacturing portion of global value chains may be informed by global standards and local labor laws, external markets, and local infrastructure limitations. Understanding the impact of global and local realities, therefore, requires sorting through a good deal of empirical data.

Analytical framework

The foregoing discussion suggests that the factors that need to be considered in the analysis of manufacturing activities are at three levels. Some of these factors are local in the sense of belonging either to the country or the cluster itself; others are sectoral, while still others are global. These are summarized in Table 5.1.

At the country level, three main factors need consideration. First, development as measured in both economic and human development terms; second, the country's geographic size and the size of its economy; and third, the nature and functioning of the main economic and social institutions, including markets, government, rule of law, family, and so forth. If the analysis is to include particular existing clusters, then cluster-level factors also need to be considered. The most important factors to include are the nature of the product(s) made in

Table 5.1 Analytical framework

Level	Specific variables
Local	Level of economic and human development
	Institutions relevant to industry
	Industrial policy
	Trade policy
	Infrastructure
	Cluster or regional characteristics
Sectoral	Main products
	Markets accessed
	Firm size structure
	Supply linkages
	Production technology
	Production linkages
	Key sectoral institutions
Global	Institutions affecting sector
	Institutions affecting country
	Regional and/or bilateral trade initiatives
	Global trends

the cluster, local and external markets for those products, size of firms in the cluster, cluster infrastructure, and existing collective efficiency.

The second level is sectoral. Some of the variables mentioned in the context of the cluster also pertain to the sector. Products, markets, firm size structure, technology, linkages, and institutions governing the sector in general can offer important insights into the environment within which a firm or group of firms operates. Finally, it will be important to consider how the country's industry is or might be affected by realities at the global level. What global institutions or external markets could make a difference to this cluster? Institutions such as the World Trade Organization (WTO) are particularly important, as are bilateral initiatives such as the African Growth and Opportunity Act (AGOA) of the US government. As discussed below, AGOA allows duty-free imports into the United States for a range of goods manufactured in qualifying African countries.

Kenya

Kenya is an East African country with a land area of 582,650 square kilometers and a population estimated at 33 million people (Kenya, 2005). Although the rate of urbanization has been more rapid than overall population growth for decades, an estimated 70 percent of the population is still rural, relying on farming, livestock, and rural employment for livelihoods. The population is unevenly distributed, with most people concentrated in the 20 percent of the land that is suitable for rain-fed agriculture, leaving the remaining arid and semi-arid lands sparsely populated. Large-scale industry is heavily concentrated in and around Nairobi and Mombasa. Smaller concentrations exist in a few other towns, including Nakuru, Eldoret, and Kisumu. Micro- and small enterprises are much more evenly distributed throughout the country, with small-scale manufacturing, including activities such as tailoring, furniture production, food processing, brick and pottery making, and metal fabrication, taking place in rural market centers and small towns, as well as in the cities and larger towns.

Politically, Kenya is a republic with a highly centralized administrative system. The eight provinces and 69 districts are administrative units dependent on the central government for funds and personnel. City and municipal councils have some ability to raise funds through various forms of levies, and local authorities vary considerably in their ability to manage their responsibilities. There is, however, no tradition of regions' competing for industry as engines of development or sources of tax revenues.

Kenya is classified as a low-income country with low levels of human development and high poverty overall. There are also significant inequalities from one part of the country to another. Per capita income in 2004 was US$460 (World Bank, 2005). When translated into purchasing power parity, per capita Gross National Income (GNI) is $1,050. The latest Kenya National Human Development Report (UNDP, 2005) shows Kenya's Human Development Index (HDI) as 0.520. The Human Poverty Index (HPI) of 0.367 suggests that more than one-third of Kenyans lack basic income, education, and health care. All of these indicators vary considerably across the country. The HDI, for example, ranges from 0.748 in Nairobi to 0.228 in Marsabit, a remote district in the Northern part of the country. Variations in the HPI are similarly stark.

Kenya has had a long history of a stated desire to promote industrialization. However, after a fairly good start immediately following independence in 1963, the pace of industrialization slowed and subsequently failed to keep up with the growth in population and the labor force. Manufacturing's current contribution of 13.6 percent to Kenya's GDP is almost identical to the 14.3 percent recorded in 1973 (UNDP, 2005). This should not be too surprising because Kenya lacks the physical and institutional infrastructure to support industry well. Physical infrastructure, especially in transport and energy, is weak and costly to use. Transport systems, including the railroad, road network, and ports, have failed to keep pace with current needs. After considerable resistance to privatization, the government has recently announced the sale of a substantial part of its interest in Kenya Railways. This is expected to have an immediate impact on the size of the labor force and, therefore, on operating costs. What is not clear is how quickly new owners can begin to address the major challenge of upgrading both track and rolling stock. The road network also needs serious updating, especially the main national highways linking the port of Mombasa with Nairobi, Kampala, and cities in Rwanda, Burundi, and eastern Congo. The poor condition of the roads is in part linked to the failure of the railways. Heavy goods are transported by road, often causing the road surface to buckle and break prematurely. Finally, the recently begun expansion and updating of the port of Mombasa itself is a step in the right direction, as are attempts by the Kenya Revenue Authority to computerize its operations at the port.

The electricity system has improved since the (literally) dark days of 2000 when drought-related power rationing forced many businesses to operate on half schedules or less. Nevertheless, power remains too costly and supplies are still erratic for those connected to the national grid, and many micro- and small enterprises either operate without power or with "informal" power supplies hijacked from nearby lines. The institutional infrastructure has many gaps and anomalies that have bred bureaucratic red tape and allowed corruption to become endemic. These have raised the cost of doing business in Kenya by increasing transaction costs and creating financial and other risks.

Kenya met all requirements for registration under AGOA in January 2001, only three months after the act was signed into law. AGOA gives duty-free access to the US market to a list of products originating in Sub-Saharan Africa. To qualify for benefits, eligible countries had to first put into place a set of procedures designed, among other things, to prevent trans-shipment. A team within Kenya's Ministry of Industry worked closely with representatives of the US Department of Commerce to ensure that all required documents were drafted and adopted to give Kenya an early start in AGOA production. This was, however, only the first hurdle. The next will be compliance with stringent rules of origin, which have been suspended for low-income countries during the initial years of AGOA, but are scheduled to take effect in a phased schedule, beginning in October 2012 (www.agoa.gov).

Study methodology

Research teams from the Institute for Development Studies, University of Nairobi carried out research into institutions and the Kenyan business system between 2000 and 2003. The overall aim of the research was to describe and analyze Kenya's business system, and out of this analysis to propose strategies that policymakers and the business community might adopt to move the industrialization process forward.

Researchers chose to view the system through the lenses of particular sectors, hoping that this approach would give depth to the study and allow for useful comparisons. The research design included both production and services, since both are necessary parts of the business system that are expected to reveal different patterns of institutional interaction. On the production side, two manufacturing and two agro-processing sub-sectors were selected. The choice of the textile and metal sectors to represent manufacturing was influenced by these sub-sectors' importance to the Kenyan economy, the expected institutional variation, and the presence of firms of different sizes within them.

Data collection methodologies varied somewhat from sector to sector. In the case of textiles, primary data gathered in 2000–2001 came from two main sources: a series of in-depth interviews of 22 textile and clothing firms, which ranged in size from five to 2,000 workers and are located in various parts of Kenya, and a survey of 125 micro- and small-scale clothing manufacturers in Nairobi drawn from a full census of Nairobi garment producers. This survey was designed to replicate an earlier study of 245 micro- and small clothing producers carried out in 1989. Secondary data and information from other studies carried out by the members of the textile team were used to supplement the primary sources.

Data collection in the metal products sub-sector was done in two parts. The first round of data collection was a scoping exercise covering 429 firms in various locations throughout the country. The firms identified were, for the most part, registered or at least large enough to be included on the enterprise lists used as a starting point for the exercise. In the second stage of data collection, four urban centers were chosen for focus. Three of these – Nairobi, Mombasa, and Eldoret – have significant concentrations of industrial activities. The fourth – Migori – is a very small urban center with only micro- and small metal products enterprises. In the four areas, the researchers identified micro-enterprises producing metal products similar to those made by the larger firms. From the resulting sampling frame, a sample of 117 firms was selected for survey interviews and 15 firms were chosen for in-depth interviews.

In both cases, data analysis was both quantitative and qualitative. This section draws from various papers that used results from such analysis.

Garment production[1]

Clothing and textiles are often lumped together. The clothing sector, however, differs from textiles in three important respects. First, there is a very large small-scale sector in clothing, which is lacking in textiles. An estimated 60,000 micro- and small enterprises produce garments in Kenya. More than 4,000 of these are located in Nairobi, with the rest spread throughout the rest of the country.[2] Another difference has to do with the other end of the size spectrum. The passage of the US African Growth and Opportunity Act in 2000 brought about a surge in Kenyan clothing exports. Kenya's exports to the US jumped from US$39 million in 1999 to $352 million in 2004 (www.agoa.gov), with most of this increase coming from garments. Finally, the generally smaller size of individual clothing firms seems to promote agglomeration.

Garment industry size, structure, products, and markets

A mapping of the industry revealed a structure with three tiers (see Table 5.2). The micro and small enterprises (MSEs) form the base of the structure. Most of these first tier firms make clothing from woven fabric. In Nairobi, about 4 percent of them make knitted garments, mostly cardigans and children's school sweaters. Some MSEs make other textile end products, including interior furnishings and industrial and other consumer products. A few specialty small enterprises produce hand-woven cloth that they use to make clothing, bags, and table and bed covers. Nearly all of the output goes to the domestic, and usually very local, market. The typical garment MSE is a custom tailor[3] who works alone or with one or two assistants to make clothes to order and do alterations and repair work. Many are minimally trained, but even fairly good ones tend to

Table 5.2 Textile and clothing firms, by tier

Tier	Approximate number of firms	Firm size	Market(s)
1	60,000	MSE	Mainly domestic; less than 10 percent export some output to neighboring countries
2	150	Small to large	Mainly domestic, with a minority of firms exporting to Africa or one or more European countries
3	45	Large to very large	Export to US, Europe

Source: Own data 2000; CBS *et al.*, 1999; Kenya, 2001; EPZ Authority; Investment Promotion Council.

Note
Tier 1 data are for mid-1999; Tier 2 are for 2001; Tier 3 data are for early 2003.

work on a "make and adjust" approach that forces the customer to return several times until the garment is satisfactory in fit and style.

The next tier consists of firms ranging in size from small to fairly large that produce mainly for the domestic market, with some forays into other countries of the region. Included here are many of the textile and garment firms established during the import substitution era that have survived liberalization and continue to aim most of their production at the local market. Firms in this tier had between ten and 400 workers at the time of our research, with most concentrated in the range of 50–150 workers. They include both textile mills and manufacturers of shirts, trousers, dresses, and uniforms. Much of the woven fabric used in garment production is imported, mostly from China and India.

The third tier consists of large to very large export-oriented firms. In 2000, there were 15 such firms, all making clothing and mainly located in Nairobi or Mombasa. By 2003, their number had tripled, mainly in response to AGOA. They range in size from 500 to 2,000 workers. These firms mainly operate as "cut, make, and trim" contractors. They receive orders from abroad, but neither do design work nor supply procurement. The importer supplies the designs and, in most cases, also sources fabric and other inputs from Asia and has them shipped directly to the Kenyan producer. Such third-country input sourcing is permissible under the current exemption to AGOA's rules of origin. The local firm then makes and grades the patterns, cuts and assembles the garments, and packages them for shipment to the buyer. The main items bought in Kenya are packaging materials.

Garment clusters

Clusters of enterprises are very common, especially among micro- and small firms. The most common form of garment cluster is the market or shopping center. Outside of the main towns clusters are too small to offer much more than market access (Billetoft, 1996; McCormick and Kinyanjui, 2000). In most cases, a few tailors are based in the local market, where they undertake a variety of production and repair services on order. These days, many, especially in rural markets, spend a substantial proportion of their time altering second-hand clothing. Tailors also make school uniforms, choir robes, and other special wear not readily available on the second-hand market.

Nairobi's large MSE agglomerations are the most developed (Ongile and McCormick, 1996, 1997; McCormick *et al.*, 1997). But even in these, the benefits attributed to clusters by Marshall (1890) and his followers – positive external economies, active networking, and complementary institutions – are weak. Some positive externalities, including market access, ready availability of materials, access to labor, and improved security, have been identified. In these clusters, as in other MSE clusters in Africa, the chief benefit appears to be improved access to the market. Traders and individual customers visit the markets regularly to purchase goods, and many producers rely almost exclusively on such passive sales. Intermediate inputs, including fabric, design sheets, thread, and buttons, are available both within the markets themselves and from input suppliers in the center of Nairobi and in the emerging market in Eastleigh. Wholesalers and retailers supply these inputs, most of which are imported from China, India, and other parts of Asia. The markets attract labor, creating a pool from which employers can choose. Although this is helpful, the employers complain that workers' skills are uneven. No systematic study of workers' skills has been done, but available information suggests that skills are very basic in all but a minority of cases (McCormick and Muguku, 2003). Another factor attracting producers to the markets is security, both the physical security of workers and machines and the security of tenure offered by presence in a city council-owned facility.

Notably absent from these clusters are technology spillovers, active networking, and complementary institutions. The market infrastructure keeps technology at a low level. One problem is the nature of the space. The markets are divided into stalls, making it impossible for firms to establish any sort of a production line. A second problem is the erratic electricity supply. To ensure that they can continue producing when the electricity fails, many firms keep one or more foot-powered machines. Not only does this add to the already overcrowded conditions of many workshops, but it also uses scarce capital that might have been invested in more modern equipment. Despite physical proximity, there appears to be little networking among the producers. A few firms indicated that they collaborate with others on buying trips to distant towns, either within Kenya or across the border into neighboring countries (McCormick 1999; McCormick *et al.*, 2002). These, however, appear to be exceptions. Most of the firms are very cautious about collaboration. Their relations with their neighbors are cordial, and they will often help each other by lending small equipment, but they do not have regular marketing or production linkages. The firms have no sectoral association and very few belong to general business associations.

Clustering appears to be less important to larger firms. At the level of market access, this is understandable. Large firms are much less likely than small ones to get walk-in customers and they, therefore, benefit less from being located near other firms in the same industry. One would expect, however, that clustering could create positive externalities in intermediate inputs and technology, as well as creating opportunities for fruitful linkages. In each case, the particular local circumstances are such that these benefits are not realized. Only in labor markets does there appear to be a positive externality. Market liberalization has created a situation in which nearly all garment inputs are imported, rather than locally produced. Furthermore, many of the East and South Asian suppliers are willing to sell in fairly small quantities, making it possible for even medium-scale producers to order directly from factories abroad.

Technology spillovers occur when firms with better technologies directly or indirectly influence the upgrading of technology by others. At the time of the main research for this chapter, there was little indication of such spillovers. The chief reasons appeared to be that garment industry technology is fairly standard, and most large firms had access to the same technology sources. More recently, however, firms have reported that the strong competition exerted by China and India in the garment markets has forced them to become more productive. Data suggest that this is indeed happening, but it appears to be the result not of local spillovers but of external pressures from their buyers (McCormick *et al.*, 2006).

Finally, clusters are expected to generate opportunities for linkages, especially subcontracting. In Kenya, the nature of the clusters in which large firms are located seems to work against this. Most are industrial areas of Export Processing Zones (EPZs) where small firms find it difficult to locate. Even where such linkages are desired, the current regulations governing export production (Manufacturing Under Bond and Export Processing Zones) discourage subcontracting. Only in labor, therefore, does clustering seem to benefit large firms. The EPZs appear to have generated a significant pool of workers with at least basic skills who can be hired on long- or short-term arrangements.

Metal fabrication[4]

Kenya's metal products sub-sector, like textiles and garments, was shaped during the import substitution era. Like their counterparts in textiles and garments, metal products firms developed inefficiencies and excess capacity. The liberalization of the 1990s affected these firms in two main ways. On the supply side, liberalization released firms from the supply constraints that had dogged them in the 1980s. As a result, the metal products sub-sector registered real growth in the mid-1990s. On the demand side, however, liberalization and the rapid growth in plastic substitutes for products such as buckets, basins, and furniture caused output to dip by the end of the 1990s.

Metal industry size, structure, products, and markets

There are fewer firms making metal products, but like garments and textiles, the sector has a large number of MSEs and a much smaller number of medium- to

Table 5.3 Metal products firms, by tier

Tier	Approximate number of firms	Firm size	Market(s)
1	7,000	MSE	Mainly domestic
2	400	Small to large	Mainly domestic, with a minority of firms exporting to Africa or one or more European countries
3	1	Large to very large	Export to US, Europe

Source: Own data 2000; CBS *et al.*, 1999; Kenya, 2001; EPZ Authority; Investment Promotion Council.

Note
Tier 1 data is as of mid-1999; Tiers 2 and 3 are for 2001.

large-scale firms (see Table 5.3). An estimated 7,000 micro- and small enterprises make a variety of metal products, including furniture and fixtures, general hardware, cutlery, hand tools, and charcoal stoves (CBS *et al.*, 1999). The metal sector also resembles garments and textiles in that its products are sold almost exclusively on the domestic market. The metal products sector has few very large firms. The largest firm is a multinational with strong roots in East Africa that claims strong coverage of the entire African continent and exports to 46 countries worldwide. It is, as Table 5.3 suggests, in a class by itself. On average, large firms export approximately 35 percent of their output, mainly to neighboring countries.

The 117 firms in the metal sector sample were involved in a variety of activities, including fabrication of metal products, general mechanical repair services, structural metal work, manufacture of furniture and fixtures, manufacture of electrical cables, and sheet metal fabrication. Many firms have a wide range of products, with only a minority specializing in one or two items. The diversity of product line that characterizes these firms has several sources. It is a way of coping with risk and uncertainty in the environment, as well as a tool for searching for new income sources, and a response to changing market conditions.

Raw materials are largely imported, though some producers use locally available steel scrap. Other inputs such as electrodes, alloying elements, coils, zinc for galvanizing, and resins for color coating are all imported. This import dependence makes the industry vulnerable to fluctuations in the world price of steel.

Firms in the metal sector seem somewhat more likely than those in textiles to enter into formal linkages with others. Approximately one-third of the firms reported subcontracting work to others and half said that they sometimes receive subcontracts. Firms cited seasonal variations in production, inadequate capacity to handle a given order, or their need for specialized skills or machinery present in the subcontracted firm as reasons for subcontracting. Capacity was the major force prompting subcontracting among small firms, while larger firms were more likely to subcontract to get specialized services or because of seasonal variations. Those that did not subcontract mainly said that they had no need either because orders were few or they had the internal capacity to produce whatever was required. Large firms have developed dealer networks for purposes of marketing their products.

More metal firms than textile firms belong to associations. Overall, half of the sampled metal firms belonged to associations, with large firms being twice as likely as small ones to be association members. The tendency for even small metal firms to belong to associations is no doubt related to the way government has chosen to relate to so-called jua kali businesses.[5] Since the 1980s, the government of Kenya has encouraged such firms to form associations, which became the vehicle for allocation of resources, especially worksites but occasionally credit and training. Many artisans joined these associations hoping to benefit from the allocations.

Clusters of metal firms

Clusters of micro- and small metal products enterprises are common, though they are often part of a mixed agglomeration that includes furniture production, vehicle repair, and other forms of metal work. This is largely because jua kali sites exist in nearly every major town. These are usually tracts of land with no services and minimal shelter located within a municipality, but often away from its commercial center.[6] As is the case with textile clusters, the main benefit of clustering for metal firms is market access (McCormick, 1999). Other theoretically possible benefits, such as the growth of manufacturing to satisfy input needs, the spillovers of improved technology, or the development of pools of specialized labor, have not materialized.

There appear to be two main reasons for this failure of the clusters to develop. The first is the nature of the product markets. Nearly all micro- and small metal firms are producing for the local market, where price rather than quality is the dominant consideration. Producers have little incentive to use higher-level technology or more skilled labor, because these would raise costs without any assurance of increased sales. The second reason why Kenya's metal clusters have not developed along a "collective efficiency" trajectory can be traced to the relative abundance of low- and semi-skilled labor. Young school dropouts with no training or only the most basic technical courses flood the clusters. Although, with time, they accumulate some skills, these tend to be better suited to the continued production of cheap metal products than to cluster upgrading.

Metal firms in some areas are also known to form temporary joint production units in order to fill large orders. The wheelbarrow makers of the Kamukunji cluster in Nairobi described in McCormick (1999) are a good example. This group of producers located within a larger metal cluster usually operates as a dozen or so independent businesses. When they receive a large order, however, they will set up a production line in order to make the wheelbarrows quickly and efficiently. Once the order is filled, the producers revert to their usual manner of operating as independent units. The preference for independent operation has been attributed to their reluctance to enter into full partnership because the institutional arrangements to protect their individual investments are lacking. Trust is important for any type of exchange, but even more so for continuing business linkages (Zucker, 1986; Platteau, 1994; Fafchamps, 1996; Schmitz, 1999, among others). Yet in developing countries, where enforcement mechanisms are weak, have been corrupted, or are only available to the rich, ordinary people exercise limited trust in their business dealings.

Large metal products firms show little tendency to cluster and even when located near one another, rarely collaborate. The most common reason given by firms of all sizes is that they have adequate resources to fill the orders they get and, therefore, have no need to subcontract. Respondents to the survey also talked about guarding against leakage of technology to competing firms by limiting the interaction of employees of different firms.

Summary and conclusions

Consideration of the two sub-sectors points to a number of issues, which in turn raise important questions about the path to industrialization in small developing countries like Kenya. The present status of Kenya's garment and metal industries can be explained in terms of the convergence of particular variables. Some of these, such as per capita income or the level of the human poverty index, are quantitative proxies for the level of development at this particular moment in time. Others are descriptions of institutions and processes of institutional change. For purposes of analysis they were grouped into sectoral, local, and global, depending on their origins and impact.

The analysis revealed some commonalities and some differences between the two sectors.

- The two industries have similar size structures.
- Both are traditional sectors with little innovation, even by large firms. Only major exporters (tier 3) use the latest technology.
- Both have seen traditional domestic markets eroded by massive imports resulting from market liberalization. In the case of garments, the biggest challenge has come from second-hand imports. In metal, the main competition is from new imports and plastic substitutes.
- In both industries, there is a tendency for small firms to be passive producers that make very similar products and then wait for buyers to come to them.
- The garment industry is linked to world markets and globalized production systems as a result of AGOA.
- Both industries rely heavily on imported raw materials.
- The more active middle-range firms (tier 2) in both sectors are attempting to access regional markets. Large metal firms have also developed dealer networks to improve their access to domestic markets.

- Large and small-scale firms are poorly linked in both industries, though there is somewhat more linkage in metal. Trust issues appear to be a barrier to linkages. These were cited in the metal industry, but probably arise equally in garments.
- Small firms in both sectors are reluctant to form and/or join business associations, though they may join credit or welfare-type associations.
- Both industries suffer from Kenya's poor infrastructure and public services. Small firms are the worst affected by these.
- Insecurity is an issue in both sectors.
- The existing education and training system does not support these sectors very well. Tier 3 firms are forced to undertake their own training. Those in other tiers rely heavily on on-the-job training and/or those trained in poorly resourced polytechnics.
- Government's stated support for industrialization is more evident in the garment sector, which is benefitting from the early qualification under AGOA and from the EPZ and MUB programs.
- Government's stated support for micro- and small enterprise development is more evident in the metal sector where many firms have benefitted from jua kali sites. The sites, however, have little or no infrastructure or services.

The findings point to a number of conclusions. The first of these is both theoretical and practical. The analysis supports the view that the Kenyan business system is fragmented, and that this fragmentation may explain some of the country's problems with industrial development. Both the garment and metal industries provide evidence of such fragmentation, with each characterized by three tiers of firms with different markets, products, and production technologies. Furthermore, the firms in each tier operate almost completely independently of one another. Even when they are geographically clustered, firms rarely subcontract or form linkages for purposes of obtaining supplies or marketing their products. Ethnicity is often a powerful factor in determining business interactions of all types. This, combined with the reluctance of firms to form marketing linkages or even to join associations, suggests that government and the more established associations may need to create new ways of bringing firms together so as to break down the barriers now dividing the business community and hindering industrial development.

The second conclusion concerns the competitiveness of Kenya's manufactured goods. Poor roads, nearly nonexistent rail transport, erratic and expensive electricity, insecurity, and tangles of bureaucratic red tape inflate the costs of goods produced in Kenya and make them less competitive on global, regional, and local markets. This is a serious problem that needs to be addressed. One approach is to focus on clusters. Existing clusters are providing only minimal benefits, but the theoretical potential of clustering is enormous. Government needs to try new approaches. Providing even the most basic infrastructure to all clusters would be hugely expensive and might not have the desired results.

One alternative would be to establish demonstration projects by upgrading a few carefully chosen existing clusters. Another, which has already been discussed by the Ministry of Trade and Industry, is to allow established small firms to enter into serviced industrial parks or Export Processing Zones. Such initiatives would have to be accompanied by the creation and/or strengthening of supportive economic institutions. Contracts and contract enforcement, business licensing, land tenure, and public service access are critical. Also useful would be links with training institutions aimed at upgrading the labor force and improving efficiency. Beyond these fairly obvious measures, both government and the private sector need to think creatively to identify ways of enhancing informal networking and promoting innovation. Both must also agree that for demonstration projects to be useful in the long run, they need to be continuously monitored to draw lessons from both their successes and their mistakes.

The third conclusion is that globalization and the nearly universal liberalization of African product markets has had the perverse effect of limiting Kenyan producers' access to regional markets. Because neighboring countries are flooded with imported new and second-hand goods, often selling at very low prices, Kenyan makers of garments and metal products face extremely stiff competition in their markets. This means that all firms, not just the very large ones aiming at so-called "global markets," need to become more efficient and adopt innovative marketing strategies. It also means that it is in Kenya's interest to strengthen its regional links so as to move quickly toward duty-free access to regional markets.

The fourth conclusion has to do with government's ability to deliver on its promises of industrial development. The government responded quickly and thoroughly to the challenge of qualifying for participation in AGOA, and it has lobbied successfully for the extension of the "third country" exemption that allows use of imported fabric in AGOA exports to September 30, 2012. It has, however, done less well in spearheading the more fundamental changes required to qualify for the benefit without the exemption. This last point is quite difficult.

Qualification for AGOA beyond 2012 requires access to African-grown cotton and African fabric. These need either to be imported from other AGOA-eligible African countries or produced in Kenya.[7] At present, few African countries have competitive textile industries, making the first option difficult to realize. Producing appropriate fabric in Kenya is technically possible, but politically difficult to organize, as it would require the concerted effort of several ministries. The Ministry of Trade and Industry has, with the help of local and foreign consultants, strengthened its industrial strategy and has now constituted a task force to develop an implementation plan. These are clearly steps in the right direction. Nevertheless, the ministry cannot achieve its goals alone and inter-ministerial cooperation has not been characteristic of the present government. The government must either act very quickly or resign itself to the loss of the US market for garments.

Finally, the analysis has revealed issues that require further investigation if the "regional question" is to be answered for African development. In particular, the analysis has skirted a key question: What is a region? The discussion has referred at one level to the entire country and at another to micro-agglomerations, such as Export Processing Zones or jua kali sites. The kinds of intermediate regions that have been the subject of focus in other – usually larger – countries do not figure in the analysis mainly because in Kenya these lack the autonomy to formulate, adopt, or implement industrialization policies. As cities like Nairobi grow and spill over into adjacent districts, it may be necessary to think differently.

If we consider a region to be any place where global, sectoral, and local forces interact to promote or constrain economic development, we can easily imagine regions of different types, sizes, and political organizations. Each will be characterized by interactions between and among firms, government, and nongovernmental actors. Each will draw on existing institutions and may, over time, craft its own rules for the particular "game" being played in the region. The challenge for all concerned with African industrialization is first, to understand and second, to shape these interactions and institutions. Only then will it be possible to turn simple geographic regions into dynamic development spaces.

Acknowledgment

The author is grateful to the Danish government, which, through its program for Enhancing Research Capacity in Africa (ENRECA), providing the funding for the research underlying this section's analysis and conclusions. Any errors and omissions remain the sole responsibility of the author.

Notes

1 This section draws heavily on McCormick, Kimuyu and Kinyanjui (forthcoming) and related papers.
2 Our own census conducted in Nairobi in 2000 identified 6,323 micro- and small firms dealing in garments, of which 4,190 were manufacturing, the rest simply trading.
3 The designation is based on a typology developed more fully elsewhere (see McCormick *et al.*, 1997). The other forms of MSE garment production – contract workshop and mini-manufacturer – are found mainly in larger urban centers.
4 This section draws mainly from Okech *et al.*, forthcoming and from CBS *et al.*, 1999.
5 The term means "hot sun" in Swahili and was first applied to informal producers working out of doors without benefit of shelter.
6 See McCormick and Kinyanjui, 2000 for description of a number of these sites.
7 AGOA also allows use of fabric in the US, but the costs of purchasing and transport render this option unrealistic.

References

Billetoft, J. (1996) *Between Industrialisation and Income Generation: The Dilemma of Support for Micro Activities: A Policy Study of Kenya and Bangladesh*, Copenhagen: Centre for Development Research.

Central Bureau of Statistics (CBS), International Centre for Economic Growth (ICEG), and K-Rep Holdings, Ltd. (1999) *National Micro and Small Enterprise Baseline Survey 1999*, Nairobi: CBS, ICEG and K-Rep.

Cherni, J. (2001) "Social-Local Identities," in T. O'Riordan (ed.) *Globalism, Localism, and Identity*, Earthscan, London.

Evans, P. (1995) *Embedded Autonomy: States and Industrial Transformation*, Princeton University Press.

Fukuyama, F. (1995) *Trust: The Social Virtues and the Creation of Prosperity*, Free Press, New York.

Fafchamps, M. (1996) "The Enforcement of Commercial Contracts in Ghana," *World Development*, 24 (1), pp. 427–448.

Gereffi, G. (1994) "Capitalism, Development and Global Commodity Chains," in L. Sklair (ed.) *Capitalism & Development*, Routledge, London.

Gereffi, G. and Memedovic, O. (2003) "The Global Apparel Value Chain: What Prospects for Upgrading by Developing Countries," Sectoral Studies Series, United Nations Development Organization, Vienna.

Gereffi, G., Humphrey, J., Kaplinsky, R., Sturgeon, T. and Timothy, J. (2001) "Introduction: Globalisation, Value Chains and Development, *IDS Bulletin*, 32 (3), pp. 1–8.

Hofstede, G. (1997) *Cultures and Organisations: Software of the Mind*, McGraw Hill, New York.

Kaplinsky, R. and Morris, M. (2001) "A Manual for Value Chain Research," www.ids.ac.uk/ids/global.

Kaufman, D. (2004) "Corruption, Governance and Security: Challenges for the Rich Countries and the World," in M.E. Porter, K. Schwab, X. Sala-i-Martin, and A. Lopez-Claros (eds.) *The Global Competitiveness Report 2004–2005*, Palgrave Macmillan, Hampshire, UK.

Kenya, Republic of (various years) *Economic Survey*, government printer, Nairobi.

Krugman, P. (1991) *Geography and Trade*, The MIT Press, Cambridge, Mass.

Kuada, J. (1994) *Managerial Behaviour in Ghana and Kenya: A Cultural Perspective*, Aalborg University Press, Aalborg.

Langlois, R.N. and Robertson, P.L. (1995) *Firms, Markets, and Economic Change*, Routledge, London.

Marshall, A. (1890) *Principles of Economics*, Macmillan, London.

Mbiti, J. (1969) *African Religions and Philosophy*, Pinter, London.

McCormick, D. (1997) "Industrial District or Garment Ghetto? The Case of Nairobi's Mini-Manufacturers," in M.P. van Dijk and R. Rabellotti (eds.) *Enterprise Clusters and Networks in Developing Countries*, pp. 109–130, Frank Cass, London.

McCormick, D. (1999) "African Enterprise Clusters: Theory and Reality," *World Development*, 27(9), pp. 1531–1552.

McCormick, D. and Kimuyu, P. (forthcoming) "Business Systems Theory: An African Perspective," in D. McCormick, P. Alila, and M. Omosa (eds.) *Business in Kenya: Institutions and Interactions*, University of Nairobi Press, Nairobi.

McCormick, D. and Kinyanjui, M.N. (2000) "Towards a Practical Understanding of Enterprise Clusters in Kenya," Report Submitted to International Centre for Economic Growth, Nairobi.

McCormick, D. and Muguku, C.W. (2003) "Labour and the Paradox of Flexibility: The Case of Garment and Metal Enterprises in Nairobi," Paper presented at Adger University College-Mzumbe University Conference, Dar es Salaam, Feb. 26–28.

McCormick, D. and Schmitz, H. (2001) *Manual for Value Chain Research on Homeworkers in the Garment Industry*, Institute of Development Studies, Sussex.

McCormick, D., Kinyanjui, M.N. and Ongile, G. (1997) "Growth and Barriers to Growth Among Nairobi's Small and Medium-Sized Garment Producers," *World Development*, 25(7), pp. 1095–1110.

McCormick, D., Kimuyu, P. and Kinyanjui, M.N. (2002) "Can Micro Enterprises Export? Preliminary Evidence from Nairobi's Garment Sector," Paper presented at the International Conference on Business Systems in Africa: Institutions in Industry and Agriculture at the Travellers Beach Hotel, Mombasa, Kenya, Sept. 26–27.

McCormick, D., Mitullah, W. and Kinyanjui, M. (2003) *How to Collaborate: Associations and other Community Based Organisations among Kenyan Micro and Small-scale Entrepreneurs*, IDS Occasional Paper No. 70, University of Nairobi, Institute for Development Studies.

McCormick, D., Kamau, P. and Ligulu, P. (2006) "Post Multifibre Arrangement Analysis of the Textile and Garment Sectors in Kenya," *IDS Bulletin*, 37(1), pp. 80–88.

McCormick, D., Alila, P. and Omosa, M. (eds.) (forthcoming) *Business in Kenya: Institutions and Interactions*, University of Nairobi Press, Nairobi.

McCormick, D., Kimuyu, P. and Kinyanjui, M.N. (forthcoming) "Textiles and Clothing: Global Players and Local Struggles," in D. McCormick, P. Alila, and M. Omosa (eds.) *Business in Kenya: Institutions and Interactions*, University of Nairobi Press, Nairobi.

North, D.C. (1990) *Institutions, Institutional Change and Economic Performance*, Cambridge University Press, Cambridge.

Okech, B., Atieno, R. and Mitullah, W.V. (forthcoming) "Linkages and Business Competition in Kenya's Metal Products Sub-Sector," in D. McCormick, P. Alila, and M. Omosa (eds.) *Business in Kenya: Institutions and Interactions*, University of Nairobi Press, Nairobi.

Ongile, G. and McCormick, D. (1996) "Barriers to Small Firm Growth: Evidence from Nairobi's Garment Industry," in D. McCormick and P.O. Pedersen (eds.) *Small Enterprises: Flexibility and Networking in an African Context*, Longhorn, Nairobi.

Pedersen, P.O. and McCormick, D. (1999) "African Business Systems in a Globalising World," *The Journal of Modern African Studies*, 37(1), pp. 109–136.

Piore, M.J. and Sabel, C.F. (1984) *The Second Industrial Divide: Possibilities for Prosperity*, Basic Books, New York.

Platteau, J.-P. (1994) "Behind the Market Stage Where Real Societies Exist – Part I: The Role of Public and Private Order Institutions," *Journal of Development Studies*, 30 (3), pp. 533–577.

Porter, M.E., Schwab, K., Sala-i-Martin, X. and Lopez-Claros, A. (eds.) (2004) *The Global Competitiveness Report 2004–2005*, Palgrave Macmillan, Hampshire, UK.

Schmitz, H. (1995) "Small Shoemakers and Fordist Giants: Tale of a Supercluster," *World Development*, 23 (1), pp. 9–28

Schmitz, H. (1999) "From Ascribed to Earned Trust in Exporting Clusters," *Journal of International Economics*, 48, pp. 139–150.

Schmitz, H. (ed.) (2004) *Local Enterprises in the Global Economy*, Edward Elgar, Cheltenham.

Schmitz, H. and Nadvig, K. (1999) "Clustering and Industrialisation: Introduction," *World Development*, 27 (9), pp. 1503–1514.

Scott, A.J. and Storper, M. (2003) "Regions, Globalisation, Development," *Regional Studies*, 37: 6 and 7, pp. 579–593.

UNDP (2004) *Cultural Liberty in Today's Diverse World*, United Nations Development Programme, New York.

UNDP (2005) *Linking Industrialisation with Human Development*, Fourth Kenya Human Development Report, United Nations Development Programme, Nairobi.

Voisey, H. and O'Riordan, T. (2001) "Globalisation and Localisation," in T. O'Riordan (ed.) *Globalism, Localism, and Identity*, Earthscan, London.

Whitley, R. (1992) *Business Systems in East Asia: Firms, Markets and Societies*, Sage, London.

World Bank (2005) *World Development Report 2005*, The World Bank, Washington, DC.

Zucker, L. (1986) "Production of Trust: Institutional Sources of Economic Structure, 1840–1920," *Research on Organisational Behaviour*, 8, pp. 53–111.

Part III

Regions and development in mixed economies

6 Promise and peril

Regional development in China's Pearl River Delta and the Northeast

Shahid Yusuf

Key regional issues

The contrasting development experience of two regions in China provides fresh insights into the role of and interaction among history, location, and policy. The Pearl River Delta (PRD) in Guangdong Province in the southwest has had the good fortune to grow at an average of over 16 percent per annum since 1979.[1] No other country or region in the world has matched this pace of GDP growth in the past 50 years. Moreover, this growth shows little sign of slackening. Suitably managed, the PRD has the economic momentum to continue expanding at double-digit rates for the balance of the decade and beyond.

In the northeast corner of China lie three provinces whose performance is lagging well behind apparent potential. The provinces of Liaoning, Jilin, and Heilongjiang, once the heartland of China's heavy industry, have since the early 1990s suffered from industrial sclerosis. The Northeast is now viewed as the country's rust belt. Liaoning and Heilongjiang provinces have slipped from fourth and fifth place in 1978 to eleventh and twentieth place in 2003, respectively, while Guangdong has risen from sixteenth place to sixth (see Table 6.1). Since the start of the 10th Plan in 2001, both central and provincial authorities have been pressing ahead with wide-ranging regional policies so as to reverse the decline, so far with modest success.[2]

What accounts for the efficacy of an earlier regional policy that pushed the PRD onto a high growth path? How has the PRD sustained its economic vitality

Table 6.1 GDP per capita ranking by province

Provinces	Rank in 1978	Rank in 1995	Rank in 2003
Guangdong	16	5	6
Zhejiang	14	4	4
Jiangsu	7	7	5
Jilin	12	14	18
Liaoning	4	8	11
Heilongjiang	5	11	20

Sources: Naughton (2002); official government Web site of Jinlin Province information, www.jlsq.gov.cn/szjl/2005/0703/40.htm.

over such an extended period of time? Why did the Northeast, which had a comfortable industrial head start over other parts of the country, start to falter and fall behind? What mix of policies could enable the PRD to deal with labor market and environmental issues and keep powering forward? And what are the policy lessons to be drawn for the Northeast from its own recent experience, from the remarkable achievement of the PRD, and from the application of regional policies by other countries?[3]

The purpose of this chapter is to explore these questions from three angles, thereby illuminating the interaction between globalization and the processes that are as Scott and Garofoli point out in the Introduction of this book, "concentrating economic growth in a few regions." First is the historical angle, which will help probe the contribution of economic and social developments in earlier periods to recent circumstances. A second, geographical angle, will factor in the impact of location, of the economic neighborhood, of production networking, and of the Chinese Diaspora. A third angle will weigh the consequences of policies pursued since the early 1950s, the specifically regional ones and the other general policies that have had regional consequences and have helped to spark a spiral of endogenous development. The former category includes policies to establish special economic zones (SEZs) in selected areas. The latter category includes fiscal policies, enterprise reform, policies toward trade and foreign direct investment (FDI), and overall industrial strategy. This chapter devotes a section to each. Prefacing these is a brief section that provides an economic backdrop juxtaposing key indicators for the two regions.

Sizing up the Northeast and the PRD

The colder northeastern region of China covers an area of 787,900 square kilometers. In 2003, the combined population of the three provinces numbered 107.1 million, giving a per square kilometer density of 135.9 persons, which is low relative to that of the coastal areas of China. The level of urbanization is 47 percent, well above the 43 percent rate (2005)[4] for the country as a whole, although urbanization varies across the three provinces, being higher in Liaoning than in the other provinces. Relative to other regions of China (see Table 6.2 for comparative data), the Northeast is richly endowed with mineral, energy, and forestry resources.[5] The Daqing oilfield in Heilongjiang has been China's principal source of petroleum since it was discovered in 1959. The industrial sector is responsible for 44.27 percent of GDP, much of it produced by the engineering, petrochemical, and metallurgical sub-sectors. Agriculture accounts for 12.4 percent of GDP and services the balance. Industrial activity is concentrated in a handful of cities. Among the leading industrial cities are Shenyang, Dalian, and Anshan, the leading center of steel production in Liaoning; Changchun in Jilin, home of First Auto Works, one of China's biggest car manufacturers; and Daqing, a center of petrochemical production in Heilongjiang (see Table 6.3).

Close to 67 percent of the manufacturing industry in the Northeast is state-owned – with a total of 12,000 state-owned enterprises in 2003 – and the state

Table 6.2 Major economic indicators by region (2003)

Area	GDP (US$ billion)	Population at year end (10,000 persons)	GDP per capita calculated (US$/person)[a]	GDP per capita (US$/person)[b]	Export (US$ billion)[c]	FDI (US$ million)[d]
North	215.17	14,931.04	1,441.11		40.59	4.99
Beijing	44.24	1,456.40	3,037.65	3,872.10	16.89	2.19
Tianjin	29.56	1,011.30	2,923.08	3,204.35	14.35	1.53
Hebei	85.73	6,769.44	1,266.45	1,269.71	5.93	0.96
Shanxi	29.67	3,314.29	895.18	897.95	2.27	0.21
Inner Mongolia	25.97	2,379.61	1,091.41	1,083.89	1.16	0.09
Northeast	156.46	10,728.70	1,458.36		19.64	3.34
Liaoning	72.49	4,210.00	1,721.96	1,721.96	14.58	2.82
Jilin	30.47	2,703.70	1,126.84	1,127.78	2.18	0.19
Heilongjiang	53.50	3,815.00	1,402.42	1,402.79	2.87	0.32
East	634.99	37,073.60	1,712.80		201.42	31.61
Shanghai	75.49	1,711.00	4,412.21	5,642.27	48.45	5.47
Jiangsu	150.49	7,405.82	2,032.09	2,030.07	59.11	10.56
Zhejiang	113.47	4,679.55	2,424.72	2,433.21	41.59	4.98
Anhui	47.98	6,410.00	748.45	779.59	3.06	0.37
Fujian	63.19	3,488.00	1,811.65	1,809.06	21.13	2.60
Jiangxi	34.18	4,254.23	803.54	806.52	1.50	1.61
Shandong	150.19	9,125.00	1,645.94	1,649.88	26.56	6.02
Central	206.39	22,331.50	924.21		7.78	3.13
Henan	85.13	9,667.00	880.60	914.27	2.98	0.54
Hubei	65.24	6,001.70	1,086.99	1,088.25	2.66	1.57
Hunan	56.02	6,662.80	840.84	912.32	2.15	1.02
South	205.70	13,621.74	1,510.08		155.68	8.66
Guangdong	164.56	7,954.22	2,068.88	2,078.87	152.85	7.82
Guangxi	33.03	4,857.00	680.11	720.89	1.97	0.42
Hainan	8.10	810.52	999.73	1,004.35	0.87	0.42
Southwest	141.46	20,345.83	695.27		7.18	0.80

continued

Table 6.2 continued

Area	GDP (US$ billion)	Population at year end (10,000 persons)	GDP per capita calculated (US$/person)[a]	GDP per capita (US$/person)[b]	Export (US$ billion)[c]	FDI (US$ million)[d]
Chongqing	27.18	3,130.00	868.39	870.65	1.58	0.26
Sichuan	65.90	8,700.40	757.41	775.12	3.21	0.41
Guizhou	16.38	3,869.66	423.24	435.14	0.59	0.05
Yunan	29.77	4,375.60	680.46	683.82	1.68	0.08
Tibet	2.23	270.17	824.76	829.83	0.12	0.00
Northwest	76.77	9,340.89	821.84		5.94	0.41
Sha'anxi	28.97	3,689.50	785.16	782.61	1.73	0.33
Gansu	15.76	2,603.34	605.22	606.48	0.88	0.02
Qinghai	4.71	533.80	882.86	878.86	0.27	0.03
Ningxia	4.65	580.30	801.98	808.09	0.51	0.02
Xinjiang	22.68	1,933.95	1,172.55	1,171.50	2.54	0.02

Source: China Statistical Yearbook 2004.

Notes

a Calculated by using total GDP and actual population (rather than registered population) from China Statistical Yearbook 2004.
b Obtained from the Yearbook directly.
c Total value of exports by location of China's foreign trade managing units by region.
d Actual foreign investment by region.

Table 6.3 Main industrial cities in the Northeast and the PRD

Liaoning	Jilin	Heilongjiang	Guangdong
Shenyang	Changchun	Harbin	Guangzhou
Dalian	Jilin	Qiqihaer	Shenzhen
Anshan		Daqing	Zhuhai
Fushun			Foshan
Benxi			Zhongshan
			Huizhou
			Jiangmen
			Zhaoqing

Table 6.4 Sources of manufacturing output (2003)

Ratio (%)	Northeast	China
Total	100	100
State-owned and holding enterprises	67.45	37.54
Collective enterprises	3.71	6.65
Others (including private enterprises and joint ventures)	28.84	55.81

Source: China Statistical Yearbook 2004.

Note
2003 current price.

sector has been slower to divest its share of industrial production than elsewhere in China.[6] Collective enterprises are responsible for a little under 4 percent of industrial output and the share of private enterprises and joint ventures is 29 percent, below the average for China and half of the share of such enterprises in China as a whole (see Table 6.4).

In the 1980s, GDP growth averaged 8.3 percent. In the first half of the 1990s, it rose to 9.6 percent, but slowed marginally during 1996–2000 to an average of 9.1 percent. As regional policies funneled more resources into infrastructure building, growth was maintained at 9.5 percent in 2002–2003, close to the average for the country as a whole. Although the Northeast might be a lagging region in the Chinese context, because of the level of industrialization and literacy, nominal per capita GDP was $1,701 as against $1,275 for China as a whole in 2004. Poverty is also low, only 8 percent of the population falls below the purchasing power parity (PPP) $1 a day line, and that mainly in a few rural pockets in Liaoning and Heilongjiang (see Table 6.5). The Northeast is less export oriented than the coastal provinces. Exports as a ratio of GDP equaled 12.5 percent in 2004. In part, this reflects the small inflow of FDI – only $3.3 billion in 2003, 6.2 percent of the total for China. In part, it is also a consequence of the lack of competitiveness of the state-owned enterprises located in the region. (See Table 6.6 for comparative data on the three northeastern provinces.)

Table 6.5 Rural poverty and inequality

	Mean (yuan)[a]	Headcount index (%)	Poverty gap (%)	Gini (%)
Liaoning				
1988	472.69	21.69	6.19	30.94
1990	451.90	19.59	4.78	27.47
1992	504.51	16.19	4.02	29.48
1996	656.22	8.30	1.87	28.54
1999	770.62	8.03	2.66	31.48
Jilin				
1988	423.73	20.47	5.93	27.33
1990	420.31	22.12	5.88	27.54
1992	386.40	26.70	7.12	27.61
1996	653.37	9.00	2.10	29.11
1999	686.47	6.40	2.57	28.34
Heilongjiang				
1988	347.74	31.81	9.71	30.12
1990	392.05	27.51	8.75	31.70
1992	439.18	21.36	6.08	31.88
1996	595.39	10.97	3.20	30.66
1999	593.06	11.70	4.53	34.10
Guangdong				
1988	432.92	21.69	4.35	31.22
1990	467.40	12.53	1.98	27.61
1992	553.89	7.57	1.22	31.07
1996	743.31	1.89	3.20	29.92
1999	871.00	0.83	0.12	29.35

Source: Data calculated by Shaohua Chen at World Bank DECRG for working paper on China's (uneven) progress against poverty.

Note
a   Mean is based on 1998 constant price and is the living expense per person per year. By using the PPP method, $1 per person per day is equivalent to 880 yuan per person per year.

At the other end of the country, almost a continent removed, the PRD is a 40,165-square-kilometer subtropical region criss-crossed by waterways that have facilitated transport. The past agricultural productivity of the deltaic region and, more recently, its industrial development, has attracted millions of migrants, swelling an already dense population (see Table 6.7). Some 41 million people (in 2000) reside in the PRD area, pushing the ratio of people per square kilometer to 1,015. A once largely rural population is moving to cities and this migration from within Guangdong and other provinces, such as Sichuan and Guanxi, is accelerating urbanization. Seventy-three percent of the PRD's population is now classified as urban, and this curve is rising steeply (see Table 6.8).

Increasingly, the delta is becoming a land of cities, such as Guangzhou, the largest (in terms of GDP), Shenzhen,[7] Foshan, and Dongguan. This upward shift in the urban share of the populace is mirrored by the percentage of GDP that originates in the industrial sector and in services, 50 and 45 percent respectively (see Table 6.7). The PRD has attracted light manufacturing and assembly indus-

Table 6.6 Major economic indicators of Northeast China (2002)

Northeast China 2002 Data	Liaoning	Jilin	Heilongjiang	Northeast	National
Land area (1,000 sq km)	145.9	187.4	454.6	787.9	9,599.2
Population (million persons)	42	27	38.1	107.1	1,284.5
GDP share of the national GDP (%)	5.21	2.14	3.70	11.05	100.00
GDP per capita (USD)	1,568.9	1,006.9	1,230.4	1,306.6	988.8
GDP per capita rank (out of 31 provinces)	8	13	10		
GDP growth (%)	8	8.9	7	8.0	7.7
GDP (USD billion)	65.92	27.13	46.89	139.93	1,270.20
Primary industry	7.13	5.39	5.40	17.92	194.65
Secondary industry	31.52	11.82	26.20	69.53	639.86
Industry	28.16	9.70	23.14	61.01	555.26
Construction	3.36	2.11	3.06	8.52	84.60
Tertiary industry	27.27	9.92	15.29	52.49	435.69

Source: China Statistical Yearbook 2003.

Note
The growth rate of Northeast China is the average of the three provinces.

tries, and in two decades has come to dominate the global production of items such as toys, textiles, small consumer electronics, computers, leather goods, eyeglass frames, footwear, and others clustered in more than a dozen cities (see Table 6.9). A region once noted for its diversified agricultural economy and trade has become China's leading exporter of manufactured and assembled goods. In fact, nearly 34 percent of the nation's total exports originate in the PRD. This makes for an extraordinarily open economy. Exports amount to 99 percent of the PRD's GDP of $114 billion in 2002, although the ratio of export value-added to GDP would be closer to 50 percent. Fueling exports is FDI that was close to $12 billion in 2002, mainly from Hong Kong (average of 20 percent) and other parts of Asia.[8] The PRD has absorbed 24 percent of the aggregate utilized FDI in China in industry, infrastructure, and real estate. This FDI is now bringing the petrochemical, IT, and auto industries to the PRD that point to a new and even more promising industrial future ("Resurgent Guangdong," 2005).

With GDP growing at double-digit rates, per capita GDP in the PRD is now among the highest in China, at $4,142, and almost three times higher than in the Northeast. Poverty rates are negligible – less than 1 percent in 1999 – and mostly affect the elderly living alone in rural villages (see Table 6.5). Inequality of incomes is also low, with the Gini coefficient falling below 30 percent, a better rate than for the nation as a whole and the average for the Northeast.

The comparison with the Northeast is stark, starting with climate, topography, and the physical appearance of the cities. Shenzhen and Guangzhou, for example, are among the most dynamic urban centers in China, with a combined GDP that is a little short of $77 billion, or almost 5.5 percent of China's

Table 6.7 Major economic indicator of PRD and other areas (2002)

	PRD	Guangdong	Hong Kong	Macao	YRD[a]	China
Land area (square kilometers)	40,165	179,757	1,102	26.8	100,200	9,597,000
Registered population 2002 (million persons)	23.65	76.49	6.79	0.44	75.71	1,284.53
Census (PRC) or actual (HK, Macao) population 2000 (million persons) (b)	40.77	85.23	6.73	0.44	82.28	1,265.83
GDP (US$ billion)	113.75	142.15	161.51	6.73	230.98	1,265.59
Primary Industry	4.9%	8.8%	0.1%		5.8%	15.4%
Secondary Industry	49.8%	50.4%	12.44%	12.6%	51.9%	51.1%
Tertiary Industry (%)	45.3%	40.8%	87.5%	87.4%	42.3%	33.5%
GDP per capita (US$)						
Official 2002 (2001 for YRD)	4,142	1,815	23,797	15,356	2,722	988
GDP 2002/registered population 2002	4,810	1,858	23,800	15,242	3,051	985
GDP 2002/Census population 2000	2,790	1,668	23,998	15,466	2,807	1,000
Real GDP growth rate 1980–2002	16.1%	13.4%	5.2%	4.9%	12.5%	9.5%
Real GDP growth rate 1990–2002	17.4%	14.0%	4.0%	3.1%	13.5%	9.7%
Retail sales of consumer goods (US$ billion)	42.05	60.55	22.67	0.65	75.45	494.09
Gross industrial output (US$ billion)	170.6	197.8	22.1	2.0	324.7	1,337.9
Value added of gross industrial output	26.3%	26.6%	31.0%	23.7%	25.6%	29.8%
Imports (US$ billion)	98.39	102.63	207.62	2.53	82.81	295.17
Exports (US$ billion)	111.55	118.46	200.1	2.36	92.4	325.6
Utilized FDI (US$ billion)	11.62	13.11	9.68	0.38	17.85	52.74

Source: Government Official Web site www.thegprd.com/about/economic.html by Department of Foreign Trade and Economic Cooperation of Guangdong Province.
Data Sources: Statistical Yearbooks of China, Guangdong, Shanghai, Zhejiang, Jiangsu, and local jurisdictions in Guangdong, Zhejiang, and Jiangsu. China Statistics Bureau, Jiangsu Statistics Bureau, Census and Statistics of Hong Kong, Statistics and Census.

Note
a YRD refers to the Yangtze River Delta Area.

Table 6.8 Urbanized population rate (%)

	1982	2000
Liaoning		46.0[a]
Jilin		43.3[b]
Heilongjiang		47.2[c]
PRD	28.2[d]	72.7[e]

Sources:
a Liaoning 2000 Population Census Assembly, rose to 56 percent in 2005.
b Jilin 2000 Population Census Assembly.
c Heilongjiang 2000 Population Census Assembly.
d Zheng Zuo, Some Thoughts on Urbanization in Guangdong (Dui Guangdong de Cheng Shi Hua Fa Zhan de Ruo Gan Si Kao), August 3, 2001, posed on the official Web site of China Department of State Development Research Center report.drc.gov.cn/drcnet/series.nsf/0/d888a6bf56ee4b9148256ab80029ecb3?OpenDocument
e Lingbing Kong, Fan Zhang, Xiaojiang Li, Changqi Chen, Pearl River Delta Area Transportation Coordination Development Research (Zhu Jiang San Jiao Zhou Qu Yu Jiao Tong Xie Tiao Fa Zhan Yan Jiu), January 2, 2005, Urban Transportation paper.studa.com/2005/1-2/113859.html

Table 6.9 Localized industries in the Pearl River region

Location	Products
Guangzhou	Autos and parts, transport equipment
Humen	Garments, electronics, electrical products
Huizhou	Laser diodes, digital electronics, CD-ROMs
Dongguan	Electronics, computers
Shenzhen	Electronics, computer products, telecommunication products
Panyu	Sports goods, textiles, garments
Zhongshan	Lighting fixtures, lamps
Jiangmen	Textiles, garments,
Shunde	Electrical appliances, woodworking
Kaiping	Water-heating equipment
Foshan	Industrial ceramics, ceramic artwork
Nahai	Textiles, aluminum products, motorcycles
Chencun	Flower farming, ornamental fish

Source: 2022 Foundation, Economic Interaction between Hong Kong and the Pearl River Delta Region.

domestic product (in 2003). No urban area in the Northeast can remotely approach the economic vigor of these cities in the PRD, their entrepreneurship, or the rapidity with which they are transforming their infrastructure. The differences between the Northeast and the PRD also extend to the degree of integration with the global market. By a rough measure, if the PRD were an independent country, it would be the world's 20th largest exporter.[9] Whereas the Northeast, especially the provinces of Jilin and Heilongjiang, has few linkages to the world economy and its trade with other parts of China is shrinking in relative terms.

The hand of history

History matters; though not always and there are instances where the influence of history on regional development is barely perceptible. However, in the case of the PRD, economic change since 1980 has antecedents that reach far back in time. Proto-industrialization in the then newly expanding deltaic region is discernible from about the time of the early Ming dynasty in the fourteenth century. The primarily rice-growing region diversified into silk production, cotton weaving, and the manufacture of porcelain. From the sixteenth century, Guangzhou emerged as the center of trade in these products with the Japanese, Portuguese, and Spanish based in Manila and with parts of Southeast Asia.

Following a prolonged downturn in the seventeenth century brought about by the fall of the Ming dynasty and the Little Ice Age (Marks, 1998), the PRD region recovered and through much of the eighteenth century and the first four decades of the nineteenth, Guangzhou was one of China's few commercial openings to the rest of the world, both directly and, more significantly, through its close connections with Hong Kong. This promoted cottage industries in the immediate hinterland, especially the production of textiles and china. Such proto-industrialization also occurred elsewhere in China, in parts of the Yangtze (Changjiang) delta area, for example, but the Lingnan region and specifically the PRD had a head start with respect to light manufacturing on a substantial scale for local and foreign markets. This inculcated traditions of entrepreneurship, production for the market, and business initiative, which have endured and flourished among the emigrant communities from other parts of China that settled in the PRD (especially the Hakka).

The abundance of local energy, initiative, and ambition also induced migration to Southeast Asia, Australia, and the US, mainly through Hong Kong, starting in the 1840s. This process was certainly assisted by contact with foreign traders and the opportunities to learn about other parts of the Pacific Basin opened by maritime commerce through Hong Kong. This

> safe haven and instrument of British Imperial policy ... became a base for supplying goods, recruiting coolies, smuggling, facilitating travel and transmitting money, information and people between the destination and the *Qaoxiang*. Bones [of the deceased] were returned through Hong Kong's Tung Wah Hospital ... and nearly all remittances from those living in the destinations went through Hong Kong.
>
> (Williams, 2003, p. 280)

With the exception of Fujian, no other province of China enjoyed such access after about the middle of the fifteenth century. Thus, as Lyn Pan observes, "Guangdong has supplied the world's largest number of overseas Chinese estimated at 8.2 million in 1957, 68 percent of the total" (Pan, 1998, p. 36). They accounted for nearly all the Chinese settled in the US at that time and more than two-thirds of all Chinese in Southeast Asia (Johnson, and Woon, 1997).[10]

This history of an early start at proto-industrialization followed by overseas trade and massive migration (an early stage of globalization) sowed seeds for future regional development with the overseas Chinese population providing vital reinforcement, a point discussed below. During the latter part of the nineteenth century and through the early decades of the twentieth, Canton (Guangzhou) and its hinterland was an important foci of trade and manufacturing activity among China's treaty ports. Shanghai experienced a more meteoric rise, gained greater notoriety, and achieved a larger economic scale; still Canton was close behind.

Had China much earlier adopted the open and decentralized development strategy that it cautiously initiated in 1979, very likely industrialization would have taken off first in the Yangtze delta area and, possibly soon after, in the PRD.[11] However, because of the of the PRD's geographical location on China's periphery adjacent to Hong Kong, the region's industrial potential was ignored or curbed by the government once communist control had been consolidated in the early 1950s and Guangdong province, like the rest of China, was insulated from the international economy (Johnson and Woon, 1997). Hutchings writes,

> In the Cold War, the [Guangdong] province's traditional links with the outside world were a source of suspicion. Beijing considered the Cantonese too parochial in outlook and moved northerners to run the province. At the same time, Guandong's position on the coast made it vulnerable to imperialist attack. Throughout the Maoist period Beijing invested little in the region relative to other, politically safe though commercially less promising parts of the country. As a result, Guangdong's rate of growth was less than the national average during the first three decades of communism.
>
> (2000, pp. 167–168)

This same wariness toward Guangdong was noted by Vogel (1969).

Neglect did not expunge commercial traditions, overseas connections or, miraculously, the preexisting foundations of a market-based industrial society.[12] When, in the second half of the 1970s, China realized the need to catch up with its rapidly industrializing neighbors, the leading reformers quickly realized that the region to be targeted for policy action was the PRD. There were several reasons. Reform-minded leaders surmised rightly that Guangdong, more so than other parts of China, was better primed for rapid industrial change. Local cadres were more ready to embrace "system reform" and to experiment with policies. The kinship links of the inhabitants in the PRD with businessmen in Hong Kong, Macau, and other Southeast Asian economies gave them access to capital, management skills, and technology that China lacked. Moreover, cooperation with the business community in Hong Kong was highly desirable to ensure the continuing prosperity of Hong Kong until and following reunion with China. Reforms that modernized the economy of the PRD and commenced its integration with Hong Kong would pave the way to a mutually advantageous reunification (Vogel, 1989, pp. 82–83).

Guangdong's location on the far periphery of China enhanced its attractiveness as a laboratory for systems reform. Were the reform efforts to run into difficulties, the Chinese leadership reasoned, China's heartland would be sheltered from much of the adverse fallout. The supporters of reform and the local cadres, who implemented what in the Chinese context was a heterodox regional policy, were proven right.

The economic history of the Northeast

Northeast China stands at the opposite pole from the PRD in more ways than one. Until early in the twentieth century, the Qing emperors attempted to restrain Han migration to Manchuria so as to preserve the distinctiveness of the Manchu people, their culture, and the privileged access of Manchus to the area's game reserves and natural resources. However, the creating of military districts maintained by the Manchu Bannermen and the use of a pass system could not restrain the rapid settlement of the area, the clearing of the forests, and the planting of soya beans by Han Chinese from the last decades of the nineteenth century (Elliott, 2000; Fairbanks, 1986; Spence, 1990).

The industrialization of the Northeast, much of it concentrated in Liaoning province, and the exploitation of the region's natural resources on a large scale was mainly the result of Japanese colonial policy in the years following the Treaty of Portsmouth, which transferred authority over southern Manchuria to the Japanese after the Russo-Japanese War of 1904–1905. Japanese investment expanded coal and iron ore mining activities and helped build the steel, engineering, and chemical industries in new towns such as Shenyang, Benxi, Fushun and Anshan. It also financed the extension of the South Manchuria Railway, originally started by the Russians, and developed mining activities.

These industries were oriented toward and complemented the Japanese economy rather than being an integral part of China's industrial system. In particular, the manufacturing sub-sectors that were established were more a reflection of Japan's industrial capabilities and were in advance of China's comparative advantage, especially that of the Northeast region. As Ho (1984, p. 380) observes

> The occupation of Kwantung [Manchuria] and the South Manchuria Railway Zone gave Japan a foothold in Manchuria and the operational base to extend its control over Manchuria's natural resources and market. Consequently, Kwantung was administered and developed with two primary aims: (1) to help Japanese businesses to capture the Manchurian market; and (2) to facilitate the development and extraction of Manchuria's natural resources for Japan's benefit.

Toward the end of World War II, Manchuria was occupied by Soviet Russian troops and, before withdrawing in 1950, the Soviets dismantled and took with them many of the factories established by the Japanese, as well as power generating plants and pumps from the mines (Spence, 1990, p. 495). However, because China adopted the Soviet model of development that emphasized steel and capital goods production, the Chinese government, with Soviet help, revived the preexisting industrial structure under state ownership. Thus, from the time of the First Five-Year Plan, the government's regional policy for the Northeast sought to develop resource- and capital-intensive industries that were import substituting. This reinforced a pattern that had emerged in the first half of the century and set the stage for the problems that surfaced from the 1990s onward.

Unlike the PRD, the Northeast was not buoyed by centuries-long commercial traditions and proto-industrialization in the rural areas. Modern economic development jump-started when heavy manufacturing was grafted onto a backward rural economy. Market forces played almost no role under the Japanese colonial administration or during the first three decades of communist rule, hence, the industries that now exist are largely creations of the state and are ill equipped to cope with competitive pressures in a market environment. Such vulnerability is exacerbated by disadvantages stemming from geographical location. The PRD, by comparison, has been greatly favored by geography.

Geography, neighborhood and the Diaspora

Cross-country empirical analysis has yielded two interesting albeit tentative findings relating aspects of location to the pace of growth. First, landlocked regions are at a disadvantage relative to regions along the coast because their integration with the global economy proceeds more slowly. Second, a region's growth performance is influenced by the dynamism of neighboring economies.

Four other findings are also of relevance in this context. One is the contribution an emigrant Diaspora can make to the development of a local economy. A second and related finding is a region's participation in global value chains, which is a function not just of the speed with which industrial capability is built but also of geographical location and the scale of the Diaspora. Urbanization and its "quality" is a third factor that has a bearing on productivity as well as the industrial geography. A fourth is the link between the distribution of mineral resources among the regions of a country and the nature of development. Each of these factors partially explains the performance of the PRD and the Northeast.

The coastal location impinges upon accessibility and through it, on transport costs.[13] In newly developing regions, the cost of logistics are higher for those areas that are far removed from the coast and this can inhibit industrialization as well as trade. The PRD has enjoyed the advantages of low intra-regional transport costs because of the network of tributaries and watercourses. More importantly, it has derived great benefit from easy access to seaborne transport and proximity to the markets of Southeast Asian countries. While the port of Dalian in Liaoning province provides a coastal link, most of the Northeast region was deprived of a coastline after nearly a million square kilometers of land north of Heilongjiang and east to Kuye Island was ceded to Russia through the Aihui and Beijing treaties of 1858 and 1860, respectively.

The PRD is ringed by some of East Asia's most rapidly growing economies, which have given rise to strong demonstration effects. The role of Hong Kong and Taiwan (China) on the development of the PRD has been critical. During the entire 25-year period, from 1979 to 2004, close to 70 percent of all the FDI in the PRD was from Hong Kong or routed through Hong Kong.[14] In addition, more than 50,000 Hong Kong-based firms employed upwards of ten million workers in the PRD area[15] (see Table 6.10) (Sit, 2004; Wikipedia, PRD). Starting in the early 1980s, Hong Kong industrialists, many of whom had emigrated from Guangdong province, began shifting production to the PRD, creating a highly advantageous division of labor (Berger and Lester, 1997; 2022 Foundation, 2003). Factories were set up first in Shenzhen and Shunde, then in areas served by the railway line extending form Shenzhen to Guangzhou and later, as infrastructure developed, to other parts of the delta.[16] Manufacturing of a wide range of products was increasingly concentrated in the PRD while packaging, marketing, and transport services were provided by businesses in Hong Kong (see Table 6.11). The latter also supplied managerial, supervisory, and technical services, which were scarce in the PRD (see Table 6.12). Each day thousands of people from Hong Kong went to work in the PRD and thousands of trucks (33,000) brought goods across the border to be shipped through Hong Kong's port.

Table 6.10 Main sources of foreign funds in the Pearl River delta region (ratio %)

Source region/country	1986–1990	1996–1999
Total	100	100
Hong Kong and Macao	73.61	67.55
Southeast Asia	0.79	2.98
Taiwan, China	1.23	3.86
Japan	12.88	4.83
Korea		0.63
Europe	4.89	6.31
North America	6.11	3.76
Australasia	0.57	0.47

Source: 2022 Foundation, Economic Interaction Between Hong Kong and the Pearl River Delta Region.

Table 6.11 The PRD region's share of PRC output, selected industries, 2000

IT and electronics		Electrical appliances	
78.8%	Telephones	80.4%	Hi-fi equipment
60.2%	Printers	72.1%	Microwave ovens
43.6%	Video recorders	64.3%	Cameras
23%	Personal computers	34.8%	Color televisions

Source: 2022 Foundation, Economic Interaction between Hong Kong and the Pearl River Delta Region.

Table 6.12 A summary of the role of Hong Kong in China's open-door policy

Financier	Direct investment	
	Indirect investment	
	Loan syndication	
Trading partner	Commodity trade	
	Services trade	
Middleman	Commodity trade	entrepôt trade
		trans-shipment
		brokerage in direct trade
	Services trade	tourism
		loan syndication
		business consultancy
Facilitator	Contact point	
	Conduit of information and technology	
	Training ground	marketing and production

Source: Sung, 1991.

Nothing comparable by way of neighborhood effects was experienced by the Northeast. The economic regions of the Soviet Union immediately adjacent to the Northeast, as well as the economy of North Korea, were and remain relatively backward. And until well into the 1980s, links with South Korea and Japan that would have generated "neighborhood effects" were limited for a variety of historical and political reasons.[17] Nor did the Northeast gain from an overseas Diaspora, as there was none; the Northeast being a region that was a focus of in-migration from other parts of China and not a source of overseas migrants. Whereas the PRD's Diaspora has been a prolific source of capital, technical assistance, and business connections, the Northeast has received no such boost. Overseas Chinese from across Southeast Asia and, to a lesser extent, in the US have buttressed the flow of capital and technology transfer enabling the PRD to build manufacturing capability in a remarkably short period of time and, from a small start in the early 1980s, to emerge as the dominant supplier of light manufactured goods such as toys, leather goods, and footwear for the global economy.[18]

Overseas Chinese were largely instrumental in hooking producers in the PRD to the global value chains. Such production networks had begun to spread through Southeast Asia in the latter part of the 1960s as manufacturers from North America began investing in lower cost production platforms and retail chains started to source garments and other items from East Asian suppliers. As the networks evolved, participation facilitated the entry of many smaller firms into the global marketplace. More often than not, the intermediaries responsible for the contracting of production, the monitoring of firms, the coordinating of payments and the integration of orders by foreign customers were Chinese businessmen with manufacturing and/or trading interests.[19] Thus, the Diaspora not only helped initiate and partly finance the virtuous cycle of development in the PRD, but also many overseas Chinese served as integrators responsible for the assembly of products and as intermediaries whose association with nascent global production networks ensured a ready market for suppliers in the PRD that could meet the quality, volume, and delivery of requirements of foreign buyers.[20] Lacking a Diaspora and an export-oriented industrial base, the North-east has remained inward looking and its connections with global value chains are of very recent origin and still fairly sparse.

The endowment of mineral resources deepens the divide between the two regions; while the PRD has rich agricultural land – rapidly being lost to urbanization and to industry – it has virtually no mineral wealth. Hence, development has been sharply skewed toward textiles, agroprocessing industries, light manufacturing, electronics, and assembly-type operations. The resource-poor PRD has depended on openness to capital flows and imports of raw materials and, in turn, that has supported the growth dynamic.

The resource-rich Northeast, in common with many other such areas, tended toward a more closed system – although resources alone do not account for the greater insularity of the region. Resource abundance and the capital intensity of the industrialization discouraged the broadening of the industrial base and the autarchic bias of the planning system made the region dependent on narrow domestic markets for its products.[21] The climate does not help. So long as labor mobility was constrained by the household registration systems (hukou) and government policies, there was limited scope for the circulation of the workforce. However, as these checks on migration have been eased, the more mobile skilled workers have begun to leave in search of better jobs in the eastern provinces. This reflects a pattern in the US, for example, where industry and the workforce have shown a tendency to move toward the warmer south and coastal areas. More then half the US population now lives within 50 miles of the coastline, although this includes the Great Lakes (Rappaport and Sachs, 2003).

The Northeast urbanized more quickly in the 1950s and 1960s because of the emphasis on industry, but the rigid planning system would not permit the urban centers to realize the many-faceted advantages of agglomeration and urbanization economies. Cities in the Northeast never developed the industrial clusters and a range of services that could have contributed to growth, productivity, technological advance, and employment. (Yusuf *et al.*, 2003) They were not allowed to evolve beyond the level of single industry towns or, at the most, cities with a narrowly industrial focus.

The rapid, unchecked, largely unplanned, Hong Kong-linked industrialization of the PRD was more conducive to the fuller realization of agglomeration economies and the formation of industrial clusters. Within a handful of years, small towns such as Shenzhen and Foshan bloomed into large cities. Initially, this process was highly chaotic, but as municipalities strengthened their finances and planning, cities in the PRD began investing in infrastructure and services and struggling to improve the quality of the environment.

While the regional impact of urbanization on growth has not been analyzed, early findings for the country as a whole suggest that the burgeoning urban centers of the PRD have lent considerable support to the development of the region. By contrast, very few cities in the Northeast have tapped the potential inherent in agglomeration economies backed by urban amenities and services of good quality. In many instances, the decay of mining or capital goods industries is triggering a spiral of decline as employment falls, the fiscal base shrinks, physical infrastructure decays, and the erosion of public services worsens the local business climate. Urban stagnation in the Northeast not only constrains growth in the near term but also, and more damagingly, the restructuring and renewal of industries. Urban dynamism depends on the entry of firms in industries where the future prospects are brightest and the exit of failing enterprises that absorb financial resources and the survival of which can contribute to excess capacity. But many cities in the Northeast are failing to provide the environment that will attract new entry. Those in the PRD very definitely are beginning to try.

These six factors have influenced the development of the two regions to varying degrees and at different times. The neighborhood effects for the PRD and the advantages from the Diaspora were strongest in the 1980s and 1990s. Rapid urbanization since the 1980s has benefitted the PRD on balance while the Northeast, by neglecting its urban centers, was unable to capitalize on an earlier lead. However, the development of the transport infrastructure in the Northeast and closer trading linkages with Japan and Korea has reduced the costs of logistics. Resource depletion and greater openness is broadening the industrial base of the Northeast but also raising the costs for traditional industries. The opening of the Northeast to trade and FDI and the flow of resources also permit the migration of labor and industry, which, if it continues, would erode future prospects in spite of policy actions to promote development. The PRD meanwhile, stands to benefit from greater national economic integration as well as integration with Southeast and South Asian economies, which are thriving and likely to be major overseas markets of the future.

Policy actions, which are the third set of factors affecting regional development, could realize the impossible – enable the Northeast to achieve double-digit growth rates and help the PRD keep its momentum alive as the push provided by history and location becomes weaker.

Pre- and post-reform regional policies in China

Policies to promote regional development have a patchy record. Successes have been infrequent, and spectacular successes, as in the case of the PRD, have been the unanticipated outcome of a series of often uncoordinated but well chosen actions that catalyzed a virtuous spiral that drew energy from several sources.

Regional policy was largely responsible for the industrialization of the Northeast, using the inherited manufacturing capacity and the abundant natural resources as building blocks. As in the case of the Soviet Union, the Chinese state was able, through massive investment, to carve out a base of heavy industries in the Northeast. The planning system also ensured that the rest of China provided a market for the steel, machinery, machine tools, aluminum, electrical and transport equipment, zinc, and other products manufactured by the factories in the Northeast. Liaoning exported half of its industrial output to other provinces, and Heilongjiang was the source of most of the petroleum consumed in China – and of China's petroleum exports until well into the 1990s.

But this proved to be a precarious achievement. Once market-oriented reforms were introduced, budget constraints were hardened, and state enterprises subjected to competition, three decades of expensively engineered regional development was placed in jeopardy. The Northeast region's share of industrial output has diminished steadily from 16 percent in 1980 to less than 9 percent in 2004. Exports of machinery, machine tools and other products to other Chinese provinces have fallen steeply, while overseas exports that amounted to a fifth of China's total in 1980 were down to 4 percent in 2004.

A comparison of two approaches to regional development is instructive because of the light it sheds on targeting regional policies and some of the necessary conditions for obtaining results that endure. China's factor endowments – industrial and research capability in the 1950s all the way through the 1980s – favored light manufacturing and some resource-intensive industries rather than the production of complex capital goods.

Thus, regional policy, as applied in the Northeast, by going partly against the grain of comparative advantage, achieved only limited success. Once the supporting structures of the command economy were dismantled, many of the industries created have not proven viable. However, regional policy in the PRD focused on an area that met certain basic preconditions, aligned more or less with market forces, permitted comparative advantage to determine the composition of industry, and triggered unprecedented rates of growth with the minimum injection of resources by the state (Lardy, 1992).

The opening policy salvo of regional development in the PRD was – with the benefit of hindsight – unusually well crafted. The establishing of four SEZs set up in greenfield sites, with a memory of proto-industrialization but with no recent history of state-led industrialization, allowed a different type of business ethics, organization, and environment to take shape.[22] The work ethics of the labor force were unaffected by the dysfunctional practices prevailing in the state-owned enterprises and, from the very outset, cadres, enterprise managers, and the rank and file sensed fresh opportunities signaling a break from past practices. Vogel (1989) quotes Ren Zhongyi, the Party Secretary of Guangdong, as declaring that, "If something is not explicitly prohibited, then move ahead, and if something is allowed, then use it to the hilt."

The SEZs in the PRD "opened the door" to the growth of light manufacturing because the region was primed for development and not excessively weighed down with the institutional baggage of the socialist economy. The SEZs alone would have been insufficient to trigger regional development. Their purpose was to attract foreign capital and technology, by offering outsiders a number of inducements, and to help China build modern manufacturing industries with export potential. To do so, authorities offered foreign investors, mainly from Hong Kong, tax concessions, low rents for factory facilities, attractively priced services and utilities, and, of course, those firms that located in the zones benefitted from labor costs that were a fraction of elsewhere in East Asia. (Eng, 1997). What made the SEZs into growth poles for the PRD, permitted them to realize fully the endogenous dynamic of agglomeration economies, and accelerated regional development were three complementary policies that greatly sharpened industrial incentives and market competition.

First, was the gradual unfolding of trade reforms that facilitated production for export or the processing of imported raw material and components for re-export. Exporters that could obtain inputs at low state-fixed prices were substantially advantaged, as export prices were significantly higher. Trade reforms that reinforced these measures included new institutions such as the Foreign Investment Advisory Commission (FIAC), China International Trust and Investment Company (CITIC), and the State Administration of Foreign Exchange Control (SAFEC). Furthermore, provinces such as Guangdong were given the powers to set up their own export–import corporations and autonomous exporting enterprises with right to export directly (Sung, 1991, p. 45). A foreign exchange retention scheme for exporters introduced in 1979 and a gradual devaluation of the renminbi through the 1980s and into the first half of the 1990s reinforced the effects of regional policies and speeded up the export-oriented industrialization in the PRD. This activity took off in the 1980s as the dismantling of trade restrictions encouraged the transfer of industries from Hong Kong and elsewhere to the PRD. As a consequence, entire industrial sub-sectors that had been flourishing in neighboring economies were transplanted in the Delta region.

Second, fiscal reforms in 1980 and 1985 decentralized fiscal responsibilities (Lin and Liu, 2000). Guangdong province, in particular, was given a favorable fiscal contract by the central government in order to encourage development. Starting in 1980, the province forwarded a fixed amount of revenue (baogan) to the center each year through 1985 rather than remitting a percentage of the taxes and customs duties collected (Vogel, 1989). This policy encouraged local officials to support industrial expansion, which could generate revenues that could then be put back into projects to promote local development. The province was also given more flexibility in allocating financial resources in distributing raw material and other inputs among enterprises, managing commercial activities, and setting wages (Vogel, 1989, p. 86).

Complementing fiscal decentralization was a third policy that eased limitations on the ownership of enterprises. Until the late 1970s, the bulk of China's industrial production was by state-owned enterprises. There were some 150,000 individually owned enterprises but these were invariably small and produced a tiny proportion of the total output. The measures introduced to attract FDI and allow foreign firms to enter into joint ventures with local producers, together with fiscal and administrative decentralization, introduced far-reaching changes in industrial organization. This resulted in the multiplication of quasi-state as well as the entry of non-state enterprises, a substantial subset of which came to be known as township and village enterprises (TVEs). These TVEs, generally under the benign eye or direct tutelage of entrepreneurial local governments, became the driving force behind the growth of the PRD and other mainly coastal provinces as well (Oi, 1999; Gore, 1998; Lardy, 1992).

The policy of openness abetted by incipient ownership reform also and very speedily transformed the market environment in the PRD and, more gradually, throughout China. With trade, FDI, and the entry of thousands of township and village enterprises, Chinese industries were exposed to competitive pressure, which had been dormant for decades. This was initially disconcerting and problematic for the inefficient firms, but it gave an immediate fillip to the productivity of enterprises. It also began raising product quality, tightening delivery schedules, and started enterprises in the PRD down the road to incremental innovation.

The impact of ownership reforms and of competition can be seen in the estimates of total factor productivity for the 1980s, relative to earlier years. TVEs outperformed state-owned enterprises and collectives, and this performance edge provided an additional advantage to the PRD region.[23] The opening of the economy to foreign direct investment delivered one further benefit to the economy of the PRD. It partially remedied the distortions in the financial market, which limited the access of non-state enterprises or enterprises with weak political connections to funding. FDI, partially at least, lowered entry barriers to new firms and provided many struggling but efficient TVEs with the financing to grow. Even though financial reforms were slow in coming to China, Yasheng Huang (2003) rightly notes that overseas capital has, in many places, served to fill the financing gaps and support regional development.

A final piece of regional policy that contributed to the PRD miracle was the government's investment in urban infrastructure. Initially, resources went mainly into developing transport and energy infrastructure and serviced land in the special economic zones. In Shenzhen, infrastructure investment was relatively lavish because it was immediately adjacent to Hong Kong and the Chinese authorities needed to convey a message regarding reforms and long-term intentions. This investment eased a number of bottlenecks that would have greatly hampered the PRD's development. Continuing investment in transport, logistics, energy, urban housing, and commercial real estate, backed in recent years by new financial instruments, has ensured that the growth momentum of the PRD was further boosted by agglomeration dynamics and not constrained by rising transport costs, although electricity shortages remained a problem for some time, now being remedied by substantial expansion of capacity.

The development policy applied to the Northeast was of an earlier vintage. The heavy industries developed gave rise to few linkages and because of the vigorously enforced policy of containing urbanization, the spillovers and spread effects from the regional policy were small. The overwhelming preponderance of state-owned enterprises also meant that no other engine of growth was able to emerge even after reform gathered strength in the 1980s and 1990s. There were collective enterprises and some TVEs in the Northeast, especially in Liaoning, but their shares of the GDP and exports were small and they provided little growth impetus.

By the time of the 10th Plan in 2001, it was becoming clear to the authorities that the Northeast region was confronting difficulties that could have serious political and social consequences. The state-owned enterprises in the area were relatively uncompetitive, unprofitable, and losing ground to imports and producers elsewhere in China. The severe environmental problems created by heavy industries in urban areas and a series of corruption scandals discouraged FDI except in Dalian, and the slow decline of the oil-producing sector centered in Daqing, starting in the late 1990s, compounded the region's problems.[24]

The future of regional policies in China

Economic growth in the Northeast continues at surprisingly high rates,[25] but there is dissatisfaction with the regional industrial policy pursued through decades. The national and provincial governments now have to decide what to put in its place. By contrast, the policies pursued in the PRD played to the region's advantages and have proven to be vastly successful in terms of growth but less so in terms of sustainability. Both regions face an industrial transition, the Northeast more urgently than the PRD, and both are in need of environmental policies to bolster their longer-term prospects.

The new recipe for the Northeast, which borrows from the mixed experience of rustbelt cities in other countries, involves raising the ante and developing high-tech manufacturing and services. This entails enhancing the quality and leveraging the pool of skills as well as the capabilities of the numerous research entities in cities such as Shenyang.[26] It also involves the investment in urban and transport infrastructure so as to draw new firms to the cities and lessen the costs of doing business in the Northeast. Complementing these are efforts to improve governance, clean up the immensely polluted environment in the major cities, and to reform state-owned enterprises or close down ones that simply cannot be salvaged. With unemployment rising and the fiscal revenues of provincial governments being squeezed, the attempt to reshape the industrial sector is inevitably constrained. Closing down state-owned enterprises leads to more layoffs and adds to the burden of social security. Leaving them in operation diverts financial resources from the task of creating a new industrial structure. There are a few bright spots. Dalian, for instance, is attracting FDI in manufacturing and off-shored services, and the combination of industrial and transport activities and a relatively attractive urban environment have sustained growth. But such examples are few.

For both national and sub-national governments, inaction is politically infeasible. But doing "something" could lead to mounting expenses with limited payoffs. Past regional policies and their industrial legacies are cautionary reminders that regional policies can go disastrously wrong, but some experience from Europe and North America provides a few pointers. Rustbelts are well-known phenomena in the OECD countries and transition economies, and a variety of policies have been mobilized to ameliorate, if not reverse, the problems of eroding competitiveness and an imploding regional economy. One trend that such economies must struggle hard to avoid is the emigration of human capital and a decline in the population, especially from the prime age cohorts. Such a trend makes it difficult to sustain positive rates of growth, to reap agglomeration economies, to ensure fiscal buoyancy, to induce new start-ups, and to diversify into other industries. When emigration exacerbates unemployment and poverty in the core urban areas, the possibility of revival is further reduced.

Where rustbelts have gained a new lease of life through industrial diversification, a few urban areas have spearheaded the process. These urban regions have derived their second wind from four interlinked policies. First, the revival has rested in public–private partnerships and political leadership focused on key industries and/or services. This makes possible the mobilizing of resources from a variety of sources that are needed to bring about a recovery that endures. These resources make possible the entry of new firms and the growth of the viable existing firms. They permit the renewal and deepening of urban and transport infrastructure. Urban investment helps arrest the emergence of deep-rooted poverty in cities. The development of transport and communication infrastructure has been shown to support growth, with state-of-the-art IT infrastructure now viewed as almost a necessity for cities that are attempting to cultivate high-tech industry (Démurger, 2001). Even a second wind for the engineering and metallurgical industries, if these remain pillars for the economy of the Northeast, will require investment in urban infrastructure that enhances the quality of life in the region's major cities (Li, 2004).

A second policy that interlaces with urban investment is the level and quality of public services and how these are buttressed through competition from private providers. Services, along with investment in housing infrastructure and public amenities, can help prevent poverty from taking root and creating an environment that is inimical to industrial renewal (Coyle et al., 2005).

A third policy supports research-oriented universities and research institutes that are a source of new technologies, training in needed skills, industrial extension, and consulting services. Research universities that are given the initiative to commercialize their findings and build linkages with the business sector can become the hubs for new industrial clusters under some quite specific circumstances. They must be located in urban areas, which are attractive for the highly skilled to reside in because of amenities, environmental quality, and the absence of poverty; there should be room in the area relatively close to the university for industrial development to occur; and a university policy of building linkages and creating a networked cluster must have strong local political support. From her study of cities of knowledge in the US, Pugh O'Mara (2005) concludes that "successful cities of knowledge were the places that applied all of their energies to the task of building university research capacity, generating industrial research and production and attracting white collar scientists and engineers" (p. 230). The suitability of the local environment was "defined by a high degree of homogeneity, a certain level of cultural vibrancy and architecture and design that created a physical separation from the rest of the urban landscape" (p. 229).

The fourth policy is the reform of state-owned industries, where these are a significant presence in declining areas. This entails privatization of firms that are viable and closure of those that are not. Moreover, the reform of state-owned enterprises (SOE) is vital in order to make way in downtown areas for new industries, services, and real estate development. Reform could also free up resources now channeled to struggling state-owned enterprises for private sector entities.

The policies associated with each of these factors are especially germane to the Northeast; however, the PRD area would also gain from improvements in the quality of the universities, public services, and the urban environment. The Northeast is greatly hamstrung by the large share of state-owned enterprises in output, presence in urban areas, and claims on financial resources. Even in Guangdong, state-owned enterprises monopolized 86 percent of lending by banks, although they accounted for no more than 30 percent of industrial output (Zhang, 2003). Measures that freed up resources for the non-state sector would accelerate industrial deepening. While both regions have issues to tackle, policy-makers in the Northeast face much more of an uphill battle.

The situation in the PRD is now altogether different. Here is an economy that has accumulated significant and competitive industrial capability and is running into problems associated with possibly too rapid a pace of expansion – there is excess capacity in certain industries, which is causing hardship; minimum wages in cities such as Shenzhen have risen 25 percent during 2003–2005, which could begin driving the more labor-intensive light industries[27] into the interior provinces, infrastructure permitting; persistent financial distortions impede the entry of new firms and the growth of dynamic non-state enterprises; urban income inequality is inching higher; and there are severe problems of air and water pollution, as well as urban sprawl that is eating into prime agricultural land. For policymakers in the PRD, these pose major headaches, but market forces and determined public policies can ameliorate them while keeping alive the tempo of industrial change and regional development.

From being one of the relatively lagging regions of the PRC in the 1970s, the PRD has moved to the front rank. It is now one of the two most industrially prosperous areas of China, the Yangtze delta being the other. The next stage of regional development involves improvements in the quality of life, particularly in the urban areas; a gradual shifting of industrial focus to electronics, biotech-nology, new materials, optomechanical-electronic devices, and environmental and oceanic technologies (2022 Foundation, 2003); and closer integration of the Pan-Pearl River Delta economy with a population of 450 million to maximize the benefits from the scale of the market (Sung, 2005; Enright *et al.*, 2005; and "String of Pearls," 2004). In the late 1980s, the Northeast was one of the most industrialized regions of China with the highest per capita GDP. A combination of history and industrial policy contributed to the region's ascent. But the pros-perity was fragile. It depended on directed resource flows and the controls insti-tuted by the planned economic system. Once reform dismantled these controls and captive markets, allowed market signals to prevail, and widened the menu of choices for buyers, the state enterprises in the Northeast had either to compete in this new milieu in terms of prices, quality, technology, and service or lose their customers. Because enterprise reforms were slow in coming and failed to revitalize the state-owned enterprises, the Northeast is now threatened with a potentially irreversible downward spiral, and China faces yet another recalcitrant regional problem calling for creative solutions.

Acknowledgments

I thank Jue Sun, Tristan Suratos and Jimena Luna for their assistance in preparing this paper. The findings, interpretations, and conclusions expressed in this study are entirely mine and should not be attributed in any manner to the World Bank, its affiliated organizations, or members of its board of executive directors or the countries they represent.

Notes

1 In 2004, Guandong's GDP exceeded that of Hong Kong ("Resurgent Guandong," 2005).
2 The decision to mount a concerted effort to reverse the decline of the Northeast was formally announced at the Third Plenum of the 16th Central Committee of the CCP in 2002.
3 The changing pattern of regional inequality in China has attracted considerable scholarly attention. Kanbur and Zhang (2005) review the evidence and underscore the importance of heavy industry development for inequality in the period prior to 1980 and the contribution of decentralization and the opening of the Chinese economy since.
4 The Liaoning provincial government estimated that the urbanization rate in 2005 was 56 percent and that the province now includes 14 cities.
5 Liaoning, for instance, produces iron ore, magnesite, diamonds, boron, petroleum, and gas. Its agricultural sector is the source of maize, sorghum, soybeans, cotton, apples, and peaches. In fact, it is the main exporter of apples from China.
6 However, a start at privatizing state-owned enterprises was made with 24 enterprises privatized in 2006.
7 Shenzhen was a small fishing village with a population of 20,000 in the late 1970s. If its huge floating population is included, the total might now exceed ten million. Dongguan was little more than a hamlet ("A new workshop," 2002). Although the four SEZs have achieved an emblematic significance, the economic reforms also privileged a number of port cities such as Guangzhou and Fushun; economic and technical development areas in selected cities (ETDAs); and open coastal economic areas (OCEAs) in the PRD and Fujian (Schmidt, 1997a).
8 See Zhang (2003), who indicates that FDI from Hong Kong was closer to 80 percent of the total. Taiwanese investment in Guangdong by the end of 2000 also approaches $7 billion in some 11,000 enterprises.
9 The greater PRD, which includes Hong Kong and Macau, was the world's 16th largest economy and the 10th largest exporter in 2003 (Enright, Scott, and Chang, 2005).
10 Williams (2003, p. 259) observes that 15 million Chinese traveled to other countries between 1842 and 1942; of these, 80 percent were from Guangdong, mainly the PRD.
11 On the limitations placed on Shanghai in the early years of reform, Naughton (2002, p. 74) has this to say: "Shanghai was restricted and limited by the enormous attention

paid to it by conservative factions in the national government and especially by Chen Yun and his group ... Chen Yun made sure that Shanghai did not establish any SEZs or grant special privileges to foreign investors. It was not until 1987–1988 that policy really shifted."

12 Industrialization, largely to meet local needs, did occur, of course. And the government invested in certain defense industries (e.g. naval shipyards, electronics, uranium mining and processing, and the manufacture of light armaments), but these fairly sophisticated industries amounted to less than 10 percent of enterprises in the province (Bachman, 2001).

13 See Gallup, Sachs and Mellinger (1998). This theme is also explored by Davis and Weinstein (1998) and Redding and Schott (2003). In the Chinese context, the relative contribution of reforms infrastructure and geography, which emphasizes the first two, is discussed by Démurger and others (2002).

14 By 1995, Guangdong had attracted over 28 percent of the FDI in China, the Northeast a little less than 4 percent (Fu, 2004).

15 In 2002, residents of Hong Kong made 55 million trips to the Mainland and more than 50,000 were living in Shenzhen (Sung, 2005).

16 The cross-border linkages between firms in Hong Kong and subcontractors that were predominantly small and medium-sized enterprises in short order developed manufacturing capability in the PRD and an unrivalled industrial network that, with Hong Kong's overseas contacts and reputation, was able to penetrate the leading international markets.

17 Since the early 1990s, Korea has invested in the Northeast with the amount rising from $11 million in 1991 to $225 million in 2004, about 10 percent of Korea's total investment in China in that year.

18 A number of factors have influenced the entry and geographical distribution of foreign firms that have invested in China. Among these, the access to markets for products and to suppliers of inputs is nearer the top, followed by wage and infrastructure costs, such as electricity prices (Amiti and Smarzynska, 2005).

19 See Yusuf *et al.* (2003) and the papers in Yusuf *et al.* (eds.) (2004); Rauch and Trinidade (2002).

20 The intermediary role played by Hong Kong's trading companies requires them to "collect information, to facilitate contracts, to provide product design and specification, to make quality controls, to secure the intermediate inputs, to bundle and distribute orders, to finance pre-shipments, and to bear the risks of non-payment from buyers" (Schmidt 1997b).

21 There is considerable literature on the resource curse. See, for instance, the recent articles by Rodriguez and Sachs (1999), and Sala-i-Martin and Subramanian (2003). On the costs to Russia of developing mineral resources in Siberia, see Hill and Gaddy (2003).

22 The three SEZs in the PRD were Shenzhen, Zhuhai, and Shantou. Xiamen, the fourth, was in Fujian province.

23 Perkins (1988) estimates that productivity increase contributed 1.4 percent to growth during 1957–1965, 0.62 percent in 1965–1976 and 3.79 percent in 1976–1985. The post-1985 findings are summarized in Yusuf, Nabeshima, and Perkins (2005).

24 The search for oil in Daqing commenced in 1955 and the first major find was in 1959. Soon, production commenced on a small scale in 1960 and mounted rapidly thereafter, exceeding 50 million tons in 1975. The peak of 56 million tons was reached in 1997 and since then has been falling to 46 million tons in 2004, with a projected 30–40 million tons through 2010.

25 It is not always easy to square the sustained regional growth rates of 8 percent or more with the scale of the industrial decline.

26 In 2003 alone, the universities in the Northeast graduated 221,000 students with a preponderance of engineers. Liaoning has 70 colleges and universities, plus 38

national-level scientific research institutes, and the ratio of scientists and engineers to the total population is 3.4 to 1,000. This compares with 106,000 graduates in Guangdong in 2003.

27 See "String of Pearls" (2004), "Resurgent Guangdong" (2005), and "Sharp Labor Shortage" (Barboza, D., 2006).

References

2022 Foundation (2003) *Hong Kong and the Pearl River Delta: The Economic Interaction*, www.2022foundation.com/reports/000001.pdf.

Amiti, M. and Beata Smarzynska, J. (2005) "Trade Costs and Location of Foreign Firms in China," IMF Working Paper WP/05/55, International Monetary Fund, Washington, DC.

Bachman, D. (2001) "Defence Industrialization in Guangdong," *The China Quarterly*, (166), June, pp. 273–304.

Berger, S. and Lester, R.K. (1997) *Made by Hong Kong*, Hong Kong, Oxford University Press, Oxford.

Coyle, D., Alexander, W. and Ashcroft, B. (eds.) (2005) *New Wealth for Old Nations: Scotland's Economic Prospects*, Princeton University Press, Princeton, NJ.

Davis, D.R. and Weinstein, D.E. (1998) "Market Access, Economic Geography, and Comparative Advantage," NBER Working Paper 6787, National Bureau of Economic Research, Cambridge, Mass.

Démurger, S. (2001) "Infrastructure Development and Economic Growth: An Explanation for Regional Disparities in China?" *Journal of Comparative Economics* (29) 1, pp. 95–117.

Démurger, S., Sachs, J.D., Woo, W.T., Bao, S., Chang, G. and Mellinger, A.D. (2002) "Geography, Economic Policy, and Regional Development in China," NBER Working Paper 8897, National Bureau of Economic Research, Cambridge, Mass.

Elliott, M.C. (2000) "The Limits of Tartary: Manchuria in Imperial and National Geographies," *The Journal of Asian Studies* (59) 3, pp. 603–646.

Eng, I. (1997) "The Rise of Manufacturing Towns: Externally Driven Industrialization and Urban Development in the Pearl River Delta of China," *International Journal of Urban and Regional Research* (21) 4, pp. 554–568.

Enright, M.J., Scott, E.E. and Chang, K. (2005) *Regional Powerhouse: The Greater Pearl River Delta and the Rise of China*, John Wiley and Sons, Singapore.

Fairbanks, J.K. (1986) *The Great Chinese Revolution 1800–1985*, Harper and Row, New York.

Fu, X. (2004) *Exports, Foreign Direct Investment and Economic Development in China*, Palgrave Macmillan, New York.

Gallup, J.L., Sachs, J.D. and Mellinger, A.D. (1998) "Geography and Economic Development," NBER Working Paper 6849, National Bureau of Economic Research, Cambridge, Mass.

Gore, L. (1998) *Market Communism: The Institutional Foundation of China's Post-Mao Hyper-Growth*, Oxford University Press, Hong Kong.

Hill, F. and Gaddy, C. (2003) *The Siberian Curse*, Brookings Institution Press, Washington, DC.

Ho, S.P.-S. (1984) "Colonialism and Development: Korea, Taiwan, and Kwantung," in R. Myers and M.R. Peattie (eds.) *The Japanese Colonial Empire 1895–1945*, Princeton University Press, Princeton, NJ.

Huang, Y. (2003) *Selling China: Foreign Direct Investment During the Reform Era*, Cambridge University Press, Cambridge.

Hutchings, G. (2000) *Modern China: A Guide to a Century of Change*, Harvard University Press, Cambridge, Mass.

Johnson, G.E. and Woon, Y.-F. (1997) "Rural Development Patterns in Post-Reform China: the Pearl River Delta in the 1990s," *Development and Change* (28) 4, pp. 731–751.

Kanbur, R. and Zhang, X. (2005) "Fifty Years of Regional Inequality in China: a Journey Through Central Planning, Reform, and Openness," *Review of Development Economics* (9) 1, pp. 87–106.

Lardy, N.R. (1992) *Foreign Trade and Economic Reform in 1978–1990*, Cambridge University Press, Cambridge.

Li, C. (2004) "China's Northeast: From Largest Rust Belt to Fourth Economic Engine?" *China Leadership Monitor* (Winter) 9.

Lin, J.Y. and Liu, Z. (2000) "Fiscal Decentralization and Economic Growth in China," *Economic Development and Cultural Change* (49) 1, pp. 1–21.

Marks, R. (1998) *Tigers, Rice, Silk, and Silt: Environment and Economy in Late Imperial South China*, Cambridge University Press, Cambridge.

Naughton, B. (2002) "Provincial Economic Growth in China: Causes and Consequences of Regional Differentiation," in M.-F. Renard (ed.) *China and Its Regions: Economic Growth and Reform in Chinese Provinces*, Edward Elgar Publishing, Cheltenham, UK.

Oi, J.C. (1999) *Rural China Takes Off: Institutional Foundations of Economic Reform*, University of California Press, Berkeley, Calif.

Pan, L. (ed.) (1998) *The Encyclopedia of the Chinese Overseas*, Harvard University Press, Cambridge, Mass.

Perkins, D.H. (1988) "Reforming China's Economic System," *Journal of Economic Literature* (26) 2, pp. 601–645.

Pugh O'Mara, M. (2005) *Cities of Knowledge: Cold War Science and the Search for the Next Silicon Valley*, Princeton University Press, Princeton, NJ.

Rappaport, J. and Sachs, J.D. (2003) "The United States As a Coastal Nation," *Journal of Economic Growth* (8) 1, pp. 5–46.

Rauch, J.E. and Trindade, V. (2002) "Ethnic Chinese Networks in International Trade," *Review of Economics and Statistics* (84) 1, pp. 116–130.

Redding, S. and Schott, P.K. (2003) "Distance, Skill Deepening and Development: Will Peripheral Countries Ever Get Rich?" NBER Working Paper 9447, National Bureau of Economic Research, Cambridge, Mass.

Rodriguez, F. and Sachs, J.D. (1999) "Why Do Resource-Abundant Economies Grow More Slowly?" *Journal of Economic Growth* (4) 3, pp. 277–304.

Sala-i-Martin, X. and Subramanian, A. (2003) "Addressing the Natural Resource Curse: An Illustration From Nigeria," NBER Working Paper 9804, National Bureau of Economic Research, Cambridge, Mass.

Schmidt, K.-D. (1997a) "Small- and Medium-Sized Enterprises in Cross-Border Networks: Empirical Evidence From the Pearl River Delta," Kiel Working Paper 808, Kiel Institute of World Economics, Kiel, Germany.

Schmidt, K.-D. (1997b) "Small- and Medium-Sized Enterprises in Cross-Border Networks: Empirical Evidence From the Pearl River Delta," Kiel Working Paper 808, Kiel Institute of World Economics, Kiel, Germany.

Sit, V.F. (2004) "China's WTO Accession and Its Impact on Hong Kong–Guangdong Cooperation," *Asian Survey* (44) 6, pp. 815–835.

Spence, J.D. (1990) *The Search for Modern China*, W.W. Norton & Company, New York.

Sung, Y.-W. (1991) *The China-Hong Kong Connection: the Key to China's Open-Door Policy*, Cambridge University Press, Cambridge.

Sung, Y.-W. (2005) *The Emergence of Greater China: The Economic Integration of Mainland China, Taiwan and Hong Kong*, Palgrave Macmillan, New York.

Vogel, E. (1969) *Canton Under Communism*, Harper Torchbooks, New York.

Vogel, E. (1989) *One Step Ahead in China*, Harvard University Press, Cambridge, Mass.

Williams, M. (2003) "Hong Kong and the Pearl River Delta," *Modern Asian Studies* (38) 2, pp. 257–282.

Yusuf, S., Altaf, M.A., Eichengreen, B., Gooptu, S., Nabeshima, K., Kenny, C., Perkins, D.H., and Shotten, M. (2003) *Innovative East Asia: The Future of Growth*, Oxford University Press, New York.

Yusuf, S., Altaf, M.A., and Nabeshima, K. (eds.) (2004) *Global Production Networking and Technological Change in East Asia*, Oxford University Press, New York.

Yusuf, S., Nabeshima, K. and Perkins, D.H. (2005) "Under New Ownership: Privatizing China's State-Owned Enterprises," Stanford University Press, Palo Alto.

Zhang, W. (2003) "The Adjustment of Economic Structure and Guangdong's Economic Growth: Past Successes and Future Challenges," in X.T. Bui, D.C. Yang, W.D. Jones and J.Z. Li (eds.) *China's Economic Powerhouse: Reform in Guangdong Province*, Palgrave Macmillan, New York.

7 Industrial clusters in China

The low road versus the high road in cluster development

Jici Wang

Dilemmas in China's industrial clusters

In recent years, there has emerged a voluminous research literature, taken from many different fields, that addresses the importance of industrial agglomeration and clusters. These concepts have also received considerable attention in China, and this chapter provides an account of the cluster concept and its uses by Chinese scholars and policymakers.

The term "industrial cluster" refers to a group of firms and associated institutions that are both geographically proximate and functionally related. The idea has two key elements. First, firms in the group must be linked by traded interdependencies (input–output relationships) or by untraded (social and cultural) relationships that form around a core activity, if not by both. Second, these interrelated firms must be located in close geographical proximity to one another. The group generates external economies, and may create opportunities for mutual learning. In successful cases, the group also enhances levels of cooperation, trust, and innovation. The competitiveness of the cluster can in many cases be strengthened by appropriate public intervention.

A big difference between clusters in developed and developing countries appears to revolve around the kinds of market niches on which they focus. Innovative and dynamic clusters in developed countries tend to specialize in higher-value niches, while clusters in developing countries tend to serve the lower end of the market where competitiveness is determined by price. In the latter case, entrepreneurs seldom share information or discuss common problems that they meet. Levels of trust in these clusters are not very high, leading to cut-throat competition. Nevertheless, the existence of industrial agglomerations means that firms are usually able to find skilled and experienced labor, secure up-to-date and relevant market information, make contact with diverse suppliers, and interact with the local institutional environment. All these factors reduce production costs, thus enhancing the competitiveness of individual firms. Industrial upgrading is another important consideration for developing country clusters. For clusters in developing countries, upgrading within global value chains is important. Only by the careful adoption of coherent policies and strategies can a cluster upgrade, avoiding the "low road" in order to take the "high road" to development.

Sources of ambiguity relating to the cluster concept in China

Growth via agglomeration is a concept rooted in the writings of Alfred Marshall (1890) and subsequent heterodox economists (e.g. Hirschman, 1958; Myrdal, 1959; Perroux, 1955). Since the early 1980s, an enormous surge of scholarship in economic geography and allied fields has greatly expanded on this earlier work, emphasizing that selected regions are capable of exerting powerful push effects on national economic development. In recent years, no one has been more influential in promoting the concept of specialized industrial localization than Michael Porter (1990, 1998, 2000), whose notion of industrial clusters has rapidly become a central analytical concept and policy tool.

In a theoretical context, the term "industrial cluster" differs from the notion of simple proximity. There is a belief that clusters reflect not only economic responses to the pattern of available opportunities and complementarities, but also an unusual level of social embeddedness and integration (Gordon and McCann, 2000).

In practice, attempts at cluster development in China have generally taken the form of conventional urban planning approaches, such as localized infrastructure projects, preferential policies, and financial assistance. These approaches usually focus on urbanization via the construction of high-cost infrastructure to attract outsiders, rather than emphasizing localization to create learning effects.

Dimensions of proximity: geographical vs. organizational

The impact of geographical proximity on interactive learning and innovation is a key issue in economic geography. In the view of the French School of Proximity Dynamics, a distinction is made between organizational and geographical proximity. While geographical proximity is defined as the spatial distance between actors, organizational proximity is associated with the functional relationships among economic actors. Economic geographers sometimes add a third form of proximity, institutional proximity, to account for the fact that interactions among players are influenced, shaped, and constrained by the institutional environment (Torre and Gilly, 2000; Boschma, 2005).

Geography alone, however, may not be enough to produce positive externalities. Boschma (2005) argues

> geographical proximity cannot be considered a sufficient condition for the exchange of tacit knowledge. This may be illustrated by the experience of multinational corporations when they try to get access to the knowledge base of a host region through the setting up of a local plant. They regularly fail to do so, because it turns out to be hard to become a member of tight networks of personal relationships through which local knowledge circulates. Another illustration is the role of gatekeepers that bring external information into their home region, but this new information diffuses only to those local agents that form part of that local network.

Boschma claimed that geographical proximity *per se* is neither a necessary nor sufficient condition for shared learning. Proximity may facilitate interactive learning by strengthening the other dimensions of proximity, but it can also have negative impact on innovation due to the problem of "lock-in." Accordingly, too much proximity may be as detrimental to interactive learning and innovation as too little. Boschma describes five dimensions of proximity: cognitive, organizational, social, institutional, and geographical (Boschma, 2005). Agglomeration that facilitates the "learning economy" will possess all five dimensions of proximity.

Global–local aspects of industrial linkages

Much of the research on the innovation process, to date, has been concerned with local networks. However, recent literature has pointed to the importance of extra-local interconnections in the context of globalization. More connections should be made between networks at these different scales, as embodied in the production networks of global firms and regional networks in specific territorial formations. Local clustering and global production networks are not only compatible, but can also be mutually reinforcing. Latecomer firms in developing countries can become functionally integrated into both global value chains and local clusters.

These questions are vital for China, because many local governments in China are eager to build local linkages, but have ignored the benefits of external linkages.

Site of operation versus site of interaction

The evolution of cluster theory has grown from a basic focus on the site of operation to a broader view entailing the site of interaction. Initial work on the issue of agglomeration held that links between firms, institutions, and other economic agents located in geographical proximity tend to generate advantages of scale and scope – development of general labor markets and specialized skills – as well as enhanced linkages between suppliers and customers (Lloyd and Dicken, 1990). These economic efficiencies are concentrated at the site of operation, and do not involve local capability for learning and innovation. In time, however, agglomeration may also facilitate the "learning economy" through interaction among actors in a cluster. In this view, industrialization is a territorial process, while innovation is a social process (Asheim and Cooke, 1999), and the relationship between innovation and regional economic development is given a far more prominent place. From this dialogue emerge a number of theoretical perspectives, such as the theory of "new industrial spaces," the "district" theory, the innovative milieu approach, and "regional innovation systems." In developing countries, however, the cluster concept continues to refer, by and large, to narrower concerns of proximity, and to focus on operational efficiencies.

In some industrial agglomerations in China, the spirit of the Schumpeterian entrepreneur has dwindled, due to increasing industrial concentration and the domination of large companies. In response, these agglomerations frequently lobby for sectoral interventions, often at a national or supranational level; but this hampers more than helps the restructuring process as it removes the incentives for entrepreneurs to take the initiative, thus paralyzing competition and protecting large industries. In these kinds of networks, status is privileged over knowledge, power over learning, and the past over the present (Eich-Born and Hassink, 2003).

Concentration and dispersion

A further problem regarding the cluster concept is the confusion about agglomeration (seen as a source of knowledge creation), and locational dispersal (which is often viewed as a way to lower labor costs). Globalization and the worldwide increase in contract manufacturing have created new trends toward concentration and dispersal in the international economy. Despite the scattering of global industry, industrial agglomeration is still a major force driving industrial geography, because of external transaction costs such as transport and administrative duties. Recent trends toward flexible specialization and associated small-scale, volatile, and highly specific contract manufacturing have also increased the incentives to agglomerate (Leung, 1993). Globalization enhances the dispersion of knowledge across firm boundaries and national borders, and can push industries to seek lower labor costs around the world.

However, industries globalizing in this sense tend to remain geographically concentrated, due to the continuous impact of agglomeration economies. Dispersed clusters at different locations can then be integrated through global production networks. In such a context, industrial clusters may be considered as facilitating factors for a number of subsequent developments (which may or may not occur): division and specialization of labor, the construction of a dense network of suppliers, the emergence of agents who sell to distant national and international markets, provision of specialized services, the materialization of a pool of specialized and skilled labor, and the formation of business associations (Giuliani *et al.*, 2005).

"Natural" and "induced" clusters

Since Porter's work on national competitive advantage in 1990, the term "cluster" has drawn great interest from scholars and officials (see Figure 7.1). Many local governments have developed cluster strategies for industrial development and upgrading, drawing on both local production systems and global resources to enhance regional competitiveness. International institutions like the United Nations Industrial Development Organization (UNIDO) and the Organization for Economic Co-operation and Development (OECD) also consistently study, advocate, and popularize strategies of industrial clustering.

It is widely recognized that public policy, whether explicitly regional or not,

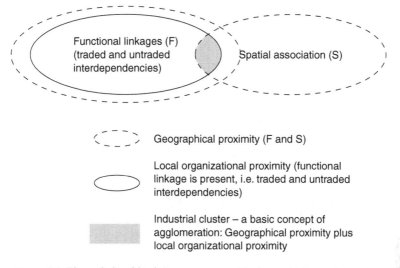

Figure 7.1 The relationship between geographical proximity and local organizational proximity.

may exert a major influence on the formation and development of clusters. There is a notion of the "inadvertent role played by public policy" in affecting cluster formation, and "...evolutionary paths for cluster creation are highly variable. Public sector decisions can affect cluster trajectories in a variety of ways, though the impacts are often unpredictable and often unintended" (Wolfe and Gertler, 2004).

According to Amsden (1989), in the "late industrialization" paradigm, a big push from the state is the main force behind successful industrialization. If this is true, the state should also use industrial agglomeration to carry out state planning and land use policy. Alternatively, Camagni (1991) argues that proximity enhances the contextual setting for intensive communication between firms, and reduces uncertainty in the interactive learning process. In short, spatial proximity enhances networking. Thus, even if an industrial agglomeration is initiated by the government, then under circumstances of rapid technical change, it improves the potential for continual learning (Scott, 1994; Storper and Walker, 1989).

As Alter and Hage (1993) argue, networking between organizations contributes to stability and reduces uncertainty. Such networks can evolve over time as "natural" clusters of firms, or they can be "induced" artificially as a result of interventions like the development of business or science parks.

Recent guidelines released by the APEC Symposium on Industrial Clustering for Small and Medium Enterprises (SMEs) highlight the possibility of governmental inducement of industrial agglomeration through regulatory or policy measures, or through the establishment of industrial parks in the early stages of development.

These strategies may include financial funding to promote incubator best practice, promoting venture capital industry, reducing market-entry barriers by simplifying regulatory and tax schemes, and pursuing international technology cooperation. Infrastructure items, such as electricity, water, telecommunications, suitable land, living environment and one stop services by the government are all important to pull potential firms and human skills together. For developing countries that lack their own resources to embark on a full-blown infrastructure development, it may be useful for them to concentrate efforts in a small region to attract investments, including foreign capital. After a cluster emerges in the region, then the area can be gradually expanded to include adjacent regions.

(APEC, 2005)

In contrast, Enright and Ffowcs-Williams (2000) argue "guidelines on policy towards clusters must be premised on a view of government as supporting existing and emerging clusters rather than trying to create them from scratch. A policy aimed at developing entirely new groups of firms in selected sectors can entail high costs, high risks, serve as a screen for outmoded forms of industrial targeting."

The debate regarding cluster creation has also proven confusing for the Chinese. Is there any way for government to drive industrial cluster formation through regulatory or policy measures, or through the establishment of industrial parks? Where can it be successful, and how can success be achieved?

Because of ambiguities in the cluster concept, there is a danger of the cluster idea becoming only a superficial fad in economic development practice. Yet large numbers of clusters do exist in developing countries and cannot be ignored; their road to upgrading must be intensively studied. While the clusters in developed countries are often global leaders and play a decisive role in innovation and product design (Schmitz, 2004), developing country clusters tend to operate under pressures that come from outside (Schmitz, 2004; Nadvi and Halder, 2005). It is urgent for these "low road" clusters, currently based on cost reduction, to upgrade and to innovate.

Problems and predicaments in the application of cluster concepts in China

The Chinese media currently give unprecedented attention to the region-centric view of development, and industrial clusters (*chanye jiqun*) are fast becoming a buzzword in national debates on regional development.

The wide interest in industrial clusters and the experience of successful clusters in Chinese coastal provinces like Zhejiang has stimulated numerous attempts to initiate industrial clusters in Chinese cities and towns. In line with movements like the Great Western Development Plan and the campaign for "Reinvigorating Old Industrial Bases," cluster creation has moved westward and northward from China's southeast coast. The term "industrial cluster" has appeared in preliminary research reports for the 11th Five-Year Plan in many provinces and cities. Efforts to plan industrial clusters are now under way in various regions, especially in underdeveloped regions. This trend is reflected in the speeches and reports of formal government conferences at the provincial and municipal levels. At the beginning of 2006, China's central government outlined several strategic tasks for building an innovation-oriented economy. The strategic importance of region-centric innovation has led China to confront issues of promoting cluster development and upgrading.

However, while cluster-based economic policy has considerable potential, it is not a panacea (Martin and Sunley, 2003). China needs to learn as quickly as possible how to shape this process, not only by adopting lessons from other clusters but also by seeking to position local industries in global value chains and by strengthening their competitiveness in the global market.

According to Schmitz, in addition to economic externalities, there is another, deliberate force at work in the generation of industrial clusters, namely, consciously pursued joint action. This force is still poorly understood in Chinese regional studies. In addition, Chinese policymakers still do not realize the importance of external linkages to the cluster in enhancing competitiveness. China has not really found any appropriate theoretical framework to balance the relationship between the heterogeneity of firms' knowledge bases with both intra- and extra-cluster knowledge systems.

The empirical background of this chapter examines two prevailing opinions about how China can promote its industrial clusters. The first is to gather scattered firms into industrial parks by local government. The second is concerned with forging an industrial chain or network (*dazao chanyelian*), by creating all the necessary backward and forward linkages of firms within a given city. What should be China's main goal – to foster "low-road" clusters or innovative clusters? This is China's key question. Rather than offering financial incentives to lure the lead firms of international production networks, China should nurture its most innovative clusters.

Spontaneous cluster development in China

Along the pathway to export-oriented industrialization in China, two types of agglomeration have emerged: those induced by top-down intervention, and "natural" clusters formed from the bottom up. The former are urban-based industrial parks created by government intervention; the latter are clusters created by market mechanisms, mostly following the "low road" to development.

Industrial agglomeration is a ubiquitous phenomenon in China. Many news reports have commented on the country's specialized agglomerations, for example:

> Buyers from New York to Tokyo want to be able to buy 500,000 pairs of socks all at once, or 300,000 neckties, 100,000 children's jackets, or 50,000

size 36B bras. Increasingly, the places that best accommodate orders are China's giant new specialty cities. The niche cities reflect China's ability to form "lump" economies, where clusters or networks of businesses feed off each other, building technologies and enjoying the benefits of concentrated support centers.

(Barbosa, 2004)

China's advantages in the global marketplace are moving well beyond cheap equipment, material, and labor. The country exploits clustering in a way that some countries just can't match. Drawing on its vast population and mix of free-market and central-command economic policies, China has created giant industrial districts in distinctive entrepreneurial enclaves such as Datang. Each was built to specialize in making just one thing, including some of the most pedestrian of goods: cigarette lighters, badges, neckties, fasteners. The clusters are one reason China's shipments of socks to the U.S. have soared from six million pairs in 2000 to 670 million pairs last year. Meanwhile, American producers, pummeled by imports from China and elsewhere, saw their share of the U.S. hosiery market fall from 69% in 2000 to 44% in 2003, according to the latest industry data.

(Lee, 2005)

The industrial clusters – e.g. Zhejiang's so-called lump economies (*kuaizhuang jingji*) and Guangdong's specialized towns (*zhuanye zhen*) – focus on one product in a locality, and are conducive to industrial linkages that form in response to market signals. Since the 1980s, these local economies have integrated with the state economic sector and have been directly involved in China's transition to a market economy, finding and filling various market niches left by the structural defects of the command economy. This remarkable specialization has helped China increase its manufacturing capacity and produce cheap consumer goods for both domestic and international markets. In the process of cluster development, entrepreneurial ability has played a significant role.

Chinese clusters are forming the institutional and social links necessary for competitive responses in a globalizing world. Yet adapting theories developed by Western scholars is problematic, because of the special properties of China's economic landscape (Wang and Tong, 2004). There are three reasons to believe that industrial clustering in China has unique features.

First, territorially embedded regional economies usually develop in areas where the legacy of the top-down bureaucratic systems is weak, and where local entrepreneurship is strong. The government has direct control over both the old industrial areas dominated by state-owned firms and the new development zones. The entrepreneurs coming out of state-owned research institutes, the leaders emerging from rural villages, or the overseas Chinese returning from abroad, all manifest themselves in different ways, in different settings. As China's tentative reforms go on, industrial clusters in different regions transform themselves constantly via industrialization and upgrading, which are not easily simplified into any single development model.

Second, investment from the outside world strongly affects the structure of local production networks in China. The global linkages between Chinese local firms and the firms in advanced countries are often stronger than the local linkages among Chinese firms within individual clusters.

Third, most of the clusters in China have formed since the beginning of economic reform and, thus, have a history of less than 20 years. China has a long way to go before it can build mature market mechanisms to facilitate competitive clusters with rich social capital.

According to data collected from news sources throughout the country and other evidence accumulated by our research group, about 740 industrial clusters with real cluster functions can be detected in China. Coastal areas, including six provinces (Guangdong, Fujian, Zhejiang, Jiangsu, Shandong, Liaoning) and two major cities (Beijing and Shanghai), have nearly 500 industrial clusters, about 70 percent of the total number.

The proliferation and performance of industrial clusters in China can be attributed to four main factors: entrepreneurship, local government, industrial associations, and foreign direct investment.

Entrepreneurship

Many of the coastal locations housing China's industrial clusters, especially in the southeast (formerly a blank on China's industrial map), have become rising stars of the new industrial economy. If resource endowments do not explain their economic performance, then differences in the quality and quantity of their human resources must. Major emphasis should be laid on that elusive factor of production called entrepreneurship.

In contrast to the success of China's southeast, plant closures, layoffs, unemployment, and rising poverty rates have hurt China's declining traditional industrial base in the northeast, a region in which a rigid system of state-owned enterprises still dominates industrial production. The main difficulties in the latter part of the country are large numbers of redundant personnel and a small number of entrepreneurial leaders who are experts in business and can deal with market competition. In such circumstances, industrial clusters cannot easily form.

Local government

Even where industrial clusters thrive, local government policy is important. In the 1980s, when Chinese clusters in coastal area were created, local governments played both a developmental and a corporate role. As local financial strength increased, some government-sponsored institutes were established to provide information about technology and markets to local firms. Local governments also provided public services for enterprises, holding trade fairs and international exhibitions of locally produced goods and creating Internet Web pages to promote local brands in national and/or global markets.

The economic performance in clusters of Zhejiang province was based primarily on local entrepreneurship, with no subsidies or support from the central government. Local governments, however, especially administrators at the county and village level, share the economic risks and opportunities with local entrepreneurs during the reform process.

As the Wenzhou footwear cluster shows, local governments also encourage people to build learning institutions. With the help of Italian businesses, Wenzhou established a footwear design center. Moreover, constructing a specialized marketplace, opening wholesale centers, and hosting regular national or international trade fairs are also important steps taken by local governments. Such efforts are rarely seen in most inland areas where bureaucratic oversight is still strong.

Industry associations

One feature that distinguishes industrial clusters in China is the existence of active industry associations. Usually, these bridge the gap between government and private enterprise. With the help of local government, a local industry association can host specialized industrial exhibitions. In addition, an association can play other roles: publicizing the regional brand to raise the reputation of the cluster, and holding lectures on new equipment, modern techniques, and other industry information. Local associations often maintain close contact with trade associations in advanced countries, inviting experts to give lectures on using new materials and equipment.

As a result of China's entry into the WTO, its industrial clusters, mostly concentrated in light industries such as textiles, clothing, and daily necessities, face the possibility of greatly increased turbulence. Chinese clusters are increasingly susceptible to external forces, including environmental regulation and antidumping cases brought by other countries. In these cases, industrial associations can play an important role.

Some local industrial associations are also concerned with the protection of intellectual property (IP). For example, Hangji, in Jiangsu province, hosts a cluster of toothbrush manufacturers. The trade association for this cluster requires its members to pay for the use of other members' patents. Members, thus, share both the intellectual property and the cost of protecting it. This is of great benefit to small private enterprises. Hangji has been a model town for IP protection; its organizational structure is shown in Figure 7.2.

Foreign direct investment (FDI)

China currently has many "low road" clusters organized around low labor costs and increasingly flexible labor markets, and connected to international markets via the increased outsourcing by multinational companies (MNCs). The southeast coastal area was the first to open up to the outside, facilitating the growth of

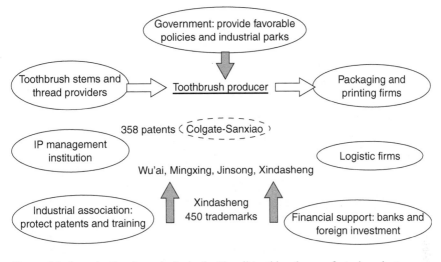

Figure 7.2 Organizational proximity in the Hangji toothbrush manufacturing cluster.

export-oriented industrial clusters. The vast majority of FDI in China was and still is directed toward the coastal provinces. From 1979 to 2003, 85.3 percent of cumulative FDI went to the 11 provinces and provincial-level cities along the eastern and southern coast. Nearly two-thirds of China's cumulative FDI went to just five provinces: Guangdong (25.8 percent), Jiangsu (14.23 percent), Fujian (8.75 percent), Shanghai (8.4 percent), and Shandong (7.1 percent). All five areas have been particularly targeted by manufacturers based in Taiwan and Hong Kong. Shandong has also been especially popular with South Korean firms (Jiang, 2003).

Global buyers have an increasing role in local industrial upgrading. Because there is limited knowledge and poor innovative capability in many clusters in China, there is a danger that numbers of them will lose their advantages unless they have interaction with the outside world. The input–output structure and institutional framework of global value chains have a profound effect on the evolution of local clusters.

Industrial parks

Industrial parks and special economic zones are two of the most important policy tools adopted by the Chinese government to attract inward investment. As the experience of traditional industrial areas shows, industrial parks in China rarely engender agglomeration economies, in spite of the close geographical proximity of many different firms. This has caused some confusion in the media and among government officials. Two questions are frequently asked: What is the difference between an industrial park and an industrial cluster? How can China turn its industrial parks into genuine industrial clusters?

Simple geographical proximity is, of course, characteristic of firms in China's traditional industrial areas and industrial parks (including high-technology parks). In many of these districts, however, firms are functionally isolated and have few local linkages.

Traditional industrial areas

Urban industrial estates constructed in the 1950s during the Second Five-Year Plan formed China's initial model for the dispersion of heavy industry. Factories with related functions – the term "firm" was not used under the planned economy – were allocated close to each other under the guidance of Soviet experts. Factories manufacturing tractors, bearings, and gears, for example, were located in the western part of Luoyang, Henan province, while electric genera-tor-related factories producing steamers, generators, and boilers emerged in the Minhang district of Shanghai. In other cases, traditional industrial areas were planned for specific urban planning concerns. The Datong industrial estate in Hefei, Anhui province, for example, was planned so workers could share shopping and educational facilities.

Yet, even during the 1960s, when industry was decentralized and moved westward due to military concerns, factories with related functions were located as close as feasibly possible. The Second Auto factory in Shiyan, Hubei province, for example, had its factory suppliers located in 27 valleys nearby. In the former Chinese command economy, however, factories were controlled by many supervisory agencies of different sectors at both the national and local levels, and this patchwork of regulation hindered interaction between firms. Bureaucratic, hierarchical organizations blocked interaction between firms and kept factories in the same locale insulated under different systems of administration. The phenomenon is called "separating the vertical and the horizontal" (*tiaotiao kuaikuai fenge*). An example is the Nanding aluminum processing area, in Zibo, Shandong province. Its production of primary aluminum, fabricated aluminum, and alumina was authorized by the Ministry of Metallurgy. Its electricity generation production was managed by the Ministry of Electricity. Its cement production fell under the Ministry of Building Materials, while the fabricated aluminum plant itself belonged to the city government.

Development zones

China's industrial parks – also called "development zones" (*kaifaqu*) – began in the early 1980s when the central government created four special economic zones (SEZs) and opened up 15 coastal cities. In the 1990s, industrial parks were specifically aimed to attract foreign companies and did so with great success. It was widely thought that any coastal city could work miracles by opening up huge swaths of land for development, forming giant industrial parks, doling out tax benefits, and developing infrastructure and transportation networks.

Fröbel *et al.* (1980, p. 302) note that "the new production zones go under a variety of designations: the most frequent are *free export zone, export processing zone* and *export industrial zone.*" In China, all such zones operate under much the same set of regulations, including open market access. In the past two decades, development zones for commercial and residential building have spread all over the country, and these zones have lured investors and competitors from many different parts of the world.

Since 2003, the central government has started to curb the rampant establishment of industrial parks. According to official statistics, by August 2004, the total number of industrial parks had reached 6,866, and covered 38,600 square kilometers. Among these parks, 171 are at the state level, 1,094 at the provincial level, and 5,671 at the city level.[1] After the central government adjusted the rules for development of industrial parks, the number fell to 2,053, and the total area occupied by industrial parks narrowed to 13,700 square kilometers.

Since the establishment of SEZs in the early 1980s, scholars have detected industrial linkages and spatial transfers of information, people, material, and administrative and communication ties among firms (Wang and Bradbury, 1986). Until now, however, local linkages within industrial parks have remained relatively weak.

China's current situation suggests that, while cluster locations may shift, the local labor market situation is likely to persist, even as capital becomes increasingly mobile. Low-skill industries like garments and footwear will move into a new generation of industrial parks with cheaper labor. Inland provinces like Jiangxi, Anhui, and Sichuan, which have low wages and low land costs, have become prime locations for new industrial parks.

Industrial clusters and industrial parks: blurring lines of distinction

In recent years, industrial parks and industrial clusters in China have become increasingly indistinct from one another. Some clusters have emerged from industrial parks, while many industrial parks are constructed in the locales where industrial clusters exist. The convergence of these two phenomena has fed into the confusion between proximity and agglomeration in Chinese regional development

Such convergent evolution can also be found in other countries and regions. Prato is a good example of an industrial park constructed within an industrial cluster. Prato, located halfway between Milan and Rome, is a classic case of an industrial cluster. Textiles pervade the life of the entire local community. The expansion of the local industry is now tied to a well-equipped industrial park, the Macrolotto, with an area of more than 98 acres (400 hectares). Evolution in the other direction, from park to cluster, can be illustrated by the cases of Stanford Research Park in California and Hsinchu Science-based Industrial Park in Taiwan. Hsinchu includes a full spectrum of firms involved in activities ranging from integrated circuit design to wafer fabrication and mask making. Recent research reveals that Sophia Antipolis has evolved from a satellite platform to a technopolis, and from a condition of simple geographic proximity of firms to organizational proximity (Lazaric *et al.*, 2004).

Although geographical proximity in industrial parks and in industrial clusters is identical in practice, to a certain degree, the origins of the two phenomena are rather different. The former is exogenous in nature and the later is endogenous. The construction of industrial parks has been identified by the government as an important infrastructural investment, capable of attracting enterprises from outside and creating jobs, while industrial clusters emerge endogenously and help generate new firms internally.

The availability of infrastructure may attract firms to certain locations, creating agglomeration economies and reducing factor and transaction costs. Infrastructure services can also contribute to the welfare of individuals. Infrastructure also involves higher level institutional capacities, including standard-setting, export control and assurance, and knowledge-fostering capacities like patent services. However, it has been long recognized that the contributions of infrastructure to economic development do not come automatically with the availability of physical facilities and structures, but require efficient operation and maintenance of those facilities, as well as supporting institutions. To turn traditional industrial parks into agglomerations of firms with interrelated functions is not easy. To turn industrial parks into innovation-oriented environments together with logistic, technological incubator, and innovation centers is even more difficult, though it remains an ideal for which to be aimed.

Hard realities about cluster building in Chinese industrial parks

At the present time, induced industrial clusters in China coincide mainly with industrial parks dominated by foreign firms. Three cases illustrate this remark.

The Nokia-created Xingwang International Industrial Park in the Beijing Economic Development Zone is a major example. Anchored by Nokia, Xingwang Park is emerging as a major Asian cluster for electronic communication devices. The 125-acre (50-hectare) Xingwang Park is being developed as a Nokia Centre for Logistics Excellence, with suppliers clustered around a central Nokia hub. The establishment of Shouxin-Nokia (Beijing) attracted more than 16 collaborating companies like Sanyo and Foxconn, locating around the lead firm. All the companies involved in the project have the same logistical operating model in common, guaranteeing flexible and efficient manufacturing. The mature industrial chain supplies Nokia with accessories, and delivers products on time. Therefore, materials and finished products inventories are close to zero; whenever a product is completed, it is delivered within the next few hours. Nearly half of Nokia's global output comes from this park, including its top cell phone. In the near future, more than 30 major material and service suppliers and R&D institutions will enter the park.

A second example is the cluster around Toyota in Tianjin. Kuchiki (2004) found that when Toyota decided to invest in Tianjin, it asked its related firms to build plants in the same region. However, Toyota's related firms were deterred from participating in the cluster due to the firm's procurement process and a "just-in-time" logistics system that decreased transportation costs from Shanghai to Tianjin. As a result, Denso, a Japanese *keiretsu* firm linked to Toyota, waited to decide on its investment in Tianjin until Toyota announced it would expand its production to 550,000 units in China. Kuchiki concludes that three factors – industrial zones, capacity building, and anchor firms – were the keys to forming Toyota's cluster in Tianjin. The *keiretsu* relationship between an anchor firm and its related firms has positive effects for the formation of an industrial cluster, and scale economies are a sufficient condition for related firms to join the anchor firm's cluster.

A third example is presented by the entry of Japanese automakers into Guangzhou. Following on the heels of Honda's purchase of a factory (operated by France's Peugeot before its withdrawal from China in 1988), Nissan and Toyota are also moving forward with plans to build factories in Guangzhou. In line with this, many Japanese auto parts manufacturers have set up local operations, and an automotive cluster is taking shape in the area around Guangzhou. The municipality has successfully attracted three Japanese automobile giants, and will continue to support the development of an auto industry, one of its nine pillar industries. Honda Automobile Co. Ltd, based in Guangzhou, will produce and market 55,000 cars and vans this year.

The above cases indicate that industrial clusters can be built on the basis of the industrial park model. Many cities and towns want to extend their industrial networks, and seek to use industrial parks to attract new upstream and downstream links in the global value chain. The reality of forging an industrial network in a particular location, however, presents serious difficulties, for at least two reasons.

First, "ownership distance" might be one of the stumbling blocks to forging an industrial network in a given region (Wang and Wang, 1998). In a recent example, it is reported that bulk steel framework required for construction of a huge building in Wuhan city had to be transported from a private company somewhere in Hangzhou, 2,000 kilometers away. Though several large, local state-owned enterprises (SOEs) exist in Wuhan, such as the Wuhan Steel and Iron Co., they could not outperform those private SMEs in Zhejiang province. It is important for Chinese leaders to know that without the vital efforts of many competent SMEs, a critical mass of firms cannot be formed, robust business linkage cannot be forged, and local economies cannot enjoy sufficient spillover effects. Without cultural and institutional proximity of related companies, such as specialized suppliers and service providers, geographical proximity can do little to promote regional potential.

Second, industries located in China's industrial parks are mainly labor intensive and have few links with their surrounding local economies, since most of their transactions are either intra-firm or are with other foreign-owned companies. An example is the Yanbu underwear industrial cluster in Guangdong province. Ideally, the town government planned a big mall with five centers –

for trade in underwear-related products and machinery, exhibitions of underwear, underwear fashion design, underwear product information, and underwear logistics. This approach of constructing market complexes in order to extend the industrial chain has been successful in many other Chinese clusters. In Yanbu, however, these have been underutilized and, thus, wasted, because underwear products are usually sold to the world market by franchisers and distributors.

Many Chinese claim that the slogan, "forging industrial networks within the region," may discourage local actors from actively exploring external markets. This line of thinking, however, is false. As Bathelt *et al.* (2002) point out, the growth of any given agglomeration is a function not only of dense local interactions, but also of the presence of trans-local linkages reinforcing the agglomeration's ties with external partners.

Conclusion: building industrial linkages

This chapter discusses the question of the role of state intervention and market mechanisms in the contrasting contexts of global and local linkages. It is urgent for Chinese regions to upgrade their industries. The agglomerations that exist in today's China appear to function largely as a means of reducing production costs, ensuring only short-term price advantage, and forcing many producers to engage in a race to the bottom. Increased exports can only be secured by means of lower wages. Cluster upgrading, in contrast, entails the manufacture of better products, making them more efficiently, or moving into more skilled activities (see Figure 7.3).

Successful upgrading involves two main strategies. The first seeks to encourage the agglomeration of different firms in industrial parks. The second is to

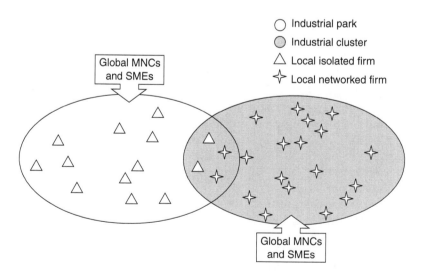

Figure 7.3 Chinese industrial parks, clusters, and their global linkages.

forge an industrial network, wherein each city or region attempts to expand its value chain by growing or attracting firms that complete its backward and forward linkages. As we know, support for regions by providing a framework and resources for the various types of zones, industrial parks, science parks, and incubators is not, in and of itself, necessarily the best way to achieve economic success. Nor can mere concentrations of firms in geographic proximity to one another, but without mutual functional integration, solve the problems of Chinese industry. In fact, the bottleneck in the Chinese regional economy is its pattern of weak industrial linkages. Therefore, the question facing Chinese central and local governments should be simple: How should they set policy that clearly encourages industrial linkages both inside and outside Chinese territory? Government policymakers have a catalytic role to play in terms of building these industrial linkages.

Two important issues need to be raised in regard to industrial linkages. First, one of the most fundamental lessons from many best-practices approaches is the extent to which success depends on the existence of close cooperation and interaction between the public and private sectors, nonprofit organizations, training and educational institutions, and community groups. Broad coalitions are needed to ensure the public and private sectors address key issues, while cooperative networks are needed to ensure the initiatives actually bring results. At the same time, in a successful developmental scenario, firms become deeply embedded in the local economy through the creation of a network of sophisticated, interdependent linkages, which support the expansion of local firms and generate self-sustaining growth of the local cluster as a whole.

Second, territory is not so much a geographic container but a set of potential interactions between different sets of actors (Coffey and Bailly 1996). The internal linkages of clusters are varied in terms of sectoral breadth, density, and permanence (Enright, 2000). Cluster policies generally concentrate their efforts on networks rather than on individual firms. Appropriate measures provide resources for a group of interrelated firms, or encourage linkages among firms and research providers. The linkages integral to cluster development are not limited to intra-regional space, but are just as likely to be national, if not international, in range (Raines, 2001).

China should pay special attention to the global linkages of its constituent regions. The value chain view of global economic integration indicates that, for many industries, access to international markets is not achieved in the first instance by designing, making, and marketing new products alone. Instead, it involves gaining entry into international design, production, and marketing networks comprising many different firms. Understanding how these value chains operate is very important for Chinese firms and policymakers.

The definition of organized proximity goes beyond simple geographical proximity, emphasizing entrepreneurial willingness to coordinate diverse production activities along the value chain. This coordination can help reduce transactions costs, create local capabilities, and generate a shared vision of business growth and potential from among the various possible technological trajectories.

Acknowledgment

This research was supported in part by the National Natural Science Foundation of China, under grant No. 40535027.

Note

1 Data source: www.mlr.gov.cn/pub/gtzyb/gtzygl/tdzy/tdly/t20041203_52147.htm.

References

Alter, C. and Hage, J. (1993) *Organizations Working Together*, Sage Publications, Inc., Newbury Park, Calif.

Amsden, A. (1989) *Asia's Next Giant: South Korea and Late Industrialization*, Oxford University Press, New York.

APEC (2005) Best practices guidelines on industrial clustering for small and medium enterprises. Prepared by the *APEC Symposium on Industrial Clustering for SMEs*, Taipei, March, 9, 2005.

Asheim, B.T. and Cooke, P. (1999) Local learning and interactive innovation networks in a global economy, in E. Malecki and P. Oinäs, (eds.) *Making Connections*, pp. 145–178, Ashgate, Aldershot.

Barboza, D. (2004) In roaring China, sweaters are west of Socks City, *New York Times*, December 24.

Bathelt, H., Malmberg, A. and Maskell, P. (2002) Clusters and knowledge: local buzz, global pipelines and the process of knowledge creation, *Progress in Human Geography*, 28, pp. 31–56.

Boschma, R.A. (2005) Proximity and innovation: a critical assessment, *Regional Studies* 39, pp. 61–74.

Camagni, R. (1991) Local "milieu," uncertainty and innovation networks: towards a new dynamic theory of economic space, in R. Camagni (ed.) *Innovation Networks: Spatial Perspectives*, pp. 121–142, Belhaven, London.

Coffey, W. and Bailly, A. (1996) Economic restructuring: a conceptual framework, in A. Bailly and W. Lever (eds.) *The Spatial Impact of Economic Changes in Europe*, Averbury, London.

Eich-Born, M. and Hassink, R. (2003) On the battle between shipbuilding regions in Germany and South Korea, paper prepared for the International Workshop *The Restructuring of Old Industrial Areas in Europe and Asia*, July 11–12, Bonn.

Enright, M.J. (2000) The globalization of competition and the localization of competitive advantage: policies towards regional clustering, in N. Hood and S. Young (eds.) *The Globalization of Multinational Enterprise Activity and Economic Development*, pp. 303–326, Macmillan Press Ltd, UK.

Enright, M. and Ffowcs-Williams, I. (2000) Local Partnership, Clusters and SME Globalization, *Local Economic and Employment Development Programme (LEED) of the OECD Territorial Development Service*.

Fröbel, F., Heinrichs, J. and Kreye, O. (1980) *The New International Division of Labor: Structural Unemployment in Industrialized Countries and Industrialization in Developing Countries*, Cambridge University Press, Cambridge.

Giuliani, E., Pietrobelli, C. and Rabellotti, R. (2005) Clusters facing competition: the importance of external linkages, in E. Giuliani, R. Rabellotti and M.P. van Dijk (eds.)

Clusters Facing Competition: the Importance of the External Linkages, Ashgate Publishing, Aldershot.

Gordon, R. and McCann, P. (2000) Industrial clusters: complexes, agglomeration and/or social networks? *Urban Studies*, 37, pp. 512–513.

Hirschman, A.O. (1958) *The Strategy of Economic Development*, Yale University Press, New Haven.

Jiang, X. (2003) Geographical distribution of foreign investment in China: industrial clusters and their significance, Special Reports, *China & World Economy*, 1, pp. 16–18.

Kuchiki, A. (2004) A flowchart approach to Asia's industrial cluster policy, in A. Kuchiki and M. Tsuji (eds.) *Industrial Clusters in Asia*, Institute of Developing Economies, Macmillan, London.

Lazaric, N., Longhi, C. and Thomas, C. (2004) From geographical to organized proximity: the case of the Telecom Valley in Sophia Antipolis, contribution to the *4th Congress on Proximity Economics*, IDEP–LEST–GRECAM, Marseille, June 17–18.

Leung, C.K. (1993) Personal contacts, sub-contracting linkages, and development in the Hong Kong-Zhujiang Delta region, *Annals of the Association of American Geographers*, 83, pp. 273–302.

Lee, D. (2005) China's strategy gives it the edge in the battle of two sock capitals, *Los Angeles Times*, April 10.

Lloyd, P. and Dicken, P. (1990) *Location in Space: A Theoretical Approach to Economic Geography*, 3rd edition, Harper and Row, New York.

Marshall, A. (1890) *Principles of Economics*, Macmillan, London.

Martin, R. and Sunley, P. (2003) Deconstructing clusters: chaotic concept or policy panacea? *Journal of Economic Geography*, 3, pp. 5–35.

Myrdal, G. (1959) *Economic Theory and the Underdeveloped Regions*, Methuen, London.

Nadvi, K. and Halder, G. (2005) Local clusters in global value chains: exploring dynamic linkages between Germany and Pakistan, *Entrepreneurship & Regional Development*, 17, pp. 339–363.

Perroux, F. (1955) Note on the concept of growth poles. in I. Livingstone (ed.) *Economic Policy for Development: Selected Resdings*, pp. 278–289, Penguin, Harmondsworth.

Porter, M.E. (1990) *The Competitive Advantage of Nations*, Free Press, New York.

Porter, M.E. (1998) *On Competition*, Harvard Business School Press, Boston.

Porter, M.E. (2000) Location, clusters, and company strategy, in G. Clark, M. Feldman, and M. Gertler (eds.) *Oxford Handbook of Economic Geography*, Oxford University Press, Oxford.

Raines, P. (2001) The Cluster Approach and the Dynamics of Regional Policy-Making, Regional and Industrial Research Paper, No. 47, European Policy Research Center, University of Strathclyde.

Schmitz, H. (2004) *Local Enterprises in the Global Economy: Issues of Governance and Upgrading*, Edward Elgar, Cheltenham.

Scott, A.J. (1994) Variations on the theme of agglomeration and growth: the gem and jewelry industry in Los Angeles and Bangkok, *Geoforum*, 25, pp. 249–263.

Storper, M. and Walker, R. (1989) *The Capitalist Imperative. Territory, Technology and Industrial Growth*, Basil Blackwell, New York.

Torre, A. and Gilly, J.P. (2000) On the analytical dimension of proximity dynamics, *Regional Studies*, 34 (2), pp. 169–180.

Wang, J. and Bradbury, J. (1986) The changing industrial geography of the Chinese Special Economic Zones, *Economic Geography*, 62 (4), pp. 307–320.

Wang, J. and Tong, X. (2004) Industrial clusters in China: embedded or disembedded? in C. Alvstam and E. Schamp (eds.) *Linking Industries across the World: Processes of Global Networking*, Ashgate, Aldershot.

Wang, J.C. and Wang, J.X. (1998) An analysis of new-tech agglomeration in Beijing: a new industrial district in the making? *Environment and Planning A*, pp. 681–701.

Wolfe, D.A. and Gertler, M.S. (2004) Clusters from the inside and out: local dynamics and global linkages, *Urban Studies*, 41, pp. 1071–1093.

8 The production organization of the automobile and motorcycle industries in Vietnam

Thi Bich Van Ho

Introduction

This chapter examines the functional and spatial production organization in the automobile and motorcycle industries in Vietnam during the transition process from central planning to market economy. Since the beginning of the 1990s, initial flows of foreign direct investment (FDI) have established the automobile and motorcycle industries in Vietnam. Import-substitution policies have been applied in order to attract FDI projects toward the protected domestic market.

The purpose of the study is to identify suitable forms of the production organization to support industrial upgrading processes of domestic firms along the production chains led by foreign firms. The wide adoption of the model of large-scale vertical integration in each domestic firm could not help to pursue industrial upgrading in the two emerging sectors due to the lack of technological capabilities of domestic firms over a wide range of involved technologies for complex engineering products, like automobiles and motorcycles. In fact, during the latter periods of industrial development, the deepening of inter-firm divisions of labor, rather than the high level of vertical integration in large firms, in the industries with complex and interactive technologies has helped build up the competitiveness of the Japanese automobile industry since the 1980s, and the American semiconductor industry in high segments since the beginning of the 1990s (Best, 2001). In the case of industrial latecomers like Vietnam, it is further needed to create clear frameworks to initiate the development of inter-firm divisions of labor in order to overcome very limited capabilities at the firm level over a wide range of involved technologies in the two sectors, and to create more possibilities for domestic firms to enter the production chains led by foreign firms.

The study is drawn on my fieldwork during the summers of 2003 and 2004 with 20 main cases, including both FDI and domestic firms, mainly in two provinces – Hanoi and Vinh Phuc (the northwestern bordering province of Hanoi) – that are the most important locations of both large FDI and domestic firms in the two industries in the North of Vietnam. Other general information on the restructuring of state-owned enterprises and trade policies in the two industries was reviewed and analyzed from daily economic news sources on the

Web sites of the Ministry of Industry, Ministry of Finance, and a number of the most important newspapers on economic issues in Vietnam during 2003–2005.

Based on the examination of the subcontracting relationships of Japanese firms in the automobile and motorcycle industries in Hanoi and Vinh Phuc, attempts have also been made to study a small cluster of Japanese suppliers in Thang Long Industrial Park located between the two provinces, close to the International Noi Bai Airport, and next door or close to their large customers, such as Denso, Toyota, Honda, etc. These Japanese suppliers and their customer firms are examined through the information available on their company Web sites and through the company profile database of Datamonitor, on the aspects of their primary product production, the internal organization of production, the network of subsidiaries and affiliates, the localization in ASEAN, leading customers in Japan and other countries. The above information usefully provides some practical basis of the organization of production, and the subcontracting network among large and smaller firms in Japan. The information about the localization of certain phases of the production chains and the replication of some supplier relationships in ASEAN is also of a great concern here.

This chapter is organized into four sections. The second section examines the impact of import-substitution policies on competition structures between FDI and domestic firms to explain the divergence in industrial upgrading paths among domestic firms in the automobile and motorcycle industries. In the third section, the results of the survey on internal and inter-firm organization of production are presented. The final section emphasizes the necessity to lower entry barriers for domestic firms; to the promotion of networking between FDI and domestic firms through the active access of domestic firms to the supplier networks led by foreign firms; and to the proposed inducement role of large state-owned firms in the development of clear frameworks, for which smaller domestic firms could specialize in multi-tier platforms of the product, module, and component levels in decentralized production networks.

The divergence in industrial upgrading paths between the automobile and motorcycle industries

The automobile industry

The automobile industry of Vietnam did not exist before 1991. That year, the first two international joint ventures were established. During 1993–1996, nine more joint ventures were set up. All 11 joint ventures were established between foreign automakers and Vietnamese state-owned enterprises. Total production capacity of those 11 joint ventures is just 148,200 units per year. But until 2002, only 18 percent of the capacity was utilized. According to the Vietnam Automobile Maker Association (VAMA),[1] in 2002 the 11 joint ventures assembled and sold 26,706 vehicle units with 37 models of 14 foreign brand-name carmakers. If we also include the imported vehicles, the total market volume was just 50,000 units in 2002.

Since January 1, 1999, passenger cars with less than 24 seats have been subject to special consumption tax with three tax rates depending on the seat number.[2] However, these tax rates were only applicable to imported completed built-ups (CBUs), while a tax break of 95 percent was set for locally assembled cars of the FDI firms.[3] This situation, however, appeared as if it was going to change by the end of 2003 after the National Assembly passed a legal decision.

But in June 2003, a new Law on Amendments and Additions on the 1998 Law on Special Consumption Tax once more extended the partial exemption for locally assembled cars from special consumption tax until the end of 2006, instead of until the end of 2003 as regulated in the 1998 law, and changed the tax break rate of special consumption tax for locally assembled vehicles at 70 percent for 2004, 50 percent for 2005, and 30 percent for 2006 (*The Publisher of Ho Chi Minh city*, August 2003; Ministry of Industry, September 13, 2004). The existence of different types of taxes, the unclear way of calculating taxes, and frequent and complicated changes of the tax rates have led to much confusion. But in general terms, the import-substitution had given too much protection for locally assembled vehicles.

The overprotection for domestically assembled vehicles has created unusual opportunities for FDI firms to pursue an overpriced strategy while the localization ratio[4] has been very low. Toyota Vietnam has achieved the highest level of localization among the 11 joint ventures at an average of 13 percent for its vehicles. It has invested in the first stamping facility in Vietnam since March 2003, which has added to its existing processes of welding, painting, and assembling, produced some parts in house and outsourced from seven foreign parts makers in Vietnam. The other 10 joint ventures have installed only the three processes of welding, painting, and assembling or just the two processes of welding and assembling of the assembling line. Because of their investment in the above production processes, the 11 joint ventures can import components and parts that are considered in the form of CKD-2 (complete knock down-2) with import tax rates of only 3–25 percent. Nearly all 11 joint ventures have concentrated on the assembling of vehicles with less than 24 seats due to the highest level of protection through taxes for these vehicles. The parts-making industry has been underdeveloped with very limited sales of vehicles (Ministry of Industry, February 3, 2005).

In order to speed up the localization process, the policy related to imported CKD kits has been proposed to change. On June 7, 2005, the government accepted the proposal of the Ministry of Finance on the application of tariff rates for single components and parts that are classified in groups for each vehicle category[5] to replace the existing policy on imported CKD kits (*Vietnam Economic Times*, June 7, 2005,). The purpose of the new policy is to promote parts production in a clearer structure. However, the new policy cannot put any pressure on the FDI firms to limit their overpriced strategy as too much difference in the import tax rates is still maintained for components/parts (on average still 25 percent) and for CBU (100 percent). Thus, once the import-substitution became hostage to the interests of the FDI firms in 1999, it became impossible for a "small" change in the policy to resolve the problem.

With very poor results gained from the overprotection of locally assembled vehicles in regard to the localization of parts production during the past ten years, by the beginning of 2005, the Ministries of Finance and Industry had planned to negotiate with ASEAN members in regard to the implementation schedule of CEPT/AFTA in order to open the auto market to ASEAN (*Vietnam Economic Times*, February 16, 2005). As soon as the normal forces of competition are resumed by the opening up of the industry to break down the overpricing strategies of the foreign auto firms, a real development path could emerge.

So far, while the 11 joint ventures have focused on the vehicles with less than 24 seats, domestic firms have made attempts to produce cheap trucks, specialized vehicles, and buses based on imported chassis, parts, and components from China, South Korea, and Russia. A number of state-owned firms have invested in production lines for these vehicles since 1999. Recently, on October 5, 2004, the government has approved the Master Plan for the Automobile Industry, in which four state-owned corporations have been chosen to play the lead role in the development of the automobile industry as follows:

- Vietnam Motor Industry Corporation (VINAMOTOR) focuses on the production of light and medium-freight trucks, buses, passenger cars, engines, gear boxes, and transmissions.
- Vietnam Engine and Agricultural Machinery Corporation (VEAM) focuses on the production of buses, light and medium-freight trucks, engines, gear boxes, and transmissions.
- Vietnam Coal Corporation focuses on the production of medium- and high-freight trucks, and specialized vehicles.
- Saigon Mechanical Transportation Corporation (SAMCO) focuses on the production of buses, specialized vehicles, components, and parts.

The four corporations will be provided state-subsidized credits for financing technology transfer contracts from well-known foreign auto firms.

Soon after the approval of the Master Plan for the Automobile Industry by the government, on October 27, 2004, the Ministry of Industry promulgated the Standard Requirements for Automakers, in which the minimum production capacity per year for an enterprise in each vehicle category is set. The requirements for technology transfer, for an assembly line, a painting process, a quality control process, for the application of quality management system ISO 9001: 2000 or equivalent quality standards (TQM, QS 9000), and environment management system ISO 14001 are also set.

By June 2005, 30 investment projects with the total registered capacity of 120,000 units of light and heavy trucks per annum had been licensed. The Ministry of Industry worries that this capacity is already higher than the estimation of additional capacity from now until 2010 at 113,000 units[6] in the Master Plan. The largest projects that include the investment in a stamping facility, cathode electro-deposit painting line, and technology transfer from South Korea, Russia, or China are of the member firms of the previously mentioned four corporations and two private companies. The remaining projects of small production scale, ranging from 5,000 to 7,000 trucks per year, are on the verge of engaging in the assembling of Chinese trucks. Although all the projects have already met with the Standard Requirements for Automakers set forth by the Ministry of Industry, the ministry has recently asked local authorities to be more conscientious in the appraisal for approval of small investment projects with simple assembling activities, and without technology transfer, for the implementation of a localization program (parts making) in their city or province (*Vietnam Investment Review*, June, 28 2005).

However, the aforementioned circumstances reveal that the requirements for technology transfer regulated by the Ministry of Industry in the Standard Requirements for Automakers are incomplete and unrealistic. In both the Master Plan and the Standard Requirements for Automakers, instead of encouraging inter-firm production linkages for parts making and service providing, the vertical integration of assembling and parts production in each firm is assumed implicitly to be the only form of the production organization. Appropriate institutions to encourage private small and medium enterprises (SMEs) to be specialized are lacking. With limited financial capabilities, private SMEs have no choice other than investing in simple assembling activities to provide vehicles directly to the market. But if private SMEs are destined by certain opportunities to be specialized in some sub-components or sub-processes created by the adoption of open architectures at both product and component levels[7] among larger member firms of the four corporations, the process of increasing specialization among private SMEs would lead to the formation of indigenous supply-bases in a better way than that of footloose FDI firms.

Rigid requirements on the production facilities, even for assemblers, should be lifted as inter-firm cooperation could help lower entry barriers into production. Firms must be left enough space to choose a suitable form of the production organization based on the consideration of their own production capabilities in relation with those of other firms. The ministry should never make attempts to impose the form of the production organization of the FDI firms on domestic firms to raise entry barriers for the latter firms. The vertically integrated model just makes it easier for the FDI firms to close their core technologies from the reach of weaker domestic firms.

The requirements for certificates on international quality management and environment management systems in a rigid calendar framework should also be lifted as they unnecessarily increase the entry barriers for domestic firms. Domestic firms should be first encouraged to learn through serving foreign firms and locally led firms, to acquire technologies through technology transfer. Acquiring certificates on international quality and environment management systems is too costly and inappropriate for domestic SMEs. Firms should be left enough space to develop their own quality management system.

The motorcycle industry

Prior to the early 1990s, Vietnam was still a country of bicycles. For most Vietnamese, the motorcycle was a luxury good, a valuable asset of a family. Despite the rapid expansion of the domestic market for imported motorcycles since the early 1990s, the indigenous motorcycle industry was underdeveloped, except for some simple spare parts. Like the automobile industry, the attraction of FDI was specially focused. In 1993, the first FDI project (VMEP) with the Taiwanese Chinfon group for motorcycle assembling was established. After that, Japanese motorcycle makers also set up their assembling plants in Vietnam, Suzuki in 1996, Honda in 1997, and Yamaha in 1999. Seven FDI firms with designed capacity of 1.73 million units per annum have so far been established. By December 2003, their implemented capital had been more than US$380 million, which accounted for 96.5 percent of the total registered capital.

In contrast to the situation in the automobile industry, the localization ratio of motorcycles has been relatively high, at 60–90 percent for the FDI firms in 2004. Another interesting point is that the selling prices of the motorcycles of the FDI firms have been decreasing at approximately 50 percent during recent years (*Vietnam Investment Review*, February 24, 2005). The large domestic market and much higher competition between the FDI and locally owned firms have been the main reasons for some initial success of the motorcycle industry contrasted to that of the automobile industry.

The rapid emergence of locally owned firms during the late 1990s in the motorcycle industry was not associated with backward and forward linkages to indigenous industries created by the FDI firms as in many cases in Singapore. But it was due to the boom in the importing of Chinese motorcycle parts and components since 1999 that immediately lowered the entry barrier for locally owned firms. As motorcycles were not until recently allowed to enter 114 coastal provinces in China, Chinese firms with already huge production capacity had to target other countries with high demand for motorcycles, including Vietnam (Hirofumi, 2003). Many Chinese parts makers, due to the pressures for liquidation of their huge stock, "generously" permitted Vietnamese firms to choose freely the "trademarks" for the parts and components, including engines, buying from them for registering with the Vietnamese legal organization (Ministry of Industry, April 2003).

As compared with to the motorcycles produced by the FDI firms, especially Japanese models, locally assembled motorcycles are made from imported Chinese kits at half the price. As with motor vehicles, motorcycles were overpriced by the FDI firms due to the import-substitution policy with the ban on imported CBUs during several years. However, the level of the overpricing could not be as high as that of motor vehicles as motorcycles are not subject to special consumption tax. The price competition between the locally owned and FDI firms during 1999–2001 had dramatically broken down the overpriced strategy of the latter firms. In addition, by January 2002, Honda Vietnam, for the first time, "pioneered" the introduction of a "cheap" motorcycle – Wave α – that was designed for the Vietnam market with a price of about US$730 in order to be competitive with the price of Chinese motorcycles of about US$600.

The only pressure for decreasing the selling prices of Honda Vietnam's existing models (Super Dream and Future) and for the introduction of "cheap" Wave α was the emergence of Chinese motorcycles that were not only much cheaper, but also very "similar" in appearance to Honda motorcycles. In China, besides the engines and motorcycles produced by the license agreements with Japan's Honda, Honda's motorcycles, engines, and other parts were widely imitated (Hoogewerf, 2003; Yoshimura, 2004). The same situation happened with other Japanese motorcycle companies, such as Suzuki and Yamaha.

However, in response to the emergence of competitive locally owned firms, Japanese firms have created many pressures on the Ministry of Industry and the Ministry of Finance to inspect locally owned firms on the matter of production facilities, localization ratios, the implementation of import quotas, and trademarks. In the inspection by the Ministry of Industry during March 2003, 45 locally owned firms were certified to have met with the ministry's technical requirements for motorcycle makers. The localization ratio was checked on only the in-house production, including the production facilities for the assembly line and the production of parts and components. By March 2003, the highest localization ratio was 65 percent; the lowest ratio was nearly 19 percent. Nine of the 45 firms had been granted ISO 9000: 2000 for their assembly and parts production activities (Ministry of Industry, April 8, 2003). By October 2004, the inspection by the ministry on 12 of the 45 firms showed that the localization ratio had been further improved. Three firms had achieved the localization ratio of 80–83 percent. The ministry believed it would be possible to achieve the localization ratio of 100 percent for locally made motorcycles in the near future (*Vietnam Economic Times*, November 2, 2004).[8]

Due to the evaluation on the production capabilities of the locally owned firms with the focus on only firms' in-house production, the role of inter-firm production linkages has not been well understood. With the narrow concept of a vertically integrated business model, the Ministry of Industry has mentioned several times that only ten of the 45 firms will survive when the tariff rates for motorcycle CBUs will be decreased from the current rate of 100 percent down to 20 percent by 2006, under the implementation of Vietnam on CEPT/AFTA for motorcycle products (*Vietnam Economic Times*, November 2, 2004; May 6, 20, 21, 2005). The 45 firms have also been encouraged to merge into large business groups as the ministry believed higher production efficiency would be achieved with large business groups.

The internal and inter-firm organization of production in the automobile and motorcycle industries in Vinh Phuc and Hanoi

Toyota Motor Vietnam

Toyota Motor Vietnam (TMV) was established in September 1995 as a joint venture between Toyota Motor Corporation (TMC), Vietnam Engine and

Agricultural Machinery Corporation (VEAM), and KUO (Asia). There was no technology transfer agreement from the two foreign partners to the joint venture. Only a member of VEAM was dispatched to the joint venture to act as vice president. The head office and the production factory is located in the Kim Hoa industrial zone, Me Linh district, Vinh Phuc province, about 30 kilometers northwest from the center of Hanoi and eight kilometers from the International Noi Bai Airport.

All the models (small and medium-sized cars, large vans) assembled in TMV are in the vehicle group with the highest level of protection under the import-substitution policy (vehicles with less than 24 seats).

By June 2003, TMV had 687 employees, including 449 production personnel plus 49 seasonal workers, 819 people working in its dealers and authorized service stations, and 6,408 people working in its supplier firms in Vietnam. However, as the production of large TMV's supplier firms has mostly been for exporting, the indirect labor of 6,408 did not reveal its scale of localization of parts making in Vietnam. Despite being the leader among the 11 joint ventures in the localization process, its localization ratio, including both in-house produc-tion and parts sourcing from supplier firms, in 2004 was only 13 percent. The TMV's suppliers include the following eight firms:

- Takanichi Vietnam
- Sumi-Hanel Wiring Systems
- Export Mechanical Tool
- Yazaki EDS Vietnam
- Technical Development and Trading Company
- Harada Industries
- GS Battery Vietnam
- Denso Vietnam.

All eight suppliers are either joint ventures with Japanese firms, 100 percent Japanese-owned, or have some partnerships with Japanese firms. Denso and Yazaki are closed affiliated suppliers of Toyota Motor. Denso and Yazaki have also served Toyota Motor Thailand (Lecler, 2002). The involvement of Japanese firms in the network of suppliers of TMV could go further if we consider the supplier relationships at the above supplier firms. Takanichi has also been sup-plying raw materials to a Japanese trading firm in Vietnam, Toyota Tsusho Cor-poration of Toyota group in Japan, to make auto seats. Denso Vietnam has sourced 100 percent of raw materials and machinery, 95 percent of components from the Japanese affiliates, either in Japan, ASEAN, or Vietnam. Harada Vietnam has also sourced from Japanese suppliers, including Okaya Vietnam in Ho Chi Minh city. Okaya Vietnam, which specializes in the production of com-ponents for auto gear boxes, is also the fifth supplier of Japanese Nidec Tosok located in Ho Chi Minh city (www.vnexpress.net, October 9, 2004). Traditional multi-tier supplier relationships between affiliated firms in Japan seem to be replicated in Vietnam between Japanese firms.

Although TMV's suppliers, except Denso Vietnam, are just for standardized parts, very few other FDI and locally owned firms could source from them for small-quantity orders as they have charged higher prices for such orders.

Locally owned firms, including the mechanical member firms of TMV's partner VEAM, could not become suppliers of TMV due to their low level of technological capabilities. Locally owned firms have also not yet participated in lower tiers to serve Japanese supplier firms. Besides the initial technical barriers, the tightly controlled, multi-tier subcontracting networks of Toyota Motor Corporation, with its strongly established intra-group division of labor, seems impermeable to the indigenous firms from developing countries, including Vietnam. The production organization at Denso Vietnam examined hereafter will further illustrate how closed networking between Japanese-affiliated firms could be replicated in their FDI projects in Vietnam.

Denso Manufacturing Vietnam and a small cluster of Japanese suppliers in Thang Long Industrial Park

Denso Vietnam received the investment license on October 4, 2001 to operate as a 100 percent-foreign-owned firm. Denso Corporation accounted for 95 percent of the capital, Sumitomo Corporation for 5 percent. The office and production plant occupying an area of 5.48 hectares is located in Thang Long Industrial Park, Dong Anh district, the northwestern part of Hanoi city. It is about 14 kilometers from Denso Vietnam to its main customer firm, Toyota Motor Vietnam. Since August 2003, Denso Vietnam has been manufacturing engine-related parts to supply TMV for its internal use and for export to Toyota IMV assemblers worldwide.

In Hanoi, a representative office of Denso Corporation was independently set up from Denso (Manufacturing) Vietnam. The Denso representative office in Hanoi has cooperated with the Hanoi representative office of Toyota Tsusho Corporation, and has been directly controlled by Denso Corporation in Japan and Denso International Singapore to implement selling campaigns through some companies in Vietnam, including Toyota Ben Thanh Motor Company (one of the 12 TMV dealer and authorized service stations), Toyota Tsusho Saigon Motor Service Corporation (a TMV dealer and authorized service station), Saigon Mechanical Transportation Corporation (SAMCO), Thang Long Ford Company, and Doan Hai Company. The components sold in Vietnam were exclusively for spare-part replacement purposes. It seems the supply of Denso's specialized components and parts exclusively for replacement purposes could be extended to authorized service stations of other car manufacturers, such as of Ford Vietnam, rather than to only those of TMV.

The tight controlling of Denso Corporation in Japan and the involvement of Toyota Tsusho Corporation over the manufacturing and trading activities of its subsidiaries and affiliates abroad may be implemented under the pressure of Keiretsu-type commitments in the supplier relationship. As one of the world's largest auto-part firms for electrical and electronic parts, and due to the new functions of modern automotive electronics in integrating other components of a car to fit together and to operate as a system, the closed Keiretsu relationship in the procurement between Denso and its main client Toyota Motor has been weakened and made vulnerable to other large auto assemblers in the United States (Ahmadjian and Lincoln, 2001; Henderson and Clark, 1990). However, it remains a big question relative to developing countries.

Denso Vietnam had 475 Vietnamese employees, including 400 workers and six Japanese directors by November 2004. The production was organized in three shifts per day. Ninety percent of its production equipment was computer-controlled and programmable. The export value during the six months prior to November 2004 was US$15 million, in which 40 percent went to Japan, 40 percent to ASEAN, and 20 percent to other Asian countries. Raw materials and machinery have been entirely sourced from the Japanese-affiliated supplier firms of Denso Corporation, in which 90 percent of the affiliated firms were located in Japan and 10 percent in ASEAN. Components and parts have been sourced 20 percent in Hanoi and Vinh Phuc, 10 percent in other provinces in Vietnam, 50 percent in Japan, and for 20 percent in ASEAN. The Japanese-affiliated firms have accounted for 95 percent of the parts and components sourcing, and ASEAN firms for only 5 percent. Thus, affiliation has been an extremely strong characteristic of supplier relationships of Denso Vietnam.

Ninety percent of raw materials and machinery sourced from Japan and 100 percent from the Japanese-affiliated firms means there has been little evidence regarding the localization of the further upstream phases of the production chain from Japan into ASEAN; and indigenous firms in ASEAN have not yet participated in the further upstream phases of the production chain. Five percent of the parts and components sourced from ASEAN firms reveal the initial participation of ASEAN indigenous firms into certain upstream phases of the production chain where about 50 percent of these upstream phases have been localized in ASEAN. Located in the same industrial park with Denso Vietnam, Kein Hing from Malaysia, which has served Denso Malaysia and other Japanese firms in Malaysia (Kein Hing International Berhad, www.keinhing.com), is an example for the participation of ASEAN suppliers into the production chains led by Denso Corporation and other Japanese firms.

With 20 percent of the affiliated parts suppliers located in Hanoi and Vinh Phuc and 10 percent in other provinces, the locational factor is relevant to some extent. Denso Vietnam has subcontracted out to other firms about 30 percent of its total production costs. As compared with other Denso production factories in Japan and in ASEAN, the factory in Vietnam is more vertically integrated backwards into the phases producing subparts/subcomponents to be used as inputs for the main production process. Several reasons for explaining the more vertical integration include weak local auto supporting industries, lack of economies of scale for the production of these subparts/subcomponents in Vietnam, and a way to prevent the leakages of proprietary knowledge about materials and process manufacturing in the environment of Vietnam.

Denso Vietnam's main subcontracting firms, including two Japanese firms, Matsuo Industries Vietnam (for plastic parts) and HAL Vietnam (for aluminum parts), are located in the same Thang Long Industrial Park (TLIP). TLIP Corporation is a joint venture between Japanese Sumitomo Corporation (accounted for by 58 percent of equity capital) and Vietnamese Dong Anh Mechanical Company (for 42 percent) to develop, market, and manage TLIP. TLIP (121 hectares) is located along the highway linking the center of Hanoi and Noi Bai International Airport in the northwest part of the city, and closed to Vinh Phuc province. From TLIP to Noi Bai International Airport is 14 kilometers, and to the center of Hanoi 16 kilometers. TLIP is one of the most successful two among the six industrial zones in Hanoi in terms of the attraction of FDI projects. Among the total of 40 tenant firms located in TLIP during August 2000 to January 2005, there are 36 Japanese firms. It is interesting to note that there is not only a concentration of Japanese firms, but also a small cluster of plastic molding parts and precision engineering Japanese firms in TLIP.

In the subcontracting relationships with its supplier firms, Denso Vietnam has always specified the characteristics of the components sourced, and also the production methods for these components. It has sometimes provided the subcontractors with raw materials. As the division of labor inside the Denso Group is among Denso Corporation, its subsidiary and affiliated firms might well be developed; it would be relatively easy for the group to integrate independent subcontractors at different points within the production chain. Denso has never provided additional machinery, financial assistance, or transferred process technology to its subcontractors. The subcontractors of Denso Vietnam that may come to Vietnam under the call of Japan's Denso Corporation are mostly strong technological firms. Therefore, the aforementioned kinds of assistance, often for junior suppliers, are no longer needed.

Besides Matsuo Vietnam and Hal Vietnam,[9] at least 15 of the total 36 Japanese firms located in TLIP are involved in plastic injection molding parts, molds for plastic parts, aluminum casting, sheet metal forming and precision machining, machine tools for the automobile, and other industries. As in the cases of Matsuo and Hal, the supplier relationships between the Japanese supplier firms and their large customer firms, such as with Denso, Yamaha, Honda, and Toyota, have been well established elsewhere in Japan, ASEAN, China, and the United States before its investment in Vietnam. Among the 17 supplier firms, some have also served customers in the electronics industry. Some of these large Japanese electronics firms include Matsushita Home Appliances, Canon, TOA and Sumitomo Bakelite. Some of the other Japanese supplier firms in TLIP have served Matsushita, Canon, etc. in Japan or in other countries.

The supplier relationships among the firms in TLIP and among some of those with nearby firms (Toyota and Honda Vietnam), and possibly among some of those with other firms located in the area surrounding Noi Bai Airport,[10] reveal the importance of geographical proximity in the localization behaviors of the supplier firms relative to that of their customer firms.

As all the 17 firms apparently do not intend to do business with local indigenous firms, it seems that the presence of these Japanese firms in TLIP would form strong supply-bases for molds, plastic, rubber parts, and precision engineering not only for large customer firms in TLIP, such as the case of Denso Vietnam with Matsuo Industries and Hal Vietnam, but also for other Japanese manufacturing firms in Hanoi, Vinh Phuc, and other surrounding provinces. All the supplier firms in TLIP express their intention to export the majority of their products. This may be related to the tax incentives granted to the firms if they export 100 percent or the majority of the products. In this case, while indigenous supporting industries are underdeveloped, a policy encouraging foreign firms to export leaves the possible supplier relationships between foreign supplier firms and locally owned firms much more tenuous. The supplier relationships between the 20 Japanese suppliers and their customer firms in TLIP (121 hectares) and the nearby area (14–20 kilometers from TLIP) are shown in Figure 8.1.

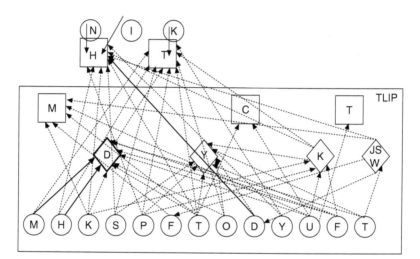

Figure 8.1 Supplier relationships between the 20 Japanese suppliers and their customer firms in Thang Long Industrial Park and in the nearby area.

If we also include others parts suppliers of automobiles and motorcycles in the Noi Bai Industrial Zone, and Yamaha Motor in the areas surrounding Noi Bai International Airport, the scale of supplier relationships will be more expanded.

In this small cluster, the replication of multi-tier subcontracting relationships between Japanese suppliers and their customer firms in Vietnam is very clear. The configuration of the network of supplier relationships is similar, but more complicated than the *hub-and-spoke* district elaborated by Markusen (1996). However, from the perspective of the local economy, it is also in the form of a *satellite industrial platform* (Markusen, 1996) as the subsidiaries and affiliates of the Japanese firms do not have linkages with indigenous firms in the local area.

Vietnam Motor Industry Corporation

Vietnam Motor Industry Corporation (Vinamotor) is one of the four main state-owned corporations that have been chosen to play the key role in the development of the automobile industry. In September 2003, Vinamotor was reestablished from the Mechanical Transportation Corporation, a state-owned corporation under the management of the Ministry of Transportation. The establishment of Vinamotor has shown the strong interests of the government in the development of the automobile industry. Vinamotor, like its former entity, is under the management of the Ministry of Transportation. By the beginning of 2004, Vinamotor had 26 member firms with more than 8,000 employees. But by the beginning of 2005, the number of its member firms rose to 34, in which 32 firms were profitable (*Vietnam Economic Times*, January 11, 2005). Its member firms are the partners in three joint ventures with foreign carmakers (VMC, VINDACO, and HINO). The head office and a larger number of its member firms are located in Hanoi, but the production factories are mostly outside Hanoi, spreading in several provinces in the North, South, and Central regions of Vietnam.

Vinamotor's main products include motor vehicles, motorcycles, parts and components, construction equipment, and steel structures. It is also involved in trading and training services. In 2002–2003, Vinamotor introduced new products into the market, including 25–50 seat vans, 40–80 seat buses, and light trucks for freight of 500 kilograms up to 2.5 tons, motorcycles, motorcycle frames, engines, clutches, and other parts.

Since the beginning of 2000, the corporation has signed an agreement with Korean Hyundai on technical license and technology transfer, for which the corporation was the only entity in Vietnam to produce Hyundai's buses and light trucks. By mid-2004, a joint stock company, Hyundai-Vinamotor (HVC), was established in which technology was contributed by Korean Hyundai and capital and personnel by Vinamotor to produce buses and trucks under Hyundai's trademarks and to do after-sale service. Since then, HVC has already built two light truck factories in Ho Chi Minh city and Can Tho province. Besides the technology transfer from Hyundai, the corporation has been looking for other sources of technologies for light trucks, including those from large Chinese firms. In 2004, the corporation sold 8,000 buses and light trucks with Hyundai's, Chinese, and its own trademarks (Transinco)[11] (*Vietnam Economic Times*, January 11, 2005).

Vinamotor will also produce 4–9 seat passenger cars with the technology from Hyundai in Dongvang Auto Industrial Zone in Bac Giang province, a further northern province, about 50 kilometers from Hanoi. The Dongvang Auto Industrial Zone, an infrastructure construction project of Vinamotor, became operational at the close of 2005. It is the first project for passenger cars produced in Vietnam by locally owned firms that would create pressure on the overpriced passenger cars of the FDI firms. Other new Vinamotor projects involving buses, trucks, and auto parts in Hung Yen province (the bordering northeastern province of Hanoi), in Ho Chi Minh city, and other provinces finalized the construction phase with operations beginning by the end of 2005 (*Vietnam Economic Times*, June 17, 2005).

Vinamotor has been authorized by the government to operate under the new model of a holding company, in which the head office of the corporation becomes the holding company with 100 percent state-owned capital, and the holding company holds majority equity stakes, at least 51 percent, in each member firm (subsidiary). The holding company may also hold equity stakes, with less than 50 percent, in each affiliated firm. Apart from the 34 existing member firms, there are some outside firms wishing to join the corporation. The possible participation of outside firms into the corporation could be in the form of affiliated firms.

The holding company has no production facilities. It plays the role of investing and coordinating the production activities among its member firms. The holding company controls the subsidiary firms in new investment projects with technology transfers from foreign firms. Depending on the size of the projects, the holding company may help its subsidiary firms in the application process with the Ministry of Transportation and other concerned ministries for financing through the subsidized investment capital of the state.

Vinamotor has so far organized 13 member firms in the production of motor vehicles, motorcycles, and parts. The 13 member firms have hosted a number of investment projects for the assembling of light trucks, buses, and parts making. The other member firms and outside firms may participate on the project basis for the production of certain parts and assembling work. Vinamotor plans to reorganize a member firm, Auto Trading and Service Company, as a sales company for the main products for the corporation, and, therefore, other member firms could concentrate on the production activities according to the orders of the clients. An automotive research and development center at the corporation level is planned to be established. Vinamotor also intends to establish a financial organization belonging to the corporation to mobilize more capital in wider social sources.

Through the implementation of new investment projects on light trucks, buses, motorcycles assembling, and parts making during recent years, a specialization structure in the production processes for these new products among

Vinamotor's member firms has been emerging. In the implementation of the investment projects on the assembling of trucks, buses, motorcycles, and motorcycle engines, the larger member firms of Vinamotor, with technology transfers from foreign firms, have gradually improved their production capabilities. And more importantly, these larger firms have also tried not to be locked into pure assembling activities by endeavoring to produce certain parts and components by themselves and to attract the smaller member firms in the production of parts and components for the final products. This process should be further encouraged in order that the member firms can develop their production capabilities not only for standardized parts, but also gradually for more specialized parts. The member firms are also encouraged to look for outside suppliers as it would help decrease the pressure for investment capital of Vinamotor for certain parts and components that could be sourced from outside firms, and to save the investment time.

Honda Vietnam

Honda Vietnam (HVN) was established on March 22, 1996 as a joint venture between Japan's Honda Motor (accounting for 42 percent of equity capital), Thailand's Asian Honda Motor (for 28 percent), and Vietnam Engine and Agricultural Machinery Corporation (VEAM) (for 30 percent). Asian Honda Motor is a 100 percent-owned subsidiary of Honda Motor; in fact, Honda Motor accounts for 70 percent of the equity capital. As in the case of TMV, VEAM's contribution to the joint venture was 20 hectares of land in the Kim Hoa Industrial Zone for use during a 40-year period.[12] Its main products are motorcycles with Honda Motor's trademarks. Production started in 1997 with Honda's Super Dream. Two more Honda motorcycle models were added, the Future in 1999, and the Wave α by the beginning of 2002.

In 2003, HVN's production capacity was 450,000 motorcycle units per year with 2,000 employees. A person from VEAM was dispatched to act as vice president of the joint venture. President and department heads were Japanese. The production was run in three shifts per day. HVN's production factory is one of the most advanced factories in Southeast Asia. The production sections are equipped with modern, computer-controlled equipment. The production factory of HVN is more vertically integrated for the phases of plastic molding components and die-castings than other Honda factories in Southeast Asia. This is due to the lack of the related supporting industries in Vietnam.

Under the pressure of competition with cheap Chinese motorcycles, the localization process of HVN has been further accelerating. By September 2004, HVN had achieved the localization ratio of more than 80 percent[13] for all its models (*Vietnam Business Forum*, December 3, 2004, vibforum.vcci.com.vn). HVN has made attempts to expand its subcontractor network from 14 local firms when it started production in 1997, to 31 local firms by the beginning of 2002, and 44 local firms by September 2004. About 50 percent of the subcontractors are FDI firms of the Japanese affiliates and subsidiaries of Honda Motor in Japan and Thailand in Vietnam.

HVN has directly selected a number of locally owned supplier firms to produce motorcycle parts meeting Honda's quality standards. To select a parts maker, HVN made an assessment process on the production capability during the course of about one year. The Purchasing Department of HVN is directly involved in the selection of parts makers, and later works with them in their sub-contracting work. However, even for small and simple parts, the headquarters in Japan makes the final approval for the selection of a new parts maker.

Two parts makers of HVN are located in the same province, but HVN's closest affiliate is GMN in Hung Yen province that borders Hanoi in the north-east. The majority of HVN's parts makers are located in Hanoi. A number of engineering FDI firms in six industrial zones in Vinh Phuc province, in Thang Long Industrial Park, and in Noi Bai Industrial Zone could also serve HVN for plastic injection molding parts, die-castings, metal and plastic parts, machine tools, etc. In fact, three foreign firms in Thang Long Industrial Park are Honda's suppliers, HAL and Sakurai in Japan, and Kein Hing in Malaysia.[14] Honda Vietnam does not reveal the list of its parts makers,[15] but does state generally that it has 2,300 employees, and nearly 22,000 laborers are working for its satel-lite suppliers (*Vietnam Economic Times*, July 26, 2005).

Conclusions

The establishment of the automobile and motorcycle industries through the attraction of FDI during the 1990s has provided very valuable feedback informa-tion about the conflicted roles of the import-substitution policies during the transition process from a command to a market-oriented economy in Vietnam. The overprotection for locally assembled cars, in which the foreign carmakers totally control the situation through their majority equity stakes in the 11 joint ventures, has created a serious enclave type of industrial development.

The typical form of the business model of the Japanese firms in Vietnam, as in other Asian countries, is more vertical integration and closed networking among their subsidiaries and affiliates (Ernst, 2000, 2002). It is the best way to avoid technological leakages to domestic firms. The Japanese firms have also tried to limit the provision of important components and parts to domestic firms. Under the import-substitution policies, the FDI firms could be closer than ever.

The policy toward the attraction of FDI so far has focused too much on the tax incentives for FDI firms and very little on the promotion of networking between FDI and domestic firms.

But even with better programs to run more automobile-specific industrial estates and their respective financial incentives in Thailand since the 1970s and throughout the 1980s and 1990s, a large quantity of the FDI of Japanese auto assemblers and parts makers did not bring in the development of Thai indigen-ous supporting industries. After more than 30 years of promoting the automobile industry based on the FDI attraction, until the late 1990s, Thai firms have been observed only in low-end parts production (Lecler, 2002). The serious problems of the enclave FDI-based industrial development have revealed that financial incentives for the FDI firms are never enough, and Asian developing countries have to make further efforts to develop their indigenous supporting industries through strengthening linkages.

For domestic firms in the automobile and motorcycle industries of Vietnam, it is necessary to combine efforts to utilize the backward linkages created through the presence of downstream (assembling) FDI firms with the attempts to approach the upstream (parts production, engineering services) FDI firms to serve them in the lower tiers of subcontracting networks, or to acquire from them components, parts, specialized engineering services, or production equipment in order possibly to participate in some points of the production chains led by the FDI, especially Japanese firms. Also, by increasing linkages with the Japanese assemblers and suppliers, domestic firms could come to understand how the Japanese firms organize the networks of multi-tier subcontracting, and how the Japanese suppliers are specialized in these networks.

In order to move further ahead from the present situation in the automobile and motorcycle industries, besides the efforts to approach the FDI firms, including the large assemblers and their suppliers, it is suggested that the adoption of nonproprietary product architectures (Baldwin and Clark, 1997) and open business models (Best, 2001) at a number of state-owned firms could help create clear frameworks for smaller locally owned firms to be specialized. Initial local supply-bases should be shared openly among all local firms for the highest possible level of consolidation in order to increase the production capabilities of locally owned firms to the level they could serve FDI firms in subcontracting activities. The development of open local supply-bases could also create more opportunities for the new firm formation and for technological fusing among firms from interrelated industries for the development of local supply-bases on an inter-industry basis.

The adoption of nonproprietary product architectures and of open business models at a number of large state-owned firms is seen as a relevant solution in response to the relatively integral feature of product architectures of the motor vehicle, and to a lesser extent, the motorcycle, that is associated with too high technical barriers for locally owned firms to enter the business. High entry barriers are also created by the high level of vertical integration in the production process by the FDI firms and closed networking among their affiliates. Only a number of large state-owned firms, not large private firms, could play the inducement role for two reasons. First, the stronger financial capabilities of the former firms compared with those of the latter firms, especially in the automobile industry, are supported by the government. Second, under the concerned legal framework, it is impossible to force large private firms to adopt nonproprietary product architectures and an open business model; but a number of large state-owned firms could be designed to adopt them as they depend largely on the financing of the government for important technology transfers from foreign firms.

In the automobile industry, initial open product architectures could be built up based on a number of platforms licensed from foreign medium-tech carmakers and parts suppliers, who the four state-owned corporations could approach through the financial support of the government in technology transfer contracts for the investment projects of trucks, buses, passenger cars, and also important modules and parts, such as engines, transmissions, and gear boxes. The post-conceptual design of platform components should encourage component sharing at the highest level among different models of the same motor vehicle. Attempts should be made to create as many opportunities as possible for the development of independent design capabilities at multi-tier platforms of the product and module, and component levels among specialized firms.

Initial successes in the motorcycle industry, mainly due to the rapid learning among locally owned firms from the Chinese motorcycle platforms that were originally built based on reverse engineering of Japanese motorcycles, should serve as a basis for the next stage – the consolidation of local supply-bases to be shared among firms from the motorcycle and automobile industries, and maybe extending further to the bicycle industry, or to the mechanical engineering sector in general. The survival of the 45 locally owned motorcycle producers will depend on whether they can abandon the vertical integration branding strategy to increase their specialization by opening themselves to each other and to other component firms for the emergence of inter-firm production linkages. More open competition with imported motorcycles from ASEAN since 2006 should not create higher pressure for locally owned firms other than that of the FDI firms at home, as imported motorcycles from ASEAN are mainly coming from the production plants of Japanese motorcycle firms, as in Vietnam.

External outsourcing could supplement the in-house production of the same components to look for flexibility in terms of both quality and quantity. External outsourcing could also promote learning among partner firms and could help to consolidate local supply-bases. The development of local supply-bases up to a certain level would attract the FDI firms for subcontracting activities with domestic firms.

The early development of the motorcycle industry has also shown that the entrance of indigenous firms, including both state-owned and private ones, into the motorcycle business was not the product of the central planning of the government, but due to their own rapid responses to market opportunities. In the automobile industry, besides the four chosen state-owned corporations, private firms have also rapidly entered the business following the promulgation of the master plan for the auto industry and of the standard requirements for auto-makers in 2004. In this sense, entrepreneurship is not lacking in Vietnam, even in a capital-intensive industry. However, without the inducement role of large firms, the rapid and simultaneous emergence of indigenous firms seems to concentrate on the pursuing of proprietary product architectures with vertically integrated busi-ness models in each firm as in the early development of the motorcycle industry. In this case, the inter-firm division of labor is underdeveloped. In addition, each vertically integrated firm is struggling to survive, as the technologies they acquired are incomplete. Therefore, the deepening of the inter-firm production linkages is needed to overcome this type of technological weakness.

With the inducement role, the large state-owned firms could invite as much participation as possible of other locally owned firms into the business. Those other locally owned firms could then enter the business through specializing in a certain component/part or process that can be plugged into modules or final products with the predetermined interfaces of the nonproprietary product architectures set by the large state-owned firms. The inducement effect could go further as nonproprietary product architectures and open business models at the large state-owned firms could be replicated in the new component firms that could induce the participation of other locally owned firms at the next tier of the supply-bases. Nonproprietary product architectures and open business models at the large state-owned firms can also be replicated in other locally owned firms that produce the same categories of the final products, modules, or parts with the large state-owned firms in order to share the supply-bases. From this perspective, the consolidation of supply-bases would be possible.

The industrial organizations for the initial development of the local supply-bases toward the locking of inter-firm production linkages inside a few dominant holding companies or cross-holding groups should be abandoned. Instead, a number of the large state-owned firms should be designed to play the inducement role to create clear frameworks for inter-firm specialization, to initiate inter-firm production linkages in an industry-wide framework, and to open more opportunities for new firm formation. The application of new microelectronics technology, information technology, or new materials technology could accelerate the technological fusion among firms from interrelated industries for further redefining of the existing industries (Best, 2001).

Acknowledgments

For helpful comments, I am grateful to Allen Scott, Gioacchino Garofoli, Antonio Vazquez Barquero and the participants of the Rockefeller Foundation workshop at Bellagio, Italy, during August 30–September 5, 2005.

Notes

1 VAMA was composed of only the 11 joint ventures until recently. The president of Toyota Vietnam, a Japanese man, is the chairman of VAMA.
2 Three categories of motor vehicles with less than 24 seats that are set for the purpose of taxation are vehicles with five or fewer seats, 6–15 seats and 16–23 seats.
3 For example, until August 30, 2003, while an imported five-seat car was subject to import tax of 100 percent of CIF price, plus special consumption tax of 100 percent above the price plus import tax, thus in total, was taxed at 300 percent of the CIF price of a CBU; the import tax for five-seat car in the form of an complete knock down (CKD) kit was only 20 percent of the CIF price of a CKD kit, and the locally assembled five-seat car assembled from that CKD kit was subject to a special consumption tax at only 5 percent of its production price, and after that to a value-added tax of 5 percent. In addition to that, corporate income tax for the FDI vehicle assemblers was totally exempted during the initial years of operation until several years after they started to make a profit. After that, favorable rates of corporate income tax at 15 or 20 percent would be applied, while the rate of 28 percent was applied to other businesses. The taxes, thus, are calculated in an overlapping way. The total protection

for domestically assembled vehicles in Vietnam is raised to an extremely high level due to this way of calculating taxes. Sturgeon (1998) in his study on the automobile industry in Vietnam could not imagine the way of calculating taxes in Vietnam. He followed a normal way of simply adding all the taxes together.

4 Localization ratio for a product of a firm is the percentage of the in-house production in that firm and of its parts sourced in Vietnam, including from both foreign and domestic supplier firms, in the total production costs to produce that product. For vehicles, imported parts still account for a very high percentage in the total production costs due to the lack of domestic suppliers and to the limited presence of foreign suppliers in Vietnam.

5 For example, a five-seat car is divided into ten technical groups that are further divided into 140 technical subgroups. The largest subgroup in terms of value is the chassis, which accounts for approximately 5 percent of the total production costs for a car (December 20, 2004, www.vnexpress.net).

6 The current estimation of quantitative demands for each product category that are set for 2010 and 2020 can be found in any current master plan for an industry. The development planning in Vietnam has not been changed in technical terms. But the scope for the participation of private firms in the industrial production has been much more open than that in the central planning during the period 1960–1986.

7 The architecture of a final product, especially for the complex engineering products in assembly industries, specifies which components, parts, or subsystems will make up the product, the function of each of these components, parts, or subsystems, and the interface rules to integrate these components, parts, or subsystems in the final product (Baldwin and Clark, 1997).

8 Besides the internal, self-made production for specialized parts inside the 45 firms, a number of standardized parts, such as tires, tubes, frames, fuel tanks, rims, exhaust pipes, and plastic parts, have also been produced by locally owned parts makers and have been openly sold in the marketplace.

9 Only the names of these two Japanese firms have been provided by a Japanese manager of Denso Vietnam. More information about the two firms, such as their location in TLIP, main products, etc. was found indirectly from other sources.

10 There is another industrial zone – No Bai Industrial Zone (NBIZ) – located in the Soc Son district of Hanoi, near Noi Bai Airport and not far from TLIP, Toyota, and Honda Vietnam in Kim Hoa Industrial Zone. Like TLIP, NBIZ is a small cluster of supplier firms for automobile and motorcycle industries with 18 firms (total of 23 tenants) specialize in precision mechanical parts, rubber molds, plastic injection and precision parts, and other parts for cars and motorcycles. Twelve of these 18 supplier firms are Japanese. NBIZ (50 hectares – the first phase) is an infrastructure joint venture between Malaysia's Vista Spectrum and Vietnam's Hanoi Industrial Construction Company. Furthermore, Yamaha Motor Vietnam is located in the same district, and also not far from Noi Bai Airport.

11 Transinco is the abbreviation of the former Mechanical Transportation Corporation, the pre-organization of the present Venamotor. Transinco is still kept as the trademark of Vinamotor.

12 VEAM is a large state-owned corporation with its head office in Hanoi and 12 mechanical and engineering member firms, two research institutes, and one trading firm located in several provinces, mainly in the North of Vietnam. VEAM is the Vietnamese partner in a total of seven joint ventures with foreign firms, including Toyota Vietnam, Mekong Auto, Ford Vietnam, Vietnam Suzuki and Honda Vietnam.

13 The localization ratio includes both in-house production and external sourcing in Vietnam.

14 This information has been found by examining these firms from their company Web sites.

15 In the interview with the managers of Honda Vietnam's purchasing department in August 2003, only some supplier names were provided.

References

17 Japanese suppliers and their customer firms in Thang Long Industrial Park (www.thanglong-ip.com): Canon (www.canon.com); Daiwa Plastic; Denso Corporation (www.denso.co.jp); Fujikin (www.fujikin.co.jp); Fujipla Engineering (www.fujipla.com); Hiroshima Aluminium Industry Co. (Hal) (www.hiroshima-cdas.or.jp); Honda Motor (www.honda.co.jp); Ikeuchi (www.kirinoikeuchi.co.jp); Japan Steel Work (JSW) Plastic Machinery (www.jsw.co.jp); Kayaba Industry (www.kyb.co.jp); Kein Hing International (www.keinhing.com); Sakurai, Ltd.: (www.sakurai-ltd.co.jp); Matsuo Industries, Inc. (www.kk-matsuo-ss.co.jp); Matsushita Home Appliances (www.panasonic.co.jp); Noi Bai Industrial Zone (www.noibaiiz.com); Ohara Plastic (www.ohara-jk.com); Parker Processing; Takara Tool and Die (www.takaras.co.jp); Toa International (www.toa.co.jp); Toho Industrial (www.toho.ne.jp); Toyota Motor (www.toyota.co.jp); Yamaha Motor (www.yamaha-motor.co.jp); Yasufuku Rubber Industries (www.yasufuku.co.jp).

Ahmadjian, C. and Lincoln, J. (2001) Keiretsu, governance, and learning: case studies in change from the Japanese automobile industry, *Organization Science*, 12 (6), pp. 683–701.

Baldwin, C.Y. and Clark, K.B. (1997) Managing in an age of modularity, *Harvard Business Review*, September–October, pp. 84–93.

Best, M. (2001) *The Competitive Advantage. The Renewal of American Industry*, Oxford University Press, Oxford.

Datamonitor, www.datamonitor.com.

Ernst, D. (2000) Evolution aspects. The Asian production networks of Japanese electronics firms, in M. Borrus, D. Ernst, and S. Haggard (eds.) *International Production Networks in Asia. Rivalry or Riches?* Routledge, London.

Ernst, D. (2002) Global production networks and the emerging geography of innovation systems. Implications for developing countries, *Economics of Innovation and New Technology*, 11 (6), pp. 497–523.

Government of Vietnam (2004) *Master Plan for the Development of Vietnam Automobile Industry*, Decision No. 177/2004/QD-TTg on Oct. 5, 2004.

Henderson, R. and Clark, K. (1990) Architectural innovation: the reconfiguration of existing product technologies and the failure of established firms, *Administrative Science Quarterly*, 35 (1), pp. 9–30.

Hirofumi, U. (2003) Vietnam motorcycle industry, in *Industrial and Trade Policy of Vietnam under Integration Framework* – the joint research project between National Economics University (NEU) of Vietnam and Japanese International Cooperation Agency (JICA), Statistical Publisher, in Vietnamese, Hanoi.

Hoogewerf, R. (2003) Yin Mingshan, *Asia Money*, November 2003, Supplement, p. 38.

Institute of Industrial Strategy and Policy (2002) *General report of the project "Overall development programming of Vietnamese industries in territorial scaling up to 2010,"* unpublished document, Ministry of Industry of Vietnam, Hanoi.

Institute of Industrial Strategy and Policy (2003) *Arguments and Urgent Demand for Building a Development Planning of the Automobile Industry up 2010, a vision of 2020*, unpublished document, Ministry of Industry of Vietnam, Hanoi.

Lecler, Y. (2002) The cluster role in the development of the Thai car industry, *International Journal of Urban and Regional Research*, 26 (4), pp. 799–814.

Markusen, A. (1996) Sticky places in slippery space: a typology of industrial districts, *Economic Geography*, 72 (3), pp. 293–313.

Ministry of Finance of Vietnam, www.mof.gov.vn, in Vietnamese.

Ministry of Industry of Vietnam, www.moi.gov.vn, in Vietnamese.

Ministry of Industry of Vietnam (April 2003) The results of the inspection of motorcycle locally owned firms, March 2003, unpublished document, Hanoi.

Ministry of Industry in Vietnam (2004) *Standard Requirements for Automobile Makers*, Decision No. 115/2004/Q_-BCN, Oct. 27, 2004.

Nhan Dan (The People), www.nhandan.com.vn, in Vietnamese.

Sturgeon, T. (1998) The automotive industry in Vietnam: prospects for development in a globalizing economy, Globalization and Jobs in the Automotive Industry – Research Projected Funded by the Alfred P. Sloan Foundation.

Vietnam Economic Times, www.vneconomy.com.vn, in Vietnamese.

Vietnam Investment Review, www.vir.com.vn, in Vietnamese.

Yoshimura, A. (2004) Motorcycle in Southeast Asia. Conflict between Japan and China on intellectual property, *TED Case Studies*, No. 724, 2004, www.american.edu/TED/honda.htm.

Part IV

Technology-intensive clusters in emerging economies

9 Contrasting regimes of regional development

The telecommunications equipment industry and computer software industry in India

Balaji Parthasarathy

The empirical question and the theoretical context

The year 1996 was a landmark for India's information technology (IT) industry. That year, the industry exported computer software worth US$1 billion (see Table 9.1), and Bangalore, a region referred to in the international press by terms such as Silicon Plateau (Fineman, 1991) or India's Silicon Valley (IDG, 2001), was the dominant center for production. While this attracted much attention, an equally significant event gave little to cheer about: 1996 was also the year when the Bangalore-based ITI (formerly Indian Telephone Industries), India's leading telecommunications equipment manufacturer, suffered the biggest loss in its history (see Table 9.2).

ITI's loss was significant for two reasons. First, by the 1990s, ITI's main product was electronic switching systems (ESS) (see Table 9.3), whose costs and functional capabilities are largely determined by software.[1] Second, in independent India's public sector-led import-substitution strategy (ISI), ITI was established in 1948 as the first public sector enterprise (PSE), with a monopoly over switching equipment production until 1991.[2]

The contrasting fortunes of the software industry and ITI raises the following empirical question: Why did a firm, making switches for nearly half a century, with no competitors, suffer a loss even though its most valuable input, software, was proving to be a source of prosperity in the same region for an independent industry that barely existed before 1985? The answer can be understood in terms of the policies that shaped the evolution of both industries and contribute to our understanding of economic development in newly industrializing countries.

The post-World War II development literature emphasized industrialization to enhance the prosperity of economically backward regions. To trigger industrial "take-off" (Rostow, 1960), and to set in motion cumulative causation and increasing returns to scale (Hirschman, 1958), autarchic, ISI policies were widely adopted. Additional arguments about the distributional inequities, and unequal sectoral and spatial development, which could result if market forces were allowed to operate freely, led to states being assigned a coordinating role in

Table 9.1 India's software revenues and exports, 1985–1986 to 2002–2003

Year	Revenues in millions of US$	Exports as % or revenues	% share of STPs	as % of all exports
1985–1986	81	29.63		
1986–1987	108	36.11		
1987–1988	130	40.00		
1988–1989	160	41.88		
1989–1990	197	50.76		
1990–1991	243	152.78		
1991–1992	304	53.95		
1992–1993	388	57.99	8.0	
1993–1994	560	58.93	12.0	
1994–1995	787	62.13	16.0	19
1995–1996	1,253	60.18	29.0	2.4
1996–1997	1,841	59.75	46.0	3.2
1997–1998	3,011	58.42	54.0	4.9
1998–1999	4,069	63.90	58.0	7.6
1999–2000	5,611	70.61	68.0	10.6
2000–2001	8,386	74.14	70.7	13.8
2001–2002	10,073	76.79	80.9	17.0
2002–2003	12,324	79.29	80.7	18.0

Source: www.nasscom.org; National Association of Software and Service Companies (NASSCOM), *Indian Software Directory, 1993–94.* NASSCOM; National Association of Software and Service Companies (NASSCOM) (1992) *Indian Software Directory, 1992.* NASSCOM; STP data from www.stpi.soft.net.

the development process (Lal, 1985). Further, drawing on the idea of a propulsive growth pole (Perroux, 1955), PSEs became a preferred instrument to implement development strategies.

The shared understanding of the problems perpetuating economic backwardness mentioned above, and the policies to overcome them, led to their widespread adoption, including in India (Chakravarty, 1987). Yet, at the turn of the millennium, if few countries matched the economic success of East Asian countries such as South Korea or Taiwan,[3] it had to do with the nature of state intervention. To Evans (1995), a state confining itself to regulation and policing, or where it takes on a direct role in production using PSEs (presuming that private capital will not) is unlikely to be effective. To be effective, the state must assist the emergence of entrepreneurs and direct them into new areas of production, including cajoling them to meet challenges in the global market.

Based on his comparative study of Egypt, India, Mexico, and Turkey, Waterbury (1993) also says that PSEs perform less efficiently in economic terms than firms in the private sector. He attributes this in part to the principal–agent problem caused by the ill-defined nature of the public property regime. Various principals and agents, including political leaders, managers, and labor, behave rationally to maximize their utility within the incentive structure offered to them.

Table 9.2 Revenues, profit before tax (PBT), value-added (V.A.) and employment at ITI (revenues in millions of current rupees, PBT and V.A. as a % of revenue)

Year	Revenues		PBT (%)	V.A. (%)	Employees
	Value	Growth			
1973–1974	498.3		13.43	n.a.	18,245
1974–1975	635.1	27.45	13.62	n.a.	19,963
1975–1976	753.7	18.67	9.70	n.a.	22,040
1976–1977	880.9	16.88	11.78	n.a.	23,771
1977–1978	921.6	4.62	10.42	n.a.	25,153
1978–1979	929.3	0.84	6.24	n.a.	26,021
1979–1980	1,093.7	17.69	11.26	62.11	26,799
1980–1981	853.9	−21.93	2.26	61.71	26,836
1981–1982	1,572.6	84.17	11.08	57.51	27,872
1982–1983	1,820.5	15.76	12.83	58.56	27,325
1983–1984	2,121.1	16.51	9.79	61.02	28,368
1984–1985	2,369.3	11.70	11.04	61.92	30,126
1985–1986	2,995.3	26.42	5.23	62.64	31,439
1986–1987	4,407.0	47.13	11.91	59.79	32.023
1987–1988	5,084.8	15.38	3.60	60.98	32,447
1988–1989	6,251.8	22.95	4.47	65.05	32,369
1989–1990	9,587.5	53.36	3.67	51.73	32,298
1990–1991	9,784.6	2.06	6.70	53.11	31,831
1991–1992	10,847.0	10.86	7.21	57.61	30,280
1992–1993	14,839.5	36.81	12.80	50.83	29,730
1993–1994	15,272.5	2.92	11.55	48.72	28,633
1994–1995	10,366.2	−32.13	−7.90	40.88	27,477
1995–1996	7,826.2	−24.50	−36.28		26,272

Source: ITI *Annual Report*, various years.

A regulatory environment typically characterized by administratively determined prices, exchange rates, and market configuration shapes this structure. Another reason for the relatively poor performance of PSEs is the multiple goals they are expected to meet: from generating surpluses for the state, to generating employment and new technologies, to promoting economic development in underdeveloped regions.

Works on the Indian economy, including Ahluwalia (1985), Nayar (1989), and Bardhan (1998), broadly agree with Waterbury's analysis about the limits to the PSE-led ISI model. Similarly, Sridharan (1996) argues that the Indian electronics industry was a relatively poor performer in comparison with its Brazilian and South Korean counterparts. He attributes the poor performance of the PSE-dominated Indian electronics industry, at least until India began to move away from ISI policies in the 1980s, to the pursuit of six major goals: growth, employment generation, exports, self-reliance from imports (including technology), promoting downstream applications and productivity, and regional balance. He adds that the industry was unsuccessful in meeting all but one of these goals and an "...unqualified yes is possible only in one sphere, regional balance. Plants

Table 9.3 Relative importance of ITI's equipment division (as a % of total revenue)

Year	Equipment					Telephone instruments	Transmission	Others
	Switching							
	Strowger	Crossbar	ESS[a]	Total				
1959–1960	63.66			63.66		22.13	12.02	2.19
1964–1965	59.28			59.28		13.64	24.81	2.27
1969–1970	44.71	19.04		63.75		11.65	22.59	2.01
1974–1975	28.86	24.39		53.25		12.74	31.65	2.36
1979–1980	28.87	17.82	0.36	47.05		17.28	27.48	8.20
1984–1985	27.89	20.86	1.14	49.89		19.52	24.94	5.65
1989–1990	10.83	5.00	48.25	64.08		9.01	26.20	5.65
1993–1994	3.30[b]		59.30	62.60		6.13	30.25	1.02

Source: ITI *Annual Report*, various years.

Notes

a ESS – electronic switching systems.

b Though the manufacture of strowger and crossbar exchanges were phased out in 1992 and 1993 respectively, ITI continued to supply spares for exchanges still in use.

have been set up in almost all states; most have their own public sector enterprises, and production has been dispersed" (p. 152).

While Waterbury's analysis provides an understanding of how the pursuit of multiple goals by the Indian electronics industry led to its relatively weak performance, this chapter will use the case of ITI to show how even the one aspect that Sridharan mentions as a success, i.e. the dispersal of production, contributed to the weakness. Establishing PSEs to achieve balanced regional development is no guarantee they will generate propulsive growth poles, unless they can also innovate. Technological and institutional innovation is crucial to ensure increasing productivity that, in turn, is the key to long-run development (Solow, 1957; Romer 1986). Competitive advantage, too, can be sustained only with continuous innovation, even if technology is initially borrowed (Porter, 1990). Yet, geography does matter for innovation, although an account of its role cannot be confined to the Perrouxian growth pole, which is based on linkages in economic space and is fundamentally not a geographical concept.

Drawing on Williamson's (1975, 1985) work on markets and hierarchies, Scott (1988a, 1988b) shows how innovation occurs in agglomerations of firms. To Scott, a technologically innovative region will contain a flexibly organized production complex with many specialized firms transacting with one another, i.e. a decentralized production network with a well developed division of labor and labor market, offering producers high levels of external economies of scale and scope. Subsequent studies, while acknowledging the importance of the firm and labor markets in innovative regions, argue that a wider array of regional institutions are essential to overcome collective action problems. These range from those that provide tangible public goods, such as physical infrastructure and education, to those that generate what Storper (1997) terms "untraded dependencies" to build trust, since economic transactions rest on social norms and novel ideas are unlikely to be shared with strangers.

For instance, Saxenian (1994) describes how the production network of large and small semiconductor firms in Silicon Valley is supported by a regional industrial system with various professional and quasi-professional institutions. These include law firms specializing in intellectual property (IP), academic institutions, from community colleges to research universities such as Stanford, and venture capitalists. Crucial to learning and innovation is the mobility of professionals across the "blurred boundaries" of the many institutions in the Valley. The mobility helps them play multiple roles, enhancing trust and leading to the sharing, validation, and diffusion of ideas, and creating a "technical community."

The second and third section will analyze, respectively, how state action affected the geography of production and technological and organizational innovation in the telecommunications equipment and computer software industries in Bangalore. The second section describes how the pursuit of regional balance crippled ITI as it was forced by the state to establish multiple plants across the country, in locations often chosen for political reasons. Then it shows how continued state interference made it difficult for ITI to cope with the erosion of its status as a monopoly producer of switching equipment following the onset of electronic switching and liberal economic policies from the mid-1980s. The problems, as the remainder of the second section will point out, were also partly due to the difficulty ITI had in obtaining reliable components from its network of small suppliers from whom it was forced to buy to comply with public policy.

In contrast to the domestic focus of ITI, the third section traces the rise of the export-intensive software service industry. The section explains why, despite becoming the center of the industry in the liberal economic climate of the 1990s, Bangalore lacked the innovative milieu of Silicon Valley. Indeed, with little local interaction between export-oriented firms and other institutions, the industry responded to surging labor market pressures and the spread of communications infrastructure with simultaneous decentralization away from Bangalore. However, as the section goes on to discuss, after 2001, alongside decentralization, forces of agglomeration began to assert themselves in Bangalore. With the global decline in demand for software professionals, following the overinvestment in IT, there was a reverse flow of expatriate Indians with entrepreneurial and technical skills, mostly to Bangalore. Their skills built on the existing labor pool in Bangalore to help move the industry into higher skill activities, especially the design of embedded systems.

This chapter concludes by pointing to some policy lessons for regional industrialization in developing countries by drawing on the experiences of the two Indian cases. It will emphasize that *local* success of a sector increasingly depends on building relations in *global* economic space. But building relations in global space and ensuring growth to cope with technological change is not merely a matter of freeing a sector or an economy from ISI policies. Sector-specific promotional intervention is necessary, although policies explicitly to achieve a politically defined "regional balance" cannot ensure the local success of a sector. For any regional policy to be effective, it must build the institutional means to ensure the continuous production and upgrading of key inputs and infrastructure. Yet, while access to inputs can draw firms and other producers to a region, a collection of firms is not a sufficient basis for an innovative region. The absence of social mechanisms to support continuous innovation is likely to hamper the effective exploitation of any advantage conferred by the access to inputs, i.e. it is akin to static comparative advantage that is eventually eroded.

Switching equipment manufacture and the case of ITI

ITI's relationship to the state and the geography of production

Nearly 50 years after independence, India had one of the lowest telephone densities in the world, and even this limited service was of relatively poor quality (Chowdary, 1997). The Indian state-dominated telecommunications served as policymaker and regulator of the industry, with the Post and Telegraph (P&T) department, an over-manned public-sector monopoly, being the service provider. Despite the poor quality, the wait lists for service were long, reflecting unmet demand. The poor quality of service also reflected the quality of equipment and technology used in the network, although much of the equipment was manufactured in the country by public sector monopolies under the P&T, primarily ITI.

ITI's problems with quality were ironic considering that, as one of the earliest and largest manufacturing firms established in independent India, it was a pioneer in introducing various techniques in industrial engineering and other systems disciplines to the country critical to manufacturing.[4] Through the years, however, the luxury of being a monopoly supplier, with a guaranteed market for its products, had exerted few competitive pressures. The lack of competitive pressures also meant that, despite having a large R&D department, research at ITI lacked focus.

ITI's problems with manufacturing quality were, however, not entirely of its own making, and must also be understood in the context of its relationship to its owner – the Indian state. ITI's manufacturing facilities were limited to its Bangalore plant until 1970, when a plant was opened in Srinagar to produce components and telephone instruments. In October 1969, the Government of India (GoI) sanctioned a plant in Naini, Uttar Pradesh (UP), 1,500 kilometers from Bangalore, a political decision that made little operational sense. Unfortunately for ITI, more such decisions followed (see Figure 9.1). In January 1976, a plant was inaugurated in Palakkad, Kerala. In April 1976, former Prime Minister (PM) Indira Gandhi inaugurated another plant in Rae Bareli, also in UP, and in what was then her parliamentary constituency. What made the Rae Bareli decision doubly absurd was the product mix. Rae Bareli started by producing strowger switches, based on improvements to an obsolete technology acquired 25 years earlier. A second plant opened there in 1982–1983 to produce crossbar switches just as negotiations with Alcatel of France were being completed for the E-10B ESS.

The fragmentation of manufacturing capacity in different plants scattered across the country prevented ITI from enjoying economies of scale and led to the under-utilization of capacity and personnel in Bangalore, even as additions to capacity and employment were taking place elsewhere. But since the locational choices, with the attendant decisions to hire staff locally, were taken for political reasons, there was little that ITI could do about them. The problems between ITI and the state became more acute in the 1980s following institutional changes at the Department of Telecommunications (DoT, as P&T came to be known) and, more importantly, the advent of new ESS technology.

The challenge of new technologies and the decline of ITI

The 1980s began for ITI with labor strife (Subramanian, 1997a, 1997b), as a result of which revenues in 1980–1981 fell by almost 22 percent (see Table 9.2). Though revenues increased by 84 percent the following year, and grew rapidly until the early 1990s, the problems that ITI faced during the 1980s eventually

Figure 9.1 The geography of ITI's facilities.

devastated it by the mid-1990s. Although a major problem ITI faced in the 1980s had to do with labor, it had little to do with industrial relations. Instead, continuing political and bureaucratic interference made it difficult for ITI to tackle the problem of overstaffing that resulted from the twin challenges of introducing new ESS technology and the erosion of its status as a monopoly producer of telecommunications equipment.

ITI's entry into electronic switching came with the manufacture of EPABX (electronic private automatic branch exchange) systems in 1976. These products, however, were not commercially successful (Meemamsi, 1993). This aborted effort was followed by a more significant effort to introduce electronic switching centered on technologies from Alcatel and the Center for Development of Telematics (C-DoT). C-DoT was established in 1984 in Bangalore as an independent body to develop ESS for Indian conditions.[5] What C-DoT promised to deliver was a family of switches based on a modular architecture, eventually leading up to a 40,000-line main automatic exchange (MAX-XL) in three years.

ITI's plan for the 6th Five-year plan (1980–1985) included the establishing of two new plants, in Mankapur in UP, and in Bangalore, with an annual capacity of 500,000 lines each, to manufacture Alcatel's E-10B ESS. Although Mankapur had little infrastructure, it was chosen because it fell within the constituency of an influential Congress party MP (Parthasarathy, 2000). This was one more disastrous political decision imposed on ITI. But more than the costs imposed by the decision to locate an ESS plant in Mankapur, it was the delay in the Bangalore ESS project that badly hurt ITI. When C-DoT started operations, the E-10B project in Bangalore was put on hold with the idea that the Bangalore ESS plant would manufacture the MAX-XL. By late 1986, however, convinced that C-DoT would not stick to its schedule, ITI began to negotiate with Alcatel. But the GoI put the negotiations on hold. ITI Chairman Nambiar then proposed that the Bangalore ESS plant manufacture 300,000 lines using Alcatel technology and rely on C-DoT technology for the remaining 200,000 lines. With crossbar phased out in Bangalore in 1987–1988, and Rae Bareli to follow, Nambiar warned that underemployment threatened ITI unless remedial measures were taken.

While Nambiar was ignored, his concerns about underemployment were vindicated. Unable to synchronize the introduction of new products following the phasing out of crossbar in Bangalore, ITI was saddled with redundant hands even as it hired afresh in Mankapur. On April 1, 1985, when production began to taper off, there were 2,774 employees in the crossbar division in Bangalore, 65.81 percent of whom were below the age of 40 (ITI, nd: 7). Though it was clear that the division was to be shut down, most employees were not terribly concerned about their future. Since it was near impossible for public sector employees to be retrenched, or be ordered to transfer to another plant, ITI's employees could afford to be complacent.

ITI's strategy to deal with this reality was to retrain and redeploy the employees rendered redundant. While redeployment was not going to be easy even in the best of circumstances, since the manufacture of electronic switches is not as labor-intensive as electro-mechanical switches, the composition of employees in the crossbar division made the process even harder. Of the 2,774 employees, only 5.4 percent had any training pertaining to electronics, while 34 percent had not completed schooling (ITI, nd: 7), reflecting the requirements of crossbar production. Similarly, 67.2 percent held unskilled positions (ibid.: 8). ITI's retraining involved one- to four-week courses in the basics of digital electronics, followed by on-the-job training. Redeployment was only partially successful and, by 1989, the crossbar division still employed 1,410 employees (see Table 9.4a). Most of those who remained were the poorly qualified, though they might have received some training (see Table 9.4b). The division was eventually renamed the Electronics Switching Division and took up the manufacture of small switches (<2,000 lines).

But ITI's overhead was such that it could not survive by merely making small

Table 9.4a Employees in ITI's Bangalore crossbar division, 1985–1989

Date	Number of employees	Redeployed	Retirement, death, etc.	Total outflow
April 1, 1985	2,774			
April 1, 1986	2,769		5	5
April 1, 1987	2,343	391	35	426
April 1, 1988[a]	2,156	394	43	437
May 27, 1989	1,410	698	48	746
Total		1,483	131	1,614

Source: ITI (nd: 13).

Note
a   250 personnel added to the division due to divisionalization of finance, administration plant, shipping, inward goods/inspection, and industrial engineering departments.

Table 9.4b Qualifications of employees in ITI's electronic switching division, 1989 (by % on 27 May)

Qualifications	%
High school or less	71.98
Trade Certificate	7.16
Engineering Diploma	11.84
Engineering Degree	2.62
Non-technical degree	6.38

Source: ITI (nd: Appendix 1).

switches; it had to manufacture a range of telecommunications equipment, especially large switches (>10,000 lines), to be profitable (Parthasarathy, 2000). ITI also had to contend with competition for small switches as C-DoT made a dent in the public sector monopoly by widely licensing its products. C-DoT's effort reflected a cautious effort to liberalize the policy regime from the early 1980s to encourage trade and private investment to address India's relatively poor economic record (Sridharan, 1996).

At the end of the 1980s, ITI was still a rapidly growing and profitable company (see Table 2). A closer look at plant-level figures, however, shows wide disparities. In 1988–1989, while the main plant in Bangalore accounted for 47.35 percent of the company's employment (ITI *Annual Report*, 1990), its per capita revenue was the lowest among ITI's major plants (see Table 9.5). The figures for Rae Bareli, the second largest plant in terms of employment, were closer to Bangalore as both locations continued to make strowger and crossbar switches. In contrast, the revenues in Palakkad and Mankapur were much higher as they manufactured the E-10B.

ITI was not unaware of the problems it faced, but confidently proclaimed it could meet any challenge, as the production targets it set for itself for the early

Table 9.5 Revenue per employee at ITI's manufacturing plants (in current rupees)

Year	Bangalore		Naini	Rae Bareli	Mankapur	Palakkad	Srinagar
	Main	EC Factory					
1988–1989	152,207	4,124	198,038	160,553	729,029	618,780	429,046
1989–1990	188,981	n.a.	262,983	149,725	1,622,238	1,230,000	315,000
1990–1991	198,557	n.a.	326,588	162,052	1,407,563	700,114	128,571
1991–1992	244,044	1,902,657	367,494	208,375	1,191,439	977,390	78,621
1992–1993	360,333	3,211,435	655,774	n.a.	1,225,573	1,088,035	55,128
1993–1994	330,803	3,393,348	647,064	204,826	1,533,400	1,808,527	85,443
1994–1995	279,457	2,261,283	264,359	154,282	1,194,800	1,353,924	77,419

Source: derived from ITI *Annual Report*, various years.

1990s indicate (see Table 9.6). If the company had met those targets, it would have commanded 41.29 percent of the national market for telecommunications equipment by 1995. But, as the table shows, the actual figure was only 13.38 percent. Although ITI's revenue grew by nearly 60 percent between 1989–1990 and 1993–1994, in the next two years, revenue fell to less than what it was in 1989–1990 (see Table 9.2). The fall meant that 1994–1995 was the first loss-making year in ITI's history. ITI's value-added, as a percentage of revenue, after fluctuating between 55 and 65 percent until 1989–1990, also dropped to 40.88 percent by 1994–1995.

ITI declined even as the state's hold on it loosened by the early 1990s. In 1991, the GoI also shed 20 percent of its equity in favor of various financial institutions. But such changes were not enough to deal effectively with an intensification of the problems of the 1980s. After crossbar was phased out in Bangalore, strowger was also phased out by 1989–1990. Similarly, both crossbar and strowger were phased out in Rae Bareli by 1991–1992 and 1992–1993, respectively. With more than 10,000 employees (4,300 from the strowger division in Bangalore and about 6,200 in Rae Bareli) having little to do, ITI had an urgent need for new technology and products. While waiting for C-DoT to deliver its MAX-XL, ITI began independently to develop its own large, state-of-the art switch, the XD-90, in 1988. By 1995, however, after having invested nearly 100 person-years, ITI talked about abandoning the XD-90 and developing a few auxiliary products with the lessons from the project (Rao, 1995b).

The XD-90 suffered from turnover in key personnel (Rao, 1995a). Ever since 1987–1988, when employment peaked at 32,447, ITI tried to reduce its workforce. A Voluntary Retirement Scheme offered in August 1991 reduced the workforce to 27,447 by 1994–1995. Welcome as this was, the problem was that the wrong people were leaving. Almost all the reduction was in Bangalore, where the main plant shrank by a third between 1988–1989 and 1994–1995, from 15,335 to 10,159, while R&D shrank by a fourth in the same period, from 1,671 to 1,263 (ITI *Annual Report*, various years). Though there was a steady loss of R&D talent when C-DoT opened its doors, the dam burst after the lack of

Table 9.6 ITI's share of national telecommunications equipment production (production figures in millions of rupees, 1990–1991 to 1994–1995)

Year	National production	ITI's target value production		Achieved
		% share	% share	
1990–1991	30,570	13,870	45.37	32.01
1991–1992	39,850	17,000	42.66	27.22
1992–1993	55,000	21,000	38,18	26.98
1993–1994	70,000	26,130	37.33	21.82
1994–1995	77,500	32,000	41.29	13.38

Source: National production data from DoT *Annual Report* (1996–1997: 37); ITI target production figures from ITI *Annual Report* (1988–1989: 5).

support to the XD-90 became evident. Thus, ITI remained overstaffed with the wrong kind of employees.

The departure of R&D talent had to do with the opportunities opening up outside the public sector. In 1991, induced by a balance of payments crisis, there was a major shift in economic policies, including devaluation of the Rupee, trade liberalization and duty rationalization, openness to foreign investment, and the announcement of a New Industrial Policy (NIP).[6] The NIP lowered entry barriers for new firms in most sectors and ended any remaining public sector monopoly in switching. After receiving DoT validation, many MNCs (multinational corporations) established production facilities in India in part because software increasingly became the critical input for switching, and for telecommunications in general. The presence of highly skilled labor pools in ITI and C-DoT drew telecommunications firms to Bangalore. *Voice and Data*, a trade journal, listed 13 MNCs that were sourcing telecommunications software from India by August 1996.[7] This list, however, included only those MNCs that had either a subsidiary or a joint venture with an Indian partner. It did not include the many Indian firms developing software on contract. Thus, a number of significantly better-paying jobs opened up for ITI employees, especially the R&D people, in Bangalore.

MNCs began to compete aggressively with ITI not only for employees but also for a share of the domestic market when the DoT adopted an open-tendering system for large switches in 1993–1994.[8] Though 35 percent of DoT orders were reserved for PSEs, the old cost-plus formula was no longer the basis for procurement. Instead, the DoT chose to buy at the lowest rate since its goal, as a service provider, was to expand the network rapidly. The damage inflicted on ITI by the drop in prices and the shortfall in orders only reflected the extent to which ITI depended on the DoT. Even as the company's annual reports in the early 1990s emphasized the need to reduce dependence on the DoT, ITI's dependence, as measured by percentage of revenues, crossed 90 percent in 1989–1990, and peaked at 95.27 percent in 1993–1994 (see Table 9.7). It fell to 82.86 percent the

Table 9.7 ITI's dependence on DoT and exports (as a percentage of revenues)

Year	DoT	Exports
1971–1972	79.19	0.96
1975–1976	83.76	1.94
1980–1981	88.27	1.32
1987–1988	89.22	0.07
1988–1989	88.05	0.05
1989–1990	91.84	negligible
1990–1991	93.33	negligible
1991–1992	93.27	0.10
1992–1993	92.80	0.06
1993–1994	95.27	0.15
1994–1995	82.86	0.27

Source: ITI *Annual Report*, various years.

following year, not because of successful diversification but due to the fall in orders from the DoT. ITI's problem was that it tended to view the vigorous pursuit of other markets as a wasteful expenditure that might create a rift with the DoT (Kaushal, 1997).

Apart from trying to expand its domestic market, ITI also decided to pay more attention to exports. As Table 9.7 shows, exports were never a significant source of revenue for ITI. This was partly because, with ITI barely able to meet the needs of DoT, there was little left to export. Furthermore, ITI could export as long as it had a well-developed technology, as was the case with electro-mechanical switches. With the coming of ESS and ITI itself struggling to obtain and absorb the technology, exports became negligible by the late 1980s.

The rise and fall of ITI's production networks

Another important reason why ITI's products were not very reliable was because it operated in an environment where the practice of ISI resulted in the production of obsolete equipment without necessarily reducing import-dependent production. This was because India relied heavily on imported components (Sridharan, 1996). Being a vertically integrated establishment, ITI did produce some of the components it needed, but the company had to rely on external sources for at least two reasons. First, since ITI manufactured a wide range of equipment for a small market, the extent to which it could economically produce components in-house was limited.

Second, ITI was forced to buy many components from small-scale industries (SSIs) and "ancillaries," which were promoted since the 1950s as an important aspect of Indian industrial policy.[9] SSIs are defined by an investment limit in plant and machinery.[10] There are various promotional measures to encourage SSIs. They are exempt from licensing procedures and are encouraged with fiscal incentives, including limited excise duty, sales tax, and concessional credit. A set of protective measures complements the promotional measures. The key protective measure is product reservation. By 1980, 836 products were reserved exclusively for manufacture by SSIs. Product reservation led to the fragmentation of production in an already tiny market and did not encourage the investments to manufacture scale-sensitive electronic components at internationally acceptable quality or prices. ITI was thus forced to produce in an environment where reliable components were difficult to obtain.

The Working Group on SSIs in 1965 defined an ancillary unit as one that supplied parts, subassemblies, components or tooling to a final producer, and permitted it higher investment limits than other SSIs.[11] Through time, the term *ancillary industry* came to refer to a firm dedicated to producing parts, components, or services for PSEs (Gupta and Goldar, 1995). In February 1971, the Bureau of Public Enterprises required all PSEs to commit themselves to ancillary development by appointing a manager for ancillary development, identifying items for ancillaries to manufacture, guaranteeing the purchase of at least 50 percent of ancillaries' output, and allowing a price preference of up to 15 percent more than landed costs. Guidelines issued in 1974 required all PSE proposals for capacity expansion or foreign technology arrangements to be accompanied by a commitment to subcontract and to extend know-how to SSIs and ancillaries. If ancillaries had any difficulty in obtaining land, land available with the PSEs had to be allotted to them. ITI, too, set up an industrial estate outside its Bangalore plant in 1972 for ancillaries. The estate started with 20 units, and many of the entrepreneurs were former ITI employees. Following a second phase of expansion, the number of ancillaries went up to 45 by 1976. By the mid-1980s, the company had more than 109 ancillaries, nearly half of which were in Bangalore (ITI *Annual Report*, various years).

Notwithstanding the policy directives forcing ITI to surround itself with ancillaries and to support them, interaction with them was characterized by arm's-length routine transactions for standardized production. When the ancillaries were first set up, ITI offered to train their employees in the relevant divisions of its plant. But the offer did not develop into any sustained program for skill upgrading. In addition to their limited skills, since the ancillaries were small and undercapitalized, and could not grow except at the risk of losing their ancillary benefits, ITI could only use them as sources of spares and components for older electro-mechanical equipment. ITI supplied the drawings and specifications, along with a list of components and sources, and carried out inspection before buying the output. The final price was settled on a cost-plus basis. Since ITI had supplied the know-how to the ancillaries, they were forbidden to sell elsewhere without permission. But the demand for components and spares from P&T was high, and the margins from the cost plus selling arrangement were good enough to make the arrangement a cozy one for both the ancillaries and ITI. The arrangement was, however, not without its limitations.

For the ancillaries, the arrangement was fine as long as there was guaranteed demand for their products. But when any change in the pattern of demand required them to acquire and adopt new technologies, as happened with arrival of ESS technology in the 1980s, the consequences were severe. Not only did the new switches have fewer components, they also had almost no mechanical components. Further, even the assembly, not to mention the manufacture, of electronic components to stringent quality standards required capital-intensive equipment, which the ancillaries could hardly afford. Thus, the introduction of the E-10B had an immediate impact. ITI's consumption of imported raw materials, components, and spares, as a share of the value of total consumption, went up just as sharply from 34.4 percent in 1984–1985 to 61.3 percent in 1986–1987 (see Table 9.8). Though this figure fell to about 44 percent in the mid-1990s, it was higher than the norm of 30 percent or less in the days when electro-mechanical switches ruled. The rise in the import content at ITI showed that the capacity to produce a range of competitively priced professional-grade components did not exist in India.

The phasing out of electro-mechanical switches brought more bad news for the ancillaries. In order to keep its own workforce occupied, ITI further cut back on purchases from ancillaries, to make the spares and components in-house (ITI,

Table 9.8 Consumption of imported raw material, components and spares at ITI (as a percentage of the value of total consumption based on current prices)

Year	Imports
1976–1979	19.70
1979–1980	30.21
1984–1985	34.40
1985–1986	47.69
1986–1987	61.30
1989–1990	63.89
1990–1991	53.01
1991–1992	46.45
1992–1993	42.57
1993–1994	41.21
1994–1995	44.11

Source: ITI *Annual Report*, various years.

Table 9.9 Sales of ITT's ancillaries (as a percentage of ITI's revenues)

Year	Bangalore	Naini	Rae Bareli	Srinagar	Total
1972–1973	3.00				3.00
1975–1976	2.81	0.46			3.28
1979–1980					5.30
1982–1983					4.94
1987–1988					1.83
1990–1991	0.56	0.42	0.43	0.02	1.43
1991–1992	0.21	0.22	0.49	0.03	0.95
1992–1993	0.14	0.21	0.15		0.50
1993–1994	0.03	0.20	0.01		0.24
1994–1995	0.04	0.18			0.22

Source: ITI *Annual Report*, various years, and data provided by company.

nd: 8). After ITI's purchases from its ancillaries peaked at about 5 percent of its revenues in the early 1980s, they fell to 0.22 percent by 1994–1995 and the share of the 46 ancillaries in Bangalore declined to a mere 0.04 percent (see Table 9.9). As a result, the problems faced by ITI since the mid-1980s, and its subsequent decline in the 1990s, led not only to a shrinking of telecommunications manufacture in Bangalore, it also hurt the region to the extent that ITI purchased inputs from SSIs and ancillaries.

Toward India's Silicon Valley? The computer software industry in Bangalore

The growth and upgrading of the Indian software industry, 1985–2000

The highlight of the Indian computing industry until the early 1980s was the failure by the Electronics Corporation of India, a PSE with a domestic monopoly, to develop a commercially successful computer, and the forcing of IBM to shut its operations in 1978 (Grieco, 1984). Following IBM's departure, many of its former employees established service bureaus, which leased out computer time, before graduating to software development (Subramanian, 1992). This was the origin of the software industry in the private sector.

The cautious efforts to liberalize the policy regime in the 1980s involved many initiatives to ensure that India, after having missed out on the globalization of the semiconductor industry (Henderson, 1989), could take advantage of the globalization of the software industry and become to software what Taiwan and Korea were to hardware (Lakha, 1990). Two key initiatives were the Computer Policy of November 1984, and the Computer Software Export, Development and Training Policy of December 1986 (Subramanian, 1992). The 1984 policy, besides easing the local manufacture and availability of computers, recognized software as an "industry," making it eligible for various allowances and incentives. It also lowered duties on software imports, and made software exports a priority. The 1986 policy aimed at increasing India's share of world software production. Industry was to be independent, with the government stepping in to provide only promotional and infrastructure support. Overall, this policy was an explicit rejection of ISI and the ideology of self-reliance in the software sector.

Despite the initiatives, exporting in this phase typically involved little more than *bodyshopping*, or the practice of providing inexpensive on-site (i.e. at customer locations overseas) labor on an hourly basis, for low value-added programming services such as coding and testing. Bodyshopping had its advantages and limitations. On one hand, it meant "input-less exports," requiring only a contact overseas, a little finance, and local programmers who could be sent on-site (Heeks, 1996). The drawback, however, was an underutilization of the skills of well-trained professionals, many of whom tended to quit seeking technically more challenging and better paying jobs once sent overseas. The high turnover only reinforced the tendency of Indian firms to compete on the basis of low costs rather than being able to fall back on a repository of technical and managerial expertise acquired from previous projects.

Although bodyshopping seems like a quick-buck strategy, for firms from a country that had hitherto not merited any attention as a source of IT products, there was no alternative to on-site services in the 1980s to gain the confidence of global customers (Parthasarathy, 2000). Furthermore, while Indian engineers had the necessary technical skills, they had trained in a closed economy. On-site services provided exposure to market trends, management processes, and socially specific communication protocols in addition to emerging technologies. The official encouragement given to bodyshopping reflected a limited understanding of the industry among policymakers: software was widely perceived as being "hi-tech" without adequate distinction made between the different stages of production or the corresponding value added.

Paving the way for a better understanding of the industry, and policy support, was a shift in the approach to policymaking. Whereas until the 1980s, it was concentrated within a closed bureaucratic apparatus, since then the state has increasingly attempted to draw on industry feedback to make policies (Evans, 1995). Based on inputs from the industry, which in 1988 formed the National Association of Software and Services Companies (NASSCOM), subsequent policy measures tried to promote the industry more proactively. The clearest instance of this was the establishment, in 1990, of the Software Technology Parks (STPs). As export zones dedicated to the software industry, the STPs offered data communication facilities that firms could use to offer offshore services, i.e. service provision from India, instead of having to work at customer sites overseas.[12] In 1991, the year after the STPs were established, came the New Industrial Policy (NIP) and the economy-wide shift toward liberal policies.

The shift to offshore services in a more liberal economic environment marked the beginning of a new relationship between the Indian software industry and global markets. According to Sen's (1994) analysis of quarterly export growth, between 1987 and 1992–1993, a linear equation provides the best fit for the growth. From 1992–1993 until 1994, however, an exponential equation provides a better fit. Although Sen had insufficient data to determine if it was a long-term trend, he projected that if exports maintained the exponential trajectory, they would reach $630 million by 1997. Since actual exports in 1996–1997 were $1.1 billion (see Table 9.1), there was clearly a change in the growth characteristics of Indian software exports.[13]

While the conscious policies since 1984 were crucial in facilitating the change, reinforcing their efficacy were certain serendipitous benefits conferred by the policies of earlier years. Despite widespread illiteracy, Indian education policies managed to create a large pool of skilled labor that, in a relatively slow-growing economy, suffered from underemployment if not unemployment. This pool offered a ready resource to meet the growing demand for high-skill, low-wage software professionals, especially in industrialized economies taking advantage of the PC and networking revolutions of the 1970s and 1980s.[14] The colonial legacy also meant that this labor was mostly educated in English. India's most pointed advantage came, however, not merely from the low-cost, English-speaking labor but from the skills embodied in it. Following IBM's departure, and the unsuccessful local efforts to build a commercially viable computer, users had to rely on imports. Since high duties were a disincentive to import, mainframes never had a significant presence in India, and the few that were imported were of various vintages and sources (Harding, 1989). The experience gained by working on a variety of platforms in the 1970s helped the

Indians win labor-intensive contracts to maintain older systems in the 1980s and 1990s.[15]

A geographical accident benefitting Indian firms is the 12.5 hours difference with the US, their main market, allowing them to undertake offshore maintenance after regular users there have left for the day. This meant lower costs and profitability as professionals in India are paid an Indian wage, whereas, once abroad, they are also paid an overseas allowance (Heeks, 1996). Offshore development also offers the advantage of having most employees under one roof, instead of them being scattered across customer sites, allowing the firm to build a repository of knowledge to compete for subsequent projects, and to move employees across projects.

It was against the backdrop of such conscious efforts and unforeseen benefits that the STPs helped transform the industry in the 1990s, and the share of offshore services in software exports increased from 5 percent in 1990 to 38.6 percent in 2000–2001 (see Table 9.10). Software factories emerged in India, with the infrastructure, technology, quality processes, productivity tools, and methodologies of the customer workplace. For instance, by June 2002, 85 firms were certified at Level 5, the highest level of the Software Engineering Institute's (SEI) five-stage Capability Maturity Model (CMM), compared with 42 in the rest of the world, with Polaris Software being the first company in the world to obtain CMMi Level 5 certification.[16]

Indian firms seek quality certification in part because a well-defined process improves their ability to estimate and manage the time and resources required for a project, helping them bid for more profitable turnkey projects (Arora and Asundi, 1999). Turnkey contracts demand substantial management skills, requiring firms to coordinate a much wider range of tasks than just programming, and

Table 9.10 Sources of India's software export revenues, 1990–2003 (as a percentage of export revenues)

Year	Onsite services	Offshore services	Products and packages
1990	90.00	5.00	5.00
1993–1994	62.01	30.05	7.94
1994–1995	60.90	29.59	9.51
1995–1996	60.32	31.63	8.05
1996–1997	58.69	30.21	11.10
1997–1998	59,00	32.20	8.80
1998–1999	58.18	33.91	7.91
1999–2000	57.26	34.69	8.05
2000–2001	56.09	38.62	5.29
2001–2002	45.21	50.69	4.10
2002–2003	38.95	57.90	3.15

Source: www.nasscom.org; National Association of Software and Service Companies (NASSCOM). (2001) *Indian IT and Software Services Directory, 2001.* NASSCOM.

Note
Data from 2002–2003 is an estimate.

to take responsibility for the overall project schedule, quality, and productivity, in contrast to bodyshopping, which is little more than resume selling.

Apart from the shift to offshore services by large Indian firms, the liberal economic climate of the 1990s also witnessed an influx of MNCs, including IBM's return, to establish offshore development centers (ODCs). The ODCs capitalized on the communications infrastructure at the STPs and on Indian skills. But when MNCs began trickling into India from the mid-1980s, they chose to put software engineers in India on a learning curve and some even started off with internal bodyshopping. By the 1990s, however, MNC ODCs shed their subordinate status and were undertaking projects either jointly or independently, as equal partners, with their parent organizations. Some even outdid their parent organizations. For instance, in 1994, Motorola's Bangalore center was only one of two software centers worldwide (the other being Loral's space shuttle software project in the US) to attain level-five SEI-CMM certification (Sims, 1994).

Within India, software factories and development centers began sprouting in regions with skilled labor and communications facilities, both of which were available in Bangalore. In the 1980s, prominent domestic firms, such as Infosys, and the early trickle of MNCs to India, located themselves in Bangalore. They were attracted by the concentration of skilled labor in the region, initially in PSEs and government laboratories in sectors such as aerospace, electronics, and telecommunications,[17] and subsequently replenished by the large numbers of graduates from the engineering colleges of the province of Karnataka (of which Bangalore is the capital) and those adjoining it (see Table 9.11).

As establishing the first STP in Bangalore provided the necessary infrastructure to reinforce the formidable skill advantages the region already possessed, Bangalore became central to the expansion plans of domestic firms, and the first choice within India for the large number of companies from Silicon Valley wanting to establish ODCs in the country (Rao, 1995a, see Table 9.12). While it is the concentration of domestic and MNCs, and the transformation of the software industry following the shift to offshore services, that have led to Bangalore being called India's Silicon Valley, Parthasarathy (2004) argues that it is more

Table 9.11 Number of approved engineering colleges and intake (as on January 21, 1999)

State	Colleges	Intake
All India	663	156,493
Karnataka	70	24,752
Tamil Nadu	129	32,160
Maharashtra	118	28,985
Andhra Pradesh	88	20,285
4 contiguous provinces as percentage of all India	405 / 61.09	106,182 / 67.85

Source: AICTE (1999: Annexure 4.1).

Table 9.12 Spatial distribution of the Indian software industry, 2000–2001 (by percentage share of exports and by location of headquarters of NASSCOM's 700 largest members)

Region	Export (%)	Headquarters[a]
Bangalore	26.64	160
New Delhi/Gurgaon/Noida	15.34	106
Chennai	10.42	72
Hyderabad	7.02	61
Mumbai/Navi Membai	5.68	148
Pune	3.39	48
Kolkata	0.88	32
Ahmedabad/Gandhinagar	0.36	10
Thiruvananthapuram	0.03	14
Chandigarh/Mohali	0.01	7
Bhubaneshwar	neg.	8
Others	29.96	54

Source: www.bangaloreit.com, NASSCOM (2).

Note

a This is admittedly a crude measure of the spatial organization of the software industry, since many firms have development centers in many cities (as with Infosys).

accurate to describe Bangalore of the 1990s as "Silicon Valley's India" because of the absence of an institutional environment to facilitate the sharing and circulation of ideas that characterizes an innovative milieu like Silicon Valley. There were at least two aspects to the absence of a supportive institutional environment that Parthasarathy identifies.

One, given the dominance of exports in Indian software production (see Table 9.1), most firms in Bangalore addressed overseas markets and their ties were to customers and other firms in the main market, as a result of which there was little interaction among firms, thereby limiting innovation. Confidentiality clauses in export contracts typically limit the ability of Indian firms to subcontract work locally. As for MNC ODCs, although many were developing new products and technologies for their parent bodies, they are often reluctant to share proprietary technologies and have almost no local ties. Further, since academic institutions and public sector firms and laboratories also operated in relative isolation, helping only to supply skilled labor, and venture capital for labor intensive service firms was limited, there were hardly any local institutions to facilitate the sharing and dissemination of ideas in the region. This placed few locational restrictions on firms.

Thus, for instance, in the 1990s, Infosys, in addition to expanding in Bangalore, established development centers in other Indian cities, including Bhubaneshwar, Chennai, Pune, and Mangalore, as well as in North America, the UK, and Japan. The global development centers

expand the capabilities of Infosys' global delivery model to leverage talent and infrastructure in different parts of the world. These centers enhance client comfort and expand ... engagement capabilities, to provide a wider range of services such as business consulting and technology architecture that involve high levels of client interaction over shorter engagement spans. They also complement larger campuses in India to accelerate engagement schedules and distribute engagement execution across multiple locations and time zones.[18]

Whereas Infosys' expansion within India reflected the continued growth opportunities offered by the offshore service provision, its expansion in other cities suggested that local ties were not crucial. The opening of development centers in its main markets suggests that for a firm trying to shift to more value-added work, greater proximity to customers and other firms was becoming essential. That the Infosys experience is not unique is evident from Table 9.10, which shows a sharp increase in the share of offshore export activity in the early 1990s, from 5 to 30 percent, with the commissioning of the STPs. However, between 1996–1997 and 2000–2001, offshore activity increased by only 8.41 percent despite the rapid spread of data communications infrastructure, and the number of STPs doubling from six to a dozen.

Underlying Infosys' moves was a tightening labor market in the 1990s and the absence of what Saxenian calls a "technical community" with a range of capabilities. Having gained a favorable reputation since the 1980s, the Indian software professional no longer depends only on firms in India for employment opportunities. In other words, with globalization, the Indian labor market for software professionals and the global labor market are no longer distinct universes. In the 1990s, with the commercialization of the Internet, the worldwide demand for skills drew Indian professionals in increasing numbers to lucrative opportunities overseas. Just one indicator of the phenomenon is that Indians became the largest recipient of H1-B visas to the US (see Table 9.13).[19] This international demand for Indian skills meant that despite the shift to offshore service provision, the problem of attrition, and holding on to those with special skills, that afflicted firms during the 1980s did not go away.

Table 9.13 H1-B visas issued to Indian nationals (as a percentage of all H1-Bs issued worldwide and rank among countries)

Fiscal year	Worldwide total	Visas to Indians	
		%	*Rank*
1992	110,193	7.48	3
1994	105,889	16.01	1
1996	144,458	20.24	1
1998	240,947	25.96	1
2000	257,640	48.40	1
2001	330,521	48.90	1
2002	197,537	33.00	1

Source: *Statistical Yearbook of the Immigration and Naturalization Service*, various years.

Thus, Parthasarathy (2004) argues, while the 1990s witnessed a quantitative expansion of the Indian software industry and Bangalore's transformation from a low-wage backwater to Silicon Valley's India, that developed software for the world market, a more limited qualitative transformation encouraged industry decentralization to inhibit the transformation of Bangalore to a Silicon Valley-like region that defines new products and technologies.

From turnkey contracts to R&D services: the case of embedded systems

Despite the global slump in demand for IT products following over-investment in the 1990s,[20] the Indian software industry and exports continued to grow after 2001 (see Table 9.1). The growth has been accompanied by a further qualitative shift, as the offerings of the industry are no longer limited to low-valued added services. Instead, it increasingly provides R&D services, which demand IP creation. According to NASSCOM, R&D service exports accounted for US$1.21 billion, or 15.8 percent of software exports, in 2001–2002. The figures grew to US$1.66 billion and 17.4 percent, respectively, in 2002–2003.[21] Central to the growth of R&D services is the provision of embedded systems that contributed US$910 million and 1.1 billion to exports in 2001–2002 and 2002–2003, respectively. The Indian embedded systems industry is centered on Bangalore, and just one indicator of this phenomenon was the formation of the Bangalore-based India Semiconductor Association (ISA) in October 2004 with 32 members to meet the specific needs of the emerging sub-sector of the software industry.[22] The ISA is distinct from the Delhi-based NASSCOM, which caters to a more broadly defined software industry.[23]

If the efforts by firms worldwide to control costs by outsourcing, not just software but everything from R&D services at one end of the skill spectrum to business processes such as voice-based customer support centers (call centers) at the other (Srinivas and Jayashankar, 2002), enabled the industry in India to grow despite the global slump in demand for IT (see Table 9.10 and note the sharp increase in offshore provision after 2001), the growth in the provision of embedded systems can be understood more specifically in terms of shifts in the organization of production in the global semiconductor industry, the changing legal framework and labor market conditions in India, and the emergence of a production network in Bangalore.

An embedded system is any computer that is a component in a larger system and relies on its own microprocessor (Wolf, 2002). The use of embedded systems has grown with more powerful microprocessors. They now find application in everything from consumer goods to transport equipment and industrial process control systems. In these devices, embedded systems not only take over what mechanical and dedicated electronic systems used to do, but they increasingly connect to the Internet. It is the ability to digitally capture and simulate various mechanical or other functions that makes the globalization of R&D in various domains technologically feasible. Thus, for instance, automobile firms such as General Motors and Daimler Chrysler have set up R&D facilities in Bangalore.

Embedded systems design is about adapting software abstractions, designed merely to transform data, to meet real-time constraints, power requirements, and safety considerations in various domains while interacting with the physical world through sensors and actuators (Lee, 2000). Designing embedded systems often requires engineers who are classically trained in the domain of application, say communications. "It is very difficult to replicate a toll-quality speech codec or a radio modem with commodity programmers" (ibid.: 19).

Facilitating the ability of Indian firms to offer their expertise globally in embedded systems, despite semiconductor-manufacturing capabilities in India being practically nonexistent, is the emergence of a new division of labor in the semiconductor industry. The vertically integrated firms that used to characterize the industry have given way to disintegrated firms occupying niches along a pro-duction continuum (Mathews and Cho, 2000). This continuum ranges from the pure play foundries at one end, which offer contract manufacture, to design houses at the other, which rely on other firms to manufacture the chips they design. Firms in India have taken advantage of the changed organization of the industry by partnering with foundries elsewhere to produce their designs.

According to NASSCOM, the global embedded software solutions market was worth US$21 billion in 2003.[24] The telecommunications, computing, and data communications segment dominated the market with a 34 percent share, thanks to voice/data convergence, which required the previously incompatible voice/data equipment of different vertically integrated manufacturers to communicate with one another. The technological and institutional trans-formation created opportunities for new firms and this was the segment that Indian firms first entered (Bhuyan, 2002). In terms of market share, this segment is followed by consumer electronics (20 percent), industrial automation (19 percent), automotive (10 percent), and office automation (8 percent). The global market is estimated to have grown 16 percent in 2004.

To exploit these emerging international opportunities, it is estimated that 30–40 firms entered the business between 1999 and 2002 with investments ranging from US$500,000 to 2.5 million (Hari and Anand, 2002). By 2003, there were more than 100 firms (Hari, 2003), and it was estimated that the IC design and validation industry employed 5,000–7,000 engineers, compared with 300 in 1997 (Menon, 2003). A different indicator of growth and size is the use of electronic design and automation (EDA) tools critical to IC design. The market for EDA tools is estimated to have grown from US$15 million in 1999 (Nair, 1999) to 60 million in 2003 (Menon).[25] Thus, a survey suggested that India is "achieving some sort of critical mass" in chip design (Hari and Anand, 2002:35).

On the domestic front, firms were helped by legal changes, important among which was the passage of the Semiconductor Integrated Circuits Layout–Design Act 2000, which provides for the registration and protection of IC layouts and designs for a ten-year period. Although the act is criticized for protecting only the layout and not going far enough to protect abstract designs and algorithms, even its critics acknowledge that this is a big leap, especially in creating confidence for the growth of the embedded systems industry (Krishnadas, 2000). However, while software patents are not permitted in India, on December 27, 2004, the GoI issued an ordinance to modify the Patent Act "to provide for patents when software has technical applications in industry in combination with hardware," i.e. embedded systems, effective January 1, 2005.[26]

There was also a deepening of the labor market to encourage firms. Thanks to the slump in demand in the US since 2001, the number of H-1B applicants has gone down sharply (see Table 9.13), and NASSCOM estimates that approximately 35,000 professionals returned to India, mostly from the US (Singh, 2003). Of the returnees, an estimated 70 percent are H1-B visa-holders, while another 10–15 percent has been abroad for at least ten years. These people are returning not only because they see international opportunities shrinking, but also because they see India as a place for innovation (Krishnadas, 2003a). One area where innovation is manifest is in R&D services, especially embedded systems, a segment where Indian firms and MNCs in India are very active.[27]

The activities of firms in India in embedded systems can be classified into three categories (Hari and Anand, 2002). First are the vendors who design entire chips. While this is the most profitable category, it also requires deep pockets and, thus, is mostly the realm of MNCs such as Intel, Motorola, and Texas Instruments (TI). In the second category are firms that generate IP to derive revenue from a customer license fee or recurring royalty payments. Although this is lucrative, especially when compared with providing software services on a man-hour basis, it is not without risks. Generating IP requires familiarity with emerging standards for which participation in the relevant international standard setting bodies is valuable. This can be expensive, especially for small firms. In the third category are firms offering contract design services for customers. This is similar to providing software services, in which Indian firms have become competitive globally, with one crucial difference. Those providing design services are very much a part of the embedded systems production chain and interact with either the customer's chief technology officer or the R&D head. In contrast, software services that are outsourced, such as maintaining databases in domains like retailing, while contributing to essential information support systems, do not typically represent the mainstream activity of most customers. Service providers in this case tend to interact with the chief information officer of their customers.

Although the data indicate that embedded systems production did not take off in India until the late-1990s, the origins of the industry can be traced back to the pool of IC designers employed by the Bangalore-based PSEs ITI and Bharat Electronics (Sridharan, 1996). It was this pool of skills that TI capitalized on when it became the first MNC to establish an ODC in Bangalore in 1985. The subsequent evolution of the ODC provides an insight into the emergence of embedded systems production in India. Despite the availability of skills, TI did not immediately plunge into design. Instead, the Bangalore center started off doing maintenance and application work and it was not until the early 1990s that TI developed a design strategy in India.[28] A design center for digital signal processors (DSPs), TI's main line of business, was set up in 1995 and Ankoor, the first commercial DSP fully developed in India, was launched in 1998. Since then, many other DSPs have emerged from the center, in addition to 225 patents and a number of industry awards.

Chip vendors such as TI, however, do not develop their products in isolation. With the growing complexity of embedded systems and the rapid proliferation in their use, the industry is moving toward a design process that integrates reconfigurable, commodity system-on-chip platforms to offer differentiated products for a wide variety of users and application domains (Martin and Schirrmeister, 2002). Platforms are a mechanism to accelerate the design and development of end-user products by providing pre-integrated, pre-verified collections of IP blocks organized into hardware–software architectures. Thus, while TI retains DSP development, globally it has more than 600 independent DSP partners from whom it either buys IP or seeks design services. Forty-seven of its partners are Indian, 31 of which are Bangalore-based.

TI's Indian partners include a mix of large, older, and established firms, as well as newer entrepreneurial start-ups. Even in the former category, one can distinguish between two classes of firms. One class is that which accumulated expertise in the design and development of hardware in the 1980s when the Indian market was protected (Evans, 1995). This includes firms such as Tata Elxsi, Wipro, and HCL. Tata Elxsi used to make peripheral cards and controllers, while Wipro and HCL produced PCs and Unix-based mini-computers. But with liberalization in the 1990s, as it became hard to manufacture locally and compete with the imports of established brands, Wipro, for instance, decided to use its available skills to work for firms whose technology it was familiar with, including Intel and Compaq (Hari, 2001). In another class are the firms that grew by exclusively providing software services. For them the shift to embedded systems is motivated less by short-term financial gain and is more an attempt to gain technological legitimacy in the long run.

If some of the bigger software service providers do not have the necessary background, a number of start-ups have emerged in niche areas to attract a chip vendor like TI to Bangalore. Start-ups include such firms as Bangalore-based Ittiam Systems, which was named the most preferred *global* supplier of DSP-based IP by the international DSP Professionals Survey of 2004 (Krishnadas, 2004). The emergence is not merely because of new market opportunities, or because firm size per se does not offer any advantage as with services; more critically, it is the availability of the right kind of people which is encouraging entrepreneurs to take risks. In many cases, the entrepreneurs are those returning home not only with years of design experience but also vital exposure to sales and marketing in the global arena. The lack of such experience previously inhibited homegrown startups and the interest of venture capitalists (Krishnadas, 2003b). If the trade press is to be believed, the pendulum has since swung to the point where VCs insist on an "India plan" from firms seeking funding.

Conclusion

The comparison of the experiences of ITI and the software industry in Bangalore offers some lessons for regional industrialization in developing countries. It shows that even amidst the current era of globalization, there is a role for states in determining how regions and firms within them cope with shifting market and technological conditions. However, as Evans (1995) points out, some forms of state action are more effective than others and the comparison in this essay shows that the *local* success of a sector increasingly depends on building relations in *global* economic space. There are two aspects to this.

One, building relations in global space means that autarchic ISI policies obsessed with self-reliance are unlikely to be effective. As the case of ITI indicates, such an obsession can backfire and lead to the import-dependent production of obsolete equipment. Ties to the global market not only provide knowledge of new markets and technologies, but also the various production arrangements that make it possible to take advantage of them. It was only after the software industry was freed from the clutches of ISI that software production and exports grew. The more Indian software professionals and firms, who despite having the technical skills were hitherto trained for a closed economy, gained exposure to market trends, management processes, and socially specific communication protocols, the more it allowed them to take advantage of the growth in demand for software.

Yet, ensuring growth to cope with technological change is not merely a matter of freeing a sector or an economy from ISI. Sector-specific promotional intervention is necessary. When the policy environment took a liberal turn in the 1980s, ITI found it hard to shake off the effect of years of state interference to take on the twin challenges of the erosion of its status as a monopoly equipment supplier, and changes in technology. But assistance from the DoT was not forthcoming. Likewise, despite the policy initiatives of the 1980s, Indian software exports in the 1980s meant little more than bodyshopping. A territorially grounded industry offering offshore services emerged only after the STPs were established to provide crucial data communications infrastructure.

Two, policies explicitly to achieve an often politically defined "regional balance" cannot ensure local success of a sector. The pursuit of such policies forced ITI to locate in regions such as Mankapur, which had little infrastructure. It not only made little operational sense, but the consequent decline of the company also left it incapable of achieving any of its other goals, such as generating new technology or surpluses for the state. In contrast, despite not having locational constraints, the software industry began to decentralize in the 1990s thanks to the spread of STPs. The decentralization of the software industry suggests that for any regional policy to be effective, it must build the institutional means to ensure the continuous production and upgrading of key inputs and infrastructure.

However, while the availability of infrastructure and inputs can draw firms and other producers to a region, a collection of firms is not a sufficient condition for an innovative region. Although there were policies that forced ITI to surround itself with ancillaries and to buy from SSIs, the interaction between them was characterized by arm's-length, routine transactions for standardized production. Since SSIs and ancillaries were administrative artifices that, in spite of many promotional and protectionist measures, lacked the resources to play a supporting role in the technological transition to ESS, they could only sink with ITI when the company declined. Similarly, while there were a large number of software firms in Bangalore, their focus on export markets minimized local interaction such that it was misleading to label the region as "India's Silicon Valley."

Barriers to innovation can hamper the ability to take advantage effectively of even those inputs to produce when there are institutional mechanisms in place, i.e. it is akin to static comparative advantage that is eventually eroded. Thus, while skilled labor was available in Bangalore, ITI was unable to capitalize on it in a manner that the software industry did, although software became the key input for switches. Similarly, while the software industry could claim competitive advantage on the basis of low-wage but high-skill labor, as long as it was confined to providing relatively low-skill services it was forced to confront labor market pressures as professionals sought more lucrative opportunities elsewhere. It was not until the rapid growth in demand for embedded systems coincided with the decline in the global demand for labor that the Indian software industry (and, even if not ITI, certainly other segments of the telecommunications industry) was able to capitalize on its global ties to attract expatriate Indians and venture capitalists from Silicon Valley to foster a network of producers for IP creation. This, in turn, led to the creation of new institutions such as the ISA and even a transformation in the role of NASSCOM.

The transformation of the software industry points to challenges in facilitating regional industrialization in developing countries. On one hand, freeing an industry and supporting it to compete globally means exposing it to the vicissitudes of the global economy, with the labor market pressures of the 1990s being a case in point. On the other hand, without those global connections, it also becomes difficult to take advantage of a change in circumstances, as with the fall in global demand for IT and the rise of the embedded systems industry. When and in what circumstances to free and support an industry, or the kind of support to provide, remain matters of judgment for which there seems to be no simple formula.

Notes

1 This reliance on software makes the ESS functionally versatile but more expensive to develop than the electro-mechanical switches, such as the strowger and the crossbar systems, which were in use earlier (*The Economist*, 1985). Strowger and crossbar systems were relatively slow, consumed a lot of power, and occupied plenty of floor space. Their large number of moving parts required considerable maintenance, making them unsuitable for high volume traffic (Feder and Spencer, 1962).

2 ITI was established when the Indian government entered in to an agreement with

Automatic Telephone and Electric of England, for the technology to manufacture telecommunications equipment. The goal was to achieve self-sufficiency in equipment that, until then, had been imported. The agreement with ATE was for 15 years. ITI started off by manufacturing strowger switching equipment and telephone instruments. In 1953, the company also started manufacturing transmission equipment.

3   In the Indian case, one outcome of pursuing a state-dominated, autarchic, ISI strategy, with a commitment to self-sufficiency and self-reliance, was the shrinkage, between 1950 and 1985, of India's share of world trade from 1.8 to 0.63 percent (indiabudget.nic.in/es96-97/CHAP6.HTM). Although India began to liberalize its policy regime from the mid-1980s, its gross national income in 2000, based on purchasing power parity, ranked 153 out of 207 countries (www.worldbank.org/data/databytopic/GNPPC.pdf).

4   The history of ITI is drawn from COPU (1973) and COPU (1982), the annual reports of the company and the Department of Telecommunications, interviews with former ITI officials, and Parthasarathy (2000), unless otherwise mentioned.

5   C-DoT was the brainchild of an expatriate Indian, Satyan Pitroda. With a number of patents to his name in switching, following years of work experience in the United States, Pitroda had the technical expertise to deliver. His proximity to former PM Rajiv Gandhi also gave him the political clout. Details of C-DoT are drawn from Pitroda (1993) and Meemamsi (1993) unless otherwise mentioned.

6   See Acharya (2002), and the essays in Oman (1996) for details of these policy changes.

7   These included Alcatel, AT&T, BellSouth, BNR, British Telecom, Hewlett Packard, Hughes Communications, Multi-tech, Nepostel, Samsung, and Siemens (*Voice and Data*, 1996b).

8   In this round of tendering, the DoT's procurement price was Rs.4,723 per line (*Voice and Data*, 1996a), whereas ITI felt that Rs.5,500 was a reasonable price (Urs, 1995). The ITI Employees Union and other former ITI officials accused the MNCs of forming a cartel to quote a rate that was lower than ITI's material costs in a desperate bid to enter the Indian market (DH News Service, 1997). There may have been more than a grain of truth to this accusation since, in the next round of tenders for 1.3 million lines in March 1996, the lowest quote per line was 55 percent higher at Rs.7,298.51 (*Voice and Data*, 1996a).

9   Details of Indian SSI policy are drawn from Tyabji (1989) and Gupta and Goldar (1995) unless otherwise mentioned.

10 This limit was Rs.0.75 million in 1966. It increased to Rs.1 million in 1975, to Rs.2 million in 1980, to Rs.2.5 million in 1980, to Rs.3.5 million in 1985, and to Rs.6 million in 1990.

11 The investment limit in plant and machinery for ancillaries was Rs.1 million in 1966. This was raised to Rs.1.5 million in 1975, to Rs.2.5 million in 1980, to Rs.4.5 million in 1985, and to Rs.7.5 million in 1990. Ancillaries as a separate category were abolished in 1997.

12 For details of all the benefits offered by STPs, visit www.stpi.soft.net.

13 The share of software in Indian exports grew from 1.9 percent in 1994–1995 to 18 percent in 2002–2003 (see Table 9.1). Rising software exports also helped increase India's share of world exports from 0.5 to 0.7 percent between 1985 and 2001. See indiabudget.nic.in/es2003-04/chapt2004/tab75.pdf.

14 Although the question of the skills shortage is controversial, in the United States at least, there is agreement that there was a shortage of people with specific skills, such as the ability to maintain older code for mainframe computers (Koch, 1998). See the main text for more on this issue.

15 An example of such contracts were those requiring the reconciliation of formats, such as those involving dates, of which the Y2K problem received the widest publicity. Jones (1998) points to other format problems with older software that manifest them-

selves in the 1990s. One date problem had to do with resetting the counters of global positioning system (GPS) satellites used for global fund transfers. The shift to the Euro, replacing 12 European currencies, from January 1, 1999, posed a different kind of format problem.

16 www.nasscom.org/artdisplay.asp?cat_id=205. Although SEI upgraded the CMM model to CMMi (Capability Maturity Model Integration) in 2000, the broad philosophy of the five-stage model remains the same. For details, see www.sei.cmu.edu/cmm/cmm.html.

17 Besides ITI and C-DoT, there are five PSEs in Bangalore, including three administered by the Ministry of Defense, and two by the Ministry of Heavy Industry and Public Enterprises. The Defense Research and Development Organization has nine of its 49 laboratories in Bangalore, while the Council of Scientific and Industrial Research has two. A laboratory of the Centre for Development of Advanced Computing and a location of the National Centre for Software Technology, both under the Department of Information Technology, are in the city. Finally, the Indian Space Research Organization, of the Department of Space, is also located in Bangalore. For the detailed list, see Parthasarathy (2004).

18 www.infy.com. The essay describes Infosys not only because it was India's second largest software exporter by 1999–2000, with SEI-CMM level five certification, but also because it is widely admired. It was started in 1981 by professionally trained entrepreneurs with little capital and became the first Indian firm to be listed on the NASDAQ. Other accomplishments include being the first company to be awarded the "National Award for Excellence in Corporate Governance" conferred by the GoI, being rated the "Best Employer of India" in a study by *Business Today*-Hewitt Associates in 2001, and ranking first in 2002 in *Business World*'s survey of "India's Most Respected Company." In 2004, *Time* magazine named N R Narayana Murthy, Infosys' chairman of the board and its main founder, as one of the ten most influential global executives helping shape the future of technology. For more about Infosys' history, see the company Web site. The listing of these accomplishments here is to merely make the point that if a firm as accomplished and successful as Infosys faces constraints in Bangalore, dealing with them becomes as challenging, if not more so, for other firms.

19 This visa program, established by the Immigration Act of 1990 to enable the employment, for up to six years, of workers in "specialty occupations," and used extensively by the US advanced technology sector, is widely identified as an "Indian program" (Alarcon, 1998).

20 For instance, in the US, spending on IT, after growing by 16 percent in 2000, fell by 6 percent in 2001 (*The Economist*, 2002) and, in aggregate terms, technology spending declined from nearly 5 percent of GDP in 2000 to about 4 percent by 2003 (*The Economist*, 2003).

21 www.nasscom.org/artdisplay.asp?cat_id=314.

22 For details, visit www.indiasemiconductorassociation.org.

23 The role of NASSCOM has also changed in the recent past. Between its founding in 1988 and 2000, it focused almost exclusively on lobbying for benefits, based on personal contacts in the government. Since 2000, it has transformed itself into a more professional organization, increasingly relying on research to influence policy (Kanavi, 2004). It has also become more actively involved in promoting startups, innovation, and incubation, all of which encourage firms in different niche areas.

24 www.nasscom.org/artdisplay.asp?cat_id=615.

25 For instance, Cadence Design Systems, the largest EDA tools vendor in the world, had only nine customers in India in 1997 (Nair, 1999). By 2002, it had 100 (Hari and Anand, 2002), and 11 of its 12 largest customers had R&D facilities in India (Kumar, 2003).

26 pib.nic.in/release/rel_print_page1.asp?relid=6074.

27 According to Singh (2003), one industry representative believes that one in three joining the chip industry is a returnee from the US.
28 Unless otherwise mentioned, details of TI's activities are from a personal discussion that followed a presentation by Dr Biswadip Mitra, managing director, TI India, at the International Institute of Information Technology, Bangalore on April 10, 2004, and from www.ti.com/asia/docs/India.

References

Acharya, S. (2002) Macroeconomic Management in the Nineties, *Economic and Political Weekly*, 37(16), pp. 515–1538.

Ahluwalia, I.J. (1985) *Industrial Growth in India: Stagnation Since the Mid-Sixties*, Oxford University Press, New York.

Alarcon, R. (1998) *The Migrants of the Information Age: Foreign Born Engineers and Scientists and Regional Development in Silicon Valley*, Ph.D. dissertation, Department of City and Regional Planning, University of California, Berkeley.

All India Council for Technical Education (AICTE) (1999) *Reshaping Postgraduate Education and Research in Engineering and Technology*, AICTE.

Arora, A. and Asundi, J. (1999) *Quality Certification and the Economics of Contract Software Development: A Study of the Indian Software Industry*, Working paper 7260, National Bureau of Economic Research, Cambridge, Mass.

Bardhan, P. (1998) (expanded edition) *The Political Economy of Development in India*, Oxford University Press, New Delhi.

Bhuyan, R. (2002) Chipping in, www.dqindia.com/content/search/showarticle.asp?arid=39564&way=search.

Chakravarty, S. (1987) *Development Planning: The Indian Experience*, Oxford University Press, New York.

Chowdary, T.H. (1997) Telecommunications in India, in E.M. Noam, (ed.) *Telecommunications in Western Asia and the Middle East*, Oxford University Press, New York.

Committee of Public Undertakings (COPU) (1972–1973) (1973) *Indian Telephone Industries Ltd. (Ministry of Communications), 5th Lok Sabha, 34th Report*, Lok Sabha Secretariat, New Delhi.

Committee of Public Undertakings (COPU) (1981–1982) (1982) *Indian Telephone Industries Ltd.: R&D and New Projects (Ministry of Communications), 7th Lok Sabha, 38th report*, Lok Sabha Secretariat, New Delhi.

Department of Telecommunications, *Annual Report*, various years.

DH News Service (1997) ITI employees reject charge on low tender, *Deccan Herald*, Sept. 6.

Economist, The (1985) The world on the line: telecommunications, a survey, Nov. 23.

Economist, The (2002) High-tech companies: IT grows up, Aug. 24, p. 45.

Economist, The (2003) Spending on information technology: some like it cold, Oct. 4, p. 62.

Evans, P.B. (1995) *Embedded Autonomy: States and Industrial Transformation*, Princeton University Press, Princeton, NJ.

Feder, H.S. and Spencer, A.E. (1962) Telephone Switching, *Scientific American*, 207(1), pp. 133–143.

Fineman, M. (1991) India's new middle class finds home in Bangalore, *The Los Angeles Times*, Dec. 17.

Grieco, J.M. (1984) *Between Dependency and Autonomy: India's Experience with the International Computer Industry*, University of California Press, Berkeley.

Gupta, D.B. and Goldar, B.N. (1995) *Ancillarisation and Sub-Contracting in Indian Industry*, Paper No. 18, Studies in Industrial Development, Office of the Economic Adviser, Ministry of Industry, Government of India.

Harding, E.U. (1989) India: After IBM's Exit, an Industry Arose, *Software Magazine*, 9(14), pp. 48–54.

Hari, P. (2001) Indian software version 2.0, *Business World*, Aug. 27, pp. 28–36.

Hari, P. (2003) Embedded technology: the crossover, *Business World*, April 14, pp. 28–32.

Hari, P. and Anand, M. (2002) Chip's of the block, *Business World*, March 18, pp. 34–41.

Heeks, R. (1996) *India's Software Industry: State Policy, Liberalisation and Industrial Development*, Sage Publications, New Delhi.

Henderson, J. (1989) *The Globalisation of High Technology Production: Society, Space and Semiconductors in the Restructuring of the Modern World*, Routledge, London.

Hirschman, A.O. (1958) *The Strategy of Economic Development*, Yale University Press, New Haven.

IDG (2001) India's Silicon Valley lures foreign companies, *The Industry Standard*, www.industrystandard.com/article/0,1902,27396,00.html.

Indian Telephone Industries (ITI), *Annual Report*, various years.

Indian Telephone Industries (ITI), nd. Change of Technology, Retraining, Deployment: A Case Study in Indian Telephone Industries Limited, internal company document.

Jones, C. (1998) Bad Days for Software, *IEEE Spectrum*, 35(9), pp. 47–52.

Kanavi, S. (2004) Coming of age, *Business India*, Feb. 16–29, pp. 55–58.

Kaushal, H. (1997) Indian Telephone Industries: Gasping for oxygen, *Economic Times*, Feb. 18.

Koch, K. (1998) High-Tech Labor Shortage, *CQ Researcher*, 8(16), pp. 361–384.

Krishnadas, K.C. (2000) Indian readies laws to protect IC designs, www.eedesign.com/article/showArticle.jhtml?articleId=17405970.

Krishnadas, K.C. (2003a) India's design centers buck economy's trend, www.eetimes.com/article/showArticle.jhtml?articleId=18308505.

Krishnadas, K.C. (2003b) Indian EEs show you can go home again, www.eetimes.com/article/showArticle.jhtml?articleId=18309505.

Krishnadas, K.C. (2004) India's Ittiam named top DSP IP provider, www.eetimes.com/showArticle.jhtml?articleID=54200821.

Kumar, V.R. (2003) Touching base, www.blonet.com/ew/2003/07/02/stories/2003070200070100.htm.

Lakha, S. (1990) Growth of Computer Software Industry in India, *Economic and Political Weekly*, 25(1), pp. 49–56.

Lal, D. (1985) *The Poverty of "Development Economics,"* Harvard University Press, Cambridge, MA.

Lee, E.A. (2000) What's Ahead for Embedded Software? *IEEE Computer*, 33(9), pp. 18–26.

Martin, G. and Schirrmeister, F. (2002) A Design Chain for Embedded Systems, *IEEE Computer*, 35(3), pp. 100–103.

Mathews, J.A. and Cho, D-S. (2000) *Tiger Technology: The Creation of a Semiconductor Industry in East Asia*, Cambridge University Press, New York.

Meemamsi, G.B. (1993) *The C-DoT Story: Quest, Inquest, Conquest*, Kedar Publications.

Menon, R.K. (2003) IC design houses swing into high gear, http://economictimes.india-times.com/articleshow/331891.cms.

Nair, C. (1999) Cadence inks multi-year pacts with Indian design houses, www.eetimes. com/article/shiwArticle.jhtml?articleId=18303272.

National Association of Software and Service Companies (NASSCOM) (1999) *Indian IT Software and Services Directory, 1999–2000*, New Delhi.

Nayar, B.R. (1989) *India's Mixed Economy: The Role of Ideology and Interest in its Development*, Popular Prakashan, Mumbai.

Oman, C. (ed.). (1996) *Policy Reform in India*, OECD.

Parthasarathy, B. (2000) *Globalization and Agglomeration in Newly Industrializing Countries: The State and the Information Technology Industry in Bangalore, India*, Ph.D. dissertation, University of California, Berkeley.

Parthasarathy, B. (2004) India's Silicon Valley or Silicon Valley's India?: Socially Embedding the Computer Software Industry in Bangalore, *International Journal of Urban and Regional Research*, 28(3), pp. 664–685.

Perroux, F. (1955) Note sur la notion de pôle de croissance, *Economie Appliquée*, 7, pp. 307–320.

Pitroda, S.G. (1993) Development, Democracy, and the Village Telephone, *Harvard Business Review*, 71(6), pp. 66–79.

Porter, M.E. (1990) *The Competitive Advantage of Nations*, Macmillan, London.

Rao, R.L.R. (1995a) Second wave of software investments to flow into Bangalore, *Economic Times*, May 10.

Rao, R.L.R. (1995b) ITI's ambitious XD-90 switch project fails to switch on, *Economic Times*, April 24.

Romer, P.M. (1986) Increasing Returns and Long-Run Growth, *Journal of Political Economy*, 94, pp. 1002–1037.

Rostow, W.W. (1960) *The Stages of Economic Growth: A Non-Communist Manifesto*, Cambridge University Press, Cambridge.

Saxenian, A. (1994) *Regional Advantage: Culture and Competition in Silicon Valley and Route 128*, Harvard University Press, Cambridge, Mass.

Scott, A.J. (1988a) *Metropolis: From the Division of Labor to Urban Form*, University of California Press, Berkeley.

Scott, A.J. (1988b) *New Industrial Spaces: Flexible Production Organization and Regional Development in North America and Western Europe*, Pion, London.

Sen, P. (1994) Software Exports from India: A Systemic Analysis, *Electronics Information and Planning*, 22(2), pp. 55–63.

Sims, D. (1994) Motorola Self-assesses at Level 5, *IEEE Software*, 11(2), p. 92.

Singh, S. (2003) India calling, www.businessworldindia.com/Nov1003/coverstory02.asp.

Solow, R.M. (1957) Technical Change and the Aggregate Production Function, *Review of Economics and Statistics*, 39(3), pp. 312–320.

Sridharan, E. (1996) *The Political Economy of Industrial Promotion: Indian, Brazilian and Korean Electronics in Comparative Perspective 1969–1994*, Praeger, Westport, CT.

Srinivas, A. and Jayashankar, M. (2002) Hard times, hard lessons: The new software solutions, *Business World*, Feb. 25, pp. 24–29.

Storper, M. (1997) *The Regional World: Territorial Development in a Global Economy*, Guilford Press, New York.

Subramanian, C.R. (1992) *India and the Computer: A Study of Planned Development*, Oxford University Press, New Delhi.

Subramanian, D. (1997a) Bangalore Public Sector Strike, 1980–81, A Critical Appraisal II: The Strike, *Economic and Political Weekly*, 32(16), pp. 843–853.

Subramanian, D. (1997b) Bangalore Public Sector Strike, 1980–81, A Critical Appraisal I: The Settlements, *Economic and Political Weekly*, 32(15), pp. 767–778.

Tyabji, N. (1989) *The Small Industries Policy in India*, Oxford University Press, Calcutta.

Urs, S.Y. (1995) ITI draws up a survival strategy, *Business World*, May 3–16, p. 63.

Voice and Data (1996a) Switching, 3(2), www.voicendata.com.

Voice and Data (1996b) Communication Software, 3(2), www.voicendata.com.

Waterbury, J. (1993) *Exposed to Innumerable Delusions: Public Enterprise and State Power in Egypt, India, Mexico and Turkey*, Cambridge University Press, New York.

Williamson, O.E. (1975) *Markets and Hierarchies: Analysis and Antitrust Implications*, The Free Press, New York.

Williamson, O.E. (1985) *The Economic Institutions of Capitalism: Firms, Markets, Relational Contracting*, The Free Press, New York.

Wolf, W. (2002) What is Embedded Computing? *IEEE Computer*, 35(1), pp. 136–137.

10 Clusters and regional industrial synergies

The electronics industry in Penang and Jalisco

Rajah Rasiah

Introduction

Governments in developing economies have since the 1950s focused extensively on attracting firms to particular locations to "stimulate agglomeration" economies or "cluster" synergies. International organizations such as the World Bank, United Nations Industrial Development Organization (UNIDO) and United Nations Conference for Trade and Development (UNCTAD), and Asian Development Bank have encouraged governments to launch industrial estates (including export processing zones) to attract investment (including foreign investment) to stimulate industrial development and employment generation.

Whereas the promotion of export processing essentially arose from efforts to stimulate agglomeration economies in newly industrializing economies, clustering emerged from abstractions of successful industrial districts in the developed economies. The successful expansion of Silicon Valley, revival of Route 128, and the continued dynamism seen in Emilia Romagna are the products of both approaches (Best, 2001; Sabel, 1995; Saxenian, 1994, 1999). Although local firms were the pillars of industrial dynamism in these regions, the application of clustering policies has produced similar synergies in Ireland and Singapore where multinational corporations (MNCs) have remained the engine of industrialization.

Malaysia and Mexico are good examples of MNC-driven clusters where differences in systemic coordination have produced contrasting consequences within their national borders. Export-oriented MNCs began relocating on a large scale in Malaysia and Mexico in the early 1970s. Following the initial waves in the early 1970s, subsequent massive relocation of MNC activities to Malaysia and Mexico took place since 1986 and 1995, respectively. The Plaza Accord of 1985 marked a watershed where both external pressures that forced the floating of the Yen, Won, New Taiwan Dollar, and Singapore dollar and the withdrawal of the Generalised System of Preferences from the Asian NIEs in February 1988 and domestic fiscal (tax holidays), and monetary policies (depreciation of the Ringgit) attracted a massive relocation of foreign direct investment into Malaysia.[1] Mexico benefitted extensively from the opening of the North Atlantic Free Trade Area in 1995 as giant firms, especially, from the United States,

Japan, Korea, and Europe relocated operations to access essentially the North American market.

Extensive work on *maquila*-type low value-added production operations in Malaysia and Mexico where little human capital synergies have been generated and appropriated already exists (Lim, 1978; Rasiah, 1993; Kenney and Florida, 1994; Wilson, 1992). Unlike moribund operations where few production linkages were created in the host economy that typified the MNC-led manufacturing, significant government-firm initiatives in both locations assisted upgrading and some amount of integration. Jalisco in Mexico and Penang in Malaysia – enjoying dynamic coordination from developmental organizations – have appropriated significant cluster synergies. Interestingly, these experiences differ considerably from the nature of MNC production in these economies – which is dominated elsewhere by truncated operations.

This chapter examines how systemic coordination helped stimulate dynamic clustering in Penang and Jalisco. While extensive federal emphasis helped raise basic education – primary and secondary schooling levels – to high standards, ineffective governance of tertiary and technical institutions constrained the supply of technical personnel and engineers and scientists in both countries. Nevertheless, strong systemic coordination by local institutions helped Penang and Jalisco produce greater skilled, technical, and entrepreneurial synergies for differentiation and division of labor. The rest of the chapter is organized as follows. The second section discusses the theory. The third section presents the regions and the details on the empirical information used in the chapter. The fourth section evaluates comparatively against data on other economies' basic and R&D infrastructure, and the consequent registration of patents in Malaysia and Mexico, and analyzes systemic coordination and the dynamics of cluster synergies in the states of Penang and Jalisco. This is followed by conclusions.

Analytic framework

Three critical concepts have dominated region-centered industrial promotion: clusters, agglomeration economies, and value chains. Marshall (1890) provided the earliest known elements that constituted clusters using the concept of industrial districts. Young (1928) articulated the advantages industry offers from its differentiating and division of labor potential. Best (2001) developed this further by examining the conditions that drive entrepreneurship and new species of industries regionally. Rasiah (2002) discussed the synergistic advantages Silicon Valley and Route 128 have introduced to the continuous reinvention of old firms and the birth of new ones in clusters where there exists ease of movement of human capital – tacit to start new firms and to galvanize old firms. Guerreri *et al.* (2001) summarized the three dominant types of industrial clusters that have emerged to compete at the global frontier: one, the atomized Marshallian small firms that typify Italy and Taiwan; two, a handful of large firms defining the roles of suppliers in Detroit; and three, the single large mother firm defining the roles of suppliers in Japan.

There has been a parallel but converging development of the theory of agglomeration economies. Theories of state power and regional organizations have focused on the role development organizations play in stimulating industrial activities by concentrating infrastructure in particular locations. Early work from geographers and development economists examined the advantages of developing growth-pole strategies (Perroux, 1950, 1970; Boudeville, 1966; Hirschman, 1958, 1970; Myrdal, 1957) on regional development. Unlike the concept of clusters, which examines the regional dynamics as a network, a growth pole was referred to by Perroux (1950) as an industry or group of firms that drive the growth of other firms and economic activities most in the region: polarization arising from the propulsive development of a firm or industry. Growth poles eventually assumed the meaning of growth polarization-stimulated external economies and linkages. The synergy effects of agglomeration economies have subsequently been documented quite lucidly by Friedmann (1972), Cooke and Morgan (1998); Garofoli (1992); Porter (1998); Scott (1988); and Storper (1995).

Work on agglomeration economies shows that regions endowed with a dynamic set of economic agents connected and effectively coordinated – firms and institutions (e.g. provision of utilities such as power, water, telecommunications, education, training institutions, and R&D labs) – drive innovation and competitiveness through flows of circular and cumulative causation. UNCTAD and UNIDO saw such regional development initiatives through strong government intervention – either through supporting import-substitution in industrial estates or export-orientation in free trade zones – as a major instrument to improve the terms of trade and balance of payments of developing economies. Hirschman (1958, 1970) emphasized the importance of exports – to appropriate the economies of scale and competition – and, hence, called attention to backward linkages. Development policy was also linked to the concepts of spread (diffusion of spillover at host sites) and backwash (destructive displacement of economic agents at host sites) and the circular tendencies of these processes. Some economists worked on crowding in and crowding out and the circumstances (including policy initiatives) that led to these developments (Lall and Streeten, 1977).

The literature on value chains addresses changes both by geographical location and technological sophistication as measured by value added that take place in the division of labor of global production networks. Gereffi (1994, 2002) identified drivers that differ in particular products with consequences both over control and implications for upgrading at host sites. The relevant value chain question relating to regional development will be on how changes in the dynamics of global value chains have affected clustering or agglomeration at host sites. The trend toward manufacturing-less operations in flagship firms such as Dell and Cisco, but serious differences in the general models of other large firms such as Intel, Advanced Micro Devices, National Semiconductor, Hitachi, and Samsung, where some rely extensively on global service providers (both original equipment manufacturers as well as contract manufacturers), has produced different impacts at host-sites.

Governments' role has increased from the neoclassical focus on simply basic infrastructure to heterodox economists working on missing or inadequate markets (including market failure) or simply a mix of all to *dirigistes*. Modern industrialization requires the employment of human capital with at least minimal communication skills so that conception, organization, coordination, and execution of tasks are carried out smoothly. Primary and secondary schools offer the initial mass of labor for large-scale, but low value-added mass production operations. Export-oriented MNCs relocated simple assembly operations in economies that offered large reserves of cheap but educated (trainable) labor. American, Japanese and European MNCs relocated in Jamaica, Barbados, Malaysia, Mexico, Singapore, China Taipei and Korea in the late 1960s and 1970s to access cheap literate labor (Sciberas, 1977; Lim, 1978; Rasiah, 1988).[2] Political instability and restrictive policies discouraged similar relocations in China and India in the 1970s. China became a major manufacturing target of MNCs from the 1980s (World Bank Institute, 2001). MNCs did not figure strongly in the economies of Korea and China Taipei (Lall, 1996; Hamilton, 1983). Singapore and Malaysia relied heavily on MNCs to generate where considerable clustering had taken place with ramifications for human capital synergies.

While the contributions of cluster and value chain exponents have been important, evolutionary economists made a major contribution to the understanding of regional development (albeit much of the focus has been on sites with fairly developed infrastructure on a national scale) by addressing institutional and systemic differences that define regions' (nations') location in the technology ladder (Nelson and Winter, 1982; Nelson, 1993; Lundvall, 1992; Freeman, 1988). From basic and secondary schooling, the demand for technical and professional skills rises as firms move up the technology ladder (Pavitt, 1984). MNC-driven regions (e.g. Ireland and Singapore) have typically managed to stimulate spillovers and industrial upgrading by matching demand conditions with the supply of technical, tertiary, scientific, and engineering human capital. Institutions associated with education often face collective action problems. Private agents are unlikely to participate in market-driven activities when the risks involved are not matched by returns. R&D scientists and engineers have increasingly become important to support innovative activities. Arrow (1962) noted that interventions in markets are necessary when social returns exceed private returns. Schumpeter (1934) argued that rents are necessary to motivate innovators. Kaldor (1957) contended that markets generate sub-optimal outcomes when addressing investments that generate dynamic increasing returns.[3] Rasiah (2004) argued that markets hardly function when they are missing or lack effective cohesion with institutions (especially the government) in underdeveloped economies. Contrary to the transaction costs arguments of Coase (1937) and Williamson (1985), markets, trust, and command (through hierarchies and directives from collection action agents such as government) play equally important roles in ensuring sufficiently effective allocation, coordination, and distribution of economic activities (Richardson, 1972; Piore and Sabel, 1984; Brusco, 1982; Wilkinson and You, 1992; Rasiah, 1994).

The production of technical personnel, scientists, and engineers involves considerable acquisition of knowledge. Given the uncertainty associated with R&D activities, R&D labs, especially those engaged in basic knowledge, will hardly attract private investment. The situation is even worse in underdeveloped economies with missing or vaguely operating markets where it is impossible to attract significant participation in information and communication technology (ICT) activities owing to the lack of basic infrastructure and a community willing to pay for the costs of installing it. Because knowledge is a public good – its consumption by one does not exclude that by others – the synergies associated with it clearly fit Arrow's distinction of social returns exceeding private returns. Hence, learning institutions such as universities, R&D labs, and technical schools that generate high tech human capital fall under the category of public goods. Intermediary organizations such as development corporations and chambers of commerce play a critical role in coordinating information and knowledge flows between government and markets (Aoki, 2001; Rasiah, 1999; Doner, 2001). South Korea and Taiwan shortened the experience of the Western economies and Japan with strong government focus on human capital development (Amsden, 1989; Wade, 1990).

The literature on clusters – particularly from the effects of interaction between employees (rubbing-off effects) as articulated by Marshall (1890) and the cohesion of knowledge flows as advanced by Best (2001) and Rasiah (2002) – are critical dimensions that help trigger and drive both the creation and appropriation of knowledge synergies. Considerable learning takes place through doing and interacting. Given the tacit nature of some knowledge, integrated clustering enables dynamic learning. While domestic institutions are necessary to increase the supply of high tech human capital, tacit and experiential knowledge is critical to run even innovating firms. Penrose (1959) and Polanyi (1997) made distinctive contributions to the understanding and significance of experiential and tacit knowledge, respectively, which overlap and are specific to individuals. Porter's (1990) notion of clusters simply included the different economic agents (e.g. firms, institutions, etc.) in a region, while Best (2001) considered further elements such as degree of integration, network cohesion, organizational and technical change, and drivers of differentiation and division of labor (for new growth). The last element relates considerably to the original explication of the growth pole exponent Perroux (1950). Rosenberg (1982) established the peculiar characteristics of human capital where coordination and extraction of performance cannot be bounded. Schumpeter (1934) and Hirschman (1958) discussed extensively the role of entrepreneurs in economic development.

However, conventional economic theory tended to confine the term "entrepreneurship" to a black box (Rasiah, 2002). Given the spontaneous nature of a number of human capital actions, formal contracts can never be exhaustive and, thus, will always involve moral hazard problems (Rosenberg, 1982; Rasiah, 1995). Hence, trust has become a critical mode of governance to stimulate entrepreneurial synergies. Business theory helped define and differentiate entrepreneurs, with the focus largely on the evaluation and management of entrepreneurship. Management courses equip entrepreneurs with technical and professional knowledge so that they become better managers. Critical elements of the theory of entrepreneurship can be traced to Mills (1848), Marshall (1890), Penrose (1959), and Chandler (1962), albeit without specific definitions and methodological instruments for empirical inquiry. The application of theory to the creation and growth of entrepreneurs became more dynamic with the works of Saxenian (1994, 1999) and Best (2001).

The term "clustering" refers to a network of interconnected firms, institutions, and other organizations whose synergy strength depends on systemic coordination and network cohesion. Clusters of firms and institutions enjoying strong network cohesion are likely to offer greater flexibility and technological and market synergies than those characterized by truncated operations of individual firms. Causation involving the propellants of synergies in clusters is complex and is not unidirectional (Smith, 1776; Young, 1928). Porter (1990) discussed clustering alongside the four diamonds that drive competitiveness, but offered vague reference to systemic instruments and network cohesion. Marshall (1890), Brusco (1982), Wilkinson and You (1992), Piore and Sabel (1984), Sabel (1995), Pyke and Sengenberger (1992), Hirst and Zeitlin (1991), Rasiah (1994) and Best (2001) offered a much more dynamic feel of the synergies associated with clustering.[4]

The role of systemic instruments in driving cluster cohesion has been important in the development of dynamic industrial districts. Inter-firm pecuniary relations through sales and purchases are only one channel of inter-firm interactions (Rasiah, 1995). Knowledge flows – rubbing-off effects from the interaction between workers (Marshall, 1890) and the movement of tacit and experiential skills embodied in human capital – produce systems synergies (Penrose, 1959). Open integrated clusters encourage inter-firm movement of tacit and experiential knowledge embodied in human capital, which, *inter alia*, distinguishes dynamic from truncated clusters (Best 2001; Rasiah, 2002). New firms benefitted from gaining managerial and technical personnel from older firms in Silicon Valley irrespective of national ownership. American-owned Intel, Dell and Solectron, and Japanese-owned Sun Micro Systems hired technical and managerial personnel from old firms in Silicon Valley.[5] Mature firms gain new ideas and processes to ensure continuous organizational change as some old employees are replaced to make way for fresh ones with new ideas, while new firms benefit from the entrepreneurial and technical – tacit and experiential – knowledge to start new firms (Rasiah, 2002).[6] Saxenian (1994, 1999) offered an impressive documentation of inter-firm movement of human capital, which helped support new firm creation capabilities in Silicon Valley.

While the prime propellants of cluster dynamics in the successful industrial districts of Emelia Romagna and Silicon Valley are local firms, five important developments have made this approach applicable even to MNC-driven clusters. First, host government investments in basic infrastructure and bureaucratic coordination helped resolve customs, security, and labor problems. Second, where the embedding environment is strong, MNCs have increasingly integrated production at selected host-sites (e.g. Ireland and Singapore). Third, falling production and product cycle times in electronics production has encouraged MNCs to subcontract out dissimilar activities to suppliers and contract manufacturers, thereby offering the room for further differentiation and division of labor. Fourth, growing horizontal integration has diffused synergies to several layers of firms in complementary activities at host sites (e.g. Israel and Singapore). Fifth, MNCs increasingly rely on host-site institutions to access scarce high tech human capital, through relocation and immigration (e.g. software in India).

Four important propositions are identified here to examine the production and distribution of human capital in Penang and Jalisco. First, effective institutional coordination is necessary to stimulate demand–supply conditions for driving differentiation and division of labor regionally. Second, cohesive clusters, as defined by the degree of connections and coordination between firms and institutions, matter in driving inter-firm linkages and new firm creation. Third, the requisite high tech infrastructure is critical to provide the public goods necessary to stimulate learning and innovation at host sites. Fourth, regions benefit from open national frameworks so that human capital deficiencies can be overcome through selective immigration as experienced by the United States, Singapore, Israel and Ireland.

The setting and data

The Malaysian electronics industry is characterized by three major regional agglomerations, and moribund operations in Sarawak and Sabah. Penang is the largest of them in terms of firm numbers, employment, and value added, followed by the Kelang Valley and Johor. Penang's electronics industry employed more than 90,000 people, followed by the Klang Valley with more than 85,000 in 1995 (MITI 1996, p. 38). Electronics assembly in Mexico is more scattered with much of the operations carried out under maquiladora arrangements, two-thirds of which are located close to the US–Mexican border. Location where maquila-type operations occur on a large scale include Chihuahua, Baja California, Tamaulipas, Coahuila, Sonora and Nuevo Leon. Jalisco is a rare state in Mexico where much of electronics manufacturing does not qualify as maquila-type activities. Although some firms such as IBM have either subcontracted out or sold their manufacturing operations to other American Taiwanese companies, the density of operations of electronics firms in the state have remained high.

Table 10.1 shows the breakdown of firms studied in 2002–2003. All firms in the Penang sample and three firms in the Jalisco sample were interviewed by the author. The information on the remaining firms in Jalisco was provided by CADELEC. In addition, interviews were also carried out with training institutions, industry associations, state planning corporations, the University of Guadalajara, and a standards organization.

Table 10.1 Breakdown of interview sample, 2001–2005

Sub-sectors	Penang	Jalisco
Component electronics	19	12
Consumer electronics	16	0
Industrial and peripheral	10	14
Plastic	16	9
Machine tools	31	11
Packaging	3	3
Total	95	49

Source: Author's survey.

Note
The Penang interviews were carried out directly by the author. Except for three firms where the interviews were carried out by the author and Pedro Lara-Martinez, the remaining information from Jalisco firms was provided by Jakobo. The author and Pedro Lara-Martinez interviewed a component, industrial and peripherals, and machine tool firm each in January 2003.

Regional growth dynamics

The empirical investigation of regional synergies and its appropriation in the electronics clusters of Penang and Jalisco is undertaken here. The first examines the provision of basic and high infrastructure in the two states. Most of the institutional services related to government action are provided on a national scale in both nations.[7] However, local state autonomy in the provision of some services, including initiatives to support clustering and other forms of inter-firm and institutional networking have differentiated these two states considerably from the other states within these economies. The chapter focuses on the latter where the dynamics of clustering is most appropriated. Despite dynamic efforts to strengthen clustering, the chapter also argues that there are limits to local coordination initiatives, which explains why both states have failed to stimulate strong participation in upgrading and R&D activities.

Institutional support

Basic infrastructure in both countries is fairly similar owing to the provision of the essential services in export processing zones located in more underdeveloped states. Besides, the formal education institutions in both countries have been governed directly by the Federal Ministry of Education – general, vocational, and technical education. Educational institutions in Penang and Jalisco faced similar coordination problems (Rasiah, 2004). Basic education offered the cognitive, judgmental, and communication skills which helped Malaysia and Mexico develop a labor force attractive for labor-intensive low value-added activities for MNCs. However, little effort has taken place to coordinate supply from technical institutes and universities to stimulate industrial upgrading in firms.

Malaysia and Mexico have enjoyed excellent basic education – primary and secondary schooling – standards. Enrolment in primary schools exceeded the global mean (see Table 10.2). The index of primary school enrolment (see Table notes) remained slightly above one between the years 1970–1998 in both countries. The relative position of Malaysia and Mexico on secondary schooling remained at the mean of one or close to one. Strong basic schooling has attracted labor-intensive transnational corporations since the early 1970s. A combination of the exhaustion of labor reserves (and its consequent impact on rising wages) and increasing skill-intensity levels in electronics manufacturing stifled further inflows of electronics foreign direct investment into Malaysia from the late 1990s, and in Mexico the target shifted to the maquila-type operations close to the US–Mexican border. Both Penang and Jalisco have intensified efforts to overcome skills development limitations since. Rising wages and the emergence of low-cost sites, such as China and the Philippines and maquila locations in Mexico, severely undermined the capacity of Penang and Jalisco to retain such operations. With a similar primary and secondary schooling index but with a massive labor reserve, China easily overtook other developing economies as the prime target for labor-intensive MNCs from the 1990s. Integration into the North Atlantic Free Trade Area (NAFTA) since 1995 has helped retain MNC interest in Mexico.

In addition, component and computer firms began to experience production changes that required the utilization of high technology, opening the way for industrial upgrading. However, local institutions failed to expand the supply of engineers and technicians, and the requisite technical support from high tech institutions to match demand. Malaysia's and Mexico's tertiary education enrolment was well below the global mean in the period 1975–1999 (Rasiah, 2002). There have been improvements in Malaysia since the late 1990s.

Aggressive efforts in Malaysia have helped raise the share of R&D engineers and scientists in the population – exceeding that of Mexico in 1998. However, the index of R&D scientists and engineers of both countries remained well below the global mean (see Table 10.3). The emphasis on science and technology in Mexico was higher than in Malaysia historically, with the patent office opened in 1809. However, federal emphasis on higher education – both tertiary and the supply of R&D scientists and engineers – has not experienced increasing emphasis. Interviews with the Science and Technology director in 2002 suggested that Mexican institutions lack authority and institutional coordination to implement plans to stimulate innovation in industry. Hence, whereas in Malaysia strong federal focus has translated into the expansion of graduates – including scientists and engineers from the late 1990s – the intensities have stagnated in Mexico. Hence, whereas the rapidly developing economies of Korea and Singapore have successfully raised their R&D scientists and engineers index from 0.4 and 0.3, respectively, in 1981 to 1.5 and 1.6, respectively, in 1998, Malaysia and Mexico remain significantly down the technology intensity ladder (Rasiah, 2002).

Using the R&D infrastructure index, estimated from R&D investment as a

Table 10.2 Education enrolment, 1970–1998

	1970	1975	1980	1985	1990	1998
Net primary	n = 60	n = 57	n = 78	n = 78	n = 72	n = 89
Malaysia	1.2	n.a.	1.2	n.a.	1.2	1.1
Mexico	1.1	n.a.	n.a.	1.2	1.3	1.4
Republic of Korea	1.3	1.2	1.3	1.2	1.3	1.1
Singapore	1.3	1.2	1.3	n.a.	n.a.	1.1
Hong Kong	1.2	1.1	1.2	n.a.	n.a.	1.1
Japan	1.3	1.2	1.32	1.3	1.2	n.a.
South Africa	0.9	n.a.	n.a.	n.a.	n.a.	n.a.
China	n.a.	n.a.	n.a.	n.a.	1.2	1.2
Philippines	n.a.	1.2	1.2	1.2	n.a.	1.2
Indonesia	n.a.	0.9	1.1	1.2	1.2	1.1
USA	n.a.	n.a.	n.a.	1.2	1.2	1.1
Ireland	1.3	1.1	1.1	1.1	1.1	1.1
Gross secondary	n = 132	n = 137	n = 153	n = 156	n = 152	n = 145
Malaysia	1.1	1.2	0.9	1.0	1.0	1.0
Mexico	0.6	n.a.	n.a.	0.9	0.8	0.9
Republic of Korea	1.3	1.5	1.5	1.7	1.6	1.6
Singapore	1.4	1.3	1.2	1.1	1.2	1.2
Hong Kong	1.1	1.3	1.2	1.3	1.4	1.1
Japan	2.7	2.4	1.8	1.7	1.7	1.6
South Africa	n.a.	n.a.	n.a.	n.a.	1.3	1.5
China	0.8	1.2	0.9	0.7	0.8	1.0
Philippines	1.4	1.4	1.2	1.2	1.3	1.2
Indonesia	0.5	0.5	0.6	0.8	0.8	0.8
USA	2.6	2.2	1.8	1.8	1.6	1.5
Ireland	2.3	2.3	1.7	1.8	1.7	1.8
Thailand	0.5	0.7	0.6	0.6	0.5	0.9
Israel	1.8	1.7	1.4	1.5	1.5	1.4
Gross tertiary	n = 118	n = 120	n = 144	n = 141	n = 129	n = 110
Malaysia	n.a.	n.a.	0.3	0.4	0.4	0.7
Mexico	n.a.	n.a.	n.a.	n.a.	n.a.	0.6
Republic of Korea	1.1	1.0	1.1	2.4	2.2	2.3
Singapore	0.9	0.9	0.6	1.0	1.0	1.5
Hong Kong	1.1	1.1	0.8	n.a.	n.a.	n.a.
Japan	2.7	2.9	2.3	2.0	1.7	n.a.
South Africa	0.6	n.a.	n.a.	n.a.	0.7	0.8
China	n.a.	0.1	0.1	0.2	0.2	0.2
Philippines	2.6	1.8	1.8	1.8	1.6	1.3
Indonesia	0.4	0.3	0.3	n.a.	0.5	0.5
USA	7.2	6.0	4.2	4.3	4.2	3.6
Ireland	1.8	1.8	1.4	1.6	1.6	1.8
Thailand	0.5	0.4	1.1	1.3	n.a.	0.9
Israel	2.8	2.6	2.2	2.3	1.9	1.8

Source: Computed from World Bank (2002); National databases.

Note

Figures calculated using the formula $x_i[\Sigma(x_i \ldots x_n)]^{-1}n$ where x_i refers to the % of enrolment of country i, and n the number of countries reporting data.

Table 10.3 R&D scientists and engineers per million people, 1981–1999

	1981 (n = 31)	1985 (n = 36)	1990 (n = 2)	1996–1999 (n = 65)
Malaysia	n.a.	n.a.	0.1	0.2
Mexico	n.a.	n.a.	0.1	0.1
Republic of Korea	0.4	0.8	0.8	1.5
Singapore	0.3	n.a.	0.7	1.6
Hong Kong	n.a.	n.a.	n.a.	n.a.
Japan	2.8	3.5	2.8	3.6
South Africa	n.a.	0.3	n.a.	n.a.
China	n.a.	n.a.	n.a.	.2
Philippines	0.1	n.a.	n.a.	n.a.
Indonesia	n.a.	0.1	n.a.	n.a.
USA	2.1	2.7	n.a.	2.5
Ireland	0.6	0.8	0.7	1.6
Thailand	n.a.	n.a.	n.a.	0.1
Israel	n.a.	n.a.	n.a.	2.6

Source: Computed from World Bank (2002).

Note
Figures calculated using the formula $x_i[\Sigma(x_i \ldots x_n)]^{-1}n$ where x_i refers to R&D scientists and engineers per million people in country i, and n the number of countries reporting data.

share of gross national investment and R&D scientists and engineers in the population, it can be seen that both Malaysia and Mexico rank very low among the selected economies (Rasiah, 2002). The index for Malaysia (0.13) and Mexico (0.23) were significantly lower than even China (0.47), Mauritius (0.33), and Brazil (0.32). The lack of R&D support institutionally has obviously restricted the capacity of firms in Penang and Jalisco to quicken their movement toward the technology frontier in the electronics industry.

The lack of a sufficiently strong emphasis on R&D infrastructure is reflected in the low residents' patents index recorded by Malaysia and Mexico (Rasiah, 2004). Residents were reluctant to file patents so as to avert distortions arising from the registration of patents by foreigners in a number of countries from R&D work carried out primarily at home sites. RPI is the better proxy of patent intensity owing to adjustment with the population of the country involved. It can be seen that the RPI of Malaysia (0.05) and Mexico (0.03) were lower than that of China (0.07) (despite its huge population), Brazil (0.34), South Africa (0.86), and Israel (0.34).

Hence, although the basic infrastructure is good enough to attract significant multinational relocation to Penang and Jalisco, this advantage is disappearing with the emergence of low wage sites with almost equally good basic infrastructure. Weaknesses in the provision of high tech and R&D infrastructure have severely restricted the capacity of these states to upgrade and participate in higher value activities. The formal institutions of human capital development have generally only managed to supply primary and secondary education, which was instrumental in attracting large-scale MNC operations in labor-intensive manufacturing activities from the early 1970s until the early 1990s in Malaysia and Mexico. The lack of high tech human capital restricted industrial upgrading, which became necessary from the mid-1990s when labor reserves were depleted and wages rose. Despite aggressive government efforts, both Penang and Jalisco lack sufficient supplies of high tech human capital. Federal institutions neither produced sufficient numbers nor effectively coordinated supply and demand conditions.

Cluster synergies

Penang and Jalisco have enjoyed strong MNC operations in electronics manufacturing for a number of decades. In addition, both locations have developed systemic coordination and network cohesion to support flexibility and inter-firm technological interface. MNCs in Penang and Jalisco enjoy strong linkages with local firms and are better connected with support institutions. State-initiated program centers have played a critical role in stimulating skills and supplier development in Penang and Jalisco. In addition, designing has also been promoted extensively in Jalisco.

Penang

The Penang government established the Penang Development Corporation (PDC) to undertake and promote socioeconomic development (PDC 1974, p. 4), which included the extensive promotion of export-oriented MNCs. MNCs helped raise Penang's manufacturing share in GDP from 13 percent in 1971 to 46 percent in 2000 (PDC, 2001). The Penang region built high volume production capability in electronic components, consumer appliances, hard disk drives, and PC components, by inserting in MNC-driven global production chains. Changes in the dynamics of MNC production coincided with improvements in systemic coordination in Penang, which helped strengthen clustering since the 1980s.

Although Penang achieved dynamic clustering, the lack of R&D infrastructure (including a serious shortage of engineers and scientists) – where federal institutions headquartered in the Kelang Valley hold governance jurisdiction – restricted industrial upgrading. Strong systemic coordination helped the cluster generate and appropriate considerable network synergies. Integrated business networks with PDC's pivotal intermediary role fueling cluster cohesion helped movement of tacit and experiential knowledge embodied in human capital for new firm creation, differentiation, and division of labor.

Penang: speciation synergies

Systemic coordination was instrumental in the relocation of industrial sub-species new to Penang, which helped sustain differentiation and extended the platform for human capital development in firms. A deliberate effort to promote subspecies to strengthen inter-firm links in Penang emerged from the late 1980s when a massive influx of electronics firms offered the state the opportunity to be selective. Personal approaches by the Penang government since the early 1970s attracted MNCs. Penang Electronics – opened as a symbolic spur – was started in 1970, which was followed by the relocation of Clarion and National Semiconductor in 1971 and, later, by Intel, Motorola, Hewlett Packard, AMD, and Hitachi by 1974. While myriad firms relocated, the early 1970s was dominated by the microelectronics subspecies. These firms used cutting-edge process technologies with extensive application of flexible production techniques from the 1980s.

Consumer electronics became important from the late 1970s, but particularly since the late 1980s. Sony, Toshiba, and Pensangko were some of the consumer electronics firms. Disk drive companies were actively wooed from 1989 with Maxtor, Conner Peripherals, Seagate, Quantum, Komag, and Read-Rite starting operations from the early 1990s. Many of them have either closed down or had relocated by the late 1990s, but Quantum, Seagate, and Komag were still operating in 2002. In addition to product transitions in old subsidiaries such as Komag and Osram,[8] the Penang government was promoting the opto-electronics subspecies in 2000–2002.[9]

The development of synergies from MNC operations also drew participation from Dell, which reported relocating in Penang to integrate around its product chain and strategically customize product development for the Asia Pacific market. Dell's movement to Penang attracted contract manufacturers such as Solectron and raised demand for other local suppliers. Subspecies of industries – not new to the universe – have also evolved domestically to stimulate differentiation and diversity in Penang. Machine tool and plastic molding species evolved from technological constraints emerging in the production dynamics of MNCs operating in Penang. The development of several tiers of firms in these industries has enabled the workforce to expand further embodied knowledge development and movement in the Penang cluster. Intel, AMD, Fairchild, and Hewlett Packard subcontracted out a number of older products to Globetronics, Unisem, and Carsem (the latter two located in Ipoh). MNC synergies initiated and stimulated the development of precision engineering, machinery, and plastic injection molding subspecies of firms in Penang, especially from the 1980s.

However, the lack of engineers, scientists, and technicians has restricted Penang's capacity to stimulate horizontal integration. The Penang government is keen on a pro-active strategy to step up the supply of engineers, scientists, and technicians with complementing imports from abroad, which are necessary to ameliorate the problem, but the jurisdiction for adoption and application rests with the federal government. China has already emerged as the biggest single threat to labor-intensive industries in Penang. In fact, four MNCs reported shifting operations from Penang to China in 2001.[10]

Penang: training ground

Changes in MNC strategies from the 1980s helped widen and deepen the production of tacit and experiential knowledge in Penang. Intel's, Motorola's, and AMD's progressive efforts from simple assembly to continuous improvement capabilities from the 1980s made it possible for greater technology transfer to Penang, which helped local plants upgrade to more complex and higher value-added activities (Rasiah, 1987; Lim 1991). Intel, Motorola, and AMD have been managed completely by Malaysians from 1980, the late 1980s, and the mid-1990s, respectively. Just-in-time (JIT) and the shift toward flexible production systems took place in the 1980s, which enabled semiconductor firms in Penang to avoid massive capacity restructuring during business downswings. New firm creation – primarily by ex-MNC employees – helped MNCs externalize dissimilar assembly and test lines easily facilitate organizational and process integration and reintegration.

In addition, MNCs such as Motorola, Intel, AMD, and Hitachi introduced redesigning activities in Penang, but were confined to adapting older technologies. Motorola Penang enjoys design leadership in Asia for the CT2 cordless telephone. The center does new product design, product–process interface, and advanced manufacturing processes. Motorola's R&D center, which started with four engineers in the 1980s, had nearly 120 in 1998 (Ngoh, 1994). However, Penang's short supply of R&D scientists and engineers made similar expansion by other MNCs difficult. Penang does not have a critical mass of scientists and engineers to support rapid product innovation or institutional support for industrial upgrading.

Dell has developed a mass customization system to reproduce in Penang its "produce to order" model that combines the Toyota production system (cellular manufacturing, JIT, Kanban, quick changeover, continuous improvement, self-directed work teams) with the Internet to integrate production and distribution into a single high-throughput process. Dell's factory is being geared to respond directly to the final customer so that all intermediary distribution links are eliminated. Its managing director reported that Penang stood out not only because of the smooth coordinating approach of the state government and PDC, but also because of its cultural mix that offered regional customization potential for much of Asia (Rasiah, 1995). Dell's unique fusion of design, process flow, and final demand facilitated by the Internet has offered production and marketing flexibility. Dell's inter-firm production network has generated considerable information and knowledge synergies for stimulating differentiation and division of labor in Penang. However, Dell does not have a sufficiently large pool of engineers and scientists in Penang to drive rapid product innovation and systems integration capabilities, which has constrained its efforts to achieve integrated manufacturing operations.

In addition, all electronics MNCs interviewed are engaged in cutting-edge competition, which has forced them to raise skill levels of employees using a long-term vision of human resource development. Company CEOs reported that the application of Total Quality Management (TQM) requires that employees continuously improve operations at all levels. National Semiconductor's subsidiaries in Penang, i.e. Dynacraft and Micro Components Technology, started to support its chip assembly subsidiary, i.e. Fairchild in Penang, trained many of Penang's engineers in precision engineering and metal working technology who now own and manage Prodelcon, Metfab, and Rapid Synergy. The founders of these three firms also acquired their tacit and experiential knowledge from working in Micro Machining, which was a subsidiary of National Semiconductor until 1989. Former employees of Intel managed Shinca, Shintel, Sanmatech, Unico, Globetronics, and Solectron in 1999. Former employees of Micro Machining (then a subsidiary of National Semiconductor that changed its name to Fairchild in 1989) started the local firms of Prodelcon, Polytool, Rapid Synergy and Metfab. Komag, Quantum and Seagate also benefited from absorbing managers from older MNCs in Penang.

Redesigning operations in MNCs also produced human capital synergies for other firms. Two of Motorola's Penang staff joined the R&D division of Sapura, a local firm located in Kelang Valley, in the late 1980s. Two of Intel's R&D personnel left for AMD's NVD design center in the mid-1990s. However, restrictions on immigration involving R&D personnel have limited MNCs capacity to upgrade in Penang. Intel, Motorola, AMD, HP, and Fairchild, and the supplier firms of Eng Technology, Trans Capital, and Unico reported trying in vain to bring foreign experts to expand R&D activities.[11]

The creation of entrepreneurs, managers, technicians, and skilled human capital has helped MNCs upgrade their own operations as the continuous movement out of older employees allowed the entry of fresh human capital with new ideas and willing to acquire new knowledge. Employees moved out to help start and support new firm creation in Penang. The increased inter-firm movement of human capital stimulated greater outsourcing of dissimilar activities while allowing MNCs to upgrade and specialize in higher value-added operations. The increasing outsourcing of dissimilar products alongside inter-firm movement of employees helped increase the number of suppliers to MNCs.

Penang: differentiation and division of labor

The expansion and movement of embodied knowledge in employees helped intensify differentiation and division of labor. Entrepreneurs and professionals, and technical and skilled employees developed in MNCs moved to start or strengthen new firms. Employees of Intel established Globetronics, Shinca, Shintel, and Unico, while Motorola launched BCM. Eng Technology, Metfab, Prodelcon, and Choong Engineering grew strongly from technological diffusion from Intel. Wong Engineering grew with support from Motorola. The founder of Loshta gained his tacit and experiential knowledge working in Motorola. Polytool and Rapid Synergy absorbed considerable precision engineering technology from Intel and AMD. Complementary but dissimilar product lines were relocated as new firm creation expanded, which was accompanied by the emergence of a locally owned supplier base with increasing differentiation and division of labor.

Strong systemic coordination and the flow of embodied knowledge stimulated localization of inputs by MNCs. Local supporting firms in Penang sourced 46 percent of their inputs locally in 1996 (Narayanan, 1997). Differentiation and the development of tacit and experiential knowledge worked both ways. The economic advantages of introducing flexible production systems encouraged lead suppliers actively to differentiate and intensify the division of labor. Rasiah (1994) had reported only three stages in 1990.

The first-tier vendors (those who had the first links with the electronics sector firms) have, in time, chosen to specialize in certain functions, and passed on some of their previous tasks to second-tier machine tool firms whom they helped foster. These second-tier firms have gone on to spawn their own third-tier sub-contracting firms, giving them simple tasks like parts fabrications, which were no longer sufficiently profitable for the former.

Increased differentiation and division of labor helped deepen and widen the movement of tacit and experiential knowledge embodied in employees. Most supplier firms in Penang have passed through the third and fourth stages of technology absorption and diffusion (Rasiah, 1994). In the first stage, suppliers did simple grinding, machining, welding, and stamping operations to supply trolleys, components, and parts to MNCs, using imported machinery and designs and drawings supplied by MNCs. This stage characterized the local machine tool firms in the 1970s. In the second stage, supplier firms upgraded to assemble semi-automated machinery and precision tools using imported machinery and designs and drawings from MNCs. In the third stage, supplier firms adapted and reverse-engineered imported machinery for their own use, and high precision foreign components and machinery for sale to MNCs in Malaysia and subsidiaries abroad. In the fourth stage, suppliers developed their own original equipment manufacturing capabilities to supply precision components and machinery to MNCs in Malaysia and their subsidiaries abroad. In the fifth stage, suppliers introduced original designs, though much of production is oriented toward subcontract demand operations.

Several first-tier firms – operating at stage four – evolved from simple backyard workshops to modern firms, and later to MNCs themselves. Eng Technology has subsidiaries in China, the Philippines, Malaysia, and Thailand, while Atlan has subsidiaries in Malaysia and Indonesia. The network of suppliers in Penang shows a generally vertical division of labor with firms confined to all the five stages of technology utilization. Nevertheless, a handful of firms (e.g. Eng technology, BCM, Unico, and SEM) show strong potential for horizontal integration. Strong technological interface between MNCs and suppliers encouraged simultaneous inter-firm engineering activities.

Firms exploited the local systemic synergies and open but integrated business network of Penang to encourage the exit and entry of entrepreneurial, technical, and skilled human capital to support new firm creation. The number of plastic, machine tool, and packaging firms linked directly or through first-, second-, and third-tier suppliers to electronics MNCs in Penang expanded from around 45 firms in 1989 to around 155 in 1993 and 455 in 2001.[12] The spread of MNC-driven synergies could not have reached high levels without the active intermediary role of the PDC. The PDC also matched potentially capable local firms with MNCs in the 1980s. The PDC helped solve collective actions involving scale and scope (e.g. training) by coordinating the formation of training centers and encouraging active consultation between suppliers, institutions, and MNCs. The PDC's role helped translate MNC demand into the formation of the Penang Skills Development Centre (PSDC) in 1989. The PDC initiated the opening of the PSDC by offering a highly subsidized building – charging a symbolic rent of RM1 a year instead of the market rate estimated at RM1 million a year.[13] The PSDC is particularly important in offering specialized and generic skills training. In addition, Intel and Motorola have specialized continuous training centers where employees can also access training and skills unrelated to their formal work. Following the demonstration effects from Intel and Motorola, locally owned Atlan established its own training center in the late 1990s. The PDC was instrumental in attracting capitalization of Globetronics from Malaysian Technology Development Corporation (MTDC).

The founding of Trans Capital, Unico, and Globetronics in the 1990s, all managed by former MNC employees, added a new dimension to Penang, which helped raise local demand for skills for "front-end" operations like chip design, surface mount technology (SMT), and applications engineering. In addition to offering demand for the absorption of R&D personnel from MNCs, these firms helped widen knowledge accumulation in local firms, though the lack of R&D scientists and engineers in the country has restricted horizontal integration.

Local suppliers achieved rapid process and product upgrades through in-house and simultaneous engineering links with MNCs. A larger number of local suppliers linked to electronics MNCs in Penang have also developed stronger technological capabilities and recorded generally higher value-added and labor productivity growth than supplier firms elsewhere in Malaysia (Rasiah, 2002). Penang's open cluster encouraged employees gaining tacit and experiential skills to support new firm creation.

Strong systemic coordination helped network cohesion and dynamic clustering in Penang, which stimulated inter-firm flows of embodied knowledge in Penang. The inter-firm movement of human capital – exposed to cutting-edge manufacturing practices – helped the appropriation of considerable tacit knowledge embodied in employees in Penang. The systematic promotion of electronics subspecies and open integrated business network with strong employee movement to support new firm creation helped increase differentiation and division of labor. However, limitations in the coordination of high tech and R&D support institutions have restricted firms' participation in R&D activities. In fact, the Malaysian Institution of Microelectronics Systems – originally started under the Prime Minister's Department and late corporatized in the 1990s to facilitate greater integration with the private sector – has failed to create the coordination and incubation synergies necessary to support innovation in firms. The Industrial Technical Research Institute (ITRI) of Taiwan has successfully produced a series of new innovating firms, *inter alia*, in the electronics industry (Mathews and Cho, 2000; Rasiah and Lin, 2005). The MTDC has not managed capitalized new start-ups to drive their entry into high tech activities. The role of the Malaysia, Industry, Government, High Technology (MIGHT) forum to establish and drive industry–government collaboration in high tech industries has hardly gained any currency. The government's clustering initiatives under the Second Industrial Master Plan (IMP2) in 1995 and the launching of the Multimedia Super Corridor (MSC) in 1997, despite their newness, have also provided little impact on technological dynamism in the industry. Hence, rising production costs and competition from cheap cost sites such as China and the Philippines are threatening to stall further differentiation and division of labor in Penang.

Jalisco

The governor and the state economic planning secretary have played a dynamic role to target MNCs and coordinate the development of linkages in Jalisco. Although the earliest MNCS in electronics relocated in the early 1970s, import-substitution was still the prime propellant of growth as oil revenue accounted for more than 80 percent of exports. Falling oil prices by the mid-1980s and the debt crisis led the Jalisco state government and Economic Development Board to promote export-oriented manufacturing – including electronics MNCs – from the mid-1980s. This expansion was further strengthened following the opening of the North Atlantic Free Trade Area (NAFTA) in 1995. The Jalisco region has since experienced a massive build-up in high volume production capability in industrial electronics, consumer appliances, hard disk drives, and PC components and supplier firms, by inserting in MNC-driven global production chains.

Although Jalisco achieved dynamic clustering, the lack of R&D infrastructure (including a serious shortage of engineers and scientists) – where governance of tertiary institutions and R&D support institutions is held by federal institutions headquartered in Mexico City – restricted industrial upgrading. Strong systemic coordination helped the cluster generate and appropriate considerable network synergies. Integrated business networks with Jalisco Development Corporation's (JDC's) pivotal intermediary role fueling cluster cohesion helped the movement of knowledge embodied in human capital for new firm creation, differentiation, and division of labor.

Jalisco: speciation synergies

Systemic coordination was instrumental in the relocation of industrial subspecies new to Jalisco, which helped sustain differentiation and extended the platform for human capital development in firms. A deliberate effort to promote subspecies to strengthen supplier networks emerged from the late 1990s when a massive influx of electronics firms offered the state the opportunity to be selective. Although the relocation of giant electronics firms had already created the momentum, strong negotiations on strengthening the infrastructure to source domestic supplies, especially of low value-added components, attracted both local firms and smaller MNCs. While myriad firms relocated, the early 1970s was dominated by the microelectronics subspecies. These firms use cutting-edge process technologies with extensive application of flexible production techniques from the 1980s.

Low value-added consumer electronics firms gradually expanded far more at the US–Mexico border where maquila-type operations locally produced little value added other than the wages paid to local employees. Higher value-added operations, such as computer and peripheral assemblies, and contract manufacturing, expanded more in Jalisco where wages were higher than at the US–Mexico border. The development of synergies from flagship firms such as IBM, HP, and Motorola attracted contract manufacturing MNCs such as Sanmina, Solectron, Flextronics, Natsteel, and SCI. The Guadalajara High Tech Park is expected to attract further inflows of contract manufacturers.

Subspecies of industries have also evolved domestically to stimulate differentiation and diversity in Jalisco. Machine tool and plastic molding species evolved from technological constraints emerging in the production dynamics of MNCs operating in Jalisco. The development of several tiers of firms in these industries has enabled the workforce to expand further embodied knowledge development and movement in the Jalisco cluster. Motorola, HP, IBM and Siemens subcontracted out a number of product lines to contract manufacturers.

However, the lack of engineers, scientists, and technicians has restricted Jalisco's capacity to stimulate horizontal integration. The Jalisco government has introduced a plan to step up the supply of engineers, scientists, and technicians in the state to enable upgrading. As the Economic Planning secretary put it: "We must solve this problem before the NAFTA effect evaporates. We have seen the elimination of the apparel industry from Chinese exports to the American market. Electronics will follow this if we do not build our high tech infrastructure. We cannot compete on wages."

Jalisco: training ground

The Jalisco government introduced and helped coordinate programs at the state level to ameliorate skills and technical human capital deficiencies the state was facing in its efforts to promote industrial upgrading. The integration of Mexico with North America as a free-trade area helped transform MNC strategies on sourcing, training, and market orientation. Motorola, HP, and IBM's efforts to shift from simple assembly to continuous improvement capabilities across their subsidiaries worldwide made it possible for greater technology transfer to Jalisco. Value-added activities far more complex then the maquila operations typical of Mexican offshore operations have expanded. JIT and the shift toward flexible production systems in American electronics firms took place in the 1980s. Although entrepreneurs have been discouraged by high interest rates facing borrowers from banks, new firm creation – primarily by ex-MNC employees – has helped MNCs externalize dissimilar assembly and test lines to facilitate organizational and process integration and reintegration.

The following comments from Guadalajara's economic development board chief provide further insight:

> We had a plan even before the integration of Mexico into NAFTA to increase the supply of skilled personnel and designers in Jalisco state to stimulate industrial upgrading. NAFTA merely allowed us to seek this alternative without us having to offer tax holidays. Unlike the maquiladoras in Mexico, we have consciously strengthened the basic [e.g. ICT access and connectivity, and loan facilities to support local supplier networks] and high tech infrastructure [e.g. designing and training centers].

In addition, MNCs such as Motorola, IBM, and HP have introduced designing activities in Jalisco, but confined to adapting older technologies. IBM Guadalajara produced around 2.5 million laptop computers to become IBM's largest manufacturing operation in 2001. Guadalajara enjoys design leadership in Mexico. State initiatives to deepen the high tech infrastructure at the Guadalajara High Tech Park promises to further expand designing synergies in Jalisco.

IBM's integration strategy in Jalisco attracted global service providers (GSPs) such as Sanmina and SCI to supply critical completely knocked down (CKDs) parts such as motherboards and monitors and even assemble desktop computers in Guadalajara. IBM reported having established a horizontal division of labor where its focus has increasingly shifted to designing and market emphasis. At the time of the author's visit to the plant in Guadalajara, laptops for the US market were still assembled by IBM but significant shares of the value added previously carried out in China was being outsourced to Sanmina and SCI under the produce-to-order framework typical of cellular manufacturing. IBM's designing center was being geared to absorb customer tastes so that the chain it drives in the division of labor matches markets with production.[14] Its senior engineer reported that Jalisco stood out in Mexico because of smooth networking links with state government officials who even responded to higher skills requirements and supplier support by directly supporting such activities.

In addition, CARDENAS reported that all electronics MNCs in Jalisco are engaged in cutting-edge competition, which has forced them to raise skill levels of employees using a long-term vision of human resource development. The focus on higher value-added activities to meet rising wage demands has driven out maquila-type activities in electronics from Jalisco. Unlike the border locations where electronics firms typically source their inputs from the US, firms in Jalisco increasingly source from the state – from both foreign GSPs and local suppliers.

Designing operations in MNCs also produced human capital synergies for other firms. The Jalisco state economic planning director reported that employees from older MNCs such as IBM, HP, and Motorola have moved to run critical functions in new firms such as SCI and also start local suppliers. In fact, this official reported stepping up programs in Jalisco to increase the supply of high tech human capital so that turnovers in incumbent firms do not undermine their upgrading operations. However, much of the designing activities do not involve frontier R&D and, hence, have hardly yielded patents. A Siemens official reported that it requires a different batch of R&D engineers and technicians and critical numbers for MNCS to enter such patentable activities.

The creation of entrepreneurs, managers, technicians, and skilled human capital has helped MNCs upgrade their own operations as the continuous movement out of older employees allowed the entry of fresh human capital with new ideas and willing to acquire new knowledge. Employees moved out to help start and support new firm creation in Jalisco. The increased inter-firm movement of human capital stimulated greater outsourcing of dissimilar activities while allowing MNCs to upgrade and specialize in higher value-added operations. The increasing outsourcing of dissimilar products alongside inter-firm movement of employees helped increase the number of suppliers to MNCs such as Motorola, HP and IBM.

Jalisco: differentiation and division of labor

The expansion and movement of embodied knowledge in employees helped intensify differentiation and division of labor. Entrepreneurs and professionals, and technical and skilled employees who developed in MNCs moved to start or strengthen new firms. Complementary but dissimilar product lines were relocated as new firm creation expanded, which was accompanied by the emergence of a locally owned supplier base with increasing differentiation and division of labor. Despite an unattractive financial environment where firms faced domestic annual interest rates of between 15 and 20 percent in 2003, suppliers registered under the CARDENAS program have enjoyed preferential loans and interest rates to support production and designing activities in Jalisco.

Strong systemic coordination and the flow of embodied knowledge encouraged the relocation of foreign suppliers as well as localization of inputs by MNCs. CARDENAS officials reported the growth of significant foreign and local suppliers engaged in manufacturing motherboards, monitors, keyboards, and components in Jalisco. Differentiation and the development of tacit and experiential knowledge worked both ways. The economic advantages of NAFTA and the introduction of flexible production systems encouraged suppliers actively to differentiate and intensify the division of labor. A senior engineer of a leading American computer company in Guadalajara reported in 2003:

> It is now the norm with companies using cutting-edge technologies. When a flagship company relocates in a region with good high tech infrastructure it triggers a snowballing effect as different layers of firms in the supply chain either relocate from abroad or emerge locally to support its operations. Outsourcing contracts with an American and a Taiwanese firm has already meant that motherboards and even desktop computers are assembled outside my company. When you add microchip, capacitors, resistors, diodes, machine tool, plastic, and packaging, the number simply multiplies. We expect further outsourcing in the near future.

Increased differentiation and division of labor helped deepen and widen the movement of embodied knowledge from firm to firm. Jakobo reported that several suppliers in Jalisco have designing capabilities. Advanced precision engineering and plastic injection molding firms have developed to service electronics and automobile firms in Jalisco. Liberalization has had the effect of forcing low value-added firms to concentrate more at the maquila locations by the US–Mexico border, but supplier firms remaining in Jalisco have tended to rationalize and even export to the US.

Apart from GSPs from abroad, unlike firms in Penang, local suppliers in Jalisco have not internationalized production operations. Instead some Jalisco suppliers have expanded operations to displace maquila-type manufacturing at the US–Mexican border. The secretary of the state planning department noted that Jalisco suppliers' further upgrading in the value chains requires them to expand operations across borders – to other parts of Central America.

Firms exploited the local systemic synergies and open but integrated business network of Jalisco to encourage the exit and entry of entrepreneurial, technical, and skilled human capital to support new firm creation. The number of plastic, machine tool, and packaging firms linked directly or through first-, second-, and third-tier suppliers to electronics MNCs in Jalisco easily reached more than 300 in 2003.[15] The spread of MNC-driven synergies could not have reached high levels without the active intermediary role of the state government, and The National Chamber of Business (CARNIETI) and Supplier Development Organization (CARDENAS). CARDENAS has also actively sought support from the state government and the MNCs to match local suppliers with electronics firms. The state government helped solve collective actions involving scale and scope (e.g. training and designing, contract R&D, and curriculum development with universities) by establishing coordination councils to encourage active consultation between suppliers, institutions, and MNCs.

CARNIETI, CARDENAS, and the state government's initiatives helped attract training and design suppliers to meet growing MNC demand for training and designing. In addition, MNCs have started designing centers in Jalisco to support higher value-added activities in the state. Following the demonstration effects from IBM, HP, and Motorola, local firms also established designing centers in the late 1990s. CARDENAS was instrumental in attracting preferential loans for local suppliers in Jalisco.

Learning and technology acquisition by local suppliers and e-commerce firms in the 1990s provided further impetus for differentiation and division of labor in Jalisco. In addition to offering demand for the absorption of technical personnel from MNCs, these firms helped widen knowledge accumulation in local firms. However, the lack of R&D scientists and engineers in the country has restricted horizontal integration.

Local suppliers achieved rapid process and product upgrades through in-house and simultaneous engineering links with MNCs and the use of specialized design centers in Jalisco. Not only are a larger number of local suppliers linked to electronics MNCs, but stronger technological capabilities and value adds have developed in Jalisco compared with the maquila-type locations elsewhere in Mexico (Kenney and Florida, 1994; Sklair, 1993; Ernst and O'Conner, 1992; Wilson, 1992). Jalisco's differentiation process has further been aided by substantial experience in automotive manufacturing. World-class automotive suppliers require specialization in a range of technologies – machinery and plastic engineering, glass, and electronics – which helped the progression of local suppliers in component manufacturing. The aggressive efforts by the state government and economic planning department helped match and drive the development of suppliers in Jalisco.

Strong systemic coordination helped network cohesion and dynamic clustering, which stimulated inter-firm flows of embodied knowledge in Jalisco. Inter-firm human capital flows – exposed to cutting-edge manufacturing practices – helped the appropriation of considerable embodied knowledge in Jalisco. The government's initiatives to strengthen proactively the high tech infrastructure in the state further strengthened the cluster, thereby offering the critical mass and connectivity for the movement of experienced employees to support new firm creation. However, limitations in the science and technology infrastructure have restricted expansion into upgrading and R&D activities. The 27 public centers of research and technology development under the Mexican National Science and Technology Council (CONACYT) have hardly contributed to new product development in the electronics firms located in Mexico. Managers from three firms in Guadalajara reported in 2003 the lack of connection between these public research centers and firms. Indeed, officials from the Mexican Patent Office reported in 2003 the dismal record of registration of patents from R&D undertaken in Mexico by local firms.[16] Unless there is an increase in R&D human capital and development research to support higher value-added operations, local officials' concerns about the evaporation of the NAFTA effect may reverse the synergy gains achieved in industrial upgrading in Jalisco.

Conclusions

The findings offer ramifications for policy. While basic infrastructure in both countries has achieved universal standards, weak federal coordination has constrained the supply of R&D and high tech infrastructure, which is critical to stimulate firms' participation in upgrading and innovative activities. Hence, MNCs expanded into labor-intensive operations in Malaysia and Mexico in the 1970s until the early 1990s – accessing low-wage literate workers. However, when the labor reserves were exhausted by the mid-1990s, both MNCs and local firms lacked a sufficient supply of technical labor, engineers, scientists, and R&D institutions to stimulate industrial upgrading to higher value-added activities. Although maquila-type, lowly integrated operations typify electronics manufacturing in most locations in Malaysia and Mexico, strong systemic coordination locally has produced strong clustering and human capital synergies in the states of Penang and Jalisco. However, the lack of R&D engineers and technicians has restricted strong participation in R&D activities even in Penang and Jalisco. Because high tech and R&D infrastructure generate important synergies that are not substitutable, the differentiation and division of labor that has emerged in Penang and Jalisco has not attracted or produced higher value-added segments in value chains and the consequent horizontal integration necessary to drive regional synergies to higher levels.

Strong systemic coordination in Penang and Jalisco has nevertheless created differentiation and division of labor, and integration with institutional support from economic agents. The strong intermediary role of the PDC and the state government in Penang, and the economic and planning department and state government in Jalisco helped bring together the business associations and firms, giving the systemic coordination necessary to raise the rate of systemic knowledge flows and inter-firm links as well as motivating new firm creation. Despite the lack of innovative activities, the Penang and Jalisco experience supports the proposition that MNCs can integrate and participate in dynamic clustering.

Both Penang and Jalisco failed to engender a critical mass of high tech technical personnel and engineers and scientists as well as the requisite incubation, *à la* Taiwan, to stimulate the birth of firms to carry out R&D activities. The instruments introduced by the Malaysian (e.g. MOSTI, MIMOS, MDC, MTDC, and MIGHT) and the Mexican governments (e.g. MST, Science Council, and CONACYT) have yet to support tangible new product development in the electronics industry. Selective immigration has been instrumental in overcoming demand–supply human capital deficits in the US, Singapore, Israel, and Ireland. However, the higher education institutions of learning in Malaysia and Mexico have lacked effective supply–demand coordination to produce technical graduates, engineers, and scientists. Constraining immigration policies have also restricted imports to overcome shortages. Thus, growing deficits in technical and R&D scientists and engineers have undermined the capacity of MNCs and local entrepreneurs in Penang and Jalisco to introduce higher value-added activities.

Despite the shortcomings, network cohesion and the intermediary role of local development corporations and local government have driven strong clustering effects in the MNC-dominated states of Penang and Jalisco. MNCs have been important training grounds for the development of tacit and experiential knowledge embodied in entrepreneurs, professionals, technicians, and skilled human capital for new firm creation in Malaysia and Mexico. The relatively underdeveloped high tech and R&D infrastructure in both Malaysia and Mexico has restricted the capacity of systemic forces to drive firms' participation in innovative higher value-added operations in Penang and Jalisco. Unless these deficiencies are met, Penang and Jalisco will continue to lose industrial synergies to competing sites with lower wages such as China.

Acknowledgments

I am grateful to Pedro Lara-Martinez, and Ganesh Rasagam, Rohan Felix, and Vigneswarer for helping with the fieldwork in Jalisco and Penang, respectively.

The study was financed from grants provided by UNU-INTECH and OECD. The usual disclaimer applies.

Notes

1 External influences were arguably more important since FDI relocation also expanded into the other Southeast Asian economies of Indonesia and Thailand.
2 In fact, the US Customs items of 806.7 and 807 specifically offered generous exemptions to stimulate the relocation of low value-added manufacturing activities to developing economies (Scibberas, 1977).
3 Abramovitz (1956) produced a similar argument about increasing returns. New growth economists such as Romer (1986) and Lucas (1988) demonstrated these ideas using elegant models. See Scherer (1992, 1999) for a lucid account.
4 Variants of these arguments related to transactions costs to explain the existence of firms were advanced by Coase (1937) and Williamson (1996), and the relevance of non-market modes of coordination by Richardson (1960, 1972) and North (1991).
5 Author interviews (1995).
6 Author interviews (1995, 1999).
7 Ganesh Rasagam assisted in opening doors of firms in Penang, and Pedro Lara-Martinez and Raquel Partida of the University of Guadalajara assisted with establishing contacts in Jalisco.
8 Osram was renamed from Siemens Litronix.
9 Author interviews (2001) with Penang's Chief Minister.
10 Author interviews (2001).
11 Author interviews (2002).
12 Author interviews (1995, 2001).
13 Author interviews (1999, 2001).
14 Some officials reported the likelihood of IBM outsourcing all manufacturing activities in Jalisco – a move that will transform it to the form taken by Dell.
15 Interviews with CARDENAS officials in January 2003.
16 Interviews by author and Pedro Lara-Martinez in Guadalajara in 2003.

References

Abramovitz, M. (1956) "Resource and Output Trends in the United States Since 1870," *American Economic Review*, 46(2), 5–23.

Amsden, A. (1989) *Asia's Next Giant: South Korea and Late Industrialization*, Oxford University Press, New York.

Aoki, M. (2001) *Towards Comparative Institutional Analysis*, MIT Press, Cambridge.

Arrow, K. (1962) "The Economic Significance of Learning by Doing," *Review of Economic Studies*, 29, pp. 155–173.

Best, M. (2001) *The New Competitive Advantage*, Oxford University Press, Oxford.

Boudeville, J.R. (1966) *Problems of Regional Economic Planning*, Edinburgh University Press, Edinburgh.

Brusco, S. (1982) "The Emilian Model: Productive Decentralisation and Social Integration," *Cambridge Journal of Economics*, 6(2), pp. 167–184.

Chandler, A. (1962) *Strategy and Structure: Chapters in the History of the American Industrial Enterprise*, MIT Press, Cambridge.

Coase, R. (1937) "Nature of the Firm," *Economica*, 16(4), pp. 386–405.

Cooke, P. and Morgan, P. (1998) *The Associational Economy: Firms, Regions, and Innovation*, Oxford University Press, Oxford.

Doner, R. (2001) "Institutions and the Tasks of Economic Upgrading," paper prepared for delivery at the 2001 Annual Meeting of the American Political Science Association, San Francisco, Aug. 30 to Sept. 2.

Ernst, D. and O'Conner, D. (1992) *Competing in the Electronics Industry: The Experience of the Newly Industrializing Economies*, OECD, Paris.

Freeman, C. (1988) "Japan: A new system of innovation," G. Dosi *et al.* (eds.) *Technical Change and Economic Theory*, Pinter Publishers, London.

Friedmann, J. (1972) "A General Theory of Polarized Development," in N.M. Hansen (ed.), *Growth Centres in Regional Economic Development*, Free Press, New York.

Garofoli, G. (ed.) (1992) *Endogenous Development and Southern Europe*, Aldershot, Avebury.

Gereffi, G. (1994) "The Organization of Buyer-Driven Global Commodity Chains: How US retailers shape overseas production networks," in G. Gerrefi and M. Korseniewwicz (eds.) *Commodity Chains and Global Capitalism*, Greenwood Press, Westport.

Gereffi, G. (2002) "Prospects for Industrial Upgrading by Developing Countries in the Global Apparel Commodity Chain," *International Journal of Business and Society*, 3(1), pp. 27–60.

Guerrieri, P., Iammarino, S., and Pietrobelli, C. (eds.) (2001) *The Global Challenge to Industrial Districts: SMEs in Italy and Taiwan*, Edward Elgar, Cheltenham.

Hamilton, C. (1983) "Capitalist Industrialization in East Asia's Four Little Tigers," *Journal of Contemporary Asia*, 13(1), pp. 35–73.

Hirschman, A.O. (1958) *Strategy of Economic Development*, Yale University Press, New Haven.

Hirschman, A.O. (1970) *Exit, Voice, and Loyalty: Responses to Decline in Firms, Organizations, and State*, Harvard University Press, Cambridge.

Hirst, P. and Zeitlin, J. (1991) *Reversing Industrial Decline? Industrial Structure and Policy in Britain and Her Competitors*, Berg Publishers, Oxford.

Kaldor, N. (1957) "A Model of Economic Growth," *Economic Journal*, 67, pp. 591–624.

Kenney, M. and Florida, R. (1994) "Japanese Maquiladoras: Production Organization and Global Commodity Chains," *World Development*, 22(1), pp. 27–44.

Lall, S. (1996) *Learning from the Tigers*, Macmillan, Basingstoke.

Lall, S. (2001) *Competitiveness, Technology and Skills*, Edward Elgar, Cheltenham.

Lall, S. and Streeten, P. (1977) *Foreign Investment, Transnationals and Developing Countries*, Macmillan, Basingstoke.

Lim, L.Y.C. (1978) "Multinational Firms and Manufacturing for Export in Less-Developed Economies: The Case of the Electronics Industry in Malaysia and Singapore," unpublished doctoral dissertation, Michigan University, Ann Arbor.

Lim, P. (1991) *From Ashes Rebuilt to Manufacturing Excellence*, Pelanduk Publications, Petaling Jaya.

Lucas, R. (1988) "On the Mechanics of Economic Development," *Journal of Monetary Economics*, 22, pp. 3–22.

Lundvall, B.A. (ed.) (1992) *National Systems of Innovation: Towards a Theory of Innovation and Interactive Learning*, Pinter Publishers, London.

MITI (1996) *Second Industrial Master Plan*, Ministry of International Trade and Industry, Kuala Lumpur.

Marshall, A. (1890) *Principles of Economics*, Macmillan, London.

Mathews, J.A. and Cho, D.S. (2000) *Tiger Technology: The Creation of a Semiconductor Industry in East Asia*, Cambridge University Press, Cambridge.

Mills, J.S. (1848) *Principles of Political Economy, with some of their Applications to Social Policy*, John W. Parker and West Strand, London.

Myrdal, G. (1957) *Economic Theory and Under-Developed Regions*, Methuen, New York.

Narayanan, S. (1997) "Technology Absorption and Diffusion among Local Supporting Firms in the Electronics Sector," *IKMAS Working Papers*, No. 9, Bangi.

Nelson, R. (ed.) (1993) *National Innovation Systems*, Oxford University Press, New York.

Nelson, R.R. and Winter, S.G. (1982) *An Evolutionary Theory of Economic Change*, Harvard University Press, Cambridge, Mass.

Ngoh, C.L. (1994) *Motorola Globalization: The Penang Journey*, Lee and Sons, Kuala Lumpur.

North, D. (1991) "Institutions, Transaction Costs and Economic Growth," *Economic Inquiry*, 25(3), pp. 419–428.

Pavitt, K. (1984) "Sectoral Patterns of Technical Change: Towards a Taxanomy and a Theory," *Research Policy*, 13(6), pp. 343–373.

PDC (1974) *Annual Report*, Penang Development Corporation, Penang.

PDC (2001) *Annual Report*, Penang: Penang Development Corporation.

Penrose, E. (1959) *The Theory of the Growth of the Firm*, Oxford University Press, Oxford.

Perroux, F. (1950) "Economic Space: Theory and Applications," *Quarterly Journal of Economics*, 64, pp. 89–104

Perroux, F. (1970) "Note on the Concept of Growth Poles," in D. McKee, R. Dean and W. Leahy (eds.), *Regional Economics: Theory and Practice*, The Free Press, New York.

Piore, M.J. and Sabel, C.F. (1984) *The Second Industrial Divide: Possibilities for Prosperity*, Basic Books, New York.

Polanyi, M. (1997) "Tacit Knowledge," in L. Prusak (ed.), *Knowledge in Organizations*, Butterworth-Heinemann, Boston.

Porter, M.E. (1990) *The Competitive Advantage of Nations*, Free Press, New York.

Porter, M. (1998) *Competitive Advantage: Creating and Sustaining Superior Performance*, Free Press, New York.

Pyke, F. and Sengenberger, W. (eds.) (1992) *Industrial Districts and Local Economic Regeneration*, International Institute for Labour Studies, Geneva.

Rasiah, R. (1987) *Pembahagian Kerja Antarabangsa: Industri Separa Konduktor di Pulau Pinang*, Masters thesis submitted to Science University of Malaysia (Published in 1993 by the Malaysian Social Science Association, Kuala Lumpur).

Rasiah, R. (1988) "The Semiconductor Industry in Penang: Implications for NIDL Theories," *Journal of Contemporary Asia*, 18(1), pp. 24–46.

Rasiah, R. (1993) "Competition and Governance: Work in Malaysia's Textile and Garment Industries," *Journal of Contemporary Asia*, 23(1), pp. 3–24.

Rasiah, R. (1994) "Flexible Production Systems and Local Machine Tool Subcontracting: Electronics Transnationals in Malaysia," *Cambridge Journal of Economics*, 18(3), pp. 279–298.

Rasiah, R. (1995) *Foreign Capital and Industrialization in Malaysia*, Macmillan, London.

Rasiah, R. (1999) "Malaysia's National Innovation System," in K.S. Jomo and G. Felker (eds.), *Technology, Competitiveness and the State*, Routledge, London.

Rasiah, R. (2002) "Systemic Coordination and the Knowledge Economy: Human Capital Development in Malaysia's MNC-driven Electronics Clusters," *Transnational Corporations*, 11(3), pp. 89–129.

Rasiah, R. (2004) *Foreign Firms, Technological Capabilities and Economic Performance: Evidence from Africa, Asia and Latin America*, Edward Elgar, London.

Rasiah, R. and Yin, Y. (2005) "Learning and Innovation: The role of market, government and trust in the information hardware industry in Taiwan," *International Journal of Technology and Globalization*, 1(3/4), pp. 400–432.

Richardson, G.B. (1960) *Information and Investment*, Oxford University Press, Oxford.

Richardson, G.B. (1972) "The Organisation of Industry," *Economic Journal*, 82, pp. 883–896.

Romer, P. (1986) "Increasing Returns and Long-run Growth," *Journal of Political Economy*, 94, pp. 1002–1037.

Rosenberg, N. (1982) *Inside the Black Box*, Cambridge University Press, Cambridge.

Sabel, C. (1995) "Design, Deliberation, and Democracy: On the New Pragmatism of Firms and Public Institutions," paper presented at the conference, *Liberal Institutions, Economic Constitutional Rights, and the Role of Organizations*, European University Institute, Florence, Dec. 15–16.

Saxenian, A.L. (1994) *The Regional Advantage: Culture and Competition in Silicon Valley and Route 128*, Harvard University Press, Cambridge.

Saxenian, A.L. (1999) *Silicon Valley's New Immigrant Entrepreneurs*, Public Policy Institute of California, San Francisco.

Scherer, F. (1992) *International High Technology Competition*, Harvard University Press, Cambridge.

Scherer, F. (1999) *New Perspectives on Economic Growth and Technological Innovation*, Brookings Institution Press, Washington, DC.

Schumpeter, J. (1934) *The Theory of Economic Development*, MIT Press, Cambridge.

Sciberas (1977) *Multinational Electronic Companies and National Economic Policies*, JAI Press, Connecticut.

Scott, A.J. (1988) *New Industrial Spaces: Flexible Production Organization and Regional Development in North America and Western Europe*, Pion, London.

Sklair, L. (1993) *Assembling for Development: The Maquila Industry in Mexico and the U.S.*, Centre for Mexican Studies, San Diego.

Smith, A. (1776) *The Wealth of Nations*, Pelican Books, London.

Storper, M. (1995) "The Resurgence of Regional Economies, Ten Years Later: The region as a nexus of untraded interdependencies," *European Urban and Regional Studies*, 2(3), pp. 191–221.

Wade, R. (1990) *Governing the Market*, Princeton University Press, Princeton, NJ.

Wilkinson, F. and You, J.I. (1992) "Competition and Cooperation: Towards an Understanding of the Industrial District," Small Business Research Center, Cambridge University, Working Paper No. 88.

Williamson, O.E. (1985) *The Economic Institutions of Capitalism*, Free Press, New York.

Williamson, O. (1996) *The Mechanisms of Governance*, Oxford University Press, New York.

Wilson, P. (1992) *Exports and Local Development: Mexico's New Maquiladoras*, University of Texas Press, Austin.

World Bank Institute (2001) "World Development Indicators," CDROM, World Bank Institute, Washington, DC.

World Bank (2005) *World Development Indicators*, World Bank Institute, Washington DC.

Young, A. (1928) "Increasing Returns and Economic Progress," *Economic Journal*, 38: pp. 527–542.

Part V

Cluster-based strategies for development

11 Policymaking for local production systems in Brazil

Wilson Suzigan, João Furtado and Renato Garcia

Introduction

In a continent-sized country like Brazil, regions and development are intrinsically connected. Regional inequalities are rooted in natural resources endowment as well as in historical processes of territorial occupation and economic and social development. The establishment of large plantations of agricultural staples for export in the Southeast and of cattle-raising in the South brought about industrialization to those regions from the late nineteenth and early twentieth centuries onward. As industrialization advanced, a symmetrical retardation or even economic decline occurred in the Northeast and North regions, while the center and western regions remained as unexplored frontiers.

Until the end of the 1970s fast economic growth, fostered by industrial policies, was accompanied by regional policies aimed at compensating for regional inequalities. The most conspicuous example is that of the fiscal incentive system for investments in the Northeast under the aegis of SUDENE – the Superintendence for the Development of the Northeast, created in 1959. Other examples include sector-specific policies with regional objectives, such as those for petrochemicals and steel, regional development programs, and even the political decision to transfer the capital city of the country to the central region.

With the breakout of the debt crisis of the 1980s, followed by hyperinflation, all industrial, regional, science, technology, and other policies were either phased out or greatly reduced. Macroeconomic stabilization policies became predominant and even in the present time restrictive macroeconomic policies impair economic growth. Per capita GDP growth rates have not reached 1 percent on average in the past 25 years. Gains in the financial markets are prime movers of capital accumulation, and social assistance policies are made to compensate for regional and social inequalities.

In the vacuum of federal government regional policies, state governments in deprived regions started a location tournament[1] to attract investments by granting tax holidays and other benefits. This practice has been extremely deleterious to state budgets and to investment location. And in recent years federal government itself, through financing agencies and development banks, together with some semi-public institutions have launched a number of initiatives to stimulate what has been called, somewhat improperly, "local productive arrangements." Our concern is with the inadequate way this instrument of regional policy is managed. First of all, it is considered by many to be the solution for promoting economic and social development in the absence of regional, industrial, or more general development policies. Second, it lacks any coordination mechanism to deal with policy implementation by a great number of institutions (23 in our last survey), leading to a possible waste of public resources.[2] Third, the selection of the arrangements to be the object of policy measures is entirely ad hoc. Finally, there are no criteria for policy measures.

This chapter addresses that policymaking problem specifically by suggesting a comprehensive methodology for the study of local production systems in Brazil. We believe that the application of such methodology is a necessary step for creating knowledge that supports adequate policy measures for geographical agglomerations of firms and institutions. We understand, however, that the dynamics of such agglomerations are geographically limited. Successful policies will improve local or adjacent regional development, but not that of larger mesoregions or of the entire country. The resumption of national economic development depends on the country's capability to practice less restrictive macroeconomic policies, and to implement concomitant policies for education, science and technology, regional development, and infrastructure.

The chapter is organized as follows. First, a brief review of the literature is presented to highlight analytical approaches that are relevant for the study of local production systems with the purpose of suggesting policy measures. Second, methodologies are described for quantitative indicators, for surveying local capabilities embedded in local institutions, and for field research work. Third, the results of an experimental application of such methods to data and information for manufacturing industries and institutions at micro-region level in the state of São Paulo are discussed, showing the regional distribution of a selected number of local production systems, classified for policy purposes into four types of local systems, and the regional distribution of supporting institutions. The results of a number of case studies are then illustratively summarized, highlighting problems identified at systems level and at firms level. Finally, the paper suggests policy guidelines aimed at those problems, with chapter of general application and some specific measures differentiated according to the typology of local systems that resulted from the quantitative and other indicators.

Fundamentals for the analysis of local production systems

Present knowledge about the relationships between geography and industry evolved from two main sources: Marshallian localized external economies and W.B. Arthur's theories of increasing returns and positive feedbacks in the economy. Based on those two original contributions, several groups of authors gradually added new analytical tools emphasizing: the importance of social, political, and cultural ties in industrial districts; deliberate joint actions to achieve collective efficiency in clusters; interrelated factors that determine the competitiveness of firms in clusters; the modeling of Marshallian externalities; dynamic interrelationships between geography and industry; governance structures in local production systems and networks; the correlation between geography and innovation; and the cognitive and evolutionary nature of local production systems.

The next paragraphs summarize the flow of contributions by those groups of authors with the specific purpose of understanding which analytical elements are relevant for the study of geographical agglomerations of firms and institutions. It is on the basis of such analytical elements that the methodology for the study of local production systems is structured and, as the ultimate objective, policy guidelines are established.

Alfred Marshall's seminal analysis of English industrial districts inspired a great deal of literature devoted to explain agglomerations of small firms in geographically bounded areas. Marshall explained *localized external economies* as those derived from knowledge spillovers, specialized labor skills, and interdependencies or linkages in the local markets.

Several Italian authors have pioneered modern studies of *industrial districts* in Italy since the 1970s following Marshall's ideas. However, those studies demonstrated that Marshallian external economies are not sufficient to explain the origin and development of Italian industrial districts. In fact, their development was also based on region-specific characteristics such as a territorial concentration of a large number of small firms specialized in one specific industry, with an extensive division of labor among them, embedded in a local community with strong socio-cultural ties that facilitated cooperation based on trust and local governance by private-firms organizations and public bodies. These special characteristics made them unique as forms of spatial organization of industrial production. Later on, evolution in the 1990s changed substantially the structural characteristics of Italian industrial districts, turning them into more hierarchically organized production systems and lessening the importance of regional social, political, and cultural ties (Lazerson and Lorenzoni, 1999).

An extension of the purely Marshallian construct was developed by H. Schmitz and his associates by combining incidental external economies with those derived from joint actions, leading to the *collective efficiency*[3] of local firms. The argument is summarized by Schmitz and Nadvi (1999, pp. 1504–1505): "... Marshallian external economies are not sufficient to explain cluster development. In addition to incidental external economies, there is often a deliberate force at work, namely the conscious pursuit of joint action," and so those authors "brought together the incidental and deliberate effects into the concept of collective efficiency defined as the competitive advantage derived from external economies and joint action." After using this approach in case studies in many countries, the authors concluded that collective efficiency can only emerge when local producers are connected to external markets through trade networks, and when inter-firm relations are subject to sanctions and sustained by trust (Schmitz and Nadvi, 1999, pp. 1506–1507). This led Schmitz and other authors in this approach to develop new research lines to investigate the performance of industrial clusters connected to global commodity or value-added chains, and to discuss the role of trust in exporting clusters.[4] In connection with those new research themes, the authors extended their analyses to study governance problems and governance structures in clusters (discussed below).

The other analytical building block is the *increasing returns* theory. In the 1980s, W. Brian Arthur, recovering old contributions neglected in mainstream economics, brought into the field the dynamic analysis of self-reinforcing mechanisms in spatial economics, as well as in international trade theory and in industrial organization, with possibilities of multiple equilibria, inefficient solutions, lock-in, and path-dependence (Arthur, 1988). An industry location pattern may result from the location decision of the first firm that enters the industry, and the sequence of location decisions by subsequent entrant firms. The first firm decision is based "purely on geographical preferences," influenced by local external economies or some "historical accident." Subsequent entrants' location decisions are "based on preference modified by the benefits of locating near the first firm(s)," and, thus, "industrial concentration becomes self-reinforcing." One region may dominate the industry if there is no limit to positive feedbacks, and this may not be an efficient solution. But usually one region cannot offer increasing returns indefinitely because of, for instance, agglomeration diseconomies. So, other regions share the industry (Arthur, 1988, 1990). More important for the study of local production systems is the assertion that positive feedback mechanisms confer advantages of initial agglomeration and strong historicity to the spatial evolution of the economy.

Working with the three sources of Marshallian external economies as centripetal forces that favor spatial concentration, and immobile factors, land rents, and congestion as three opposing centrifugal forces, Krugman (1999) modeled the so-called *new economic geography* as a new wave in the "increasing returns-imperfect competition revolution" of economic theory. The modeling was extended by Fujita *et al.* (1999) to cover spatial issues related to urban, regional, and international economics. However, recognizing that the trinity of Marshallian external economies "has proved to be notoriously hard to model in any formal way" (Fujita *et al.*, 1999, pp. 18–19), those authors modeled just one pair of centripetal and centrifugal forces, namely linkages, "when producers are subject both to transport costs and to increasing returns, and immobile factors. The bulk of theoretical and empirical work on this line of research is still to be done before it can be useful for explaining the "complicating realities" of the spatial economy, characterized by a multiplicity of dynamic processes that are usually under way concurrently (David, 1999, p. 111).

The analysis of regional agglomerations of firms was enriched by contributions in the field of *business economics* (Porter, 1990, 1998). On the basis of his "competitive advantage of nations" approach, the author developed the analytical argument that the competitiveness of firms in local clusters is determined by four sets of favorable conditions prevailing in the local business environment: (1) factors of production (supply, cost, quality, and specialization of inputs:

natural resources, skills, knowledge, capital, physical and science and technology infrastructures, information and management infrastructures); (2) demand:
sophisticated customers, with needs of specialized goods or services that could
also be internationally supplied; (3) presence of suppliers and related industries
and business services; and (4) a context of rivalry and competition strategies of
local firms. In such an environment, multiple local actors "make up a complex
web of relations that tie firms, customers, research institutions, schools and local
authorities to each other. The interaction between economic, socio-cultural,
political and institutional actors in a given location triggers learning and
enhances the ability of actors to modify their behavior and find new solutions in
response to competitive changes" (Porter and Sölvell, 1998, p. 443). Policies
should ensure the supply of high quality inputs (educated citizens, physical
infrastructure, information), eliminate barriers to competition (protection of
intellectual property rights, anti-trust laws), stimulate the creation of norms and
standards for product certification, promote related business meetings, and
encourage the attraction of suppliers and service firms.

Authors in the *economic geography* tradition have brought geography back to
the core of the debate on industrial clusters. Many authors have contributed in
this field, but we will focus the contribution by Scott (1998). Our interest in this
specific contribution is based on two important points: first, the paper demonstrates quite clearly that industrial performance and location patterns in modern
capitalism are intrinsically related to geography, despite globalization, and
second, it strongly suggests that non-market coordination and public action are
necessary to adjust the "social bases of production" of localized industrial complexes (regional industrial clusters).

To demonstrate that industrial performance is grounded in geography, Scott
(1998, p. 386) starts by arguing that: ". . . we can only start fully to decipher the
locational logic of industrial landscape when we approach it in terms of its
origins as a pure social construct, and more specifically as a question about
external economies and locational agglomeration." Then the argument proceeds
by showing that, besides those static spatial issues, constrained by counter-
forces (agglomeration diseconomies) that limit locational convergence, complex
dynamic and historical determinants also influence industrial location. Localized
increasing returns effects, dynamic learning effects, and cumulative causation
characterize the evolution of regional clusters as a path-dependent process in
which history, historical "accidents," lock-in and branching points caused by
radical shifts in markets and technologies play an important role. The conclusion
is that "Regions are once again emerging as important foci of production and as
repositories of specialized know-how and technological capability, even as the
globalization of economic relationships proceeds apace" (Scott, 1998, p. 394).

The paper ends with a detailed and comprehensive set of policy considerations. Although recognizing that market mechanisms are efficient in activating
agglomeration economies, Scott (1998, pp. 394–399) considers that they can be
enhanced by non-market coordination and collective action. In general, regional
policies should aim at building institutional infrastructures "that lie outside of

the sphere of market relations," and at providing urban equipment, planning the use of industrial land, and mitigating pollution problems. Collective action, in turn, could bring "significant augmentation of market capability" in localized industrial complexes. It should be organized to adjust "the social bases of production in at least three main fronts," namely (1) the supply of critical inputs and services such as technological research, labor-training activities, information, and marketing; (2) cooperation among local firms to increase efficiency in transactional interactions, and to facilitate learning processes and pooling of technologies and labor skills; and (3) organization of forums for strategic choice and action to secure regional trademarks, create producers' associations to manage short-term adverse conditions, and organize regional economic councils to discuss long-term trends and strategies. All the participants should be local "agents of collective order" such as government bodies, firms' and workers' associations, and private–public consortia and partnerships. Thus, all major local actors would be committed and social cohesion in the regional industrial cluster would be reinforced. This approach, according to Scott (1998, p. 397), is cost-effective because it does not involve large financial commitments, and it does not preclude market mechanisms from eliminating firms that fail.

Other important contributions in the field have been made by several authors who studied forms of *governance*, emphasizing the role of actors in territorial agglomerations of firms. From the standpoint of policymaking, the most important analytical contributions are: (1) the taxonomic classification of production structures in territorial agglomerations and their relationships with governance structures; (2) the characterization of global commodity chains or production networks and their connection with successful exporting clusters under chain or network governance; and (3) the importance of local governance, even if as a complementary action by local actors. Policy issues stemming from those analytical constructions can be summarized as follows.

Storper and Harrison's (1991) paper offers a comprehensive classification of production systems that are differentiated according to the division of labor, the size of firms, and their interrelationships and territorial agglomeration, and then connects this classification of production structures to different forms of governance. The result is the well-known set of four types of governance structures, namely all-ring, no core; core–ring with coordinating firm; core–ring with lead firm; and all-core, no ring. At the root of this typology are structural characteristics such as hierarchy, leadership, and command, as opposed to market relationships and cooperation. Such characteristics define the space for policy action. When Storper and Harrison (1991, pp. 419–420) come to policy discussion they recognize that, although the region may be formed by a complex set of production systems, "in most cases the 'view from the region' is different from the standpoint of the production system, and it is the regional standpoint that must inform local policy makers." Thus, the degree of division of labor, the degree of hierarchy, and whether connections among firms are local or not are the relevant dimensions for policymaking.

After Gereffi's (1994, 1999) analysis of producer- and buyer-driven global commodity chains, Humphrey and Schmitz (2000) and other authors, following the clue about the need of governance studies made by the works in the collective efficiency approach, made several contributions on the implications of local–global interactions for cluster upgrading. Humphrey and Schmitz's (2000) paper is very important for policy discussion because it adds a new layer in the theoretical construction of cluster analysis: the interaction of global value chain governance and local governance. The central question addressed in their paper is "whether insertion in global value chains enhances or undermines local upgrading strategies." Three stages of upgrading are considered: in production, in marketing, and in strategic functions such as design and own brand manufacture. A new notion of chain coordination is introduced: the quasi-hierarchy governance, which describes more properly developing countries' asymmetrical cluster structures participating in global value chains. Local governance and local industrial policy can help in different ways according to different cluster upgrading strategies. In case the strategy aims merely at strengthening the existing position of the cluster, then governance can take the form of (1) collective initiatives to promote upgrading in production through, for example, the creation of a local technology institute, and upgrading in marketing through, for example, the formation of an export consortium, or (2) a hub-and-spoke structure in which upgrading in production and in marketing depend on R&D activities and the opening up of new markets by the local lead firm. In this case local industrial policy could play a role in "expanding infrastructure and strengthening training, testing and certification facilities" (Humphrey and Schmitz, 2000, pp. 28–29). But when the strategy aims at repositioning the cluster through functional upgrading, "local industrial policy requires building a coalition of the key actors in the public and private sector" (p. 29). Business associations and lead firms in more symmetrical networks can be major players in such coalitions. Other essential policy ingredients are local institutional support, firms' own strategies for functional upgrading and, at higher policy levels, human resource formation and concurrent national industrial policy.

Another important set of contributions came from authors who study the relationship between *geography and innovation*. Feldman (1993, 1994) and Audretsch and Feldman (1996), for example, show that there is a clear relationship between the localization of innovative activities, measured by the number of patent citations, and the geographical concentration of innovative inputs such as R&D in universities, industrial R&D, the presence of related industries, and the presence of firms that provide specialized business services, showing that there are important "geographically mediated spillovers." However, it is the presence of related industries that is more relevant for innovation activities. The reason is that geographical proximity facilitates the transmission of new knowledge characterized as complex, tacit, and specific to certain production and innovation systems and activities. This type of knowledge is best transmitted through interpersonal contacts, frequent interaction, and mobility of workers from one firm to another, which explains why firms agglomerate in local production and innovation systems. In such systems, according to Breschi and

Malerba (2001, pp. 819–820), the following characteristics are evident: (1) learning through networking and interacting, including user–producer relationships, formal and informal collaborations, inter-firm mobility of skilled workers, and spin-offs of new firms from existing firms, universities and research centers; (2) deep embeddedness of local firms in a very thick network of knowledge sharing, supported by close social interactions and facilitated by shared norms, conventions and codes, and in institutions that build trust and encourage informal relations among actors in a collective learning process; (3) availability of a common set of resources, such as universities, research centers, technology centers, and a pool of specialized and skilled labor, all of which help reduce the costs and uncertainties associated with innovative activities.

Finally, in the last decade a new, *cognitive and evolutionary approach* to analyze local production systems has been developed. The most important contributions on this line of thought are those by Belussi (1995, 2000), Belussi and Gottardi (2000), and Lombardi (2000, 2003). Our discussion will be centered on Lombardi's contribution, specifically the 2003 paper, where the new theoretical framework is explained in greater detail. His paper analyzes the evolution of Italian local production systems[5] in the past three decades as the result of the "dynamic matching between systemic properties of local production systems . . . and the characteristics of the competitive environment" (Lombardi, 2003, p. 1443). After a stylized description of the evolutionary phases in the development of traditional local production systems, the author discusses the evolutionary dynamics of such systems, which he characterizes as adaptive, self-organized, complex systems of collective order. In such complex systems, he argues, evolution is determined by "how information and knowledge flows are created and organized" (p. 1444). Thus, the focus of the approach is on the key idea of the "centrality of information" in the "interactions between agents and entities which exercise functions" that must be specified by information and knowledge (p. 1444). Information asymmetries between strategic agents, who have access to market trends and other information, and operational units in the production network, create an "informational divide." The strategic agents become holders of hidden information, which they translate into parametric information for the operational units. Coordination is automatic, organized by an "invisible mind."

However, the informational divide led to traditional local production systems being incapable of innovation. Technological choices and investment decisions had to be made by operational units that did not have access to market information. Thus, when new competitive factors emerged from late 1980s onward, the systemic properties and the adaptive behavior of local production systems were weakened. A new cognitive architecture then emerged, in which the informational divide tends to disappear, the techno-organizational structures become vertically integrated, and coordination becomes explicitly designed as "more visible minds" (Lombardi, 2003). This means that production structures in local systems are becoming more hierarchical and increasingly dominated by large firms that control knowledge and information flows. Traditional local production systems are becoming a thing of the past. Thus, policies, especially in less developed countries, should reinforce systemic properties and improve the capacity to innovate, especially that of small independent firms.

A methodology for the study of local production systems in Brazil

Our methodology was designed with the objective of producing evidence on the existence and characteristics of local production systems for purposes of policy-making in Brazil. It comprises three consecutive steps: (1) the use of quantitative indicators for the identification and structural characterization of those systems; (2) a statistical account of the regional distribution of educational institutions, labor training courses, laboratories, research centers, and technology support institutions as a proxy for regional or local capabilities; and (3) field research work, collecting data and information about the local production system as a whole and the firms that operate in it. Our final aim is to develop a typology of local production systems for policy purposes, claiming that differences in the local system relevance for regional development and its share of the industry, production structure, industrial organization, technical and innovative capabilities, trading and governance structures, institutional infrastructure and social and cultural contexts, all justify different policy approaches and specific measures, according to different types of local systems.

This section presents only a brief summary of those three methodological steps. A more detailed description is presented in the next section, which describes the application of the methodology to the state of São Paulo. Indicator formulas and other details can be seen in our previous works, especially Suzigan (2005) and Suzigan *et al.* (2003, 2004, 2005).

At first, two *quantitative indicators* are calculated to identify, geographically delimit, and structurally characterize local production systems: locational Gini coefficients and location quotients. They are calculated using the database of the Brazilian Ministry of Labor's RAIS (*Relação Anual de Informações Sociais*). This is a very detailed database, covering the whole country and containing data on employment, number of plants, and other information for manufacturing industries as well as for other economic activities. Data are broken down at four-digit industry class and micro-regions. Each micro-region contains a few municipalities, and usually the larger and/or hegemonic municipality centralizes and names the micro-region. Both indicators are combined with control variables or filters in order to add additional quantitative criteria to select relevant geographic agglomerations of firms. The most commonly used filter variables are the requirements of a minimum share of the micro-region in the total employment of the industry and a minimum number of plants of the same industry in the micro-region.

As a second step in the methodology, we compiled data and information on the geographical distribution of educational and labor training institutions, laboratories, research centers, and technology support institutions as proxies for *local capabilities*. Those institutions provide firms with support in educational, scientific, technical, and technological services, and perform functions that enable firms to enhance their technical, technological, and innovation capabilities. The most important ones are: universities and research centers, technical high schools, professional training schools, research labs, and technology centers. Data and information from the RAIS database and direct collection from institutions were consolidated and shown in maps that could be compared with the map of local production systems.

Finally, *field research work* was carried out to capture the specific features of each agglomeration, such as history, evolution, morphology, industrial organization, role of supporting institutions, and governance structure, among other characteristics. To know those specificities is the last, albeit indispensable, step in laying the foundations for support actions and public policy measures. Our method for case studies is carried out at two levels of analysis: first at the aggregate level, i.e. that of the system as a whole, and second at the level of the firms that constitute the local production system. At each of these levels, collection of data and information is organized as a survey based on questionnaires, interviews, and visits to firms and local institutions.

Such methodology to study local production systems is instrumental for guiding policy measures. We used such methodology in a sector-specific study covering several Brazilian states, and in two research projects for mapping local production systems in the states of São Paulo and Paraná.[6] An illustrative discussion of the results for the state of São Paulo is presented next.

Local production systems in the manufacturing industry of São Paulo state

The state of São Paulo is the most industrialized region in the country. Manufacturing industries are spread over 63 geographic micro-regions in the state, with higher concentrations in the metropolitan areas of São Paulo city and Campinas, and along the axes of the main highways. The use of our methodology allowed us to map a great number of local production systems, characterize their production structure in statistical terms, and elaborate a typology of local systems. Additionally, it brought information on the regional distribution of firms' supporting institutions in the state. The results of the statistical work, and the regional distribution of institutions, served as primary information for field research work in a selected number of local production systems. Case studies produced a rich and varied spectrum of system features and problems. The methodological steps are summarized below.

The statistical work to *map, characterize and classify local production systems* consisted in taking RAIS employment and other data for 267 four-digit manufacturing industries, spread about the 63 micro-regions in the state, to calculate locational Gini (LG) coefficients and location quotients (LQ). The first results showed that in excess of three-fourths of the industries had LG coefficients greater than 0.5, indicating some degree of regional concentration. This is not of much help for policymaking. Thus, we proceeded to apply filters requiring that, to be considered as regionally concentrated, an industry with a LG coefficient greater than 0.5 must have an LQ equal or greater than 2 in one micro-region, must account for at least 1 percent of the total employment of the industry in the state, and must have at least 20 plants in the same micro-region. The latter is intended as a criterion to select agglomerations of firms, avoiding the cases in which concentration results from the presence of a large, integrated unit. The result was the selection of 64 industries. Next we classified those 64 industries into four types according to the respective share of the total employment (equal to or less than 10 percent, and greater than 10 percent) and to the respective LQ (equal to or less than 5, and greater than 5). Those four types constitute the basis for our typology of local production systems for policy purposes, discussed later in this chapter. The next step was to identify the micro-regions where those 64 concentrated industries are located. The result was 27 micro-regions, some of them with more than one industry. Next, the industries and respective micro-regions were allocated in the four types of local systems.[7] Finally, a vertical, cross-section of industries for each micro-region allowed us to capture statistically the presence of related industries and to have an approximate idea of the local production system structure.

The gathering of data and information on firms' *supporting institutions* covered (1) educational establishments offering technical, technological, and professional qualifications at various levels, from university degrees to certificates in different areas of technology via technical high schools and industrial training courses, and (2) technology institutes and centers, and R&D labs. Broken down by micro-region, the data show the distribution of those institutions throughout the state. The number of courses and students in science and technology areas show a high level of concentration in the micro-regions of São Paulo and Campinas. However, when the quality of courses is considered,[8] a different regional pattern emerges. The outstanding regions are Campinas, S. José dos Campos in the Paraíba Valley, and several towns in the interior where state university fields are located, following approximately the axes of the main highways. In or around several of those towns, local production systems are embedded. Technological courses and technical schools are also concentrated in the São Paulo micro-region, but they have greater importance in micro-regions like Campinas, S. José dos Campos, Sorocaba, Limeira, Ribeirão Preto, São Carlos, Franca, and Jaú where they are linked to the productive activities that predominate locally.

Technical high schools and industrial training institutions are more evenly spread out. Collected data show industrial training courses are disseminated throughout the state, whereas technological courses are strongly concentrated in a few micro-regions, especially São Paulo. A regional breakdown of technical and industrial training courses shows concentration in São Paulo and adjacent micro-regions, especially Campinas, São José dos Campos, Sorocaba, and Santos, but in this case concentration in such areas is far less intense than in that of the technological courses or even the college-level courses. The greater degree of regional dispersion of technical and industrial training courses has to do with the regional distribution of industrial activities and, above all, with the existence of local production and innovation systems, as shown by the Limeira, Ribeirão Preto, São Carlos, Jaú, and Franca micro-regions, among others. Finally, data and information collected on technological centers and R&D laboratories that provide services in areas such as technological information, product development, management of production processes, technical and technological assistance, and consulting, testing, and laboratory trials show an even higher level of concentration. Four high-tech micro-regions (São Paulo, Campinas, S. Carlos, and S. José dos Campos) concentrate the majority (133) of the 151 labs and technology centers of the state in 2004. This concentration is related to agglomerations of firms in high tech industries and to regional centers of education and research institutions. The remaining 18 labs and technology centers are spread into 13 micro-regions in the interior of the state, some of them (Franca, Araraquara, Tatuí, Jundiaí) showing a clear relationship with local production systems.

The last step of our methodology was *field research*. The previous steps allowed us to start with some detailed knowledge about the local production structure, number of plants and formal jobs, size of firms (measured by the number of employees), presence of related industries, and education and training (and other) institutions. By interviewing people and filling in questionnaires in local firms and institutions, we were able to confirm our statistical work and acquire new knowledge about the system and the local firms, to complement the previously gathered data and information.

The results support not only our quantitative methods, but also the various analytical approaches discussed earlier in this chapter. A stylized description of the studied cases may be summarized as follows.

All of them have deep historical roots: they started either by some historical accident, for example the development of local skills or knowledge, or by initial conditions related to, for example, a pioneer entrepreneur, the presence of education and research institutions. External economies attract the first firms. A development process ensues when the site becomes an attractive location in the investment decisions of other firms in the industry, forming an agglomeration. As it grows and supplies regional markets, the agglomeration of firms becomes attractive to other related industries. Local interrelationships in production increase, facilitating cooperation with suppliers, knowledge spillovers among firms, and collective actions to organize business associations and labor unions. As local production structure diversifies to include suppliers of raw materials, parts, and equipment, a greater division of labor takes place and a sophisticated industrial organization is shaped, with more interrelationships in production that, in turn, enhance learning processes, but with fewer horizontal interactions and cooperation. Increasing returns reinforce the process and stimulate new firm entries. Competition increases and new competitive factors other than price become relevant. Local firms increase their demand for higher skills and technical and technological services that would enable them to improve their capacity to differentiate their products and to develop new products and processes.

Professionals, institutions, and firms providing those services are attracted. Some firms become dominant for their capacity to control market information, to open new domestic or international market channels, and to dominate strategic assets like capabilities in R&D and brand names. The morphology of the system tends to change, and some form of governance is established, either by system self-regulating mechanisms or intentional planning. In the latter case, governance may be exercised by local dominating firms with their own market channels, production networks, and brand names, or by domestic or international firms controlling buyer- or producer-driven commodity or value chains, or by a collective organization of local firms and institutions.

Field research work also showed clearly the *problems* that usually affect most of the local systems. To facilitate policymaking discussion, those problems are summarized below first at system level and then at firm level.

At *system level*, there are five major problems that could be the object of policy measures or collective action. The first has to do with infrastructures. In most cases, there is no planning of land use for industrial plants. The urban area becomes congested, urban infrastructures deteriorate, transportation costs increase, logistic problems start to weaken firms' competitiveness, and agglomeration diseconomies halt growth and development. This is worsened by additional urban infrastructure problems related to water supply, sewage, and pollution. Other more general infrastructure problems like the cost and quality of highway transportation and port services also diminish firms' competitiveness.

The second major problem at system level is insufficient development of local institutions. In general, local government bodies are not relevant actors in the local systems studied, but this is a political and cultural, rather than a policymaking problem. More important from a policymaking point of view is the insufficiency of local technology-service institutions, collective R&D centers and laboratories, and local-specific technology-focused degree courses.[9] Local educational systems are also deficient in the supply of undergraduate and graduate management and business administration courses. Labor training, on the other hand, is well structured in most local systems, either by firms' on-the-job training schemes or by technical and professional schools.

The third usual problem at system level is the absence of a collective organization to deal with crises and evolutionary trends. All local systems studied at some time had to overcome crises caused by domestic or international market trends, or face major technological or organizational changes, and usually the crises were lengthened and deepened and the adaptation to changes was slow for lack of an adequate forum to discuss this kind of system problem, which also impairs foresight and strategic actions of a collective nature. In some cases, organizational changes like the decision of firms to enter a production or value chain network breaks the system social cohesion and undermines trustful relations. The consequences are increasing difficulties for collective actions with a view to, for example, create an export consortium or a technology services center, and more generally for local governance.

The fourth problem is precisely governance. Evolutionary changes produced hybrid structures in most of the local systems studied, in the same way and by the same mechanisms as those observed by Humphrey and Schmitz (2000) and Lombardi (2003). Hybrid structures brought with them hybrid forms of governance. Usually there is a structural divide of firms: on one side are some large, lead firms that either operate their own network of local producers and have their own market channels, or are themselves producers for domestic or international buyers or subcontractors, and on the other side are a great number of small (in some places also large) independent firms. The firms in the first segment have their own governance structure or are subordinated to external, domestic or international governance structure. The firms in the second segment usually have greater and varied local interactions, are socially more embedded, as they are usually the product of spin-offs from other local firms, and tend to cooperate or act collectively. But in many local systems we visited the initiatives of small firms of the second segment are impaired by the firms of the first segment, which usually have the political control of the local business association.[10] Thus, what in this case is the policy problem? It is to make possible for the small, independent firms to organize themselves in a local governance structure. We suggest the best way to do that is for firms to have a coordinating agent to organize collective actions and to bridge local firms and institutions with state or federal government financial or technological institutions.[11]

Finally, the fifth problem at system level, although not in all local production systems, is environmental pollution. The local systems of industries that produce toxic residues or effluents, such as leather and shoes, leather products, and jewelry, or that exploit natural resources, such as ceramic tiles and wood furniture, must not only comply with state environment legislation but also have their own environment control policy in order to avoid social costs. Problems are aggravated where the number of informal firms is larger. Cluster policies could stimulate firms and local governments to build adequate disposal sites, to treat effluents in the industrial plant, and to exploit only environmentally certified natural resources.

At the *firms level*, the problems are more numerous, albeit easier to solve from the point of view of policies. They have been observed in all local systems that we have visited, but are more frequent and more intense in the types of local production systems we described as embryonic and as vectors of local development. The most frequently observed problems are listed and briefly commented on below.

A problem that affects most firms, especially small firms, is related to plant layout and production and technology bottlenecks. Production lines are inefficiently organized, increasing production time, or are bottlenecked because one or more pieces of equipment have incompatible production capacity or inadequate technology. Another frequently observed problem is the deficiency in management and business administration. Many entrepreneurs are former blue-collar workers who acquire only rudimentary knowledge in those areas. Thus, many small firms are cost-inefficient and badly managed. A third problem is that most of the small firms, but some of the large ones too, are trapped in competition based on low prices, usually combined with production of a large quantity of low-quality products. That happens because they get locked into subordinate trade relations with retailers or network producers and into inferior technologies. Fourth, as price competition becomes fiercer, firms tend to be unwilling to cooperate, although production interrelations and learning interactions continue to exist. This makes collective actions more improbable. Fifth, there is a general deficiency in the so-called strategic assets: R&D structures, product development knowledge, design, patenting, and brand names. Again, firms producing for supply chains or production networks, although they manage to upgrade in production, fail to develop capabilities in those strategic assets.[12]

Sixth, although information and communication technologies have been widely diffused lately, most firms still find it difficult or costly to gather information on new products, technologies, and market trends. A creative solution was found in Birigui micro-region, a local system that manufactures children shoes made mainly out of synthetic material. There, a specialized service firm was created by the former owner of a manufacturing concern, who travels abroad twice a year to gather information on new products and market trends for a number of local manufacturers. Data and information are then compacted in a CD-ROM and supplied to the manufacturers, which pay a fraction of the cost they would have to pay to collect those data and information by themselves.[13] Seventh, quality problems are widespread. Firms, mainly the small ones, tend to focus on end-of-production-line quality control, with a considerable rate of rejection and re-elaboration. There is insufficient quality control in the production chain, and few firms get ISO certificates. Eighth, there is a general scarcity of specialized professionals or firms in services related to the local production. This includes design, total quality control, production management methods, and professionals like laboratory technicians, financial managers, and other business administration specialists. Ninth, environmental problems: in local systems where production processes generate toxic residues and effluents, environmental control at plant level is usually deficient.

Policymaking for local production systems: a suggested approach

The same methodology was used to study local production systems in the manufacturing industry of Paraná state, and the same is presently being done to study other states, with similar results. For this reason, we believe the policy guidelines suggested below are generally useful to study all Brazilian local production systems in manufacturing industries.

Before going into detail about policy measures, it is important to emphasize some basic principles that should be observed in policy implementation. First of all, the methodological approach we developed, by mapping and characterizing existing local production systems, respects market principles and does not consider it feasible simply to create such local systems. Thus, policies should preferably not have this objective. Second, some general rules must be observed:

(1) Policies must offer the conditions for local actors – firms, entrepreneurs, workers, government bodies, private institutions, and society – to make use of their capacity to mobilize the system in favor of development. That means policies should never substitute for local actors, and must avoid measures that could inhibit the autonomous development of the system and its social forces. (2) Policies must require local actors to commit themselves to policy measures either by contributing with a fraction of the allocated public resources, or by taking up complementary collective actions. (3) Specific policy measures must be differentiated by types of local production systems and according to their stage of development. There are, however, some policy measures of general application to all kinds of local production systems. Keeping those principles in mind, and considering the local systems' problems enlightened by our case studies, the remainder of this section suggests some policy guidelines.

Policy measures of general application

At first, policies should address general problems that are common to most of the local systems. Such problems include: (1) the five areas in which we identified problems at system level, namely infrastructures, local institutions, organization for strategic actions, governance, and environmental pollution, and (2) some problems that usually affect the efficiency of almost all firms. Why are those two kinds of general policy measures necessary?

By tackling infrastructure problems, the policy would eliminate sources of external diseconomies to local firms. In order to do that, it would be necessary first to identify those sources of external diseconomies and then mobilize local actors to invest and/or find the means of bringing in investors. Financial mechanisms or incentives could be adequate instruments to start the process.

Deficiencies in services related to the main local economic activity, which are provided by specialized service firms and institutions, increase firms' costs of labor training, R&D, and other technology and managing activities and limit firms' abilities to absorb new knowledge and develop learning processes. Policy measures in this area should facilitate the assessment of such deficiencies and offer support for the development of existing institutions or the establishment of firms and institutions that could match the needs of the local system.

General policy measures should also stimulate local actors to organize some form of collective organization for the discussion of problems and long-term trends.[14] This would help them anticipate major crises and evolutionary changes, and limit their costs by finding collective forms of strategic action. In addition, the system social cohesion would be strengthened and the building of trust reinforced.

Policies aimed at the governance of the system should focus on small firms and give them support to organize a local governance structure of their own. The role of a coordinator, a leading local entrepreneur or a hired professional, may be decisive for the success of this initiative. It would help build ties that could lead to joint actions in exports, gathering of information on market trends, creation of a labor training school, establishment of an R&D and technology services center, and other related activities.

Finally, system-level environmental policies should include regulations that require the local public sector and firms associations to build disposal sites, and firms to introduce pollution control equipment and effluent treatment systems at the plant level. In addition, a clause should condition the benefit of any policy measure to compliance to government environmental norms and regulations.

Firm-level general policies, on the other hand, should aim at eliminating the most common sources of inefficiencies observed in case studies. In all local systems there is a need of professional services to assist in methods of planning and control of production processes, total quality control, and other related techniques. There is also a general need of courses in management practices and business administration methods. Equally necessary in almost all local systems are the means (tangible and intangible) to acquire information that enable firms to follow market trends, technologies, export markets, and other relevant knowledge. Capabilities in product development and in other strategic functions are equally needed, and policies should stimulate upgrading in these areas.

Policies differentiated by types of local production systems

Local production systems have characteristics that enable them to be raised to the status of industrial, regional, and social development vectors. Moreover, they can also make a valuable contribution to the effort to enhance the nation's balance of payments if their production capacity can be complemented with new capabilities in trade and if they are directed to new markets.

While there is broad agreement on the importance of local production systems, this consensus is lacking with regard to how such agglomerations of firms and institutions should be quantified and qualitatively assessed on an industry-wide and regional basis. As mentioned at the outset of this chapter, in the absence of a true regional development policy, some government agencies and other institutions in Brazil launched a program to support a large number of badly defined and ad hoc selected local agglomerations of firms. Our methodology, in contrast, allows us to map, identify, and characterize local production systems and classify them for policy purposes according to a typology. Our typology of local systems results from the combination of two variables: the importance of the local system to the region (measured by the location quotient), and the importance of the region to the industry (measured in terms of the micro-region's share of total production and employment throughout the state in that industry). Table 11.1 summarizes the four types.

Using this proposed typology, the various local production systems in São Paulo state manufacturing industry identified by our methodology were classified in one of the four quadrants. Some local systems of each type are shown in Table 11.2.

Such classification may be valuable when formulating a comprehensive and consistent industrial policy for the highly diverse local production systems

Table 11.1 Typology of local production systems

		Importance to the industry	
		Low	High
Importance to the region	High	Vectors of local development	Centers of industrial and regional development
	Low	Embryonic local production systems	Advanced vectors

Table 11.2 Typology and examples of local production systems in São Paulo state

		Importance to the industry	
		Low	High
Importance to the region	High	Araraquara (textile and clothing) Amparo (knitwear) Campos do Jordão (knitwear) Dracena (structural ceramic) Jaú (leather goods) Votuporanga (furniture) São José do Rio Preto (jewelry)	Franca (leather footwear) Jaú (leather footwear) Birigui (plastic footwear) Limeira (semi-precious jewelry and bijouterie) Ribeirão Preto (medical equipment) S. José Campos (electronic material)
	Low	Ourinhos (leather footwear) Pirassununga (ceramic tiles) Limeira (machine-tools) Mogi Mirim (ceramic tiles) Ribeirão Preto (farm machinery)	Campinas (textile) Campinas (optical, information and communication equipment) São Paulo (clothing) São Paulo (printing) São Paulo (precision instruments)

universe. There are so many of those systems in São Paulo state and throughout Brazil that an industrial policy designed to foster their development would have to include differentiated "incentive packages" capable of encouraging local actors to offer active responses and effective commitments. The success of industrial policy depends on the involvement of private agents and social actors. Ensuring this involvement must be built into the policy and its instruments from the start of the design process.

Centers of industrial and regional development have developed vigorously and have a long history in almost every case. Given the intrinsic characteristics of this development process, their manufacturing dimension is hyper-developed in relation to their commercial functions, including marketing. For this very reason, an appropriate industrial policy designed to help these systems reach a higher stage of development and competitiveness would include a combination of commercial and industrial functions geared toward moving beyond dependency on channels and other forms of selling, and to encouraging a focus on product development, brand equity, patent registration, design, certification, and quality.

Overcoming subordinate market insertion and a production function tied to high volume coupled with low price requires integrated and consistent development in both dimensions. The industrial policy "package" offered to systems of this type should include these two aspects and treat them in an integrated manner. A typical strategy for promoting these centers of industrial and regional development would include education and training in higher technical skills and autonomous selling and marketing capabilities. Extending present education and training facilities can provide the former, but the latter involves bringing together dispersed competencies and setting up new business associations or special legal vehicles.

Embryonic local production systems are the most numerous types, although the number of cases can be reduced if more rigorous filters are included in the methodology. If the resources required for a policy of fomenting these embryonic systems can be considered modest in individual terms, the number of such local production systems and the probable incipient nature of the local fabric of organizations entails greater risks. Thus, the industrial policy package for embryonic local systems should be associated with a concatenated sequence of conditioned stages, each clearly requiring matching local contributions in the form of funds, resources, or some other involvement. Although embryonic local systems are diametrically opposite to the previous type described above (centers of industrial and regional development) in several respects, it is important to avoid making the mistake of trying to force them to follow in a linear way all the developmental stages of their developed "predecessors." After all, today these veterans find themselves in the "blind alley" of high volume and low prices, and it will be no easy task to find a way out.

To avoid this trap, industrial policy must encourage embryonic local systems to conduct market research that will help identify segments or even niche markets capable of being exploited by coordinated promotional activities. This is the best way to sidestep the temptation to focus on mere expansion of production capacity and downward competition, which drives down prices and quality. Industrial policy should include coordinated measures to provide the conditions for acquiring the necessary technical and production-related capabilities for them to develop these market segments.

The systems comprised by *local development vectors* are those industrial policy is better equipped to foment. On one hand, they have passed the embryonic stage and have the critical mass for their local importance to be recognized. On the other they do not yet face the difficulties inherent in centers of industrial and regional development, such as having to act as trailblazers and possibly make mid-course corrections. Because they are at a certain distance from these centers, local development vectors can avoid repeating mistakes and more easily identify opportunities. Their main challenge is to build a trajectory on the basis of sporadic or localized opportunities.

Advanced vectors, unlike all the other types mentioned, pose considerable difficulties for policymakers aiming to integrate them with a predominant dimension of regional development. They have minimal significance in regions normally much more developed and with a diversified and integrated economic (and social) fabric. This does not mean this type of local system is less structured or does not have strong links and relationships among its constituent elements, although they may not be very visible. However, the fact is that the surrounding economic fabric has multiple ingredients that can be mobilized to promote the development of the constituent elements of advanced vectors: this is a characteristic that differentiates them clearly from local development vectors and *a fortiori* from the other types.

Thus, policy measures to foment advanced vectors should focus on mobilizing local resources to prevent the erosion of competitiveness that insertion of their products at the bottom of the market would inevitably cause if these systems were to depend on a cheap and plentiful supply of factors in areas (urban or metropolitan) where such factors are certainly far more expensive.

The policy instruments best suited to each of these types of local production systems are evidently very different. The activities to be considered for embryonic local systems may be numerous but they will certainly be more basic. Experience in the field shows that, in these cases, basic ingredients such as courses on cost accounting and management are extremely useful and can be inserted in the initial stages of longer, more ambitious development programs. As for the more advanced types of local systems, be they centers or vectors, the appropriate policy instruments will involve larger volumes of funding and other resources, while also entailing greater risk in terms of the resources involved.

In any of the four cases discussed, policy should offer conditions for local protagonists to use their capacity for mobilization in favor of development. This means the policy cannot and must not take the place of local actors. Moreover, if it is to avoid failure from the start it must not include measures that weaken or stultify the autonomous development of the local system and its social forces. Local institutions must be preponderant protagonists in any policy for local production systems.

In addition, it is of crucial importance from the initial stages on to set a priority in the policy for embryonic local production systems. It is commonplace in Brazil to acknowledge that local production systems have developed only to a limited extent the cooperative mechanisms that, according to the paradigmatic view, characterize these configurations in other countries, especially in Europe and, above all, Italy.

Cooperation is not something you invent, of course; nor can it be created by decree. But through incentives associated with local involvement and collectively assumed commitments, policy can lay the foundations for a strengthening of the local fabric and local associative spirit, allowing cooperation and more effective collective actions to grow out of that. Thus, the incentive package that is part of industrial policy for local systems should be geared toward creating collective spaces and institutions, with shared management and public funding (to be phased out over time) as well as private funding (to be phased in over time). The initial stimulus provided by the policy through competition should explicitly and contractually require tangible matching contributions and institutional mechanisms of collective management, preferably shared among the social groups.

The mechanisms introduced to foster competition among local systems should ensure two significant results from the policy perspective. The first is tangible reciprocity, i.e. the contribution of local matching funds in proportion to public funds allocated to local systems under the policy. Thus, for example, the right to join a program of technical and industrial labor training centers or management courses should also be evaluated in terms of the local contribution. The second is evaluation of local membership (a priori), which could be used to prioritize demands from local systems, and evaluation of the results obtained (a posteriori) to help decide whether a program continues and/or should be redesigned.

At the opposite end of the local systems spectrum, i.e. for the promotion of centers of industrial and regional development, the same system of public competition for the resources offered by the development policy should produce responses in both dimensions, tangible and intangible. With regard to the former, it is possible to imagine reciprocity in each relevant aspect of local system development, even if the system through its collective institution(s) applies for resources under the policy only for some of the programs offered. Thus, application for collective facilities for technology development should be approved only in exchange for efforts in other dimensions, for example education, training, and the development of new commercial competencies. In respect of intangibles, it is both desirable and feasible that projects submitted for approval by public-sector development agencies should be appreciated in terms of a global vision of local system development and expansion strategy.

Concluding remarks

The methodology that has been developed proved to be a useful tool for identifying, locating, structurally characterizing, and surveying local production systems through field research work in Brazil. It aims primarily at classifying the numerous local systems according to a typology, and at knowing the most typical problems that affect their development both at system level and at the level of its firms, which could be the object of public policies and of actions by semi-public institutions and private entities. The knowledge thus created allows for the organization and coordination of those policies and actions, avoiding ad hoc criteria, unnecessary super-positions, excessively dispersed actions and, consequently, waste of public and private resources.

A word of caution is necessary, however. Although the approach to regional development problems discussed in this chapter may be useful for promoting local development, it should not be seen as a panacea for national or even regional development problems. It cannot replace a national economic and social development policy; neither can it be a substitute for industrial and regional policies.

In fact, local production systems are naturally limited in dynamic terms, in the sense that their capacity to promote greater diversification of the production structure and to lead the development of other activities is limited, especially when they are not connected to regional industrial complexes. Yet, in all cases we have studied it was observed that, in spite of the limited dynamics and of problems like the ones commented on above, economic and social development in the system's region of influence is undeniable. In all cases, the system's main activity pays better wages, average growth rates have been higher than those of the respective industry in the country, unemployment rates are lower, social problems are lessened, the labor force has better opportunities for technical and industrial training, more attention is given to innovation and technology upgrading as well as to exports, and a great number of new, spin-off firms confer dynamism to the local business environment. Thus, to make policies with a focus on local production systems in Brazil seems to be relevant and highly promising, and the methodology developed in this chapter may be a useful guide to such policies.

Acknowledgments

The authors acknowledge financial support from CNPq (National Council for Scientific and Technological Development) in the form of research grant – Process No. 478786/2003-5. They are also grateful to Sérgio E.K. Sampaio, who participated in the development of the methodology.

Notes

1 This expression is borrowed from P.A. David (1999). The state government's bids for investments became known as "fiscal war."
2 One of the institutions announced in 2003 that it would support 500 clusters throughout the country.
3 The notion of collective efficiency is also Marshallian. See A. Marshall, *Principles of Economics: An introductory volume*, Macmillan, New York, eighth edition (1949), Book IV, Chapter XIII, p. 314. Garofoli (1983) introduced it to the analysis of Italian industrial districts. Hubert Schmitz (1995, 1997) elaborated on the original concept and, later on, Schmitz and Nadvi (1999) reviewed the concept in light of a large number of applications to several case studies, published in the excellent Special Issue on Industrial Clusters in Developing Countries they edited for *World Development*, 27 (9), September 1999.
4 The role of trust in exporting clusters is discussed in Schmitz (1999). Contributions to the study of cluster performance in global chains are summarized below.
5 The concept of local production systems was primarily introduced in the Italian context by Garofoli (1983), and has been widely used since then mostly by Italian and French authors.

6 Case studies have been made in eight states, covering several manufacturing industries (leather and shoe, furniture, jewelry, information and communication equipment, ceramics, medical equipment, clothing, marble stones, wood products, agriculture machinery, plastics) and software. Approximately 400 firms and institutions have been visited in the past five years.

7 Namely: (1) those that are very important for the industry and also very important for the region, which we named as *centers of industrial and regional development*; (2) those that are very important for the industry but not so important for the region, which we named as *advanced vectors*, usually located in highly industrialized metropolitan areas; (3) local systems that are not important for the industry, but are very important for the region, named as *vectors of local development*, and (4) local systems that are not yet important either for the industry or for the region, but are already relevant geographic agglomerations of firms in the industry, which we named as *embryonic local production systems*.

8 Course quality is assessed by a national test applied to final-year undergraduates in selected subjects.

9 In some local production systems the interaction with the educational system is better focused. For example, the Information and Communication Technology (ICT) industry cluster of Campinas benefits from courses in that industry area at UNICAMP (State University of Campinas) and other local educational institutions. ICT firms in Campinas also interact intensively with the local R&D centers and labs, which have been historically present in the region. In Votuporanga, the furniture local production system has managed to create a specific furniture technology degree course in a local university.

10 The most conspicuous example is that of Franca, a men's leather shoe manufacturing local system, where several initiatives of smaller, independent firms to organize collective actions were sabotaged by the large, dominating firms that are subcontracted producers for international buyers.

11 We base our suggestion on the successful experience of a group of 25 small firms from Votuporanga who hired a coordinator to manage them out of a crisis. The coordinator organized a total quality control program, introduced management best practices, helped create a course of furniture manufacturing technology in the local university, and managed the financing and establishment of a technology, R&D, and labor training center that became the second most important in the country. The results were production growth, increasing exports and technological progress, with several firms ISO certified.

12 The case of Franca comes to mind once more. Most of the large firms producing for foreign buyers are technically upgraded but devote much less attention to product innovation. Small and large independent firms, on the other hand, are innovative and successful in opening their own market channels with their own brand names all over the world. The same happens in other local production systems such as Votuporanga (furniture) and Limeira (jewelry).

13 The service was so successful that it was extended to firms in competing local production systems in the country, which was of course against the interests of the local manufacturers.

14 This is in agreement with Scott's (1998, p. 396) suggestion for the creation of "forums for strategic choice and action," and with Lombadi's (2003, p. 1459) similar suggestion for the "creation of agencies specialized in favoring the adaptation of decentralized production systems to radical challenges."

References

Arthur, W.B. (1988) Self-reinforcing mechanisms in economics, in P.W. Anderson, K.J. Arrow, and D. Pines (eds.) *The Economy as an Evolving Complex System*, SFI Studies in the Sciences of Complexity, Addison-Wesley Publishing Company, Reading, Mass.

Arthur, W.B. (1990) Positive feedbacks in the economy, *Scientific American*, 262, February, pp. 92–99.

Audretsch, D.B. and Feldman, M.P. (1996) R&D spillovers and the geography of innovation and production, *American Economic Review* 86 (3), pp. 630–640.

Belussi, F. (1995, 2000) Policies for the development of knowledge-intensive local production systems, *Cambridge Journal of Economics*, 23, pp. 729–747, updated version published in Belussi and Gottardi (2000), Chapter 5.

Belussi, F. and Gottardi, G. (Orgs.) (2000) *Evolutionary Patterns of Local Industrial Systems, Toward a Cognitive Approach to the Industrial District*, Ashgate, Aldershot.

Breschi, S. and Malerba, F. (2001) The geography of innovation and economic clustering: some introductory notes, *Industrial and Corporate Change*, 10 (4), pp. 817–833.

David, P. (1999) Comment on "The role of geography in development," by Paul Krugman, in B. Pleskovic and J.E. Stiglitz (eds.) *Annual World Bank Conference on Development Economics 1998*, The World Bank, Washington, DC.

Feldman, M.P. (1993) An examination of the geography of innovation, *Industrial and Corporate Change*, 2 (3), pp. 451–470.

Feldman, M.P. (1994), *The Geography of Innovation*, Kluwer Academic Press, Dordrecht, The Netherlands.

Fujita, M., Krugman, P. and Venables, A. (1999) *The Spatial Economy: Cities, Regions and International Trade*, The MIT Press, Cambridge.

Garofoli, G. (1983) *Industrializzazione difusa in Lombardia*, Irer-Franco Angeli Editore, Milano.

Gereffi, G. (1994) The organization of buyer-driven global commodity chains: how U.S. retailers shape overseas production networks, in G. Gereffi and M. Korzeniewicz (eds.) *Commodity Chains and Global Capitalism*, Praeger, Westport.

Gereffi, G. (1999) International trade and industrial upgrading in the apparel commodity chain, *Journal of International Economics*, 48, pp. 31–70.

Humphrey, J. and Schmitz, H. (2000) Governance and upgrading: linking industrial cluster and global value chain research, IDS Working Paper 120, IDS, Brighton.

Krugman, P. (1999) The role of geography in development, in B. Pleskovic and J.E. Stiglitz (eds.) *Annual World Bank Conference on Development Economics 1998*, The World Bank, Washington, DC.

Lazerson, M.H. and Lorenzoni, G. (1999) The firms that feed industrial districts: A return to the Italian source, *Industrial and Corporate Change*, 8 (2), pp. 235–266.

Lombardi, M. (2000) The cognitive approach to the study of local production systems, in Belussi and Gottardi (eds.), Chapter 3.

Lombardi, M. (2003) The evolution of local production systems: the emergence of the "invisible mind" and the evolutionary pressures towards more visible "minds," *Research Policy* 32 (8), pp. 1443–1462.

Porter, M.E. (1990) *Vantagem competitiva das nações*, Campus, Rio de Janeiro.

Porter, M.E. (1998), *On Competition*, Harvard Business School Press, Portuguese edition: *Competição = On Competition: Estratégias Competitivas Essenciais*, Campus, Rio de Janeiro.

Porter, M.E. and Sölvell, Ö. (1998) The role of geography in the process of innovation and the sustainable competitive advantage of firms, in A.D. Chandler, Jr., P. Hagström and Ö. Sölvell (eds.), *The Dynamic Firm: the role of technology, strategy, organization, and regions*, Chapter 19, Oxford University Press.

Schmitz, H. (1995) Collective efficiency: growth path for small-scale industry, *The Journal of Development Studies*, 31 (4), pp. 529–566.

Schmitz, H. (1997) Collective efficiency and increasing returns, IDS Working Paper, 50, IDS, Brighton.

Schmitz, H. (1999) From ascribed to earned trust in exporting clusters. *Journal of International Economics*, 48, pp. 139–150.

Schmitz, H. and Nadvi, K. (1999) Clustering and industrialization: introduction, *World Development*, 27 (9), pp. 1503–1514.

Scott, A.J. (1998) The geographic foundations of industrial performance, in A.D. Chandler, Jr., P. Hagström and Ö. Sölvell (eds.), *The Dynamic Firm: the role of technology, strategy, organization, and regions*, Chapter 16, Oxford University Press.

Storper, M. and Harrison, B. (1991) Flexibility, hierarchy and regional development: the changing structure of industrial production systems and their forms of governance in the 1990s, *Research Policy*, 20 (5), pp. 407–422.

Suzigan, W. (Coordinator) (2005) The Regional Dimension of ST&I Activities in São Paulo State, *Science, Technology & Innovation Indicators in the State of São Paulo/Brazil 2004*, Chapter 9, FAPESP, São Paulo.

Suzigan, W., Furtado, J., Garcia, R. and Sampaio, S.E.K. (2003) Local production and innovation systems in the state of São Paulo, Brazil, *43rd Congress of the European Regional Science Association (ERSA)*, University of Jyvaskyla, Finland.

Suzigan, W., Furtado, J., Garcia, R. and Sampaio, S.E.K. (2004) Local production systems in Brazil: mapping, typology and policy suggestions, *44th Congress of the European Regional Science Association (ERSA 2004)*, University of Porto, Portugal.

Suzigan, W., Furtado, J., Garcia, R. and Sampaio, S.E.K. (2005) Knowledge, innovation and agglomeration: regionalized multiple indicators and evidence from Brazil, *45th European Congress of the Regional Science Association (ERSA 2005)*, Vrije Universiteit (VU), Amsterdam, Holland.

12 Regional development and cluster management

Lessons from South Africa

Mike Morris and Justin Barnes

Introduction

Regional and local development cannot be separated from globalization. For the defining characteristic of this era of globalization (differentiating it from earlier periods of internationalization) is the international dispersal of the production of manufactured components, globally coordinated, and oriented toward supplying industrialized country markets (Dicken, 1998; Kaplinsky, 2005). Most enterprises in developing countries do not engage in spot market, arm's-length trade with their export customers, i.e. thin, transient relationships. They are instead locked into various hierarchical outsourcing arrangements, i.e. "thick" relationships where lead firms determine production parameters, specifications, and design over the outsourced enterprises (Gereffi *et al.*, 2004; Kaplinsky, 2005). Consequently, issues of operational performance, competitiveness, learning, upgrading, or innovation at a regional level are interlinked with global value chain determinants (Humphrey and Schmitz, 2002). Furthermore, collective efficiency (i.e. clustering and learning through networking) has played a crucial role in local firms enhancing their productivity, rate of innovation, and competitive performance (Bell and Albu, 1999; Maskell *et al.*, 1998; Bessant *et al.*, 2003; Lawson and Lorenz, 1999; Morosini, 2004; Nadvi and Schmitz, 1999; Schmitz, 1999a, 1999b, 2004).

On a policy level, this is reflected in the importance of developed country governments promoting *existing* regional clusters (Peck and McGuinness, 2003). However, the same cannot be said about developing countries attempting to *create* clusters and learning networks, for the Washington Consensus has marginalized industrial policy in developing countries (World Bank, 1997). Even though the World Bank has recently come to accept that governments can act as a "facilitator of networking, as a catalyst of dynamic comparative advantage and as an institution builder, creating an efficient incentive structure to remove systemic and market inefficiencies in (national) systems of innovation." However, "The creation of clusters should not be a government-driven effort but should be the result of market-induced and market-led initiatives" (World Bank, 2004). According to the Bank, developing countries must strategically shift from policies of direct interventions to ones of indirect inducement, such as creating supporting network, dialogues, and knowledge exchange structures and schemes. Government should not subsidize firms or sectors in setting up clusters, nor should cluster policy be about limiting market rivalry. Furthermore, government should not create clusters from scratch in declining markets or industries. It also should not try to take the direct lead or ownership in cluster initiatives. Instead, government should work as a catalyst, a broker bringing actors together, creating forums for dialogues, supplying supporting structures and incentives to facilitate the clustering and innovation process. In short, "supporting existing and emerging clusters rather than trying to create them from scratch" (Enright and Ffowcs-Williams, 2000: 4).

In contrast, exponents of industrial policy are relatively silent on governmental purposive action to create clusters. Chang, although a major advocate of industrial policy, basically ignores clusters in his published work (Chang, 1994, 1998, 2002). The development literature has cluster advocates and descriptions of the operations of existing clusters (Altenburg and Meyer-Stamer, 1999; Humphrey and Schmitz, 1995, 1996; Lall, 2004; Helmsing, 2001; Morosoni, 2004), which contains useful policy advice but there is not a huge amount on how to create, sustain, and manage them in a regional framework.[1] UNIDO's Web site (www.unido.org/clusters) goes the furthest, containing a policy framework for supporting and facilitating cluster development in developing countries. The importance of neutral external intermediaries and brokers in building cluster cooperation is a strong thrust of the policy recommendations. However, much of the UNIDO literature is silent on allocating specific responsibilities to external public sector role players (such as government, donors, business associations, international agencies, etc.) and especially on the specific role that developing country governments can or should play in the process.

So, from the perspective of regional development, conventional economic orthodoxy warns against an active government policy, and is very chary of allocating substantial resources to create clusters and networks from scratch. While those who differ with this orthodoxy tend not to be very specific about the manner in which purposive action to create clusters fits in as an integral part of industrial and regional policy. If we are, therefore, to understand purposive action and agency from a policy perspective, we need to tease apart the concept.

First, there are two distinct aspects to purposive action to facilitate clustering and networking. The public sphere concerns government policies and implementation activities, while the private sphere revolves around external intermediaries (business development services, cluster and network facilitators, consulting firms). Thus, the question is how to allocate different roles to each. Is government merely a facilitator, a funding agency, and how should the private sector play a leading role?

Second, should one eschew starting clusters from scratch, or only work with existing clusters/networks? The answer may be best gleaned from empirical case studies. If this has been done in a developing country, as we argue is the case in South Africa, then it certainly opens up a much wider scope for policy initiatives.

Third, in the process of creating clusters/networks, is it best to do so from above or below? Do we have case study experiences of creating clusters and learning networks that can help pose appropriate questions and inform us of relevant answers regarding the dynamics of the process of cluster/network creation and development?

Fourth, which level of governance (central or local) is best positioned to formulate and implement cluster industrial policy? There is often, in our experience, a huge gap between the policy supportive framework articulated and the institutional arrangements the state puts in place to implement them. How can we ensure that state support policy for clusters and networks is implemented in a way that facilitates policy objectives rather than obstructs them?

Fifth, is policy different in creating clusters or learning networks? That is, collective action sharing activities/costs to create collectivized scale economies, or cooperative activities to facilitate learning and raise operational competitiveness within each enterprise. In order to unpack these questions, we examine clusters and learning network experience in the automotive, clothing, and textile sectors in South Africa.

The automotive component benchmarking clubs

In the mid-1990s, South Africa shifted from import-substituting industrialization to trade liberalization, a major drop in tariff protection and rapid integration into the world economy. This posed major challenges for the automotive component sector, which was faced with the urgent need to become internationally competitive. With government support measures providing 65 percent funding, a learning network was established in 1998 called the "KwaZulu-Natal Benchmarking Club" (KZNBC), comprising 11 component makers and one assembler, facilitated by a private service provider,[2] and operating as a manufacturing excellence learning network (Barnes and Morris, 1999). Central to this was the use of a benchmarking model of key competitiveness drivers (see Table 12.1).

The executive consisted of firm representatives controlling policy, budget, and payments, with two facilitators as nonvoting members. The following services were provided to members:

- A confidential diagnostic report of each firm providing confidential, evidence-based feedback on performance. The report measured operational performance, major customers' assessment of its performance, the firm's perception of its major suppliers' performance, as well a benchmark against a "like for like" international competitor.
- A monthly newsletter outlining aggregate benchmark data for the whole network.
- Quarterly "best practice" inter-firm workshops discussing generic findings, common problems, and emerging solutions.
- Encouraging information sharing between firms through inter-plant visits, etc.

Table 12.1 The critical success factor/market driver matrix measuring operational performance

Market drivers	Operational performance measures	Linked organizational practices
Cost control	Inventory use (raw materials, work in progress, finished goods)	Single unit flow, quality at source, cellular production, kanbans
Quality	Customer return rates, internal reject, rework and scrap rates, return rates to suppliers	Quality control structures, statistical process control, quality circles, team working, multi-skilling
Lead times (value chain flexibility)	Time from customer order to delivery, delivery frequency of suppliers and supplier delivery reliability, delivery frequency to customers and delivery reliability	Business process engineering, cellular structures, processing and dispatch, value chain relationships and supply chain management
Flexibility (operations)	Manufacturing throughput time, machine changeover times, batch sizes, inventory levels, production flow	Production scheduling, JIT, single minute exchange of dies, multi tasking and multi-skilling, cellular production in manufacturing
Capacity to change (human resources)	Literacy/numeracy, suggestion schemes, employee development/training, absenteeism rates, labor/management turnover, employee output	Continuous improvement (kaizen), work organization, worker development and commitment programs, industrial relations
Innovation capacity	R&D expenditure (process and product), Contribution of new products to total sales	Concurrent engineering, R&D

The first difficulty encountered was a lack of trust, an unwillingness to share information, and a tendency to blame others for emerging problems – government, suppliers, customers. This changed as members took ownership of the network, and workshops were run in the factories themselves, signaling a shift toward more open experience sharing and trust building.

The Club's success led to four similar networks being established in other industry centers: Port Elizabeth, Gauteng, East London, and Cape Town. In total, 70 firms belong to these networks, linked by a common service provider and sharing generic resources. Although each has differing agendas, depending on the local assemblers, there is considerable interchange with inter-firm visiting and participation in workshops between regions. Consequently, knowledge sharing has developed into a national capability across the sector.

The risk with concepts like "learning networks" is that they become synonymous with general meetings and gatherings that would happen anyway arising from day-to-day sectoral operations. We suggest it is possible using these key indicators to measure the concept and assess network effectiveness in supporting learning and knowledge development:

- Increasing *knowledge sharing*, e.g. willingness to present to other member firms on achieving significant success on some of the key performance indicators.
- Significant *knowledge transfer*, e.g. recorded spontaneous firm visits between members, involvement in joint projects with confidential information sharing.
- Major improvement in *operational performance*, e.g. reflected in the competitiveness indicators measured annually.
- Spread of the clubs as *new members* were attracted.

However, the two most significant criteria of success are network sustainability and demonstrable internalization of firm-level learning. The former is clearly apparent by the decision to become completely self-reliant in January 2004, after national government reneged on the promise of three-year funding and the clubs were faced with dissolution. The various club executives decided to ensure long-term sustainability by creating a national South African Auto Benchmarking Club with branch chapters solely dependent on private firm subscription fees.

Considerable qualitative data exist to measure knowledge sharing and information transfer. There is clear evidence of growth in the network's popularity through membership expansion – firms clearly perceived the activities as beneficial. But the most significant indicator of learning success is actual improvements in operational performance that member firms attributed to their participation in the network. The clubs are primarily based on firms wanting to ensure continuous improvement and operational performance enhancement in order to make them more internationally competitive. The driving force underlying knowledge sharing and upgrading is benchmarking the operational performance of member firms against other club members as well as against international comparators. Therefore, the best quantitative indicator is the improvement in the operational performance of firms. In conjunction with internationally comparative data it is possible to see the nature and rate of performance improvement. Table 12.2 presents this in summary and aggregated format.[3]

The learning impact on operational performance has been significant even if the South African components sector has some way to go to reach the global frontier. With the exception of delivery reliability to customers, progress for all of the measures in South Africa has been significant. Generally speaking, domestic performance is better where internal factors (work-in-progress control, training, absenteeism) are involved than where they are dependent on external factors (raw material inventories, supplier performance). From a value chain perspective, this suggests that the growth of learning is still predominantly in the first-tier components suppliers and has not yet diffused sufficiently up the chain. Some of the inventory control weakness is due to value chain logistic problems, especially with regard to incoming materials (minimum-sized import quantities; problems at the ports) and distance to the export market (for stocks of finished goods). In general, there are clear indications that significant process upgrading has occurred and the firms are becoming more internationally competitive. Clearly, external factors have also contributed, but the members argue that the cooperation, knowledge sharing, and learning embedded in the operations of the clubs have played a major and critical role in the process (Barnes and Lorentzen, 2004).

There is still some distance from the international frontier, but these firms are clearly learning rapidly. A number of other factors have also contributed, but the qualitative data mentioned earlier suggest that firms perceive considerable value in shared learning as a way to accelerate learning progress. The limits to horizontal cooperation can be seen in the relative lack of impact on inter-firm issues, suggesting that some form of vertical cooperation is also needed to help with sector development (Bessant *et al.*, 2003).

How do we assess government institutional levers in this process? Without the existence of an auto sector-specific industrial policy coupled with cross-sectoral policy levers that allowed the service providers to access financial support for clustering (Barnes *et al.*, 2004), the Benchmarking Clubs would never have emerged and been sustainable in their early years. Yet one of the most striking difficulties experienced by the clubs was the institutional difficulties associated with the support received from the national government. Government abandoned import-substituting industrialization, adopted new policies, and the Department of Trade and Industry (DTI) had employed new personnel. But the administrative structure remained intact and there was insufficient reconceptualization of the deployment implications of these policies and, hence, reconfiguring of the institutional arrangements to ensure that implementation followed the policy shift.

The support measures were immersed in bureaucratic red tape and it was extremely difficult to access them. The long lead times associated with the department's previous practice – lobbying for tariff protection or requesting various licensing permits – were no longer adequate in this new era of

Table 12.2 Operational performance change – club firms (1998/1999–2001) and (2001–2004)

Market drivers Key performance indicators		South African firms							Comparator firms			
									Developed economies		Emerging economies	
	n	1998/ 1999	2001	Change %	n	2001	2004	Change %	n		n	
Cost control	Raw material (days)	24	32.33	21.77	32.7	55	23.26	20.50	11.9	12	11.42	43	18.83
	Work in progress (days)	24	12.40	8.15	34.3	55	7.10	6.92	2.6	12	6.40	43	7.18
	Finished goods	24	17.82	12.12	32.0	55	12.25	10.41	15.0	12	8.17	43	9.33
	Total inventory (days)	24	62.56	42.03	32.8	55	42.61	37.83	11.2	12	26.03	43	35.90
Quality	Customer return rate (ppm)	23	3,270	1,240	62.0	43	1,558	276	82.3	11	266	34	1,127
	Internal reject rate (%)	25	4.90	3.89	20.7	38	3.87	3.26	15.8	12	1.44	47	1.73
	Internal rework rate (%)	19	3.14	2.40	23.5	39	2.76	2.79	–1.05	11	2.14	34	1.90
	Internal scrap rate (%)	24	4.24	3.51	17.2	41	1.98	1.74	12.1	8	0.32	14	1.51
	Supplier return rate (ppm)	21	21,989	18,518	16.0	41	16,330	11,645	28.7	8	7,470	34	9,506
Flexibility	Lead time (days)	19	19.9	17.9	9.9								
	Lead time ex prod (domestic – days)					50	8.50	7.69	9.6	7	7.57	18	4.57
	Lead time ex prod (global – days)					29	43.63	43.54	0.2	6	7.83	8	27.94
	Supplier on time (%)	23	78.7	82.2	4.5	50	86.25	88.41	2.5	13	93.88	47	89.19
	On time to customers (%)	25	92.2	92.7	0.6	53	91.25	93.21	2.1	14	97.66	48	93.69
Capacity to change	Training spend as % total remuneration	30	1.3	2.0	56.2	53	2.06	1.95	–5.3	11	2.05	34	4.39
	Absenteeism (%)	27	4.4	4.0	9.4	57	4.14	3.57	13.8	12	4.01	47	5.40
Innovation capacity	R&D expenditure (%)	24	1.64	2.12	29.5	33	0.95	1.01	5.5	12	1.96	17	2.42

Source: Data provided by benchmarking and manufacturing analysts.

international competitiveness. Furthermore, the knowledge implications of the policy shift required retraining staff, shifting their center of gravity as "paper pushers" to agents of change, fully attuned to the competitiveness demands being placed on South African firms.

While it was easy obtaining formal government support, practically establishing the club was more difficult. The launch was seven months late and then took a further five months for the first government payment. Moreover, as time progressed, the clubs (and service providers incurring the actual costs) discovered that providing a 65 percent subsidy proved a double-edged sword. The DTI invariably took between three to six months to respond to invoices and, consequently, the service providers facilitating club activities constantly experienced cash-flow crises. Lengthy procedures created considerable uncertainty, payment delays threatened to derail activities – all resulting in loss of participant confidence. Furthermore, since the service provider had to pay VAT on invoice and not on receipt of government payment, this placed further pressures on the viability of the networks, incurring excessive administrative time in generating resource certainty. Ironically, the DTI reneging on its promise of block funding unintentionally forced the clubs to confront the issue of long-term sustainability. They became completely self-financing, dependent only on membership fees, finally solving the continuous recurring cash-flow crises engendered from erratic government support.

In short, there was a lack of alignment between national government policy goals, strategies, and these networking activities taking place outside its immediate ambit. Second, the inability of central government to put in place the appropriate institutional arrangements to create an enabling environment also nearly killed the initiative, but inadvertently created the conditions for the learning network to move onto another level.

The Durban Auto Cluster

The initial stimulus for setting up the Durban Auto Cluster (DAC) came from the municipality, which was keen to foster regional development. Toyota SA, the major assembler in Durban, had secured a significant export order and the opportunity presented itself to work with the firm and key suppliers to enable regional economic growth.

The existing infrastructure and high trust within the KZN Benchmarking Club was used to initiate the DAC. In June 2001, the external facilitators proceeded in the following manner:

- Firms in the local value chain (40 in total) were identified, visited, and invited to participate, without financial obligation.
- Workshops involving the major actors were held.
- International research on cluster success was disseminated.
- Local, provincial, and central government support provided political legitimacy.

- A needs survey was undertaken on key issues affecting the local industry.
- Participants voted to identify four focus areas: logistics, human resources, supply chain, and operational competitiveness.
- Technical task teams comprising firm representatives managed these focus areas, identified key issues, wrote a one-year business plan with program goals, activities, and designated budgets.
- A final workshop discussed these plans, a (firm-based) governance structure, a budget, government support, membership fees, etc. and firms voted to launch the cluster, signing up as members.

The DAC as a public–private initiative was formally launched in January 2002.[4] Most of the finance came from local government with firms also paying membership fees. The four development programs[5] were run by technical steering committees controlling program activities and expenditure, chaired by firm representatives, with technical support from the service provider. The executive comprised the technical task team chairs, government representatives, and facilitators.

Operationally, the DAC works in the following manner:

- Providing key operational services
- Enabling financial savings through joint activities
- Knowledge sharing through workshops and a newsletter
- Joint research
- Access to an online database.

The four core programs operate in the following manner:

1 *The logistics program* shares information, creates price transparency, secures fair pricing and reduces costs through consolidation and load balancing across sea, road, and air. Logistics accounts for between 5 and 15 percent of selling costs, hence critically affecting competitiveness. A logistics costs survey showed that sea freight charges for smaller firms were double those of the larger firms, affecting competitiveness throughout the value chain. Hence, the drive to cut freight costs. Freight rates were "benchmarked" and linked to average prices for member firms. A special "cluster rate" was negotiated between Europe-SA for all cluster participants[6] – $1,300 per 20-foot container compared with $2,500 smaller firms paid.

2 *Supplier development* focuses on raising purchasing skills, aligning purchasing functions, developing a supplier awareness database, and information sharing. Activities include identifying training needs, exchanging knowledge, and running purchasing and supply management "best practice" workshops. Aligning purchasing functions was achieved through a common approach to supplier management by original equipment manufacturers (OEMs) and first-tier suppliers. A comprehensive directory of all suppliers to improve selection and facilitate comparison was created.

3   *The human resource development* program established a forum to interface with the government training organization as most firms are unaware of training grants or are unable to follow their complicated administrative procedures. A local training institute has developed a basic adult education program. Finally, to achieve collective scale economies, a joint training scheme provided nine technical training courses attended by 200 staff from 22 firms, the cost savings being about 30 percent per delegate (see Figure 12.1).

While Toyota's support is important, it was agreed by all that it would take a backseat. This enabled suppliers to feel comfortable working on strategies without feeling dominated by the powerful assemblers.

The DTI offers inconsistent support and erratic interest – national representatives rarely participate in the local activities, and no funding was provided. Responses to funding applications have been inadequate, as departmental bureaucrats have little direct experience of the cluster or its participants. In any case, the DTI's funding procedures required meeting criteria too precise to allow for the flexibility necessary in facilitating firm-based clustering. Despite numerous promises, the DAC never received any earmarked funds. Requests for more direct involvement were met with a view that the DTI has to be distanced from regional processes and focus on strategic national activities. This persists despite the DAC being one of the government's most successful cluster projects.

The DAC's relationship with provincial government has also been fraught with inflexibility, beset by delays and uncertainty with respect to funding support. Furthermore, the provincial department was prone to hijacking the cluster for its own political interests. In return for funding, it was wont to issue policy directives requiring the DAC to focus on matters that were not its core businesses.

The relationship with the local Metro-level government is markedly different. The metro government, concerned with Durban's problems in regenerating its

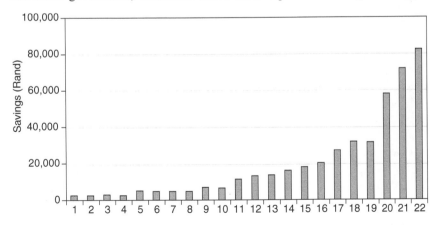

Figure 12.1   Joint training savings for participating firms: 2004 (source: data provided by benchmarking and manufacturing analysts).

industrial base, was acutely aware of the local automotive industry's importance. It was also aware, as a result of numerous interactions, of the success of the KZN Benchmarking Club. This *institutional intimacy* enabled it to play a proactive role. The Metro government has become the primary source of public funding for the DAC, and the incessant cash flow problems experienced through accessing national government funds have ceased. The Metro is embedded in the DAC, and this is apparent from the continuous presence of its representatives at the quarterly workshops, as well as the numerous occasions the deputy mayor and Metro CEO have been guest speakers. The facilitators meet regularly with local officials to discuss a variety of relevant issues, and an informal monitoring process is embedded in this working relationship

Cape Clothing and Textile Cluster, and KwaZulu-Natal Clothing and Textile Cluster

The clothing and textile industries were taking severe strain as a result of changing global circumstances (Kaplinsky, 2005). The entry of China into the WTO and the end of the quota-based Multi-Fibre Agreement resulted in Chinese imports flooding into the domestic market. Furthermore, the rapid appreciation of the Rand during the past few years (coinciding with China's entry into the WTO) resulted in clothing exporters' international inefficiency being rapidly exposed and a substantial fall in exports. In short, clothing and textiles was bleeding jobs and enterprises (Morris *et al.*, 2006,). Since these two domestic sectors were concentrated in the Western Cape and KwaZulu-Natal, there was major pressure on the respective provincial governments to assist the industry. Knowing of the successes in the auto sector, these provincial governments separately approached the facilitators (BMA) to initiate clothing clusters, providing start-up funding. These two clusters were respectively initiated in late 2004 and early 2005, and followed a similar model as the DAC.

The set up process took the following familiar form:

- Define, review, create consensus through firm level benchmarks and interviews to tease out the opportunities, constraints, obstacles, and competitiveness issues.
- Entrench support for clustering via firm level and regionally based workshops.
- Produce background analysis of the provincial clothing and textiles sectors trends and secure agreement on major problem areas.
- Develop industry-led strategies tackling key issues and areas of intervention.
- Transfer institutional ownership to sector champions, through technical steering committees, business plans, budgets, and realizable development programs.
- Set up a public–private partnership between government and firms, through the facilitation of a neutral service provider.

Both clusters were launched with programs solely focused on ensuring manufacturing excellence upgrading – collective efficiency, knowledge sharing, and continuous improvement learning activities.[7] Upgrading operational performance toward world-class manufacturing is of particular importance in this sector, for management traditionally has low knowledge levels and lacks appreciation of manufacturing excellence. Firms still tend to externalize problems, and hope that a "silver bullet" from an outside agency will save them. Hence, the stress in these two clusters on making firms focus internally on rapidly improving their operational performance to become more internationally competitive.

The differentiating feature of clothing and textiles is the critical lead role played in the domestic value chain by the large domestic retail firms that hold the future of the firms in their supply chain in their hands. Hence, the major strategic initiative has been (a) to draw the retailers into supporting local industry upgrading, (b) on this basis build a "business alliance" between all links in the value chain, and (c) massively accelerate the impact of the clusters by getting the big retailers to join them and encourage their suppliers to do likewise (*Business Report*, 7/4/2006). The success of these three initiatives place the CCTC and KZNCTC in a unique position of encompassing the entire value chain within their institutional confines and radically facilitating horizontal and vertical cooperation.

Conclusion

This chapter began by raising a number of general issues to be tested on the basis of the South African case study experience. Can clusters and learning networks, using industrial policy and government levers in developing countries, be created from scratch? Is there any proof that this is beneficial to the firms involved? If the answer is in the affirmative, then what analytic (as opposed to highly practical) lessons can be gleaned in respect of creating clusters from below or above? How should we understand the role of government (in its different tiers) and that of cluster facilitators in doing this? Finally, in understanding these processes, can one discern differences with respect to clusters and learning networks?

The first set of questions centred around whether clusters and learning networks can and should be created? The South African experience is yes; under certain circumstances and following certain processes, it is possible to create them where existing industrial capacity exists but cooperation is absent. Furthermore, as the data and descriptions clearly verify, they can lead to extremely beneficial results. The data cited and the examples provided of marshalling scale economies and internalizing learning is unequivocally positive. So why do we find resistance in the literature to government providing funding and marshalling human resources to foster clusters? There are a number of sources to such resistance. Some, such as the serious lack of institutional and human resource capacity in many developing country governments are legitimate and have to be taken very seriously. Others arise from a knee-jerk, ideological reaction to allocating public resources to pre-selected firms rather than creating policies that are available to all. The rationale behind this is a perfectly laudable concern to husband public resources and cut out rent-seekers, to which we turn later.

This is presumably also the basis for the World Bank's warning that clusters should not be government-driven or subsidized by public funds, and that government should not try and create them from scratch. However, there is a conceptual problem with this position. For it assumes stasis in the core competency of firms, takes capabilities as given, and operates without a concept of building dynamic capability (Teece and Pisano, 1994). But then how are firms in developing countries to change their capabilities, upgrade, and move onto a new innovation regime without some external facilitating process? Most firms in developing countries externalize their problems. Firms in developing countries don't understand the need to upgrade, and even when they do, they don't have the internal capacity to change or build on their core competency. This is the important role of government in regional development processes – to push firms out of their current stasis, to break vested interests, and to incentivize firm-level upgrading. As is borne out by the South African case studies, clustering is a way of doing so in a manner that is ultimately risk reducing, because it spreads risks, reduces upgrading costs and collectivizes efficiency gains.

What then about rent seeking? This is entirely dependent on the process and structure adopted. The case studies show how a process can be constructed that cuts out, or at least cuts down, rent seeking. First, the public cash contributions involved are relatively small. The South African Benchmarking Club's current annual budget is around $239,000. The Durban Auto Cluster's annual budget is around $212,000. The newly created Cape Clothing Cluster budget is around $196,000, and the recently launched KZN Clothing and Textile Cluster budget is $290,000.

Second, requiring firm contributions acts as an important check on how program monies are spent. The South African Auto Benchmarking Club is wholly funded by members, the Durban Auto Cluster depends on between 40 and 50 percent member funding, and both the clothing and textile clusters depend on 25 percent membership contributions. Firms are more careful about spending public money when their own contributions are integrally tied into the budgets.

Third, the institutional relationship between the government, firms, and the facilitators acts as an important control over expenditure. The contributions are paid into a legally constituted institution formally separated from the service provider, which the latter has to invoice for all activities and associated costs. Expenditure occurs through the cluster's executive, dependent on the program business plans managed by each technical steering committee to meet program objectives and budget targets, thereby providing substantial countervailing checks and balances.

Finally, the large contribution in kind from firms (time, energy, knowledge) builds in controls. This not only creates buy-in from the membership, but also ensures responsibility and accountability from firms for operational activities.

Indeed, some clusters are costing such contributions to offset them against the individual firm's membership payment. Essentially, this structure has created a situation where it is difficult for cluster participants to dupe government and put money into their own pockets. All expenditure falls within a business plan. One way rent-seeking can occur is if firms themselves do not take up participation in the various programs, and then it is the private sector and not the public sector that loses out. Ultimately, large-scale fraud would require the compliance of all role players for substantial rent-seeking to take place.

In thinking through the role of public funding, it is useful to contrast the differences between the clusters and the learning networks. This can be empirically captured through asking a question: What dynamics allowed for full membership payment in the South African Benchmarking Club (learning network) and would this be possible for the auto and clothing/textile clusters? The answer lies in the difference between a learning network designed to upgrade individual firm capabilities and a cluster operating to achieve collective efficiency through cooperative economies of scale. The benchmarking clubs are based on cooperation, but they are all about individual firms cooperating in order to internalize knowledge so as to upgrade. They are essentially built on a spine of enhancing private firm-level competitiveness. Hence, once the clubs had proven success, members were susceptible to them becoming wholly self-supporting. Indeed, it was wholly appropriate, if accidental and potentially disastrous in its timing, for government support to come to an end at some point.

The clusters, on the other hand, are based on achieving externally induced cooperative scale economies through substituting for what could instead have been the provision of public goods. The services the clusters provide all mirror this. For example, data provision and knowledge and enhancement are the provision of information, which should be a public good, provided by public authorities. Collective training is a public good that should be provided by government-sponsored training institutions. Brokering, joint negotiation, joint marketing, etc. are often services subsidized by government trade facilitation bodies. Member firms regard many of the clusters' collective efficiency services as partly public goods and, hence, it is appropriate for their costs to be shared with the public sector. That is also why they don't regard accessing these services through the cluster as rent-seeking.

Such issues may bother academics concerned with the theoretical questions of government's role vis-à-vis the private sector. But for those grappling with implementing regional development policies and using purposive action to create a cluster or learning network, the issues are concrete and institutionally located. As the experience of the South African case studies demonstrates, the big flaw in the relationship between government and clusters is much more mundane – it lies in government's inability to translate policy decisions into the institutional arrangements to ensure that the strategic policy goals can be implemented. While it is indisputable that without public funding these clusters would never have got off the ground, these clusters have succeeded in spite of, rather than because of, the way these resources were institutionally distributed. There are a number of reasons for this implementation failure, as well as policy lessons that flow from them.

Essentially, the South African DTI ignored reconfiguring its institutional arrangements to create a flexible delivery mechanism. Instead, it wrapped the process up in bureaucratic, time-consuming, and unnecessary activities instead of the first principles of lean manufacturing: flexible and quick response times. This was compounded by the DTI's lack of human capacity skills, and the refusal to realize that this was a way for its sector personnel to learn through an iterative relationship with the clusters. Instead, it engaged in an endless cycle of high profile and expensive management restructuring exercises. The result was that any specific training invested in the sector directorates was wasted, and the department bled demoralized staff at an alarming rate. Good industrial policy is far more than a process of abstract formulation, it also requires continuously learning, government staff embedded in sector dynamics. Furthermore, the DTI did not build internal institutional arrangements to intersect national industrial policy with locally based cluster initiatives. Hence, the local cluster initiatives were institutionally dislocated (in funding, accountability, and report back relationships) from national government initiatives, dependent on fragile personal relationships.

Correspondingly, local government's ability to create the institutional arrangements points to the issue of institutional location. Central government was too far away and distant from the firms to be institutionally embedded in their needs, problems, requirements, and cluster activities. It was unable to monitor and appreciate the cluster and network successes, and track the enterprises' movement toward international competitiveness. In short, it lacked the *institutional intimacy* to set up appropriate institutional arrangements of implementation. Delivery agencies do not have to be located at the same government level as resource-allocating tiers. In the case of the DAC, central government funds were accessed by the local tier for kick-starting the cluster. Resource allocation was located at central level while allowing for its drawdown and implementation to occur at lower government levels. Unfortunately, since it was purely accidental and ad hoc, it also illustrates the weaknesses, and policy irrelevance, of the process.

Most public–private partnerships are viewed as a relationship between two parties – government and firms. However, it is clear from the above case studies that creating clusters and learning networks from below through purposive action requires the application of particular skills on the part of external intermediaries – the facilitators. Indeed, there are actually three parties involved, and the problem is that the one that is most crucial from the perspective of agency tends to be left out of the policy equation. The facilitators are private sector, but they are distinctively different from the manufacturing enterprises, which are the real targets of industrial and cluster policy. The facilitators' task is to assist firms to upgrade, cooperate, and become more competitive. They are the conduits of policy, creating the link between state and manufacturing, the third arm of this triangle, linking the state's enabling environment and supportive financial structure and the manufacturing enterprises. Hence, a key conclusion is the need to close the magic triangle. By posing the question in terms of state vs. market – either government drives clustering or it allows the market to lead – this essential element gets lost. Instead, the central question is: How does government industrial policy build an effective business services sector to assist enterprises in building this new manufacturing economy? Supporting the private sector and creating public–private partnerships requires government to recognize, support, and reward the important role of the business services sector in delivering the sorts of direct interventions to raise the competitiveness levels of industry that government requires but, especially in many developing countries, is seldom capable of doing.

The initiative for creating clusters and networks from below through purposive action emerges from local processes. It is rarely the product of national government interventions, precisely because of the need to be sectorally embedded and establish institutional intimacy with local firms, facilitators, and supporting organizations. Hence, it is better to have government institutions involved in creating or maintaining clusters that operate at a lower level than the national structures. Whether this should be provincial or local government depends on the resource capabilities and human capacity levels of the different tiers. Central government's tendency to concentrate resources and set up bureaucratically obstructive accessing mechanisms has a major debilitating impact on the ability of firms to gain from networking arrangements. Distant and unresponsive centralized bureaucratic structures do little to enhance the building of relations essential to the uptake of programs deemed national priorities. Space barriers, distance, and limited contact between firms and central government officials do not enhance trust and mutual learning that are essential ingredients for successful networking and clustering.

A major problem obstructing building clusters from below is national government misunderstanding the various stages of creating effective industrial policy and strategy, i.e. formulation, design, promotion, and implementation. Policy formulation is usually undertaken by externally based consultants in cooperation with central government producing a coherent set of principles and guidelines that are adopted with suitable modification by government.

Policy design translates this into a legal framework as the codified policy of the government – undertaken by central bureaucrats and legislative experts. Policy promotion disseminates this to interested stakeholders. Policy implementation ensures that the bureaucratic processes and internal institutional arrangements are in place to deliver on the policy objectives. This requires government departments to reorganize internal institutional arrangements, train staff, change civil servant mindsets, speed up processes, etc. to ensure that the policies are accessed, the activities delivered to the relevant parties in the correct timeframes, and the results monitored and evaluated. Unfortunately, most policy processes stop at policy promotion, government bureaucrats assuming that dissemination equals implementation, and the crucial issue of ensuring that the necessary institutional arrangements have been put in place to implement the objectives is ignored. In respect to clustering, institutional intimacy and embeddedness suggest that these institutional arrangements and interventionist foci are best located within specialized government agencies/departments at lower government levels. A spin-off is that the increased local interaction results in major learning by local officials, building knowledge and capacity within the regional system of innovation.

Finding the appropriate level of government to situate public policy initiatives is complicated by the imperatives of globalization and the impact of global value chains on firms. In previous work we have analyzed the automotive sector using the analytic distinction between three kinds of industrial policy (macro, cross-sectoral, and sector specific) and stressed the need for systemic policy integration (Barnes *et al.*, 2004; Lall and Teubal, 1998). We have built on this by developing the following matrix (see Figure 12.2) where each cell contains a number of possible initiatives and activities. These are merely illustrative.

In conclusion, the issue of government and market in creating clusters and learning networks is particularly complicated and fraught because the terms of discussion are wrongly set. There cannot be a cluster without it being situated within a market environment, and it is highly unlikely that we can get sustainable clustering without purposive action. From the perspective of the firms involved, clusters arise because of both institutional and market failure. It is, therefore, a question of recognizing that it is an issue of finding the appropriate balance. Fundamentally, the role of government in regional development is to create an enabling environment for firms to engage in collective efficiency to upgrade systemic competitiveness on a long-term basis. In all the South African case studies of clusters the underlying rationale and logic of the cluster and the accompanying purposive action is always driven by systemic upgrading, and the role of government is not to help firms simply cut their immediate operating costs – that is a short-term agenda and doesn't necessarily contribute to upgrading systemic efficiency.

The South African clusters cited are driven by policy purposiveness, international competitiveness drivers, and an upgrading imperative, and bolstered by the systemic linkages between macro-, cross-sectoral, and sector-specific industrial policy (albeit somewhat erratically implemented). This may be the fundamental difference between spontaneous clustering and purposive clustering in the context of regional development. It is also why we believe that government has a critical role (always taking into account capacity limitations) to play in fostering purposive clusters – not because of support for a particular set of firms, but because of the congruence between the broader developmental objectives of national and/or regional government and the firm-level upgrading challenges confronting individual firms and clusters of firms in particular localities.

		Competitiveness levels		
		Micro level (Intra-firm)	Meso level (Value Chain/Cluster)	Macro (National)
Global		WTP, MFA, AGOA, EU agreement, internationally agreed certification standards (ISO, labor, fair trade, eco-labeling), value chain technical operating performance protocols		
Governance policy levers	Central	• Horizontal support policy (e.g. Competitiveness Fund) • R&D/innovation support • Resource allocation	• Sectoral stakeholder alignment • Supply side policy • R&D/innovation support • Information for VCs/clusters/sectors • Selective sector assistance levers • Cross-sectoral resource allocation	• Enabling framework • Selective sectoral policy • Cross sectoral policy • Review of industrial policies • Data collection • Policy performance review • Analyze global sectoral trends
	Province	• Export information • Firm upgrading support • Service provider directory • Information hub • Build BDS sector	• Market info on global buyers • Sector trade intelligence • Information hub to assist supply chain operational performance • Cluster/learning network support • Conduit for horizontal support measures e.g. funding, monitoring	• Lobbying • Institutional participation in national sector councils • Conduct socioeconomic impact studies
	Local	• Optimize infrastructure • Logistics costs/assistance • Data collection/analysis • Skills development	• Cluster/learning network support • Conduit for horizontal support measures, e.g. funding, monitoring • Disseminate sector information • Alignment to province strategies	• Lobby provincial government • Institutional participation in sectoral councils

Figure 12.2 Example of an industrial policy and cluster strategy levers framework.

Notes

1 Altenburg and Meyer-Stamer (1999) identify five areas in which government can help clusters. Humphrey and Schmitz advocate their Triple-C approach, but as they say, what government should do about it is less clear. Lall (2004) argues cluster facilitation as a part of industrial policy, but doesn't go much further than stressing the role of clusters in building absorptive capacity in firms and government. Helmsing (2001) makes a case for significant public policy adjustments and stresses the importance of the state's role in the process, particularly in its regional and local form. Morosoni (2004) posits a range of roles that public policymakers, through government interventions, can play in fostering the development of clusters and associated learning activities.

2 The private sector facilitation services arose from research by Justin Barnes and Mike Morris, since these were not academic activities. Justin Barnes is the full-time CEO of Benchmarking and Manufacturing Analysts (BMA – www.bmanalysts.com). He is also a research affiliate of SALDRU, University of Cape Town.

3 Presenting time series data to compare performance is difficult where membership is constantly growing. One cannot compare performance averages based on 56 firms in 2004 with 25 firms in 1998. Hence, the data are presented separately for two samples and sets of years – the original sample (1998/1999–2001) and a sample of firms joining in 2001 tracked to 2004. The discrepancy in "lead times" results from the way data are collected. International firms performance is static as no consistent time series data are available.

4 The DAC currently has 42 participating firms paying membership fees, 20 more than when it was launched.

5 This program will not be discussed here since it is simply the incorporation and expansion with new members of the KZN Benchmarking Club, which we have already discussed, into the DAC.

6 At least one of the larger firms with huge volume pays even less than the negotiated cluster rate.

7 These two clusters have not been operative long enough to assess the impact quantitatively on the competitiveness of member firms.

References

Altenburg, T. and Meyer-Stamer, J. (1999) "How to Promote Clusters: Policy Experiences from Latin America," *World Development*, 27(9)., pp. 1693–1713.

Barnes, J. and Lorentzen, J. (2004) "Learning, Upgrading and Innovation in the South African Automotive Industry," *European Journal of Development Research*, 16(3), pp. 465–498.

Barnes, J. and Morris, M. (1999) "Improving Operational Competitiveness Through Firm Level Clustering: A Case Study of the KwaZulu-Natal Benchmarking Club," working paper 24, School of Development Studies, University of Natal.

Barnes, J., Kaplinsky, R. and Morris, M. (2004) "Industrial Policy in Developing Economies: Developing Dynamic Comparative Advantage in the South African Automobile Sector," *Competition and Change*, 8(2), pp. 153–172.

Bell, M. and Albu, M. (1999) "Knowledge Systems and Technological Dynamism in Industrial Clusters in Developing Countries," *World Development*, 27(9), pp. 1715–1734.

Bessant, J., Kaplinsky, R. and Morris, M. (2003) "Developing Capability Through Learning Networks," in *International Journal of Technology Management and Sustainable Development*, 2(1), pp. 9–38.

Chang, H.-J. (1994) *The Political Economy of Industrial Policy*, St Martin's Press, New York.

Chang, H.-J. (1998) "Evaluating the Current Industrial Policy of South Africa," *Transformation*, 36.

Chang, H.-J. (2002) *Kicking Away the Ladder: Development Strategy in Historical Perspective*, Anthem Press, Wimbledon.

Dicken, P. (1998) *Global Shift: Transforming the World Economy*, Paul Chapman, London.

Enright, M. and Ffowcs-Williams, I. (2000) "Local Partnership, Clusters and SME Globalisation," Organisation for Economic Co-operation and Development, www.oecd.org/dataoecd/20/5/2010888.pdf.

Gereffi, G., Humphrey, J., and Sturgeon, T. (2004) "The Governance of Global Value Chains," *Review of International Political Economy I*, 12(1), pp. 78–104.

Helmsing, A.H.J. (2001) "Externalities, Learning and Governance: New Perspectives on Local Economic Development," *Development and Change*, 32(2), pp. 277–308.

Humphrey, J. and Schmitz, H. (1995) "Principles for Promoting Clusters & Networks of SMEs," Vienna: UNIDO, www.unido.org.

Humphrey, J. and Schmitz, H. (1996) "The Triple C Approach to Local Industrial Policy," *World Development*, 24(12), pp. 1859–1877.

Humphrey, J. and Schmitz, H. (2002) "How Does Insertion in Global Value Chains Affect Upgrading in Industrial Clusters," *Regional Studies*, 36(9), pp. 1017–1027.

Kaplinsky, R. (2005) *Globalization, Poverty and Inequality: Between a rock and a hard place*, Polity Press, London.

Lall, S. (2004) "Reinventing Industrial Strategy: the Role of Government Policy in Building Industrial Competitiveness," TIPS working paper, 9.

Lall, S. and Teubal, M. (1998) "Market Stimulating Technology Policies in Developing Countries: a Framework with Examples from East Asia," *World Development*, 26, pp. 1369–1385.

Lawson, C and Lorenz, E. (1999) "Collective Learning, Tacit Knowledge and Regional Innovative Capacity," *Regional Studies*, 33(4), pp. 305–317.

Maskell, P., Eskelinen, H., Hannibaldson, I., Malmberg, A. and Vatne, E. (1998) *Competitiveness. Localized Learning and Regional Development: Specialization and Prosperity in Small Open Economies*, Routledge, London.

Morosini, P. (2004) "Industrial Clusters, Knowledge Integration and Performance," *World Development*, 32(2), pp. 305–326.

Morris, M., Barnes, J. and Esselaar, J. (2006) "Globalisation, the Changed Global Dynamics of the Clothing and Textile Value Chains and the Impact on sub-Saharan Africa," in Memedovic (ed.), *Global Value Chains and Production Networks: Prospects for Upgrading by Developing Countries*, UNIDO, Vienna.

Nadvi, K. and Schmitz, H. (1999) "Clustering and Industrialisation," in *World Development*, 27(9), pp. 1503–1514.

Peck, F. and McGuinness, D. (2003) "Regional Development Agencies and Cluster Strategies: Engaging the Knowledge-base in the North of England," *Local Economy*, 18(1), pp. 46–62.

Schmitz, H. (1999a) "Collective Efficiency and Increasing Returns," *Cambridge Journal of Economics*, 23(4), pp. 465–483.

Schmitz, H. (1999b) "Global Competition and Local Cooperation: Success and Failure in the Sinos Valley, Brazil," *World Development*, 27(9), pp. 1627–1650.

Schmitz, H. (2004) (ed.) *Local Enterprises in the Global Economy: Issues of governance and upgrading*, Edward Elgar, Cheltenham.

Teece, D. and Pisano, G. (1994) "The Dynamic Capabilities of Firms: an Introduction," *Industrial and Corporate Change*, 3, pp. 537–556.

World Bank (1997) *World Development Report: The State in a Changing World, The World Bank*, Oxford University Press.

World Bank (2004) Web site on "Program and Project Options: Implementing LED. More Information on Cluster and/or Sector Development," www.worldbank.org/urban/led/cluster2.html.

Part VI

Regional development and global value chains

13 Knowledge, obsolescence, and product segmentation

Isaac Minian

Introduction

This chapter explores the main factors that explain the segmentation of production processes and the resulting relocation or outsourcing of these segments. These processes generate a fine international and regional division of labor that combines the different advantages of firms and of production sites. Relocation and outsourcing are part of the reorganization of MNCs (multinational corporations). They adopted strategies that pulled away from vertical organization. This included: segmenting their productive activities, relocating parts of the production process abroad, developing networks of national and international suppliers, buying specialized goods and services in the market, and even relocating the administrative services that had been previously produced in house.

This study uses data from international trade of parts and components showing the issue's importance on manufacturing. Nowadays, MNCs also relocate services and part of their administrative functions. The lack of systematic information makes it difficult to include these issues.

The second section points out some of the benefits obtained for firms and segments of production through specialization. The increasing complexity, deepness, and cost of knowledge alongside the diseconomies of scale in the management of specific intangible assets requires segmentation of production. Thus, knowledge contributes to productive decentralization.

The third section analyzes some of the impacts of the decrease in the costs to process information on the organization of firms, especially on MNCs. This reduction opened up a new range of possibilities for change in national and international organizational structures. For example, it encouraged modular organization of production, it helped MNCs to control value chains that are geographically spread, and it allowed them to seize advantages from these processes. These new possibilities abate the advantages from centralized organization and from geographical vicinity.

The fourth section analyzes the different options faced by MNCs to deal with segmentation in economies that are increasingly based on both incorporated and nonincorporated knowledge, and that have new organizational possibilities. The calculation of profitability of each single productive segment, or even of particular functions of the firm, allows corporations to choose among various economic options. These include decisions as to whether to increase investments in the "core" of the firm in order to enlarge automation and production systems or to fragment the value chain and locate segments in specialized firms or in sites with lower costs of production. These alternatives give rise to a variety of investment and organizational schemes. Decisions to locate each segment take into account the characteristics of the segment, the intangible assets of firms, and the human and productive resources from the sites of production.

The final section raises some questions about the implications of a more fine international division of labor.

Knowledge and segmentation

Knowledge has always existed in productive activities. Nevertheless, the present amount of investment to increase knowledge has no precedent in history. This comes together with a technological revolution based on information technologies that dramatically reduces the costs of production as well of those of codification and transmission of knowledge and information (M. Polanyi, 1962, 1966). Productive and organizational activities are transformed. The part of knowledge included in intermediate, capital, and consumption goods, and in services, has increased dramatically. Technological innovation that drives all these processes is created more and more by cooperative networks of firms. Innovation results from technological and organizational competencies of firms, from human capital, and from the institutional environment where firms operate. New knowledge and technology diffuse through the whole economy, allowing new waves of increases in productivity, changes in the organizational structure of firms, changes in institutions; in fact, changes in the whole social structure and cultural life (K. Polanyi, 2001).

Knowledge has several implications for the segmentation process of firms. Let's consider the relationship between knowledge and labor in the following context. Division of knowledge triggers division of labor and vice versa. Specialized production develops the capacity of workers and generates more knowledge. Specialization is necessary to use the most advanced techniques efficiently and to improve their use during the productive process. This theory comes from Adam Smith (1776).[1] These ideas have been used with different emphasis by Babbage (1835), Rosenberg (1976), and Machlup (1984). For the later author, there is a natural tendency for knowledge to fragment and disperse itself as it becomes more complex. This fragmentation comes from the division of labor: specialized works create and require fragmented knowledge. Nowadays, the creation of knowledge is more and more fragmented as it takes place in laboratories, academies, firms, and institutions in spite of the great interrelation between these agents.

Other scholars emphasize the impact of specific knowledge over specialization. The efficient use of knowledge requires specialized production. Labor is segmented due to the complexity and amplitude of the needed knowledge in the production process in relation to the limited capacity of absorption and accumulation of it by individuals, firms, and institutions (Simon, 1982; Demsetz, 1988; Beckers and Murphy, 1992; Mokyr, 2002). All innovation generates a new division of labor in order to benefit from the new specialized knowledge and to develop workers' new abilities. As a consequence, decentralization and segmentation in productive processes take place.

Industrial organization scholars suggested that technological and organizational knowledge, among other factors, disintegrate the vertical organization of production. The centralized management in firms or institutions of very specialized knowledge assets could cause diseconomies of scale. On the contrary, decentralized organization could increase total efficiency. The growing complexity, deepness, and amplitude of knowledge encourage specialization and a decentralized administration. PC (personal computer) industry is a good example of this process. Curry and Kenney (2004), when analyzing the personal computer value chain, show a production process totally disintegrated with development, design, manufacturing, and distribution activities decentralized and separated by large distances. The PC consists of a hierarchy of components, each with its own specific technology, organizational complexity, and production linkages. A PC assembler is more a logistics coordinator than a manufacturer. Some companies like IBM, NEC, Fujitsu, and Samsung do have internal integration. But "internal integration has not assisted their competitive status, and may, in fact, have hurt it" (Curry and Kenney, 2004, p. 114). Development of components in different modules results in higher efficiency. For example, the production process of some semiconductors is also organized under modular forms (Leachman and Leachman, 2004).

Specialization and segmentation are important not only in the management of intangible assets but also in the creation of new knowledge. The size of the markets restrains the degree of specialization that can be economically reached. This idea was already present in Adam Smith's work and is also used by Babbage (1835) and Mokyr (2002). The amount of resources needed to produce knowledge for many economic activities has become increasingly large, therefore segmentation or technological partnership are needed. This implies a reduction in the range of technological efforts and activities undertaken by a firm. Market size may be insufficient not only for a firm but also for a country, international markets are then required in order to introduce new knowledge and take advantage of it.

Coordinating knowledge

As a result of the above phenomena, the value chain is disintegrated and scattered. Nevertheless, in order to achieve the assembly of a good each segment must be related to the others. Weitzman (1996) develops the idea that the recombination of knowledge and existent techniques allows the production of totally new knowledge. This idea can be usefully applied to the knowledge that comes from different productive sectors, especially those that conform to the value chain, come from different institutions, and are recombined by the firms. Thus, they obtain "segments" of knowledge and information from different social and economic agents as inputs for their technological, organizational, and strategic decision making. They can then act as an integrated firm.

Coordination of different aspects (technical, designing, marketing, manufacturing, financial, etc.) of the value chain must take place. The combination of information from different agents, in order to make decisions, help coordination to take place. The sources of knowledge and information come from suppliers of equipment and material; national and international specialized expertise; national and international knowledge (patents, international publications); relationships with customers; financial and governmental institutions. For instance, Murtha *et al.* (2004) point out this aspect for the flat panel display industry.

Another type of integrative knowledge (produced by private and public committees) is norms and standards. They permit the compatibility and interoperability between systems, subsystems, and segments of production. Integrative knowledge that includes conventions and proceedings methodologies enables the transfer of information within and between organizations (David, 1987; David and Greenstein, 1990; David and Steinmueller, 1996).

Geographical clusters in the creation of knowledge

Unlike diseconomies of scale in the centralized management of the very specific intangible assets of a firm, important advantages are obtained from the localization of segments that produce knowledge and innovations, in geographical sites with technological externalities (Krugman, 1991a, 1991b; Jaffe *et al.*, 1993; Scott, 1993; Garofoli, 2002). The administration of specialized knowledge may require decentralized management but the absorption of new knowledge becomes easier with geographical proximity. Spatial concentration and geographical vicinity continue to hold a huge importance for absorption and creation of knowledge and fostering innovation. The importance of clusters of innovation is their ability to generate synergy. The transmission of new knowledge occurs more efficiently among proximate actors within a cluster. The complexity and tacit nature of the knowledge that is transmitted needs proximity in order to reduce the costs of transmission. Proximity facilitates interpersonal contacts, the mobility of human capital, and promotes technological inter-firm agreements. Spatial proximity may also create the condition for collective learning (McKendrick, 2004).

Reducing the cost of information processing

One of the central canons that guided business practice for much of the twentieth century was that a firm should aim to maximize integration (Chandler, 1977).[2] Behind this practice was the idea that, unlike decentralized structures, hierarchical organizational ones reduce communication costs because they minimize the number of communication links required to connect economic actors

(Malone *et al.*, 1987). Similarly, Chandler and Cortada (2000) have argued that since colonial times the economy of the United States has been continuously transformed by information and knowledge. These ideas have been present since 1937 in economic theory. Coase forecasted that boundaries of a firm can shift under the impact of a new communication technology: "If the telephone reduces the cost of the price mechanism more than it reduces the cost of organization, it will have the effect of reducing the size of firms."[3] The boundaries of firms are determined by the cost of transactions, especially the costs of communication. Nowadays, the cost of automated information processing has fallen more than 99.9 percent since 1960 (Brynjolfsson and Hitt, 2005). As a consequence, the ways in which firms act have changed dramatically.

Reducing the costs to process information has important implications to the functioning of firms and MNCs such as: the redefinition of the control mechanisms of firms; the decentralization of productive and organizational segments within the boundaries of a firm; the coordination of knowledge "inputs" and information that come from different economic and social agents; the vertical disintegration of production and its replacement by networks of national and international suppliers; the geographical dispersion of these networks; and the economic and financial calculations for each segment of the firm. Details will be provided for some of these aspects.

Changes in the governance of firms

The reduction in the costs to process information allows the MNC to use several mechanisms to exert direct or indirect control over its firm and over its network of suppliers. They maintain command due to their strategic assets, such as specific and proprietary knowledge and technology or to their market access capabilities (Kaplinsky, 2000). These are the intangible assets of the firms on which their monopoly power is based. MNCs determine strategies and use the information to make the productive and financial activities that are taking place in the rest of the network more transparent.

Modularity

The small costs of processing information help to split productive segments within the boundaries of a firm. The coordination of these processes – that need important flows of information – is, in certain cases, the first step before the disintegration of the value chain and relocation of productive segments. "Globalization and deverticalization strategies are enmeshed in a movement by various auto assemblers especially those in the United States to *modularize* vehicle design and production. Modularity is significant because it facilitates deverticalization: the shift of assembly tasks from the auto assembler's factory to the factories of the first-tier suppliers."[4]

Improving organizational advantages

The reduction in the costs of processing information is an important element to obtain organizational advantages; the flows of information create "organizational proximity." In some cases, organizational advantages result from interrelated firms; these are firms with a greater integration level (fusions, acquisitions, technological partnerships). In other cases, organizational advantages result from a decentralized organization of networks of firms (suppliers of specialized goods and business services; producers of parts, components, and subassemblies; subcontractors). The flows of information create conditions of organizational coordination, allowing firms to act nearly as integrated organizations.

Information networks also help improve relations with customers and in the gathering of knowledge and information coming from different economic and social agents: "... technologies such as electronic data interchange [EDI], Internet-based procurement systems and other interorganizational information systems have significantly reduced the cost, time, and other difficulties of interacting with suppliers. The Internet has opened up a new range of possibilities for enriching interactions with customers."[5]

The Internet and other technologies that reduce the cost of information processing have opened up a new range of possibilities for change in systems and work practices that emphasize flexible production with just-in-time (JIT) inventory management, speed to incorporate new computing technologies into the product, and speed to be the first arriving to the market.

Geographical dispersion advantages

Geographical dispersion of production allows firms to benefit from a fine division of labor; taking advantage of very specialized firms geographically spread and from sites with lower costs of production. These specialized firms own specific technology, have scale economies, or other advantages. The lower costs of production in these sites result from intangible assets of MNCs and national firms, from lower prices of factors of production, including lower cost of human capital, and from locative advantages. The lower costs of processing information make it possible to keep a coherent production in spite of geographical dispersion.

The fine division of labor is reflected in the regional intratrade of parts and components as shown in the matrices in Table 13.1 and 13.2.

Greater transparency

The lower costs of processing information play other roles that affect the segmentation processes. They allow firms to estimate, in a real or imputed way, the profitability of each productive segment or of each function of the firm and to make national and international financial comparisons. This makes it possible to evaluate different options: produce, buy from the network of suppliers, or purchase in an arm's-length transaction.

All reallocation of resources, such as segmentation, requires a huge amount of information about the expected profitability, prices, costs, quality of the product, and other economic and social impacts of new strategies. This information is crucial for shareholders, public institutions of regulation, labor, and financial markets. These need a great transparency over the anticipated profitability. Financial markets, in order to diversify risks, require significant flows of data and impose important restrictions to new strategies such as segmentation.

Centralized investments and disintegration of vertical organizations

Investment in information, technology, and organization

Since the 1980s, although with much more emphasis in the 1990s, manufacturer production in developed countries increasingly used incorporated and non-incorporated knowledge in information technologies. Firms invested heavily in new capital goods, intermediate goods, and communication infrastructures. As a consequence, IT investment has accelerated in most developed countries during the past decade. IT investment rose from less than 15 percent of total non-residential investment in the business sector in the early 1980s to between 15 and 30 percent in 2000, varying from country to country (Ahmad, 2003).

The rapid growth in IT investment has been fueled by a rapid decline in the relative prices of equipment owing to technology improvements (Jorgenson, 2001). The lower price of IT is only one of the factors that drive investment. In fact, firms have also invested in IT because it offers large potential benefits: productivity, a growing scope for the application that enables new strategies, new organization of work, changes in products and services, new forms of outsourcing, new relations with customers and suppliers (reducing procurement costs), and new forms of coordination of inputs of knowledge and information coming from numerous agents.[6]

IT is only a small fraction of much larger complementary investments in intangible assets: technical knowledge, software, business organization, and new skills. For example, in an "Analysis of 800 large firms, Brynjolfsson and Yang suggest that the ratio of intangible assets to IT assets may be 10 to 1."[7] IT investment in the automation of manufacturing alongside major organizational changes – business processes, decision-making structures, corporate culture – play an important role in the ability of a firm to improve productivity and provide greater product customization and variety.

International trade of parts and components

Data from international trade of parts and components show the importance of segmentation. Figures 13.1 and 13.2 display the share of parts and components

Table 13.1 The matrix of intra-trade in parts and components: participation of exporter in total regional imports of the trading partner, share of partner's exports destined to, and trade balance of the exporter: among East Asian countries, 2004

Importer partner Countries	Exporter partner (million USD)										Total region
	Japan	China	Taiwan	Korea, Republic	Malaysia	Singapore	Philippines	Hong Kong	Indonesia	India	
Value of export in parts and component (million US$)											
Japan		13,474	6,966	7,066	2,971	1,983	3,336	372	781	75	37,024
China	31,189		23,60	,981	9,707	4,822	6,423	4,083	685	106	99,657
Taiwan, China	10,344	4,604		5,960	2,743	1,950	2,118	960	202	23	28,905
Korea, Republic	11,196	5,187	4,445		1,385	2,710	1,261	995	104	23	27,307
Malaysia	6,695	4,657	3,169	2,614		4,455	2,324	1,432	680	147	26,172
Singapore	8,415	5,960	6,583	3,751	13,270		3,269	1,749		104	43,101
Philippines	4,958	1,123	1,873	1,392	1,015	1,727		1,021	67	11	13,186
Hong Kong, China	15,852	28,107	11,441	5,124	3,855	7,426	3,291		172	44	75,312
Indonesia	1,760	332	104	163	110	240	29	44		25	2,808
India	632	772	181	576	381	580	74	185	45		3,428
Total region	91,042	64,215	58,423	45,627	35,438	25,894	22,127	10,842	2,736	558	356,901
Participation of exporter in total regional imports of the trading partner, %											
Japan		36.39	18.82	19.08	8.03	5.36	9.01	1.00	2.11	0.20	100
China	31.30		23.74	19.05	9.74	4.84	6.45	4.10	0.69	0.11	100
Taiwan, China	35.79	15.93		20.62	9.49	6.75	7.33	3.32	0.70	0.08	100
Korea, Republic	41.00	18.99	16.28		5.07	9.93	4.62	3.65	0.38	0.08	100
Malaysia	25.58	17.79	12.11	9.99		17.02	8.88	5.47	2.60	0.56	100
Singapore	19.52	13.83	15.27	8.70	30.79		7.58	4.06		0.24	100
Philippines	37.60	8.52	14.20	10.56	7.70	13.09		7.74	0.51	0.08	100
Hong Kong, China	21.05	37.32	15.19	6.80	5.12	9.86	4.37		0.23	0.06	100
Indonesia	62.67	11.81	3.72	5.80	3.93	8.56	1.02	1.58		0.91	100
India	18.44	22.53	5.29	16.81	11.12	16.93	2.17	5.41	1.30		100

Share of partner's exports to, %

	Japan	China	Taiwan, China	Korea, Republic	Malaysia	Singapore	Philippines	Hong Kong, China	Indonesia	India
Japan		20.98	11.92	15.49	8.38	7.66	15.08	3.43	28.54	13.41
China	34.26		40.50	41.60	27.39	18.62	29.03	37.66	25.05	19.01
Taiwan, China	11.36	7.17		13.06	7.74	7.53	9.57	8.86	7.39	4.19
Korea, Republic	12.30	8.08	7.61		3.91	10.47	5.70	9.18	3.80	4.15
Malaysia	7.35	7.25	5.42	5.73		17.21	10.50	13.21	24.85	26.28
Singapore	9.24	9.28	11.27	8.22	37.45		14.77	16.13		18.64
Philippines	5.45	1.75	3.21	3.05	2.86	6.67		9.41	2.44	1.90
Hong Kong, China	17.41	43.77	19.58	11.23	10.88	28.68	14.87		6.30	7.85
Indonesia	1.93	0.52	0.18	0.36	0.31	0.93	0.13	0.41		4.57
India	0.69	1.20	0.31	1.26	1.08	2.24	0.34	1.71	1.63	
Total region	100	100	100	100	100	100	100	100	100	100
Trade balance of the exporter										
Value (million US$)	54,018	−35,443	29,518	18,321	9,265	−17,207	8,940	−64,470	−73	−2,870
Balance/exports (%)	59.33	−55.19	50.52	40.15	26.15	−66.45	40.41	−594.63	−2.66	−514.07

Source: Computations based on UN Comtrade, SITC rev. 3.

Table 13.2 The matrix of intra-trade in parts and components: participation of exporter in total regional imports of the trading partner, share of partner's exports to and trade balance of the exporter: among North America, Central America, and Caribbean, 2004

Importer partner	Exporter partner				
	Canada	Central America[a]	United States	Mexico	Total
Value of export in parts and component (million US$)					
Canada	–	84	34,374	2,777	37,235
Central America	8	–	1,555	48	1,610
United States	25,850	847	–	26,256	52,953
Mexico	884	717	25,214	–	26,815
Total	26,742	1,647	61,142	29,081	118,612
Participation of exporter in total regional imports of the trading partner, %					
Canada	–	0.22	93.32	7.46	100
Central America	0.50	–	96.55	2.95	100
United States	48.82	1.60	–	49.58	100
Mexico	3.30	2.67	94.03	–	100
Share of partner's exports to, %					
Canada	–	5.08	56.22	9.55	
Central America	0.03	–	2.54	0.16	
United States	96.66	51.42	–	90.29	
Mexico	3.31	43.50	42.24	–	
Total	100	100	100	100	
Trade balance of the exporter					
Value (millions US$)	–10,493	37	8,189	2,266	
Balance/exports (%)	–39.24	2.25	13.39	7.79	

Source: Computations based on UN Comtrade, SITC rev. 3.

Note
a Central America as an importer is formed by five countries: Costa Rica, El Salvador, Guatemala, Nicaragua, and Panama; and as exporter by eight countries: Belize, Costa Rica, El Salvador, Guatemala, Honduras, Jamaica, Nicaragua, and Panama.

in exports and imports of manufacturers in some developed and emergent countries. Matrices in Tables 13.1 and 13.2 show that the international division of labor in parts and components is also a regional one among countries in close proximity. The appendix includes figures that present the share of parts and components in international trade of selected industries (see appendix Figures 13.A.1, 13.A.2, and 13.A.3).

The economic logic of segmentation and relocation

Some investment took place to reinforce the core of firms; this is the segment where its monopoly power lies. Other investments were done to undertake new strategies of decentralization, relocation, and creation of networks of suppliers.

Core investments

Large levels of investment in technology, knowledge, and information allow firms to strengthen their market advantages, their monopoly power. They reinforce the "core" of a firm even in a context of organizational decentralization or disintegration of the vertical organization. Theories of industrial organization

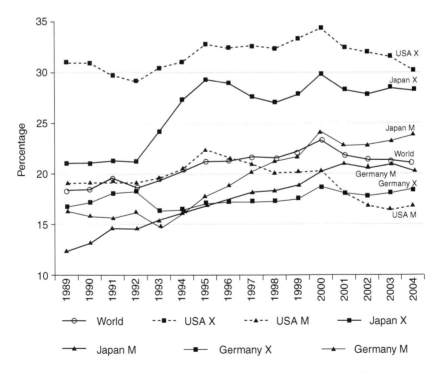

Figure 13.1 Parts and components share in total manufactured exports (X) and imports (M), world and selected developed countries (1989–2004).

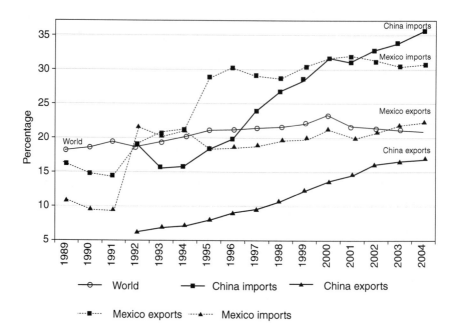

Figure 13.2 Parts and components share in total manufactured exports (▲) and imports (■), world and selected emergent countries (1989–2004).

analyze firms as an entity that owns knowledge and other specific intangible assets. Firms have "corporate core competencies" and "organizational practices" that determine their hierarchical position in a network of firms. These practices and competencies form part of the intangible assets of firms.[8]

New investments in IT along with organizational changes may create strong barriers to entry. For example, information "network effects" do so: the product becomes more valuable the more it is used. It is easier for people to use a Microsoft program if everyone else uses it too. The combination of supply-side and demand-side economies of scale in many industries, especially in high-tech industries, can be very powerful. Higher sales not only reduce production costs, but also make the product more valuable to other users. In such a market, one firm tends to become dominant for a long time.

Limits to centralized investments and new investment strategies

In spite of all the advantages mentioned in the above section, there are constraints to centralized investments. Profitability expectations mark the limits to increase investment in new technologies and in non-incorporated knowledge. Firms not only invest in their "core" but they also carry out strategies to divide the value chain and locate each segment in other organizational and geographic context. In this process of decentralization or disintegration, MNCs must undertake investments. MNCs invest in other firms and in other sites their intangible assets (technological or organizational knowledge, human capital, design, software, market access), their capital or intermediate goods, or their financial resources. These investments have different legal forms and imply different links among the firms involved, such as: direct investment, co-investment, technological partnership, production sharing (maquila), licenses, and franchises. Decisions to divide the value chain, relocate, and invest in each segment lie on the different expected profitability of centralized investments of a firm vs. the foreseen profits of relocating (under the same governance) or buying in specialized firms, in chains of suppliers, or in the open market.

There are two particular sets of elements that restrict centralized investments and favor new investment strategies: activities that severely increase both the costs and risks to firms and the heterogeneity of segments that form part of the value chain. Among the various elements that increase costs and risks figure: the rapid foreseen obsolescence of capital and intermediate goods and of intangible assets, the huge fixed costs in certain sectors faced to the volatility of demand, the increasing financial risks, and the weakening of entry barriers.

In the semiconductors industry, for example, the foreseen obsolescence of products also makes the capital goods that cannot be readapted obsolete. To minimize these costs, when it is technically feasible, labor-intensive segments are not automated. They will be located in sites with low wages. On the contrary, in spite of obsolescence, firms will invest in fixed assets in those segments that contribute to their monopoly power (Minian, 1981). This phenomenon is still present in the same industry.[9]

Obsolescence also plays another role in segmentation when it affects intermediate and final goods. In the industry of personal computers, firms try to reduce, as much as possible, their stocks and the time elapsed between production and consumption. Segmentation of production takes place and the final segments of the value chain are located in the vicinity of consumption centers.[10] Similarly, in the textile and garment industries, Abernathy *et al.* (2004) show that, in "fashion forward" garments, a dynamic obsolescence takes place because of the creativity of designers and the changing tastes of customers. A fashion item on the way from a distant low-cost production site could easily lose much of its value prior to arriving to customers.

High fixed costs in situations of volatile demand increase financial risks. In order to reduce fixed costs and risks, production is made to be modular. Costs and risks are then distributed among the network of suppliers.[11] In the automobile industry there is also a distribution of costs and risks between automakers and auto-parts producers.[12] The other element that induces new investment strategies lies in the heterogeneity of segments in the value chain. Chains are composed of segments with different characteristics: they have different intensities of a certain factor (they are, for example, knowledge, capital, labor, and material intensive). Each segment benefits in different degrees from economies of scale, of scope, of agglomeration, or from learning processes because of its distinct traits. Relocating these segments in the appropriate context will increase general efficiency.[13]

Corporations must then choose either to decentralize under the same governance or to cease production and buy from a particular firm or a network of suppliers. In the outsourcing case, production will be "located" in specialized firms, or in firms with economies of scale or with other advantages. For instance, segments intensive in technology and knowledge are located in very specialized firms and, in some cases, as in the semiconductors industry, specific components are even undertaken by only one or two particular firms with proprietary knowledge. Another example can be provided from the automobile industry, which operates in a modular form, taking advantage of economies of scale and of scope. The use of the same component or subassembly in various automobile models (platforms of production) allows automakers to save in development costs and, along with producers of automotive parts, benefit through economies of scale and of scope.[14]

Geographical dispersion also plays a very important role in segmentation strategies. Some corporations have important departments of R&D that create new knowledge and innovations. These departments benefit from spillovers when located in knowledge-intensive settings: geographical clusters or joint efforts of manufacturers, equipment and material suppliers, customers, and public and private institutions, as mentioned earlier.

Finally, some segments will take advantage from a particular geographic location that offers them lower costs of production. The existence of multiple industrial bases in Southeast Asia and in other parts of the world with low costs of production widens the options as to where productive activities can be located. The decrease in the costs of processing information allows the location of productive segments in distant places, as long as the necessary infrastructures exist. The characteristics of the productive segments, location, and intangible assets of international and local firms must match.

Labor-intensive segments are drawn to regions that have lower prices of factors of production compared with those of developed countries. However, lower wages are not the only decisive feature. Production takes place when there is a combination of intangible assets, especially from MNCs, and local resources, including human capital. MNCs relocate knowledge incorporated in artifacts and capital goods and non-incorporated knowledge of industrial processes, organizational routines, human capital, specific production techniques, design, organization, and marketing. The relocation of knowledge is done in a manner that temporarily prevents it from being diffused and copied.

MNCs and each of the relocated segments benefit from belonging to a productive network as they can take advantage from externalities of global production. Creation of knowledge in emergent countries is also an important factor when considering the location of productive segments, especially those of high and intermediate technology. Some emergent countries make important investments in R&D, IT, and in gaining international knowledge through international movements of human capital and flows of ideas.[15]

Final considerations

The segmentation, relocation, and creation of international networks of suppliers have significant implications on countries, regions, firms and, especially, labor markets. The most obvious result is the increasing interdependence among countries and regions. The productivity and competitive edge of a country or region are tightly linked to the productivity and competitive edge of all the segments that belong to their value chains. Nevertheless, this interdependency is asymmetric: value chains are composed of central segments (the core) where decisive factors of monopoly prevail and where the whole control over the value chain is exerted. The governance and location of the value chain are essential features to determine asymmetries in the assignment of resources, particularly in the international location of intangible assets (knowledge and information).

International segmentation implies substantive benefits from trade. An international division of labor made of parts and components is indeed finer than that of complete goods only and allows higher productive efficiency. However, the distribution of these benefits may be very uneven among countries. In the particular case of high tech manufactures, terms of trade show important losses for the emergent exporting countries (Minian and Luna, forthcoming).

International outsourcing has crucial repercussions on the level and quality of employment as well as on the wage level. The general conception about employment is that manufacturer jobs are departing from developed countries. Furthermore, this conception leads to the belief that developed countries not only purchase the manufactures, parts, and components they need abroad, but also relocate well paid knowledge-intensive jobs. But these issues must be studied in detail. Outsourcing does not take place exclusively in a north–south relation. Developed countries are not only importers but also important exporters and of complete manufactured goods, parts, and components. A substantial part of this trade takes place among them. Even though there are no systematic statistics about qualified services, the best paid of them are often relocated to other developed countries.

Finally, international outsourcing is not the only process that is modeling the world economy. Massive investments in IT are reshaping the productive systems in the most advanced countries. Production and organization change dramatically due to the increases in productivity, the creation of new materials, and the development of nano- and bio-technologies. These changes will make previous ways of production and of organization, including some of the activities that have been relocated, obsolete.

Appendix

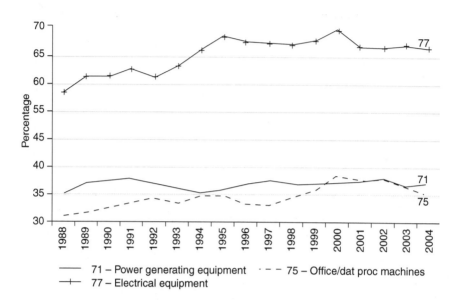

Figure 13.A.1 Parts and components share in world trade of selected industries (1988–2004).

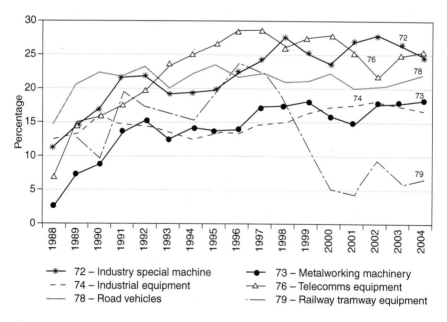

Figure 13.A.2 Parts and components share in world trade of selected industries (1988–2004).

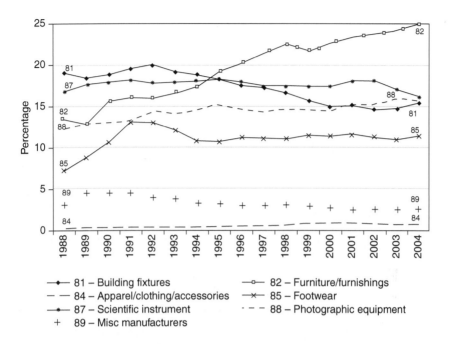

81 – Building fixtures   82 – Furniture/furnishings
84 – Apparel/clothing/accessories   85 – Footwear
87 – Scientific instrument   88 – Photographic equipment
89 – Misc manufacturers

Figure 13.A.3 Parts and components share in world trade of selected industries (1988–2004).

Acknowledgments

I wish to acknowledge the invaluable help received from the team composed of Ilana Kat (coordinator), Raúl Salazar and Isidro Victoriano. These individuals were in charge of the organization of the database, statistics, figures, tables, and the form and style of the text.

Notes

1 "But in consequence of the division of labour, the whole of every man's attention comes naturally to be directed towards some one very simple object. It is naturally to be expected, therefore, that some one or other of those who are employed in each particular branch of labour should soon find out easier and readier methods of performing their own particular work, wherever the nature of it admits of such improvement" (Smith, 1776, re-edition 1976, 13).
2 "The first proposition is that modern multiunit business enterprise replaced small traditional enterprise when administrative coordination permitted greater productivity, lower cots, and higher profits than coordination by market mechanisms. Such internalization gave the enlarged enterprise many advantages. By routinizing the transactions between units, the costs of these transactions were lowered. By linking the administration of producing units with buying and distributing units, costs for information on markets and sources of supply were reduced. Of much greater significance, the internationalization of many units permitted the flow of goods from

one unit to another to be administratively coordinated. More effective scheduling of flows achieved a more intensive use of facilities and personnel employed in the processes of production and distribution and so increased productivity and reduced costs. In addition, administrative coordination provided a more certain cash flow and more rapid payment for services rendered. The saving resulting from such coordination were much greater than those resulting from lower information and transaction costs" (Chandler, 1977, pp. 6–7).

3 Coase (1937), pp. 386–405.

4 Sturgeon and Florida (2004) p. 53.

5 Brynjolfsson and Hitt (2005) pp. 32–33.

6 "An enterprise is transformed when new knowledge or information is introduced and acted in one or more of its business processes. Knowledge is the fuel that activates a business process. Knowledge is the ultimate substitute. When it is used effectively it reduces the need for raw materials, labor, time, space, equipment, and funding in business processes" (Mason and Apte, 2005, p. 134). "In material intensive enterprises and business processes, knowledge and information are used to guide the manipulation of materials, to create new or more effective materials, to substitute for materials, or to decrease the time and costs required to process them. This is the 'substitution effect' of knowledge" (op. cit., 2005, p.142).

7 Brynjolfsson and Hitt (2005) p. 41.

8 Saviotti (1996) p. 175.

9 In the semiconductor industry, "each succeeding generation typically requires replacement of between 25 percent and 35 percent of the processing equipment used in the previous generation." Labor-intensive segments will be relocated in low wages sites. "...to complicate the business environment, the fabs depreciate very rapidly as new generations are introduced. A typical piece of wafer fab processing equipment is useful for three or four generations of process technology, where each generation involves a 50 percent reduction in the minimum feature size from the previous generation" (Leachman and Leachman, 2004, p. 205). "Over the life of the industry, the time between chip generations has averaged two to three years, and recently it has been compressed to one and one-half to two years" (ibid., pp. 205–206). "By using a foundry lab, lucrative niche markets can be tapped quickly with very little capital investment, and sales can be completed before prices seriously erode from inevitable technological obsolescence" (ibid., 207).

10 "...the rapid decline in value of its semiconductor and hard disk drive components emphasizes the importance of situating the final segment of the value chain in close proximity to the final consumer. For the PC assembler, controlling logistics is critical for commercial success. Few products experience the ravages of delay-induced devaluation as palpably as the PC" (Curry and Kenney, 2004, p. 138). "As Leachman and Leachman and McKendrick show, these two classes of components experience extremely rapid improvement, while the value of earlier generations decreases accordingly. For example, newly introduced semiconductors and hard disk drives (HDDs) experience a rate of technological obsolescence that decreases their value at up to 1 percent per week. Outside the electronics sector, as Abernathy *et al.* show, it may only be fashion-forward clothing that experiences a similar rate of value erosion. For the PC assemblers, mastering this pace of change is vital for success. Excess inventory or transit time, delays of expensive components, or any finished or semi finished product containing them, anywhere in the value chain, results in value loss" (ibid., pp. 113–114).

11 "The foundry fabless partnership offers a market-based collective solution to the imperative of decreasing each individual firm's large capital expenditures for fabrication. The capacity investment risk of a large foundry company can be diversified across the product portfolios of all of its potential customers. In the face of substantial market risk this pooling of investment risk suggests a great average return for the

fabless-foundry partnership on investment in manufacturing capacity and development of process technology than for integrated firms independently investing" (Leachman and Leachman, 2004, pp. 220–221).

12 "One of the most interesting and important aspects of globalization is the ways in which automakers use first-tier suppliers to spread the risk of new investments. First-tier suppliers are being asked to supply new offshore assembly plants locally, shouldering part of the burden of meeting local content requirements and the often onerous task of finding and developing local second-and third-tier suppliers. Global suppliers are growing to the point where operations are beginning to mirror automaker operations, with control and development centralized in core locations and globally dispersed production. Accordingly, global suppliers are facing many of the same challenges that automakers are facing, especially overcapacity risks, coordination and control problems associated with large and spatially dispersed organizations, management of multiple joint venture relationship, and operation within multiple sets of national and regional regulatory domains" (Sturgeon and Florida, 2004, p. 80).

13 In the case of semiconductors, "the industry now includes fabless firms carrying out the product definition, design, and marketing functions, partnered with foundry firms that develop process technology and provide contract-manufacturing services" (Leachman and Leachman, 2004, p. 228). In the flat panel display industry, "... successful companies moved decisively to create knowledge stakes in a new display functionality that offered myriad prospects in future product markets. They mobilized knowledge assets around the world while centering their business in Japan, where the new industry was approaching critical mass. Their technologies and manufacturing process had reached advanced stages of development when high-volume, mass product markets emerged" (Murtha *et al.*, 2004, p. 177). "Few integrated firms excel at both design/marketing and manufacturing. Vastly different management skills are needed, and each area thrives in a different kind of business culture" (Leachman and Leachman, 2004, p. 228).

14 In the motor vehicle industry, "the lead firms often seek to economize on development costs by creating global product platforms that share and reuse many common parts, modules, and subsystems. Partnering with a small number of suppliers, or even a single supplier for a particular part, enables lead firms to exploit these economies of scope more fully, while also avoiding the cost of requalifying new suppliers for each new market" (Sturgeon and Florida, 2004, p. 69).

15 "China has become the third largest R&D performer behind the United States and Japan (mainly owing to rapid growth in researchers' salaries). Investment in knowledge (comprising expenditure on R&D, software and higher education) in the OECD area reached around 5.2 percent of GDP in 2001, compared to around 6.9 percent for investment in machinery and equipment. In 2003, China had the world's second largest number of researchers (862,000), behind the United States (1.3 million in 1999), but ahead of Japan (675,000) and the Russian Federation (487,000). Non-member countries such as Brazil, China, India and the Russian Federation have a high level of internationalization compared to large OECD countries. For example, two-thirds of the Russian Federation's EPO patents are owned or co-owned by foreign residents" (OECD, 2005, pp. 8–10). "In 2003, Israel had the world's highest R&D intensity, spending 4.9 percent of GDP on civilian R&D, more than twice the OECD average. Chinese Taipei was the only other non-OECD economy with an R&D intensity above the OECD average" (ibid., p. 20). "Non-member countries like the Russian Federation, China, India and Brazil have a high level of foreign ownership of domestic inventions compared with the large OECD countries. This is mainly due to the presence of multinationals" (ibid., p. 78).

References

Abernathy, F., Dunlop, J. Hammond, J. and Weil, D. (2004) "Globalization in the Apparel and Textile Industries: What is New and what is not?" in M. Kenney and R. Florida (eds.) *Locating Global Advantage: Industry Dynamics in the International Economy*, Stanford University Press, Stanford, Calif., pp. 23–51.

Ahmad, N. (2003) *Measuring Investment in Software*, STI working papers, 2003/6, OECD, Paris, pp. 1–68.

Babbage, C. (1835) *On the Economy of Machinery and Manufactures*, reprint edition, Kelley, Fairfield, NJ.

Becker, G.S. and Murphy, K.M. (1992) "The Division of Labor, Coordination Costs, and Knowledge," *Quarterly Journal of Economics 107*, No. 4, pp. 1137–1160.

Brynjolfsson, E. and Hitt, L.M. (2005) "Intangible Assets and the Economic Impact of Computers," in *Transforming Enterprise: The Economic and Social Implications of Information Technology*, MIT Press, Cambridge, Mass., pp. 27–48.

Chandler, A.D., Jr. (1977) *The Visible Hand: The Managerial Revolution in American Business*, Harvard University Press.

Chandler, A.D., Jr. and Cortada, J.W. (eds.) (2000) *A Nation Transformed by Information*, Oxford University Press, Oxford.

Coase, R.H. (1937) "The Nature of the Firm," *Economica*, 4, pp. 386–405.

Curry, J. and Kenney, M. (2004) "The Organizational and Geographic Configuration of the Personal Computer Value Chain," in M. Kenney and R. Florida (eds.) *Locating Global Advantage: Industry Dynamics in the International Economy*, Stanford University Press, Stanford, Calif., pp. 113–141.

David, P.A. (1987) "New Standards for the Economics of Standardization in the Information Age," in P. Dasgupta and P. Stoneman (eds.), *Technology Policy and Economic Performance*, Cambridge University Press, Cambridge, pp. 206–239.

David, P.A. and Greenstein, S. (1990) "The Economics of Compatibility Standards: an Introduction to Recent Research," *Economics of Innovation and New Technology*, 1, pp. 3–41.

David, P.A. and Steinmueller, W.E. (1996) "Standards, Trade and Competition in the Emerging Global Information Infrastructure Environment," *Telecommunication Policy* 20 (10), pp. 817–830.

Demsetz, H. (1988) "The Theory of the Firm Revisited," *Journal of Law, Economics, and Organization*, No. 1 (spring), pp. 141–161.

Garofoli, G. (2002) "Local Development in Europe: Theoretical Models and International Comparisons," *European Urban and Regional Studies*, 9 (3), pp. 225–239.

Jaffe, A.B., Trajtenberg, M. and Henderson, R. (1993) "Geographic Localization of Knowledge Spillovers as Evidenced by Patent Citations," *Quarterly Journal of Economics*, 108, pp. 577–598.

Jorgenson, D.W. (2001) "Information Technology and the U.S. Economy," in *American Economic Review*, 91 (1), pp. 1–32.

Kaplinsky, R. (2000) "Globalisation and Unequalisation: What can be Learned from Value Chain Analysis?" *Journal of Development Studies*, 37 (2), pp. 117–146.

Krugman, P. (1991a) "Increasing Returns and Economic Geography," *Journal of Political Economy*, 99 (33), pp. 483–499.

Krugman, P. (1991b) *Geography and Trade*, MIT Press, Cambridge, Mass.

Leachman, R.C. and Leachman, C.H. (2004) "Globalization of Semiconductors: Do Real Men Have Fabs, or Virtual Fabs?" in M. Kenney and R. Florida (eds.) *Locating Global*

Advantage: Industry Dynamics in the International Economy, Stanford University Press, Stanford, Calif., pp. 203–231.

Machlup, F. (1984) *Knowledge, its Creation, Distribution and Economic Significance*, Vol. III, Princeton University Press, Princeton.

Malone, T.W., Yates, J. and Benjamin, R.I. (1987) "Electronic Markets and Electronic Hierarchies," *Communications of the ACM*, 30 (6), pp. 484–497.

Mason, R.O. and Apte, U.M. (2005) "Using Knowledge to Transform Enterprises," in *Transforming Enterprise: The Economic and Social Implications of Information Technology*, MIT Press, Cambridge, Mass.

McKendrick, D.G. (2004) "Leveraging Locations: Hard Disk Drive Producers in International Competition," in M. Kenney and R. Florida (eds.) *Locating Global Advantage: Industry Dynamics in the International Economy*, Stanford University Press, Stanford, Calif., pp. 142–174.

Minian, I. (1981) *Progreso técnico e internacionalización del proceso productivo: el caso de la industria maquiladora de tipo electrónica*, CIDE, pp. 57–66.

Minian, I. and Luna, M. (forthcoming) *Economía del Conocimiento y Términos del Intercambio: Estados Unidos y Economías Emergentes*, CISAN-UNAM.

Mokyr, J. (2002) *The Gifts of Athena: Historical Origins of the Knowledge Economy*, Princeton University Press, Princeton.

Murtha, T.P. *et al.* (2004) "Industry Creation and the New Geography of Innovation: The Case of Flat Panel Displays," in M. Kenney and R. Florida (eds.) *Locating Global Advantage: Industry Dynamics in the International Economy*, Stanford University Press, Stanford, Calif., pp. 175–202.

OECD (2005) "Science, Technology and Industry Scoreboard," Paris.

Polanyi, K. (2001) *The Great Transformation*, Beacon Press, Boston.

Polanyi, M. (1962) *Personal Knowledge: Towards a post-Critical Philosophy*, Chicago University Press, Chicago.

Polanyi, M. (1966) *The Tacit Dimension*, Doubleday, New York.

Rosenberg, N. (1976) *Perspectives on Technology*, Cambridge University Press, Cambridge.

Saviotti, P.P. (1996) *Technological Evolution, Variety, and the Economy*, Edward Elgar Publishing, Cheltenham.

Scott, A.J. (1993) *Technopolis: High-Technology Industry and Regional Development in Southern California*, University of California Press, Berkeley.

Simon, H. (1982) *Models of Bounded Rationality: Behavioural economics and business organization*, Vol. 2, MIT Press, Cambridge, Mass.

Smith, A. (1776; re-edition 1976) *The Wealth of Nations*, E. Cannan (ed.), University of Chicago Press, Chicago.

Sturgeon, T. and Florida, R. (2004) "Globalization, Deverticalization, and Employment in the Motor Vehicle Industry," in M. Kenney and R. Florida (eds.) *Locating Global Advantage: Industry Dynamics in the International Economy*, Stanford University Press, Stanford, Calif.

Weitzman, M. (1996) "Hybridizing Growth Theory," *American Economic Review*, 86, No. 2 (May), pp. 207–213.

14 Regional systems and global chains

Hubert Schmitz

Introduction

In their opening chapter, "The regional question in economic development," Scott and Garofoli put forward two main propositions:

1 The model of local productive systems as worked out for the more advanced economies of North America and Western Europe has – with suitable modifications – considerable relevance to the analysis of less advanced economies in Africa, Asia, and Latin America.
2 Policymakers in low-income countries need urgently to take this circumstance into account . . . considerable enhancement of economic development strategies can be expected by more vigorous pursuit of the region-centric approach.

I agree with both these propositions. Moreover, I would say that both propositions command increasing support in the developing world and from the donor organizations that provide advice and finance for development. Nevertheless, there remains skepticism and resistance and it seems useful to reflect why this is so. I would identify three factors that make it difficult to convince skeptics of the relevance of the region-centric approach for developing countries:

1 Ideological factors: the case for a regional development approach includes an argument for government intervention that goes beyond reforming the framework conditions for private enterprise. It assumes that government agencies are willing and capable of coordinating, mediating conflict, and constructing a common interest with private enterprises.
2 Role models in crisis: some of the celebrated role models in the developed world are in crisis. This seems to apply even to the Third Italy. Some of the Italian industrial districts struggle to cope with competition from the developing world, in particular China (*Financial Times*, May 25, 2005).
3 Poor academic guidance: the literature on regional development in developing countries is very rich but also confusing. Leaving aside the proliferation of concepts and terms, there are fundamental problems that typically arise

for analysts of developing country regions seeking guidance from the developed country literature.

I will concentrate here on the last of the points made above. Analysts of developing country regions often seek inspiration and guidance from the developed country experience on which there is an enormous literature. Typically, this takes the form of searching for a successful role model or the key ingredients of success. Such searching has typically been bedeviled by three problems:

1   Difference between model and reality: much of the literature is organized around stylized models of, for example, the industrial district, industrial milieu, local production system, regional innovation system, etc. Researchers working on developing countries then proceed to compare "their regions" or "their localities" with these stylized models, finding that some of the key ingredients are missing. This is rarely helpful, not least because even the developed country reality differs from the model. A good example is the research of Roberta Rabellotti, who set out to compare industrial districts in Italy and Mexico. She found that the Italian reality differed substantially from the "Third Italy" model, which had become a prominent reference point in the international debate. Rabellotti (1997) solved the problem by carrying out a threefold comparison of Italian model – Italian reality – Mexican reality, which produced many new insights, relevant for theory and policy. However, much work on developing country research consists of comparing reality with fiction.

2   "From models to trajectories." This is the subtitle of a seminal paper by John Humphrey concerning industrial reorganization in developing countries (Humphrey, 1995). It was published a decade ago, but its central argument remains valid: understanding trajectories and distilling different trajectories from the observation of the real world is probably more useful for theory and policy than comparing real cases with models. It leads to asking "what works?" instead of asking "where does region x fall short of best practice?"

3   Relationships with global players: the more the analysis shifts from static to dynamic issues the more important it becomes to include relationships which enterprises in the region have with enterprises elsewhere, especially with powerful suppliers or customers. This is a problem for much research on regional development. In spite of the proliferation of concepts, this literature has a common analytical framework that prioritizes the relationships between enterprises in the region and the relationships between enterprises and institutions in the region. At a descriptive level, relationships with the outside world are discussed but they do not constitute the core of the analysis, which tends to focus on the density and quality of relationships between regional actors.

The rest of this chapter is primarily concerned with the latter issue: how to bring external relationships into the analysis. This is not just a matter of acknowledging the importance of external linkages. The importance of trade with the outside world is not controversial. No serious analyst questions the importance of the quantity of trade for economic development. My key concern is with the way this trade is organized. Who sets the parameters for producers in the region? Are the relationships between local producers and global buyers or suppliers even or uneven? The assumption is not that working for powerful global players is a bad thing. On the contrary, as will be shown, it can provide enormous opportunities but it can also stifle particular types of development. The underlying thesis is that understanding inequality and power in the relationships between local enterprises and global buyers/suppliers is central for understanding market access, the acquisition of capabilities, and the distribution of gains from trade. These issues matter for all regions, but they are especially important for regions in the developing world. As latecomers to the global economy, dependent on fast learning, the type of relationships with the outside world are particularly critical.

The important but difficult step lies in unraveling the interaction between these global and local relationships. The task is difficult because it is not just a matter of adding the analysis of external (extra-regional) relationships to the analysis of internal (intra-regional) relationships. Frequently, the former transforms the latter, sometimes with an enabling, sometimes with a disabling, effect.

This chapter sets out some of the steps my colleagues and I took in trying to understand different local–global interfaces. The conceptual apparatus and findings come from a project that examined industrial clusters in both the developed and developing world, and that focused on the space for local upgrading strategies in a globalizing world.

The debate on this issue is torn between two lines of thinking: those who believe local relationships between enterprises and institutions are key to upgrading, and those who argue that the spaces for upgrading are defined by the sourcing strategies of global buyers. The first view comes from the literature on regional systems (industrial clusters, innovation systems) and the second from the global value chain literature, inspired by the work of Gereffi (1999). Both sets of literature provide important insights; neither can – on its own – provide adequate guidance to researchers and policymakers. The project, therefore, sought to bring the two approaches together. This proved more difficult than expected but, as will be shown in the course of this chapter, generated useful insights. While I coordinated the project, my collaborators named in the course of this chapter carried out much of the original work. I thank them for allowing me to draw on their work. The full papers can be found in Schmitz (2004).

This chapter is structured as follows: the second section recalls some of the key achievements of region-centric studies in developed and developing countries. The third section sets out the new questions that arise from taking into account global linkages and the fourth section provides a conceptual framework for addressing these questions. The fifth and sixth sections then summarize the case material, concentrating on the most significant findings. Finally, the last section poses research questions for the future.

I am aware that I have not been particularly tidy in that I use "local" and "regional" or "locality" and "region" interchangeably. Sinful as this may be to some economic geographers, I believe it does not affect the substance of the argument.

The locality matters: a convergence of views

A paradoxical feature of the recent debate on competitive advantage in globalized markets is the importance given to locality. Influential authors from a range of different disciplines have emphasized the local determinants of upgrading. Mainstream economics rediscovered the importance of locality, prompted by Paul Krugman's (1991) *Geography and Trade.* Krugman builds on Alfred Marshall's (1920) *Principles of Economics* in which he set out how clustering small enterprises can compete in distant markets owing to local external economies.

Marshall continues to be the key reference for all writers in this field, but for many writers the impact of clustering is not confined to agglomeration economies. The competitive advantage of locality also arises from the combination of rivalry and cooperation between local enterprises and from the partnerships of public agencies and private organizations aimed at supporting local enterprises.

The importance of local synergy and rivalry has for some time been stressed in Michael Porter's (1990) work on industrial clusters and has been emphatically restated in "Regions and the New Economics of Competition" (Porter, 2001). Similarly, the literature on industrial districts has for some time hailed the importance of local relationships for competing in the global economy (Garofoli, 1991). The Pyke and Sengenberger (1992) volume *Industrial Districts and Local Economic Regeneration* was particularly influential in a debate that continues to be pursued with vigor in both the academic and policy arena. Take for example, the special issue of *European Planning Studies* in which Becattini (2002), Bellandi (2002), and Dei Ottati (2002) reassert and refine their earlier analyses of Italian industrial districts. Likewise, take the EU *Observatory of European SMEs*, which is devoted to policies for "Regional Clusters in Europe" (EU, 2002).

A parallel line of work, concerned with local innovation systems, produced similar messages, even though its origins were different. In the 1990s, the literature on technological development moved from a focus on the individual firm and a strong distinction between innovation and diffusion toward a greater concern with learning-by-interaction (Lundvall, 1998). This led to the studies of innovation systems, first at the national and then increasingly at the regional and local level (Freeman, 1995; Edquist, 1997; Braczyk *et al.*, 1998; Strambach, 2002).

Even though these writers come from different disciplines, most of them share an optimistic view of the scope for local upgrading strategies. In most works there is a strong emphasis on local governance, as for example in Cooke and Morgan's (1998) *The Associational Economy* or Scott's (2000) *Regions and the World Economy*. The central message is that effective local upgrading strategies build on strong linkages between local enterprises and institutions; and that local policy networks can help local enterprises to reposition themselves in the global economy.

A very similar message came from the 1990s research on clusters, local innovation systems, and systemic competitiveness in developing countries. For example, the work on *Systemic Competitiveness: New Governance Patterns for Industrial Development* by Esser *et al.* (1996) stresses the critical role of meso-level policy in building competitive advantage. The co-authors of this work extended it in very interesting ways: Messner (1997) gave particular attention to theoretical analysis, especially the political determinants that enhance or block policy networks concerned with competitive strategies. Meyer-Stamer (2000) opted for the more practical route of making local competitive strategies work. He pioneered the "Participatory Appraisal of Competitive Advantage" (PACA) in which local stakeholders undertake their own analysis of constraints and opportunities and then jointly implement their ideas for repositioning the local economy.

These authors drew their inspiration from a number of sources, including the research on industrial clusters in developing countries by Nadvi (1999), Rabellotti (1997), and Schmitz (1995). This research helped to overcome the earlier pessimism concerning the export prospects of small firms in developing countries.[1] Conceptually, this research was organized around the idea of *collective efficiency*, defined as the competitive advantage derived from local external economies and joint action. The practical implications of this work were synthesized by Humphrey and Schmitz (1996) as the *triple C of local industrial policy*. Customer-oriented, collective, and cumulative were proposed as key features of effective approaches for fostering local development.

A wealth of further studies on industrial clusters and local innovation systems in developing countries has emerged since then (Cassiolato and Lastres, 1999; Cassiolato *et al.*, 2003; Nadvi and Schmitz, 1999; Van Dijk and Rabellotti, 1997). This body of research has made a major impact on the policy debate – within developing countries and in the donor agencies concerned with fostering economic development,[2] bringing about a welcome shift to a more systemic and region-focused approach. The problems identified in these studies often mirror those found in developed countries. However, they tend to differ in one respect. The clusters in developed countries are often global leaders and they play a decisive role in innovation and product design (Garofoli, 1994; Halder, 2004). In contrast, developing country clusters tend to work to specifications that come from outside (Schmitz, 1999; Nadvi and Halder, 2002). The observation of such differences leads to new questions: Who defines and monitors the parameters for local producers? How do these producers respond? How do power relationships change overtime? What is the connection between upgrading and different global–local power configurations?

Taking into account the new global linkages

While the old debate on clusters and local innovation systems was mainly concerned with local linkages, the new debate needs to examine the global linkages and how they affect local relationships. This is not just an add-on; it transforms the understanding of local upgrading strategies and options. Local producers do not just export into an anonymous global market; often they feed into chains that are governed by powerful global players. Chain governance means that some enterprises set and/or enforce the parameters under which others in the chain operate. How does this global chain governance affect local upgrading strategies at the enterprise and cluster level? How does it affect the scope of action for local policy networks? Does the effect differ according to type of individual or collective upgrading strategies? How are the different upgrading strategies affected by different constellations of global and local governance?

Answering these questions is an ambitious undertaking. It requires bringing together the above-mentioned work on local and regional development and the literature on global value chains. The remainder of the chapter summarizes how my colleagues and I tried to do this through both new conceptual work and a range of case studies from developed and developing countries. The objective was to understand how global and local governance interact. As will be shown, we found new forms of power and inequality in global chains but also identified scope for local action.

Conceptual framework

In order to understand the interaction between local and global governance one needs a clear understanding of how the global economy is governed. Most of the current academic literature and policy advice is informed by one of the following two views: (a) the *neoliberal view* of a free global market economy in which local advance depends on local efforts and the market friendliness of government; (b) the view that emphasizes the need for regulation and intervention and puts forward a *stratified public governance* model, that is intergovernmental organizations at the global level, national governments, local governments. Neither view is helpful for us. Local enterprises and policymakers are not operating in a free global market economy, nor in a global economy that is governed in a stratified way.

Dirk Messner (2004) proposes a different conceptualization: the *network-based global economy*. He stresses that the global economy is not just governed by a combination of reliance on free markets and rules of intergovernmental organizations. Export-oriented regions experience this most directly as they are tied into global value chains often governed by global buyers and they are faced with global standards that are defined by global policy networks. This leads Messner to develop the idea of a governance triangle comprising: (a) a local policy network; (b) lead firms of global value chains; and (c) a global policy network concerned with the setting and monitoring of standards. His key point is that local enterprises and policymakers need to interact with these sector-specific global governance structures and that the options and limits for local action arise from this interaction. He then seeks to provide a framework for working out the scope for local action, which instead of starting from an analysis of local relationships starts from the global relationships.

Humphrey and Schmitz (2002, 2004) focus on those global relationships, explaining how and why global value chains are governed. As mentioned above, central to value chain analysis is the observation that there are lead firms, notably global buyers that set and enforce the parameters under which other firms in the chain operate. The question is why these lead firms would go to the trouble and expense of setting up and supervising supply chains. No firm will incur the expense of developing arrangements with specific suppliers in order to purchase products that the market freely provides. The authors suggest that there are two reasons why the global buyers do not rely on coordination through the market and seek to govern their chains:

1   Product definition – the more the buyers pursue a strategy of product differentiation, for example, through design and branding, the greater the need to provide suppliers with precise product specification and to monitor that these specifications are met.
2   Risk of supplier failure – the increasing importance of non-price competition based on factors such as quality, response time, and reliability of delivery, together with increasing concerns about safety and standards, means that buyers have become more vulnerable to shortcomings in the performance of suppliers.

Understanding chain governance is not an objective in itself. Our project sought to understand (changes in) chain governance because it structures the upgrading opportunities of local producers. At least this was the general proposition at the outset. In order to test this proposition, a set of tools was developed which included a distinction between four types of relationships in value chains:

1   Arm's-length market relations – buyer and supplier do not need to develop close relationships because the product is standard or easily customized. A range of firms can meet the buyer's requirements and the switching costs are low.
2   Networks – firms develop information-intensive relationships, frequently dividing essential competences between them. The interaction is coordinated and the relationship is characterized by reciprocal dependence. The buyer may specify certain product performance standards or process standards to be attained, but would be confident that the supplier can meet them.
3   Quasi hierarchy – one firm exercises a high degree of control over other firms in the chain, frequently specifying the characteristics of the product to be produced, and sometimes specifying the processes to be followed and the

control mechanisms to be enforced. This level of control can arise not only from the lead firm's role in defining the product, but also from the buyer's perceived risk of losses from the suppliers' performance failures. In other words, there are some doubts about the competence of the supply chain.

4   Hierarchy – the lead firm takes direct ownership of some operations in the chain. The case of the intra-firm trade between a transnational company and its subsidiaries falls into this category.

With these distinctions one can then ask whether some types of chains offer local producers better upgrading prospects than others. Such questioning can be further refined if one distinguishes between different types of upgrading:

1   Process upgrading: transforming inputs into outputs more efficiently by reorganizing the production system or introducing superior machinery.
2   Product upgrading: moving into more sophisticated product lines (that can be defined in terms of increased unit values).
3   Functional upgrading: acquiring new functions in the chain (or abandoning existing functions) to increase the overall skill content of activities.
4   Inter-sectoral upgrading: using the knowledge acquired in particular chain functions to move into different sectors.

Equipped with these typologies one can then investigate the hypothesis that the upgrading opportunities of local producers vary with the type of chain governance.

Local upgrading in global chains

The Sinos Valley in the South of Brazil is an ideal location for testing the above hypothesis because its enterprises feed into chains that are governed in different ways. The Sinos Valley is Latin America's most significant footwear cluster. In order of importance, its main markets are the United States, Brazil, the rest of Latin America, and Europe. The relationships between the producers and customers in these four markets vary significantly – as shown in a comparative study by Luiza Bazan and Lizbeth Navas-Alemán (2004). The US chain is a clear case of quasi-hierarchy. The combination of high pressure and technical assistance from the US buyers led to fast process and product upgrading but little advance in functional upgrading. Relationships between European buyers and local producers were not quite so close and seemed to provide more space for functional upgrading. The relationships in the Latin American and Brazilian chains are more even and local producers tend to use their own design and own brands.

This research by Bazan and Navas-Alemán is the most thorough case study to date of the connection between chain governance and upgrading in that it provides both comparative and historical analysis. The analysis of the US and European chains underscores the enormous gains local producers can derive from integrating into global chains. It enabled them to become world-class producers. The downside was that they remained in a captive relationship with their buyers for a long time. But this is changing according to the authors. Their explanations of this change are of general interest even though it is difficult to establish a clear hierarchy of factors. The trigger seems to have been a shift in the main US buyer's commitment to source from Brazil that brought into focus a long recognized but neglected strategic issue; that is, the need to diversify marketing channels and destinations. Some firms found this more difficult than others. Not surprisingly, the most successful firms were those that had begun to operate in several chains simultaneously for some time. More of this was now required.

Particularly successful in exploring new markets were a number of firms that had previously prioritized the domestic market. Their key advantage was that they had developed their own design and marketing capabilities. These were essential in particular for diversifying into the Latin American market where relationships with customers tend to be market-based. These results question the widely held view that exporting provides superior learning opportunities for local firms. While this view holds for process and product upgrading, it does not seem to apply to functional upgrading.

The above case of delayed functional upgrading in Brazil contrasts with a story of functional downgrading in Italy. When Roberta Rabellotti first presented this finding at a workshop, it came as a big surprise because she was studying a world-class Italian industrial district. Is this district a casualty of globalization? Not quite. Many enterprises in the footwear district of Brenta continue to export products based on their own designs and using their own brands. However, an important new line of exports has emerged: the production of luxury shoes based on the design and brand of powerful top fashion companies. To be part of the chain, Brenta's producers accept a functional downgrading, abandoning design and marketing to focus on production. Rabellotti (2004) suggests that, in the short-term, this does not represent a step backwards because the producers inserted in this chain have higher returns than those exporting their own designs and brands. However, if one takes the long-term view one could come to a different conclusion. By abandoning their design competence, these Italian producers risk giving up the key advantage they have over their competitors in developing countries. Whether this will happen is hard to tell. It depends on whether producers dedicate themselves entirely to producing for these top brand companies or whether they engage simultaneously in other chains in which original design and branding remain important. But the space for independence seems to be shrinking. A general lesson from this case is that the growth of global buyers, design, and fashion houses changes the market conditions for all producers, even sophisticated ones. The already observable trend toward explicit chain governance arising from global branding and retailing will impact on developed country clusters as well.

The question of how global relationships affect local relationships and practices was also examined for the case of the surgical instrument cluster of Tuttlingen in Germany (Halder, 2004). There are similarities and differences to the above Italian case. Like Brenta, Tuttlingen is also a world leader, relying on interactive innovation to maintain its position. Competition from low-wage countries, especially the Pakistani cluster of Sialkot, has eroded Tuttlingen's traditional strength, which is the manufacture of handheld instruments. The cluster has responded by developing new products and services. Both require substantial investment and active management of the relationships with users. The cluster's large firms have this capability whereas most of the small firms are confined to the more traditional products in which they are struggling to survive. Some of the small firms have moved from manufacture to trade in surgical instruments – sourced from Pakistan (Halder, 2004; Nadvi and Halder, 2002).

Large firms also source traditional instruments from low-wage countries and maintain (quasi-) hierarchical relationships with their suppliers in Malaysia, Pakistan, Poland, and Hungary. Their in-house manufacture concentrates on new products such as surgical implants or instruments for minimally invasive surgery. In order to develop these products, the firms maintain network-based relationships, characterized by the sharing of competences and close coopera-tion, with leading surgeons and hospitals. Large firms have also taken on addi-tional functions by offering hospitals sterilization services and just-in-time (JIT) delivery of instrument or implant kits. Gerhard Halder concludes that the cluster has become more differentiated, that most small firms are losing out, and that large firms capable of combining internal and external knowledge flows do well. As a result of this increasing differentiation, cluster-wide upgrading initiatives have become more difficult and the management of relationships with specific external holders of complementary competence has become strategic.

There is a general lesson that emerges from the analysis of these European clusters: a leap in understanding resulting from combining the cluster and value chain approaches. At the outset of the research, this combination of approaches was thought to be important mainly for the analysis of developing country clus-ters. In the end, it was found that bringing together the two perspectives was also critical for the developed country cases.[3]

Why not go the whole way and rely entirely on the global value chain approach? Four prominent clusters analyzed in our project are outsourcing an increasing part of their production: enterprises from the South Brazilian footwear cluster in the Sinos Valley have set up subsidiaries in the Northeast of the country where wages are lower (Bazan and Navas-Alemán, 2004); enter-prises in the Italian cluster of Brenta are farming out the most labor-intensive operations to Eastern Europe (Rabellotti, 2004); the German cluster of Tuttlin-gen acquires simple surgical instruments from suppliers in Pakistan, Malaysia, Poland and Hungary (Halder, 2004; Nadvi and Halder, 2002); and the most rapid increase in outsourcing has occurred in the Taiwanese computer cluster, which has a growing share of the computer equipment produced in Mainland China (Kishimoto, 2004). Does this signify a decreasing importance in the rele-vance of clustering for international competitiveness? Kishimoto, in his analysis of the Taiwanese case, answers this question with an emphatic No. Following Bell and Albu (1999), he distinguishes between the production and knowledge system and shows that although the importance of clustering diminishes in the former, it increases in the latter. Shedding repetitive activities and concentrating on knowledge-intensive activities is seen as a sign of functional upgrading.

The analysis of the Taiwanese computer cluster is important for other reasons. By the year 2000, it had become the world's most significant industrial cluster outside OECD countries, accounting for about half of the world's output in computer hardware. Substantial progress was achieved in all categories of upgrading and the main question is how this was achieved. Kishimoto (2004) argues that the key lies in the interaction of local and global linkages. The global linkages were analyzed, as in the other cluster studies, by using the global value chain approach. Initially, local producers operated in quasi-hierarchical chains in which they were able to upgrade processes and products very fast with the assistance of their buyers. Functional upgrading was also achieved but not all the way. Many local firms acquired design capabilities but few established their own brands. Those firms that succeeded in marketing their own design and brand achieved this by maintaining the contract manufacturing for the main buyers and simultaneously experimenting with their own design and brands in other smaller markets. Such leveraging of competences across chains (Lee and Chen, 2000) was central to the functional upgrading achieved by some of the Taiwanese computer producers.

Humphrey and Schmitz (2004) pull together the findings on local upgrading in global chains. Clearly, power and inequality in global chains need explicit attention in the assessment of cluster upgrading. However, accepting a subordinate role can bring significant advantages. The case material shows that accepting foster parents offers a fast track to product and process upgrading. But integrating into quasi-hierarchical relationships is a double-edged sword. On the one hand, it facilitates inclusion and rapid enhancement of product and process capabilities. On the other hand, local producers become tied into relationships that prevent functional upgrading and leave them dependent on a small number of global buyers.

The question then is how local firms can break out of such a lock-in. This requires investment at both the enterprise and the cluster level. In the Taiwanese computer cluster and the Brazilian footwear clusters, mentioned above, some enterprises pursued a clear strategy of operating in several chains simultaneously: producing to the specifications of their big customers while also experimenting with their own designs in the production for different markets. However, most firms cannot acquire the design and marketing capability on their own. The investment requirements for breaking into new markets are high. This is where they need access to effective support offered by either collective self-help organizations such as business associations and/or by government. But do the relevant support organizations exist? How is the development of the institutional infrastructure – and of the policy networks that produce it – affected by the insertion of the cluster in the global economy? The next section summarizes the insights coming out of our project.

The scope for local policy

What is the scope for local development strategies in a world where trading relationships are increasingly global? Messner (2004) argues against the pessimism of those capitulating in the face of the new global governance structures; equally, he argues against the unguarded optimism reigning in many agencies concerned with fostering local development. He calls for a new type of analysis that locates the local economy in the global networked economy and helps to identify where the scope for local action is expanding and where it is shrinking. Key factors to consider are: the specific governance pattern in the relevant global value chain; the core competence of the global lead firms; and the manner in which global standards are implemented. Messner's key message is that there are not only restrictions but also new opportunities for local action through coalitions with global actors.

This analysis builds on his earlier work (Messner, 1997), which shows that, in order to be effective, local industrial policy requires building a coalition of the key actors in the public and private sector. He refers to this as building policy networks across the public–private divide and shows the context within which they are likely to work. His new work (Messner, 2002, 2004) emphasizes that such policy networks increasingly need to be formed along a local–global axis. More importantly, it provides a new framework for analyzing the scope of action for such policy networks.

Collective actors such as business associations are essential players in such policy networks, both because of their sector-specific expertise and their ability to mobilize political and financial support. Individual actors can also play a major role, notably the lead firms of hub-and-spoke clusters. The more clusters are integrated into global markets, the more heterogeneous they become and the more they move toward a hub-and-spoke organization in which the lead firms become the gatekeepers of both material and knowledge flows. The surgical instrument cluster of Tuttlingen is perhaps the clearest example. Halder (2004) shows that institutions concerned with strengthening existing competences, for example the highly specialized local training institute (BBT), have the support of all local enterprises. In contrast, an institution concerned with developing new competences (competence center) does not have the backing of the local lead firm; the fear is that through participating in the new competence center, other firms could avail themselves of the fruits of its (the lead firm's) R&D investment.

In other words, the scope for building policy networks depends on the type of upgrading they seek to promote. This applies even more to clusters in developing countries that operate in global chains coordinated by external actors. The issue is straightforward where the policy aim is the *strengthening of the existing position* of a manufacturing cluster in a global chain. This requires process and product upgrading that is usually incremental in nature. The insertion in a global chain ensures that a great deal of learning occurs in the course of making products defined by external buyers (provided that the local manufacturers make the corresponding investment in people and equipment). Clustering facilitates the rapid diffusion of the knowledge thus acquired. Local industrial policy has an important role to play in expanding infrastructure and strengthening training, testing, and certification facilities. Such local industrial policy can usually count on the support of all actors, including the buyers, because its aim is to strengthen and reinforce the position that the cluster occupies in the global chain.

Upgrading aimed at *repositioning* the cluster requires a more active search and risky investment in capabilities aimed at reaching new markets or reaching old markets in new ways. What scope is there for local industrial policy to foster the radical product upgrading or functional upgrading? A key issue is whether the local lead firms support the repositioning of the cluster. Which is stronger, their allegiance to the local policy network or the relationship to their customer(s) in the global chain? The answer depends on the way in which the chain is organized. If local firms sell to a few buyers to whom they are in a quasi-hierarchy relationship, their risk in supporting a project of repositioning is particularly high. The risk lies not only in the investment of exploring new markets but also in jeopardizing sales to existing markets. It is precisely for this reason that a local policy network in the Sinos Valley collapsed in the mid-1990s (Schmitz, 1999). As pointed out by Bazan and Navas-Alemán (2004), the local policy network became stronger again a few years later when the connection between the main global buyer and local lead firms had loosened.

Marcia Leite (2002) also examines the relevance of the value chain for the formation of policy networks. Her study focuses on the auto and plastics sectors in the ABC region of São Paulo. These two sectors differ substantially in their involvement in the regional industrial chamber, a major public–private upgrading initiative. Leite shows how and why the active participation of the plastics firms contrasts with the passive attitude of the auto and auto-parts producers. A reason for this lack of interest can be found in the relationship of the auto-parts producers with their clients, who are few in number and pursue global sourcing strategies. Local producers prioritize this relationship over all others. In contrast, the plastics producers have many clients operating in many different chains and are, therefore, less dependent on specific vertical relationships. It gives them greater freedom, but the challenge of raising their competitiveness remains. Since individual efforts are rarely sufficient, they support collective efforts and participate actively in the regional chamber.

Further supportive evidence is provided by Meyer-Stamer *et al.* (2004). Their study of tile clusters in Italy, Spain, and Brazil suggests that symmetrical relationships with external customers have facilitated the emergence and functioning of local policy networks. However, change is under way. In two of the three clusters, the local policy networks have weakened. The authors link this weakening to the upgrading strategies of the main local producers. Their competitive strategy has shifted from prioritizing excellence in production to controlling marketing channels and, thus, increasing their market share. This strategy has intensified competition among local firms and has weakened their interest in the local policy network. This conclusion applies to both the Italian and Brazilian cluster. In contrast, the Spanish tile producers, who are not pursuing such marketing strategies, continue to participate actively in collective initiatives.

The circumstances in which local policy networks can make a difference are discussed further in "Paradoxes and Ironies of Locational Policy in the New Global Economy" by Jörg Meyer-Stamer (2004). He highlights the enormous current interest in local and regional upgrading strategies and then assesses the likelihood of these strategies becoming successful. He does this by drawing attention to a number of paradoxes that have not been given sufficient attention in recent debate. First, there is the "lifecycle paradox": pursuing active local policy is crucial in the early stage of economic development but effective local policy networks are more likely at a late stage. Then there is what one could call the "integrationist paradox": local policy networks that seek to achieve close relationships between local producers and global producers will be marginalized if they succeed. Finally, the "location paradox": firms are increasingly demanding when it comes to locational quality but show a decreasing propensity to invest in local policy networks. The main message of this insightful contribution is not one of pessimism but realism. It provides many insights that help to define the circumstances in which local or regional upgrading strategies can be expected to succeed – or fail.[4]

Questions for the future

Reading across the project papers one finds increasing similarities between developed and developing regions. The conflicts, trade-offs, and paradoxes are often the same for local enterprises and policy networks in developed and developing countries. In a way this is not surprising. They operate in the same global economy and the old division of labor has changed. Export manufacturing is no longer concentrated in the developed world; Asian and Latin American regions have become major exporters of manufactured products, forcing European and North American regions to abandon some industries and restructure others. Low labor costs are not sufficient to explain this transformation. Global value chain analysis, with its emphasis on the coordination of seemingly fragmented production sites, helps to explain global redistribution of manufacturing. It helps in particular to explain the speed of change. The speed at which production capabilities have spread from developed to developing countries is historically unprecedented.

However, progress in other capabilities has been much slower. R&D, design, branding, and systems integration have remained largely concentrated in the developed countries. The question is how long this knowledge and power divide in the global economy will last. Some regions in the developing world are beginning to accumulate significant innovation capabilities, for example, the software cluster of Bangalore, the computer cluster in Taiwan, and various industrial clusters in Mainland China. Their experience gives rise to new questions: What enabled these clusters to make the transition from production to innovation?

Under what circumstances is the growth of industrial production capabilities in developing regions transformed and extended into the growth of innovation capabilities? Are there common patterns in the evolution of these innovation capabilities and systems in developing regions? In what ways does the governance of global value chains influence these common patterns or diversity around them? How do policy networks and support organizations of emerging innovation systems contribute to these patterns of commonality or diversity?

Notes

1 The new export optimism rarely extended to enterprise clusters in Africa (McCormick, 1998).
2 For example, in Brazil, the Instituto Metas produces *Clusters – Revista Brasileira de Competitividade*, a journal for the many policymakers and practitioners concerned with strengthening local production systems. In KwaZulu-Natal, South Africa, Barnes and Morris (2000) have improved operational competitiveness of manufacturing firms through firm-level clustering. In India, UNIDO supported a program for strengthening the export competitiveness of clusters. In Indonesia, JICA (Japan International Co-operation Agency) supported a project for strengthening the capacity of SME clusters.
3 One of the best examples of using this combination of approaches is the comparative analysis of German and Pakistani clusters by Nadvi and Halder (2002). They show that the two clusters occupy different stages in the same value chain and that the relationships between them are both conflictual and complementary.
4 Mike Morris and Justin Barnes have shown through practice and analysis how combining the industrial cluster and value chain approaches enriches local industrial policy (Barnes and Morris, 2000; Morris, 2001; Morris and Barnes, 2004).

References

Barnes, J. and Morris, M. (2000), "Improving Operational Competitiveness Through Firm-Level Clustering: A Case Study of the KwaZulu-Natal Benchmarking Club," CSDS Working Paper 24, School of Development Studies, University of KwaZulu-Natal, Durban.

Bazan, L. and Navas-Alemán, L. (2004) "The Underground Revolution in the Sinos Valley: A Comparison of Upgrading in Global and National Value Chains," in Schmitz (ed.).

Becattini, G. (2002) "Industrial Sectors and Industrial Districts: Tools for Industrial Analysis," *European Planning Studies*, 10 (4), pp. 483–493.

Bell, M. and Albu, M. (1999) "Knowledge Systems and Technological Dynamism in Industrial Clusters in Developing Countries," *World Development*, 27 (9), pp. 1715–1734.

Bellandi, M. (2002) "Indian Industrial Districts: An Industrial Economics Interpretation," *European Planning Studies*, 10 (4), pp. 425–437.

Braczyk, H.-J., Cooke, P. and Heidenreich, M. (eds.) (1998) *Regional Innovation Systems*, UCL Press, London.

Cassiolato, J. and Lastres, H. (1999) *Globalização e Inovação Localizada – Experiências De Sistemas Locais No Mercosul*, IEL/IBICT, Brasília.

Cassiolato, J., Lastres, H. and Maciel, M.L. (eds.) (2003) *Systems of Innovation and Development – Evidence from Brazil*, Elgar, Cheltenham.

Cooke, P. and Morgan, K. (1998) *The Associational Economy: Firms, Regions and Innovation*, Oxford University Press, Oxford.

Dei Ottati, G. (2002) "Social Concertation and Local Development: The Case of Industrial Districts," *European Planning Studies*, 10 (4), pp. 451–466.

Edquist, C. (1997) *Systems of Innovation: Technologies, Institutions and Organizations*, Pinter, London.

Esser, K., Hillebrand, W., Messner, D. and Meyer-Stamer, J. (1996) *Systemic Competitiveness: New Governance Patterns for Industrial Development*, Frank Cass, London.

EU (2002) *Observatory of European SMEs No 3, Regional Clusters in Europe*, Office for Official Publications of the European Union, Luxemburg.

Freeman, C. (1995) "The National System of Innovation in Historical Perspective," *Cambridge Journal of Economics*, 19 (1), pp. 5–24.

Garofoli, G. (1991) "Local Networks, Innovation and Policy in Italian Industrial Districts," in E. Bergman, G. Maier and F. Tödtling (eds.) *Regions Reconsidered*, Mansell, London.

Garofoli, G. (1994) "The Industrial District of Lecco: Innovation and Transformation Processes," *Entrepreneurship & Regional Development*, 6, pp. 371–393.

Gereffi, G. (1999) 'International Trade and Industrial Upgrading in the Apparel Commodity Chain," *Journal of International Economics*, 48, pp. 37–70.

Halder, G. (2004) "Local Upgrading Strategies in Response to Global Challenges: the Surgical Instruments Cluster of Tuttlingen, Germany, pp. 200–232 in H. Schmitz (ed.).

Humphrey, J. (1995) "Industrial Reorganization in Developing Countries: From Models to Trajectories," *World Development*, 23, (1), pp. 149–162.

Humphrey, J. and Schmitz, H. (1996) "The Triple C Approach to Local Industrial Policy," *World Development*, 24 (12), pp. 1859–1877.

Humphrey, J. and Schmitz, H. (2002) "How Does Insertion in Global Value Chains Affect Upgrading in Industrial Clusters?" *Regional Studies*, 36 (9), pp. 1017–1027.

Humphrey, J. and Schmitz, H. (2004) "Chain Governance and Upgrading: Taking Stock," in Schmitz (ed.) *Local Enterprises in the Global Economy: Issues of Governance and Upgrading*, Elgar, Cheltenham.

Kishimoto, C. (2004) "Clustering and Upgrading in Global Value Chains: The Taiwanese Personal Computer Industry," in Schmitz (ed.) *Local Enterprises in the Global Economy: Issues of Governance and Upgrading*, Elgar, Cheltenham.

Krugman, P. (1991) *Geography and Trade*, MIT Press, Cambridge, Mass.

Lee, J.-R. and Chen, J.-S. (2000) "Dynamic Synergy Creation with Multiple Business Activities: Toward a Competence-Based Growth Model for Contract Manufacturers," in R. Sanchez and A. Heene (eds.) *Theory Development for Competence-Based Management, Advances in Applied Business Strategy*, JAI Press, Greenwich, Conn., pp. 209–228.

Leite, M.D.P. (2002) "The Struggle to Develop Regional Industry Policy: The Role of the Plastics and Auto Sectors in the Regional Chamber of Abc, São Paulo," IDS working paper, No. 154, Institute of Development Studies, Brighton.

Lundvall, B.-A. (1998) "Innovation as an Interactive Process: From User-Producer Interaction to the National System of Innovation," in G. Dosi, C. Freeman, R. Nelson, G. Silverberg and L. Soete (eds.) *Technical Change and Economic Theory*, Pinter, London, pp. 349–369.

Marshall, A. (1920) *Principles of Economics*, 8th edn, Macmillan, London.

McCormick, D. (1998) "Enterprise Clusters in Africa: On the Way to Industrialisation?" IDS discussion paper 366, Institute of Development Studies, Brighton.

Messner, D. (1997) *The Network Society: Economic Development and International Competitiveness as Problems of Social Governance*, Frank Cass, London.

Messner, D. (2002) "The Concept of the 'World Economic Triangle': Global Governance Patterns and Options for Regions," IDS working paper, No. 173, Institute of Development Studies, Brighton.

Messner, D. (2004) "Regions in the 'World Economic Triangle,'" in Schmitz (ed.) *Local Enterprises in the Global Economy: Issues of Governance and Upgrading*, Elgar, Cheltenham.

Meyer-Stamer, J. (2000) "Participatory Appraisal of Competitive Advantage: A Methodology to Support Local Economic Development Initiatives," mimeo, www.meyer-stamer.de.

Meyer-Stamer, J. (2004) "Paradoxes and Ironies of Locational Policies in the New Global Economy," in Schmitz (ed.) *Local Enterprises in the Global Economy: Issues of Governance and Upgrading*, Elgar, Cheltenham.

Meyer-Stamer, J., Maggi, C. and Seibel, S. (2004) "Upgrading in the tile industry of Italy, Spain, and Brazil: insights from cluster and value chain analysis," in Schmitz (ed.) *Local Enterprises in the Global Economy: Issues of Governance and Upgrading*, Elgar, Cheltenham.

Morris, M. (2001) "Creating Value Chain Cooperation," *IDS Bulletin*, 32 (3), pp. 127–136.

Morris, M. and Barnes, J. (2004) "Policy Lessons in Organising Cooperation and Facilitating Networked Learning in Value Chains and Industrial Clusters," School of Development Studies, University of KwaZulu-Natal, Durban.

Nadvi, K. (1999) "The Cutting Edge: Collective Efficiency and International Competitiveness in Pakistan," *Oxford Development Studies*, 27 (1), pp. 81–107.

Nadvi, K. and Halder, G. (2002) "Local Clusters in Global Value Chains: Exploring Dynamic Linkages between Germany and Pakistan," Institute of Development Studies Working Paper No. 152, Sussex, UK.

Nadvi, K. and Schmitz, H. (1999) "Industrial Clusters in Developing Countries," *World Development*, 27 (9) (special issue).

Porter, M. (1990) *The Competitive Advantage of Nations*, Macmillan, London.

Porter, M. (2001) "Regions and the New Economics of Competition," in A. Scott (ed.) *Global City-Regions: Trends, Theory and Policy*, Oxford University Press, Oxford, pp. 139–157.

Pyke, F. and Sengenberger, W. (eds.) (1992) *Industrial Districts and Local Economic Regeneration*, International Institute for Labour Studies, Geneva, ILO.

Rabellotti, R. (1997) *External Economies and Cooperation in Industrial Districts. A Comparison of Italy and Mexico*, Macmillan, London.

Rabellotti, R. (2004) "How Globalization Affects Industrial Districts: the Case of Brenta," in Schmitz (ed.) *Local Enterprises in the Global Economy: Issues of Governance and Upgrading*, Elgar, Cheltenham.

Schmitz, H. (1995) "Collective Efficiency: Growth Path for Small-Scale Industry," *Journal of Development Studies*, 31 (4), pp. 529–566.

Schmitz, H. (1999) "Global Competition and Local Cooperation: Success and Failure in the Sinos Valley, Brazil," *World Development*, 27 (9), pp. 1627–1650.

Schmitz, H. (ed.) (2004) *Local Enterprises in the Global Economy: Issues of Governance and Upgrading*, Elgar, Cheltenham.

Scott, A.J. (2000) *Regions and the World Economy: The Coming Shape of Global Production, Competition, and Political Order*, Oxford University Press, Oxford.

Strambach, S. (2002) "Change in the Innovation Process: New Knowledge Production and Competitive Cities: The Case of Stuttgart," *European Planning Studies*, 10 (2), pp. 215–231.

Van Dijk, M.P. and Rabellotti, R. (eds.) (1997) *Enterprise Clusters and Networks in Developing Countries*, Cass, London.

Index

An environmentally friendly book printed and bound in England by www.printondemand-worldwide.com